INHERITING
SYRIA

Syrian President Bashar al-Asad attends a ceremony marking the one-year anniversary of his father's death.

INHERITING SYRIA

BASHAR'S TRIAL BY FIRE

Flynt Leverett

BROOKINGS INSTITUTION PRESS
Washington, D.C.

Library of Congress Cataloging-in-Publication data
Leverett, Flynt Lawrence.
   Inheriting Syria : Bashar's trial by fire / Flynt Leverett.
      p. :   ill., maps ; cm.
   Summary: "A detailed analytic portrait of Syria under the Asad dynasty,
offering a new strategy for achieving American foreign policy and security
objectives in the Middle East, largely independent of the Arab-Israeli peace
process"—Provided by publisher.
   Includes bibliographical references and index.
   ISBN-13: 978-0-8157-5204-2 (cloth (isbn-13) : alk. paper)
   ISBN-10: 0-8157-5204-0 (cloth (isbn-10) : alk. paper)
   1. Syria—Politics and government—2000– 2. Asad, Bashar, 1965–
3. Geopolitics—Syria. 4. United States—Foreign relations—Middle East.
5. Middle East—Foreign relations—United States. I. Title.
   DS98.6.L48 2005
   320.956918 098 0511—dc22   2005006453

9 8 7 6 5 4 3 2 1

The paper used in this publication meets minimum requirements of the
American National Standard for Information Sciences—Permanence of Paper
for Printed Library Materials: ANSI Z39.48-1992.

Typeset in Minion

Composition by R. Lynn Rivenbark
Macon, Georgia

Cartography by Meridian Mapping
Minneapolis, Minnesota

Printed by R. R. Donnelley
Harrisonburg, Virginia

To Hillary

Contents

Foreword

S YRIA HAS ONCE AGAIN come to the top of the U.S. policy agenda, despite conventional wisdom not too long ago that it was finally taking its rightful place on the margins of Middle East affairs. At the beginning of his second term, President Bush has made Syria a focus for the next phase in his administration's global war on terror.

Much of the renewed attention on Syria has concentrated on the leadership qualities and strategic intentions of the country's president, Bashar al-Asad. It has become a rhetorical commonplace to question whether Bashar has the same degree of authority and tactical savvy displayed by his late father and predecessor, Hafiz al-Asad. In this context, it is worth recalling that Hafiz al-Asad was not perceived as the uncontested master of his country and an astute player of the regional game until he had weathered a series of defining challenges: establishing Syrian hegemony in Lebanon, defending that hegemony against both Israel and the United States, and putting down serious challenges to his authority within Syria from Sunni fundamentalists and ambitious family rivals.

Perhaps the current controversy over Syria's position in Lebanon will be a similarly defining crisis for Bashar. If Bashar is able to maintain a capacity to influence events in Lebanon in the face of mounting international pressure, he could emerge as a stronger figure, domestically and regionally. If, on the other hand, Bashar is judged to have made missteps that cost Syria its ability to protect its interests in Lebanon, he will be significantly weakened;

this could have serious consequences for Syria's position in the region and Bashar's position at home.

At this critical moment, Flynt Leverett's *Inheriting Syria: Bashar's Trial by Fire* could not be more timely or needed. A senior fellow with the Saban Center for Middle East Policy here at Brookings, Flynt draws on rich experience as a scholar, policymaker, and intelligence analyst to assess Syria's unavoidable importance for U.S. foreign policy, the enduring and evolving dynamics of Syrian politics and policymaking, and Syria's regional role. He paints a comprehensive portrait of Bashar al-Asad as national leader. He also offers thoughtful recommendations for U.S. policy toward Syria, proposing a strategy of conditional "carrots-and-sticks" engagement with Damascus. On all these counts, his work follows in the best tradition of Brookings scholarship and adds to the growing list of contributions that the Saban Center has made to national and international discussion of U.S. policy in the Middle East.

STROBE TALBOTT
President

March 2005
Washington, D.C.

Preface

T HE SYRIAN ARAB REPUBLIC is a comparatively small, internally conflicted, economically underperforming, and resource-poor Arab state. It nonetheless factors prominently in U.S. foreign policy toward the greater Middle East. For three decades before the September 11, 2001, attacks, Syria, under the leadership of President Hafiz al-Asad, "boxed above its weight" as both subject and object of America's Middle East policy. At least since the 1973 Yom Kippur war, Syria has been an inevitable focus for the ongoing American quest to place the region on a more peaceful and positive strategic trajectory. This is true both with regard to resolving the Arab-Israeli conflict and, more broadly, to shaping the overall balance of power in the Middle East.

Under the leadership of Hafiz al-Asad's son and successor, Bashar al-Asad, Syria has become even more salient for U.S. policy in the context of America's post–September 11 war on terror. For the Bush administration, Syria falls into the particularly problematic category of states that simultaneously sponsor terrorist activity, pursue weapons of mass destruction, and repress their people. Moreover, even though Syria offered intelligence and other assistance to the United States in its post–September 11 crackdown against al-Qaeda, Damascus has opposed other aspects of the administration's global war on terror. In particular, Bashar al-Asad opposed the U.S. military campaign to unseat Saddam Hussein in 2003. Reflecting that opposition, Syria has both before and after the military conflict acted at times to undermine the pursuit of U.S. objectives in Iraq. All of this has made Syria a challenge for U.S. policymakers seeking to chart an efficacious course for global counter-terrorism efforts and develop a "grand strategy" for the greater Middle East. Finally, the furor following the assasination of former Lebanese prime minister Rafiq al-Hariri has focused U.S. and international attention on the issue of Syrian hegemony in Lebanon.

At the same time that Syria's problematic behaviors have posed a significant policy challenge, the degree of analytic consensus in the United States and elsewhere about the country's leadership dynamics and strategic agenda has declined noticeably. Analysts and policymakers in the West had thirty years to scope out Hafiz al-Asad's regime and his approach to internal and foreign policy issues. They have had just four years to make sense of Bashar's leadership and approach to policy matters, and have interpreted the experience and evidence of Bashar's presidency to date in widely divergent ways. Not surprisingly, the uncertainty and lack of consensus in analytic discussions of Syrian affairs have made it more difficult to achieve any meaningful consensus about policy.

Against this backdrop, the key objectives of this book are to reduce the level of analytic uncertainty about Syrian politics and policy today, to develop an actionable analytic portrait of the Asad regime under Bashar's leadership, and to draw the implications of that portrait for U.S. policy. The book contains five chapters. Chapter 1 examines in greater detail Syria's regional significance and the challenges that problematic Syrian behaviors pose for U.S. policy. Chapter 2 sets the stage for analyzing Syria under Bashar al-Asad's leadership by looking at the nature of the regime that Hafiz al-Asad created and passed on to his son as well as the elder Asad's substantive policy bequest to his son regarding both internal economic and political issues and foreign policy. Chapters 3 and 4 concentrate on Bashar al-Asad's tenure as president of Syria. Chapter 3 focuses on the internal challenges confronting the new president and examines his handling of domestic economic, political, and social issues. Chapter 4 pursues a similar examination of Bashar's stewardship of Syrian foreign policy. Finally, chapter 5 evaluates options and makes recommendations for U.S. policy toward Syria.

Acknowledgments

LIKE OTHER AUTHORS, I have accumulated many debts in writing this book; it is my pleasure to acknowledge them here. First of all, I thank Martin Indyk, the founding director of Brookings's Saban Center for Middle East Policy. Martin took me in at the Saban Center and gave me a professional home when I left government service in May 2003. More than anyone else, he gave me the idea for this book, and provided much encouragement and intellectual support while I was writing it. Casey Noga was an exemplary research assistant, whose contribution to the final product went well beyond the conventional definition of a research assistant's job. He was also responsible for compiling this book's timeline, whose thoroughness will certainly be as appreciated by future scholars of Syria as it was by me. Additionally, I thank my Brookings colleagues Ivo Daalder, Ken Pollack, and Jim Steinberg for their many inputs into the project; Jim also offered insightful comments on an early draft of the manuscript. Janet Walker and Larry Converse at the Brookings Institution Press were instrumental in guiding this book through the publishing process. To Susan Woollen I owe credit for devising an ideal cover concept. Martha Gottron's meticulous editing and constructive suggestions significantly improved the quality of the text.

This book grows out of almost a decade of involvement with Syrian affairs in the U.S. government. I am grateful to George Tenet, who, during his tenure first as deputy director and then as director of Central Intelligence, gave me the opportunity to serve as the CIA's senior expert on Syria for the last half of the 1990s. In the process, I was able to learn much about the (not always productive) intersection of intelligence analysis and policy-making. During the first year of the Bush administration, Richard Haass asked me to serve as the Middle East specialist on the State Department's policy planning staff, where Syria was an important part of my portfolio. Both before and after the September 11 attacks, Richard helped me to think through the problems associated with a strategy of conditional engagement with state sponsors of terrorism. In his postgovernment life at the Council on Foreign Relations, Richard took the time to read the first draft of the manuscript and offer comments.

At the beginning of the second year of the Bush administration's tenure, Condoleezza Rice gave me the once-in-a-lifetime opportunity to serve as senior director for Middle East affairs on the National Security Council staff. I held this position during a critical time when President Bush made many of his most important decisions about U.S. policy toward Syria and other Middle Eastern issues. I had, literally and figuratively, the best seat in the house from which to observe the administration's policymaking on those issues. In the end, I disagreed with enough of those decisions to leave the administration. In this book, I have sought to convey analytic truth as best I can and to give an intellectually honest recommendation about opti-mal U.S. policy toward Syria. In the process, I have been very critical of Bush administration policies I consider dysfunctional for the achievement of U.S. interests. Nevertheless, I remain grateful to the president and to Dr. Rice for the chance to have served at the White House.

I thank those former and currently serving U.S. government officials who have continued to discuss Syrian affairs and U.S. policy toward Syria with me in my postgovernment incarnation. Dennis Ross kindly let me see pre-publication drafts of the Syria chapters from his indispensable *The Missing Peace*. I am also grateful to officials in the British, Dutch, Egyptian, French, German, Iranian, Israeli, Jordanian, Lebanese, and Turkish governments, at the European Commission and European Council in Brussels, and at the United Nations who shared their perspectives on Syrian developments. In virtually all cases, I have refrained from citing U.S. and foreign officials by name, but without their input this book would have been deprived of valu-able information and insights.

A number of official and nonofficial Syrians have contributed to the book. I am grateful to all but will only single out a few for individual mention. Starting at the top, I thank President Bashar al-Asad for taking the time to talk with me in January 2004 about the range of challenges confronting him and his country. Dr. 'Imad Mustafa, the Syrian Arab Republic's ambassador to the United States, has also been very generous with his time and insights. Additionally, I thank Minister for Expatriate Affairs Dr. Buthayna Sha'ban and Deputy Foreign Minister Walid al-Mu'allim for their frank and insightful conversation. Those engaged in Syria's civil society movement who took the time to talk with me about their experiences have not only my gratitude but also my profound respect for what they are doing to create a better future for their country.

I thank the outstanding quartet of reviewers who evaluated the manuscript for the Brookings Institution Press. As a scholar-practitioner, Itamar Rabinovich is a model for anyone wanting to write on contemporary Syria; his comments were of immense value. Martha Kessler first set me to work on Syrian issues at the CIA in 1995 and taught me much of what I know about the country, its politics, and its foreign policy; as usual, her comments made my work better. In government, I had no better colleagues than Bill Burns and David Satterfield; their comments on the manuscript have sharpened the final version in countless ways.

Finally, I offer wholly inadequate words of gratitude to my wife, Hillary Mann Leverett, to whom this book is dedicated. Meeting her was definitely the best part of my service in the Bush administration. Her influence is reflected on every page of this book. Moreover, she made writing it a joy, as she does every other aspect of my life.

Syria: Political Divisions

TURKEY

al-Hasaka
• al-Hasaka

al-Raqqa

Halab (Aleppo)
Halab
• Idlib
• al-Raqqa

al-Lathaqiya
(Latakia)
Idlib
Euphrates

Qordaha

Banyas
Hama •
Hama
• Dayr al-Zawr

Tartus •
Dayr al-Zawr

Mediterranean Sea
• Homs
al-Lathaqiya

IRAQ

Homs

Beirut ★
LEBANON

Dimashq

ISRAEL
• Damascus ★
al-Qunaytra
• al-Qunaytra

Dar'a al-Suwayda
Dar'a •
• al-Suwayda

West
Bank
JORDAN

★	Capital
•	City
Homs	Province
———	International Boundary
- - - -	Disputed International Boundary
–·–·–	Provincial Boundary
———	Major Roads
+++++	Railroads
✈	Airports

0   75 kilometers
0   75 miles

CHAPTER ONE

The Syrian Paradox

L ITTLE ABOUT SYRIA's natural endowments would lead an analyst to predict that it would have such a central role in Middle Eastern affairs. By most indicators of strategic importance—including size, internal cohesiveness, and wealth—Syria would seem destined to be no more than a minor player, relatively easy for greater powers inside and outside the region to marginalize and ignore.

Despite these apparent manifestations of insignificance, vulnerability, and weakness, Syria has long been an important consideration in U.S. foreign policy toward the greater Middle East. Understanding this paradox is essential to understanding the challenges that Syria poses for U.S. policymakers. To that end, this chapter offers an overview of Syria's strategic place in the greater Middle East as well as an overview of the principal analytic questions surrounding Bashar al-Asad's presidency.

Apparent Weakness

Syria today has a population of about 18 million, placing it only in the middle third of Arab League states in terms of size.[1] More than most Arab states, Syria's population is a "fragile mosaic" of ethnic and sectarian communities.[2] Arguably, among Arab states, only Iraq and Lebanon present comparable arrays of distinct communities.

Ninety percent of Syria's population is Arab in ethnicity; another roughly 9 percent is Kurdish, with Armenians, Circassians, and Turkomans filling out the mix.[3] Syria's Arab majority, however, is riven with sectarian cleavages that diminish its coherence as a definer of individual identities. Sunni Muslims are 74 percent of Syria's overall population, but Kurds represent probably 8 percent of that figure, reducing the core Sunni Arab majority to roughly two-thirds of the populace.[4] Another 16 percent of the population, while Arab in ethnicity, consists of various offshoots of Shi'a Islam—Alawis, Druze, and Isma'ilis.[5] (This figure almost certainly includes a few tens of thousands of Twelver Shi'a who are not captured as a distinct community in official Syrian demographic data.) The Alawis are by far the largest community in the category of non-Sunni Muslims; demographers usually estimate Syria's Alawi community at 11–12 percent of the overall population.[6] Christians, of various Orthodox and Uniate traditions and the Latin Rite, along with a smattering of Protestants, make up another 10 percent of the population.[7] Syria's small but historic Jewish community has all but disappeared as a result of emigration in the early 1990s. (For maps of ethnic and religious demography, see p. 3.)

These ethnic and sectarian cleavages have for centuries been the source of considerable social tension in Syria.[8] Even today, there are palpable, historically grounded antagonisms between the Sunni Arab majority and non-Sunni communities. Through much of the twentieth century, these antagonisms were reinforced by the traditional economic dominance of Sunnis in Syria's major cities. They have been reinforced as well by Sunni perceptions of non-Sunni Muslims as heretical and of Christians as willing collaborators with non-Muslims seeking to rule Syria.[9]

In such a climate of ethnic and sectarian antagonism, it was virtually impossible for the entity that emerged as the modern nation-state of Syria in 1946 to integrate its society successfully or forge a cohesive political community. Of course, the difficulties of forging a coherent state structure and national identity in a culturally pluralist society are not unique to Syria; such problems have been felt in other places in the Arab world and, indeed, throughout the postcolonial third world. But these pressures have been undeniably acute in Syria.[10]

To be sure, what many Syrians considered the lack of legitimacy of their country's territorial parameters exacerbated the problem of forging a state structure and a national identity. Most politically aware Syrians viewed their

Syria: Ethnic and Religious Demography

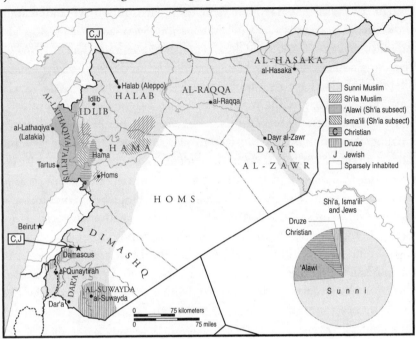

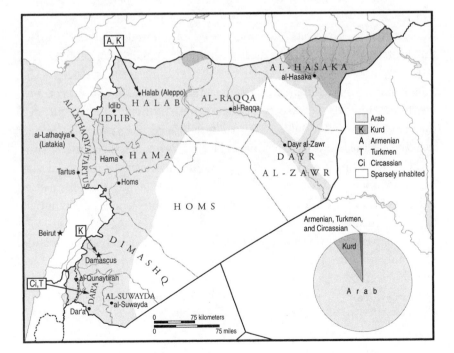

state's territory as having been truncated through Western imperialist intervention. This sense of deprivation went beyond frustration over the creation
of the state of Israel in 1947. Politically conscious Syrians shared a historically
grounded perception, rooted in the experience of the Arab revolt of 1916–20,
that a single state should have been created in historic Syria—*bilad al-Sham*
(literally, the northern region, in Arabic)—joining what are today Syria,
Lebanon, Jordan, Israel, the West Bank, and Gaza in one sovereign entity.[11]

The gap between the proposition that the Levant should be a single political unit (the notion of *suriya al-kubra*, or Greater Syria[12]) and the far more
modest territorial reality of postindependence Syria increased the difficulties in forging a stable state structure or overarching national identity within
a fractured society. Of course, difficulties in forging such structures and
identities in polities whose borders are incongruent with their social structure and political orientation have also been common experiences among
postcolonial nations in other regions of the third world. But this problem
was intensified for emerging polities in the Arab world by the apparent contradictions between the existence of individual nation-states, on the one
hand, and deep attachments to a common Arab-Islamic culture and a pan-
Arab political vision, on the other.[13] And, in the case of Syria, the task was
further complicated by the addition of a more specific pan-Syrian political
construct.

Since Syria achieved its independence as a modern nation-state in 1946,
this accumulated historical baggage has made it a challenging place to govern, always to some degree at apparent risk of coming apart as a society. The
pull of supranational identities, whether Arab or Muslim, and subnational
identities, either to minority sects or non-Arab ethnicity, has complicated
the consolidation of a stable state structure or a genuinely national Syrian
identity. For the first quarter-century of its independence, these internal difficulties helped to keep Syria weak and politically unstable, making it vul-
nerable to manipulation by outside actors.[14] Today, nearly sixty years after
independence, the traditional tensions within Syrian society still lie not far
below the surface of Syrian politics.

Islamic revivalism among Sunni Muslims, while clearly a regionwide
phenomenon during the last three decades or so, has had special resonance
in countries like Syria, with a Sunni majority but also significant non-Sunni
and non-Muslim communities. Historically, the main exponent of politi-

cally oriented Islamism among Syria's Sunnis has been the Syrian Muslim Brotherhood, a *salafi* movement self-consciously modeled on the Muslim Brotherhood in Egypt.[15] The Brotherhood has a long history in Syria, originating before independence, and made a forceful play for political power in the late 1970s and early 1980s.[16] Although the Brotherhood as an organization has been suppressed in Syria for more than two decades, the strength and persistence of Islamic revivalism among a significant segment of Syria's Sunnis continues to reinforce the country's sectarian cleavages and adds another layer of complexity to the maintenance of political stability by secular (and non-Sunni) rulers.

Syria's problematic internal political environment is matched by an undistinguished economy. After more than five decades of effort at economic development, Syria remains comparatively unprepossessing in its economic performance. Its gross domestic product per capita is $3,300 a year, less than that of the most important non-oil-producing economies in the region, including Egypt ($4,000), Jordan ($4,300), Morocco ($4,000), and Tunisia ($6,900), and nowhere near that of the major oil-producing states of the Persian Gulf.[17] More than a quarter of the labor force still works in the agricultural sector, which is focused on cultivation of cereals, cotton, fruits, and vegetables. Almost 30 percent of the labor force works in industry, but Syria's industrial sectors have long been either state-owned (the model for heavy industries) or heavily protected and subsidized by the state (the tendency for light industries, active predominantly in food processing and textile production). For the most part, these industrial enterprises are not internationally competitive. Syria has failed to develop substantial nonagricultural exports, and its agricultural exports do not earn sizable amounts of foreign exchange.

Syria's most important natural resources are deposits of oil and gas, but its proven reserves of both make it at best a second- or third-tier energy producer for international markets.[18] Syria earns at least 50 percent of its trade revenues from crude oil exports; without this windfall, Syria's overall economic performance would be far less positive. More ominously, without development of new sources, Syria's current proven reserves of oil are projected to run out within a decade, prospectively setting the stage, barring compensating changes, for a precipitous deterioration in the country's economic situation.

Challenges for U.S. Policy

These apparent manifestations of weakness notwithstanding, Syria has long been an essential consideration in U.S. foreign policy toward the greater Middle East. Syria's centrality to the U.S. agenda in the region stems in part from its strategic location—at the heart of the Levant, in the heart of the Middle East as a whole. But Syria's regional status also stems from the ability of the regime established by Hafiz al-Asad in 1970 to consolidate a sufficiently stable domestic platform from which to assert Syrian interests on the regional stage. As he tenaciously worked to make Syria a real player in regional affairs, Asad frequently challenged and almost always complicated the efforts of U.S. policymakers dealing with the Middle East. Since Bashar al-Asad succeeded his father, in July 2000, these challenges have continued into the post–September 11 environment.

The Asad regime's inclination to challenge U.S. Middle East policy has not stemmed primarily from the personal obstreperousness of Syrian leaders, but from a particular assessment of what defending Syrian interests required in the face of the U.S. posture toward the region. The United States is, of course, the chief external backer of the state of Israel—from a Syrian perspective, an expansive power seeking regional hegemony. U.S. military and political support has been critical to allowing Israel to expand its territorial holdings and occupy these lands in defiance of what Syrian leaders frequently describe as "international legitimacy." From a Syrian vantage point, U.S. policy in the Middle East for much of the last thirty-five years has aimed principally at ensuring Israel's ability to consolidate and maintain its hegemonic position in the region.

Given this interpretation of the underlying rationale for America's Middle East policy, the Asad regime has long been concerned to forestall a worst-case scenario in which Syria would be encircled by regimes hostile to its interests, allied to the United States, and docile toward Israel (that is, a Lebanon that has made a separate peace with Israel, a pro-Western Turkey cooperating strategically with the Jewish state, an Iraq with a regime supported by and supportive of the United States, a Jordan ruled by pro-American Hashemites who have sold out the Palestinian cause and forged security ties to Israel, and a rump Palestinian entity). Under these conditions, Syria would be marginalized in regional affairs, with other states free to ignore or undermine its interests. The Asad regime's efforts to forestall such a scenario have frequently brought it into conflict with U.S. efforts to promote stability in the Middle East, whether in the Arab-Israeli arena or the region as a whole.

Syria and Regional Stability

Syria has long been a focus for U.S. efforts to stabilize the Arab-Israeli arena. Syria is a leading frontline state, and the Arab-Israeli diplomatic record contains important acknowledgments that a comprehensive peace between Israel and the Arab world cannot be achieved without the conclusion of a peace agreement between Israel and Syria.[19] More recently, the Arab League's 2002 peace initiative made clear that a settlement between Israel and Syria is a predicate condition for peace between Israel and the Arab world as a whole.[20]

U.S. policy toward Syria in the Arab-Israeli context has fluctuated between efforts to facilitate Israeli-Syrian agreements and attempts to isolate and pressure Damascus to change its terms and tactics for achieving a peaceful settlement.[21] The 1974 Israeli-Syrian disengagement agreement brokered by Henry Kissinger marked the beginning of serious U.S. involvement in Israeli-Syrian diplomacy.[22] Jimmy Carter, who came to office eager to pursue a comprehensive Arab-Israeli settlement, certainly recognized Syria's centrality to that project; in the face of Egyptian and Israeli pressure, however, Carter ultimately gave up on the quest for comprehensive peace, pursuing instead a separate Egyptian-Israeli settlement.[23] During the Reagan administration, when Syria's isolation became an important objective of U.S. Middle East policy, the United States pursued a "Lebanon First" option for Arab-Israeli peacemaking as well as a "Jordanian option" with regard to the Palestinian question; neither course proved productive.[24] The administration of George H. W. Bush returned to the goal of a comprehensive peace, with a concomitant refocusing of diplomatic effort on Syria, by convening the 1991 Madrid Peace Conference.[25] President Bill Clinton picked up on his predecessor's efforts and worked until his last year in office to broker an Israeli-Syrian settlement.[26] The administration of George W. Bush, by contrast, has declined to engage on the Syrian track, preferring to press Damascus in the context of the war on terror. In the end, no administration, Democratic or Republican, has been able to escape the ineluctable logic of Kissinger's observation that the Arabs cannot make war without Egypt and cannot make peace without Syria.

More generally, Syria has been, and almost certainly will continue to be, an unavoidable point of reference for U.S. efforts to forge a regional order that is both more stable and more favorably disposed to the interests of the United States and its allies. Syria has long been considered a critical "swing state" in the regional balance. For the first two and a half decades after World War II, Syria was a constant point of struggle between and among Arab republics and their conservative monarchical rivals in an ongoing contest for regional influence.[27] After 1970, when Hafiz al-Asad came to power, Syria became a considerable player in its own right in this contest. In looking at the evolution of Arabism and dynamics within the Arab League since the 1967 Arab-Israeli war, a number of scholars have argued that the dominant trend has been incremental departure away from the overburdening conflict with Israel and toward greater autonomy for individual nation-states to pursue their own interests.[28] Overall, such a generalization seems undeniably true, but throughout the post-1967 period, Syria has often been able to slow the pace of this evolution and in some cases to define its outer limits.[29]

For the United States, Syria has been a long-standing factor in assessments of the regional balance of power. Washington has long considered Syria, in terms of the region's strategic environment, as somewhere in between those states well-disposed toward a negotiated peace with Israel and strategic cooperation with the United States (Egypt, Jordan, the states of the Gulf Cooperation Council, and the more moderate North African regimes, along with Turkey on the region's perimeter), on the one hand, and those states opposed or strongly resistant to such developments (the Islamic Republic of Iran and Iraq under Saddam Hussein), on the other. U.S. efforts to broker an Israeli-Syrian settlement have been motivated not only by an interest in completing the "circle of peace" between Israel and its Arab neighbors, but also by an interest in anchoring Syria squarely in the moderate Arab camp and tipping the regional balance of power against more radical or revisionist actors.[30]

Of course, as the United States has sought to promote these interests following the establishment of the Asad regime in 1970, it has had to cope with Syrian resistance on a variety of fronts. Under Hafiz al-Asad, the Syrian leadership was chronically concerned that the U.S. approach to Arab-Israeli peacemaking would not decisively address the issue of the return of occupied territory. From this perspective, if Syria were not steadfast in defending its diplomatic position, it risked not regaining the Golan Heights lost to Israel during the 1967 war (this suspicion intensified after the government of Menachem Begin annexed the Golan in 1981). There was a concomitant concern that stateless Palestinians might someday act to destabilize Syria; this scenario played itself out in 1970 in Jordan and later that decade in Lebanon, and the Asad regime was determined to forestall a similar turn of events in Syria. Prodded by these concerns, Syria pushed consistently for more than two decades for a comprehensive settlement to Israel's conflicts with its Arab neighbors on a basis that ensured Syria would regain the territory on the Golan Heights.[31]

This meant that Damascus often opposed the preferred direction of U.S. administrations with regard to Arab-Israeli peacemaking. Most notably, in the late 1970s, Asad was bitterly opposed to Egyptian president Anwar al-Sadat's peace initiative toward Israel, and resented President Carter's abandonment of a prospective reconvening of the abortive 1973 Geneva peace conference to shepherd separate Israeli-Egyptian peace talks that culminated in the Camp David Accords of 1979.[32] Asad was concerned throughout the 1980s about a possible deal between Israel and the Palestinians or some sort of Jordanian-Palestinian confederation and, in the 1990s, was sharply critical of Palestinian leader Yasir Arafat's pursuit of a separate peace through the Oslo process.[33]

Chronic concern about possible strategic marginalization also prompted Syria to act, at times forcefully, to thwart what Damascus interpreted as further steps by the United States and Israel to encourage its regional isolation. During the cold war, Hafiz al-Asad was adept at playing on the U.S.-Soviet rivalry to forestall Syria's diplomatic isolation in the region, but he was also willing to act unilaterally against U.S. interests in defense of Syria's regional position.[34] Asad's largely successful campaign to repulse Israel's 1982 invasion of Lebanon, undermine the 1983 Israeli-Lebanese peace treaty, and drive U.S. military forces out of Lebanon was a direct challenge to the Reagan administration's initial strategy for the Levant and the Arab-Israeli arena.[35] Syria's inauguration of a strategic alliance with Iran during the Iran-Iraq War—while motivated by a range of considerations, including an interest in winning Iranian clerical endorsement for the Asad regime's legitimacy as it confronted a Sunni Islamist insurgency—ran against American moves throughout the 1980s to bolster Iraq as a bulwark against the Islamic Republic's revolutionary influence.[36]

Such resistance continued after the end of the cold war. During the 1990s Syria's continued alliance with Iran and, in the second half of the decade, its progressive entente with Iraq threatened the integrity of the Clinton administration's policy of "dual containment."[37] More recently, the intensification of Syria's economic ties to Iraq during 2000–03—which gained most of its momentum after Bashar al-Asad had succeeded his father as president and made Syria the leading violator of UN sanctions against Saddam Hussein's regime—was viewed in Washington as a challenge to the Bush administration's efforts in 2001 to reform the sanctions regime and, subsequently, to U.S. preparations to unseat Saddam.[38] As the Bush administration launched its military campaign against Saddam's regime in 2003, Bashar not only opposed the war but authorized actions that worked against U.S. pursuit of its objectives in Iraq.

Problematic Behaviors

As Syria has resisted U.S. efforts to stabilize the region, it has employed means that the United States considers threatening in themselves to regional and international security. The most problematic of these from a U.S. perspective are Syria's support for terrorism and its pursuit of weapons of mass destruction.

Syria is a charter member of the U.S. government's list of state sponsors of terrorism, a status that Damascus has enjoyed since 1979.[39] Historically, the Asad regime has provided various levels of support to an array of terrorist organizations, including the Kurdistan Workers Party and the Japanese Red Army in addition to a range of secular and Islamist Palestinian rejectionists and Lebanese Hizballah. The regime has consistently viewed its connections to these groups as sources of leverage and pressure for pursuing a range of strategic and tactical goals, mostly in the Arab-Israeli arena.

Syria's involvement in international terrorism began in a serious way in the late 1970s and early 1980s, when Asad used his intelligence apparatus to build contacts and extend operational guidance and support to a variety of radical Palestinian groups that defined themselves in opposition to Yasir Arafat's Palestine Liberation Organization (PLO) and its interest in a diplomatic settlement of the Israeli-Palestinian conflict; Asad even brought these groups together in 1984 in a Damascus-based coalition of secular nationalist factions.[40] Syria used these groups as proxies to carry out terrorist attacks, in the region and abroad, not only against Israeli targets but also against

Jordanian and PLO targets. Damascus sponsored these attacks for a variety of tactical aims, all supporting Asad's overarching strategic goals of pressing for a comprehensive Arab-Israeli settlement and preventing Syria's diplomatic marginalization. These tactical aims included undercutting Arafat's standing as the preeminent Palestinian leader, pressing Jordan's King Hussein and Arafat not to conduct direct talks with Israel, and limiting support for Jordanian-PLO cooperation.

Asad's regime also developed links to terrorist organizations in Lebanon— both Palestinian and indigenous Lebanese groups, including the nascent Hizballah—to carry out attacks against Lebanese, Israeli, and Western targets in Lebanon following Israel's 1982 invasion.[41] Again, Damascus encouraged these attacks in support of various tactical goals: preventing the emergence of a Lebanese government willing to sign a separate peace treaty with Israel, undermining U.S. willingness to stay the course in supporting a genuinely independent Lebanese government, and increasing the price that Israel would have to pay to maintain a military presence in southern Lebanon.

Asad overplayed his hand on the terrorism issue in 1986. Spurred by Israel's interception of a Libyan airliner returning Syrian officials to Damascus in February 1985 and Israel's downing of two Syrian fighters in Syrian airspace in November 1985, Syrian Air Force intelligence—almost certainly with Asad's approval—launched two "special operations" to blow up Israeli jetliners in Europe by having passengers unwittingly smuggle bombs aboard the aircraft. The first of these plots, the so-called Hindawi affair, was uncovered at Heathrow Airport in London in April 1986; the second, in Madrid, was thwarted in June of that year. The international reaction to these attempted terrorist acts was severe. Britain broke relations with Syria over the Hindawi affair, and Asad, mindful of the Reagan administration's strike against Libya earlier that year in response to Libyan complicity in terrorist operations in Europe, worried that Syria might also be attacked.[42]

The failed operations in London and Madrid and the international reaction to them forced the Asad regime to change the nature of its support for the terrorist organizations to which it maintained ties. Indeed, according to official U.S. government statements, Syria has not been directly involved in an incident of international terrorism since 1986.[43] Instead of direct involvement in the planning and conduct of terrorist operations, Syria has focused for the last eighteen years on less direct modes of support for groups that the regime can describe as prosecuting guerrilla campaigns of "national liberation." By providing indirect support, Damascus still seeks to derive tactical leverage from its ties to terrorist organizations, particularly in the Arab-Israeli arena, but also hopes to minimize the risks of international "blowback" from specific terrorist operations.[44]

Syria has continued to provide safe haven to a range of secular Palestinian radical groups, most significantly the Popular Front for the Liberation of Palestine-General Command (PFLP-GC), which maintains its headquarters in Damascus.[45] As Islamist rejectionism emerged as a force in Palestinian politics in the late 1980s and early 1990s, Syria began extending similar backing to Hamas and Islamic Jihad; in 1993, after the signing of the Israeli-Palestinian Declaration of Principles, Damascus created a new rejectionist coalition encompassing both secular and Islamist groups. At this point, both Hamas and Islamic Jihad effectively maintain offices in Damascus.[46] Harboring these groups in Syria allowed (and continues to allow) the Asad regime to demonstrate its support for the Palestinian cause, to exercise some degree of tactical leverage vis-à-vis Israel, and to maintain some residual leverage in its dealings with the PLO.

At the same time, the Syrian leadership appears to have imposed restrictions on the groups' activities in order to make it harder—but not impossible, in a number of specific instances—to establish a clear operational link between rejectionist figures based in Damascus and specific terrorist attacks in Israel or the West Bank. Training activities, for example, have been relocated to Hizballah and PFLP-GC camps in the Biqa'a Valley in eastern Lebanon. It also appears that Damascus has prohibited Palestinian groups under its sway, such as the PFLP-GC, from deliberately attacking U.S. or Western targets, either inside or outside the region.[47]

Similarly, in the Lebanese context, Syria has used its ties to Hizballah to pursue tactical aims in support of its strategic goals of compelling Israel to negotiate peace on a basis acceptable to the Asad regime and bolstering Syria's dominant position in Lebanon. Damascus has for many years been the principal conduit for Iranian military supplies going to Hizballah fighters in southern Lebanon. This has given Syria considerable influence over the group's activities and allowed the Syrian leadership to play the Hizballah "card" in a modulated way, turning up the heat when it wanted to press Israel and moderating Hizballah's paramilitary operations when it wanted to emphasize the desirability of winning Syrian cooperation.[48] (Of course, Damascus has had to take into account the potential costs it might accrue from alienating Iran by constraining Hizballah overly much from an Iranian perspective, but the fundamental point about the Asad regime's tactical perspective on Hizballah's paramilitary activities remains valid.)

Even after Israel's withdrawal from southern Lebanon in May 2000, Syria, under the leadership of Bashar al-Asad, has continued to see its ties to Hizballah as an important tactical tool in its posture toward Israel.[49] And, as will be seen, Bashar has allowed Hizballah to become increasingly involved in supporting anti-Israeli terrorist activity in the West Bank and Gaza in the context of the second intifada, formally known as the Intifada al-Aqsa.

As with the Palestinian terrorist groups it supports, Syria has placed limits on Hizballah's terrorist activities in an effort to manage the risk of regional or international blowback. Over the years, Damascus has sought to manage the pace and scope of Hizballah's anti-Israeli operations in Lebanon and across Israel's northern border to forestall direct and extensive military confrontation between Israel and Syria.[50] Syria has little apparent influence over Hizballah's terrorist activities outside of the region, which are carried out by the group's international wing, the so-called Islamic Jihad Organization, with extensive support from Iran. Nevertheless, Syria seems to have barred Hizballah from targeting U.S. or other Western targets in the region.[51] In addition, Syria has overseen Hizballah's evolution as a political party and major player in Lebanon's parliamentary politics since 1992, helping the group to establish an identity apart from its paramilitary and terrorist functions.[52]

On another important issue, Washington has for many years been concerned about Syria's pursuit of weapons of mass destruction (WMD) capabilities. U.S. government assessments have concluded that the Asad regime's efforts to develop WMD capabilities are focused on the achievement of a "strategic deterrent based on ballistic missiles and chemical warfare capabilities, as the ultimate guarantor of regime survival."[53] There is no evidence that Syria has seriously pursued, or is currently pursuing, a nuclear weapons capability, although some analysts continue to raise the possibility of a covert nuclear program.[54]

The heart of Syria's WMD posture is its indigenous chemical warfare (CW) program. Hafiz al-Asad's quest for a CW capability began before the 1973 war, when Egypt transferred munitions filled with mustard agent to Syria; these munitions were not used during the course of the war. Following the 1973 war, Syria began to develop an indigenous CW program, with assistance from a range of countries, including India, North Korea, and the Soviet Union (and subsequently Russia). These efforts intensified during the 1980s and included the production and weaponization of both blister (mustard) and nerve (sarin) agents.[55] By the 1990s Syria was also producing and weaponizing a more deadly and persistent nerve agent (VX).[56]

Syria's CW arsenal today is assessed by both governmental and non-governmental analysts in the United States and Israel to include stockpiles of mustard, sarin, and VX agent, CW warheads for delivery on surface-to-surface missiles, and aerial bombs for delivery by aircraft.[57] Analysts have also concluded that Syria currently has the largest and most advanced CW program in the Middle East and the most active offensive CW testing program in the region.[58] Syria is not a signatory to the Chemical Weapons Convention.

Syria's development of CW capabilities was accompanied by procurement of ballistic missiles to serve as potential delivery systems for weaponized CW agent. Syria began to build up its ballistic missile capabilities in the late 1960s, focusing originally on battlefield support and tactical missiles. During the 1973 war, Syria used conventionally armed, Soviet-origin, Frog-7 battlefield support missiles against civilian settlements in northern Israel. After the 1973 war, Syria sought to develop a more strategically capable missile force, starting with the procurement of its first SCUD-B missiles from North Korea in 1974.[59] The expansion of Syria's missile force continued during the 1980s and 1990s with the procurement of additional SCUD-Bs, SCUD-Cs, and SCUD-Ds from North Korea.

Currently, Syria's ballistic missile arsenal is assessed by nongovernmental analysts in the United States and Israel to include 200 SCUD-Bs, 60–120 SCUD-Cs, and an uncertain but still small force of SCUD-Ds.[60] These platforms give Syria a capability to deliver conventional or CW warheads against targets in countries in the region allied to the United States, including Israel. In addition, Syria continues to maintain a force of two hundred SS-21 tactical missiles (the Frog-7 follow-on). Beyond this, Syria has over the years developed the capability to produce its own specimens of the various missiles in its inventory and both liquid and solid propellants through acquisition of necessary technology from North Korea and Iran, according to congressional testimony by U.S. intelligence officials.[61]

To this list of Syrian behaviors that are problematic from an American policy perspective, one should add Syria's long-standing domination of its Lebanese neighbor. Starting with Syria's intervention in the Lebanese civil war in 1976, Hafiz al-Asad worked tenaciously to build up an essentially hegemonic position in Lebanon. The elder Asad defended this position throughout his presidency, and it has been maintained by Bashar.

The U.S. posture toward Syria's domination of Lebanon has evolved over the last three decades, moving from an attitude of acceptance and even support during the 1970s to one of criticism and resistance for the past twenty years. Effecting Lebanon's autonomy from Syrian influence was one of the goals behind President Reagan's intervention in Lebanese affairs in the early 1980s. Although the Reagan administration effectively abandoned Lebanon to Syrian hegemony in the mid-1980s, the United States has never subsequently accepted Syria's controlling role there.[62] Since the 1980s the removal of Syrian troops from Lebanon and the promotion of greater effective Lebanese independence have been stated U.S. policy goals, even if successive administrations were not especially assiduous in pursuit of these goals.[63] More recently, the adoption of United Nations Security Council Resolution 1559 in September 2004, calling for the withdrawal of Syrian forces from Lebanon, has renewed debate over how high a priority U.S. policymakers should ascribe to this goal.[64] This debate has intensified in the aftermath of former prime minister Rafiq al-Hariri's assasination in February 2005.

The Post–September 11 Agenda

As the foregoing rehearsal makes clear, most Syrian behaviors that the United States considers threatening or offensive originated well before September 11, 2001. Those behaviors include not only support for terrorism, development of WMD capabilities, and maintenance of a hegemonic posture in Lebanon, but also (until 1997) involvement in narcotics trafficking.[65]

This long record makes Syria, in many ways, a paradigmatic "rogue regime."[66] That record notwithstanding, the United States has never, at least until recently, treated Syria in the same manner as other Middle Eastern rogues, such as the Islamic Republic of Iran or Iraq under Saddam. Washington has consistently maintained normal diplomatic relations with Damascus; even after the notorious Hindawi affair of 1986, the United States, unlike Britain, which broke diplomatic relations altogether, only recalled its ambassador for consultations. Similarly, while the designation of Syria as a state sponsor of terrorism brings the automatic imposition of specific U.S. sanctions on Damascus, Syria is the only state sponsor that has never been placed under comprehensive trade and economic sanctions.[67] And successive administrations have usually left Syria out of their more categorical statements about rogue regimes.[68]

For much of this period, the centrality of Syria to Arab-Israeli peacemaking and its status as a "swing state" in the region have kept successive administrations from any fundamental rupture with the Asad regime. However, the September 11 attacks and the prosecution of the global war on terror have made undesirable Syrian behaviors increasingly problematic from a U.S. standpoint.[69] In the context of the global war on terror, Syria's prominence is almost self-generating. Indeed, Syria falls into that particularly troublesome category, identified by the Bush administration, of states with terrorist links simultaneously maintaining or pursuing weapons-of-mass-destruction capabilities.[70] Moreover, Syria's authoritarian order stands in sharp contradiction to U.S. interests—as part of a program for attacking the roots of Islamist violence—in promoting greater political openness, popular participation in decisionmaking, and economic and social liberalization in the Arab and Muslim worlds.[71]

Syria's status as a state sponsor of terrorism pursuing WMD capabilities was bound to become a source of increasing friction between Washington and Damascus. And, without an active and ongoing Syrian track of the peace process, Damascus lost an important part of its protection against American opprobrium. Syria, under the new leadership of Bashar al-Asad, offered the United States intelligence cooperation against al-Qaeda and related groups in the aftermath of the September 11 attacks, but did nothing to reverse its own terrorist ties.[72]

Increased U.S. frustration with Syrian behavior was clearly reflected in the groundswell of congressional momentum after the September 11 attacks that ultimately led to the enactment of the Syria Accountability and Lebanese Sovereignty Restoration Act. The legislation was designed to mandate the imposition of more punitive restrictions on U.S.-Syrian diplomatic and economic interaction. For at least some of its supporters, the measure was also meant to serve as a precursor for subsequent legislation, modeled after the Iraq Liberation Act and the Iran-Libya Sanctions Act, which would mandate support for Syrian oppositionists and impose secondary sanctions on countries continuing to do business with or invest in Syria.

For two years the Bush administration fended off congressional pressure to pass the Syria Accountability Act. In 2002 State Department officials cited

Syria's cooperation against al-Qaeda to forestall congressional action on the bill.[73] As the administration worked in 2002 and early 2003 to define its approach to Arab-Israeli peacemaking and prepare for war in Iraq, the White House continued to hold Congress at bay by citing the need for maximum diplomatic flexibility.[74]

Of course, during the same period, Syria was adding to the list of U.S. grievances against it by its continuing violations of UN sanctions imposed on Saddam's Iraq, by official Syrian complicity in the transfer of military and dual-use items to Iraq, and by Syrian facilitation of the movement of so-called "foreign fighters" across the border into Iraq in the early days of the war.[75] Once the war had been fought and Syria did not meet U.S. demands to change several problematic behaviors, especially with regard to Syrian links to Palestinian terrorist organizations and Lebanese Hizballah, the administration's willingness to oppose congressional action on the Syria Accountability Act weakened. The effective suspension of U.S.-Syrian information sharing on al-Qaeda further diminished the executive's inclination to resist new legislative measures against Syria.[76] Ultimately, Congress completed action on the Syria Accountability Act in November 2003, and President Bush signed the bill into law the following month.[77] Pursuant to the law, President Bush issued an executive order imposing new economic sanctions on Syria in May 2004.[78] The Bush administration's frustration with Syria mounted in the second half of 2004, as the security situation in Iraq continued to deteriorate. As the president began his second term, the assasination of Hariri sparked a further downward spiral in U.S.-Syrian relations, with Washington withdrawing its ambassador from Damascus.

Thus, Syria's standing in Washington has declined significantly since September 11, 2001. In a very pointed way, the decline underscores that the current approach to dealing with Damascus is not working to achieve U.S. policy goals. As the U.S.-Syrian relationship has deteriorated, disagreements within the U.S. policy community (and between the United States and its allies) over the optimal course for dealing with Syria have intensified.

This situation raises fundamental questions about the appropriate direction for U.S. policy toward Syria. What is the optimal course for changing problematic Syrian behaviors in the context of the global war on terror?

—Should Washington continue ratcheting up economic, political, and rhetorical pressure on Damascus? How likely is such a course to produce significant changes in Syrian behavior?

—Or, should the United States place Syria in the same category as Afghanistan under the Taliban and Iraq under Saddam Hussein—states for which the only way to stop threatening policies was through coercive regime change? If so, how should regime change be pursued in the Syrian case, and what sort of political structures might replace the current order?

—Alternatively, could the United States get Syria to alter problematic behaviors through carrots-and-sticks engagement, along the lines that the Clinton and Bush administrations pursued toward Libya? If so, what would an effective package of incentives and disincentives include and how much change in Syrian behavior could that package induce?

It will be difficult for a U.S. administration to continue indefinitely a course that does not address and resolve the challenges to U.S. interests posed by problematic Syrian behaviors, given the ongoing war on terror and the elevated importance of the Middle East as the principal battle-ground in that war. Thus, the United States will have to come to grips with the problem of formulating a coherent Syria policy.

Analytic Uncertainties

Obviously, American policymakers cannot make sound decisions about U.S. policy toward Syria unless their choices are grounded in genuinely in-sightful assessments of Syrian intentions, motivations, and constraints. Yet, at precisely the time that U.S. officials need to be making sound choices about policy toward Syria, the level of analytic uncertainty about Syria's leadership and regional agenda has risen precipitously.

For thirty years, from 1970 until 2000, U.S. officials concerned with Syria and the Middle East dealt with the increasingly familiar and, in retrospect, rather steady figure of Hafiz al-Asad. Asad's longevity in office, his unques-tioned authority in Syria, and his usually careful and strategic approach to regional affairs gave American policymakers a relative degree of analytic clarity about Syria's long-term goals, tactical preferences, and perceived con-straints. However, since Hafiz al-Asad's death in June 2000 and the accession of his son Bashar to the presidency, that relative degree of analytic clarity about Syria has declined significantly.

Much of the current uncertainty revolves around questions about Bashar al-Asad's leadership. Four and a half years into Bashar's presidency, there is little analytic consensus about the quality of his leadership, his inclinations on key domestic and foreign policy issues, or the degree of influence he really exercises over Syria's internal and external policies. Perceptions of Bashar outside of Syria have fluctuated significantly since his inauguration. Initially, there was appreciable optimism about Syria's new leader. Despite widespread awareness of the constraints on Bashar and the challenges he would face in consolidating and maintaining his position, there was also a sense that he was potentially a different sort of leader from his father. Some observers expected that Bashar's exposure to the West during his postgraduate medical education in Britain would give him a more progressive outlook than his father or the surviving members of the inner circle.[79] Others anticipated that generational succession in Syria could ultimately have a transformative impact on the nature of the Syrian regime.[80] At this point, however, there is a widely held perception that political and economic reforms have not come as fast under Bashar's leadership as some had anticipated or as Syria's many pressing problems demand.[81]

Why has change come so slowly and what does that mean about Bashar al-Asad as a national leader? Several competing and, for the most part, contradictory explanations have been advanced for the current state of affairs, each with its own implications regarding future possibilities for reform in Syria. Three conflicting images of Bashar as national leader currently dominate analytic debates and policy arguments about Syria. These may be summarily described as "Bashar as closet reformer," "Bashar as loyal son," and "Bashar as neophyte."

Bashar as Closet Reformer

The first image presents Bashar as someone who recognizes Syria's backwardness, wants to reform the system he inherited from his father, and seeks to improve Syria's relations with the West, particularly the United States. In this image, however, Bashar is constrained in acting on these impulses by his continuing need for support from an old guard of senior officials in the government and security apparatus. These officials, who served Hafiz al-Asad for decades, are not interested in reforms that would undermine their authority or reduce their families' opportunities for gain through corruption and control over lucrative sectoral monopolies.

The closet-reformer view has two variants, one relatively optimistic and the other relatively pessimistic about Bashar's chances for changing Syria. The more optimistic variant suggests that, over time, as Bashar is able to consolidate power and replace the old guard as it passes from the scene with younger officials who share his interest in reform, he may be able to implement fundamental changes in the system he inherited from his father.[82] The more pessimistic variant presents Bashar as, effectively, Syria's Gorbachev, presiding over a system so fraught with internal tensions and contradictions that he cannot pursue fundamental change without risking either removal from office or a collapse of the established order.[83]

Bashar as Loyal Son

In contrast to the first view, this image presents the Syrian president as a force for continuity and stasis (if not retrogression) in Syrian domestic and foreign policy. From this perspective, Bashar is a thoroughgoing product of the system his father built up over three decades, whose principal goal as president is to protect the core constituencies of the Asad regime and preserve the main elements of his father's foreign policy. In this view, Bashar's disinclination to pursue fundamental reforms in Syria's economic and political order makes him very much part of the "problem" in Syria; he can in no way be considered a prospective part of the solution.[84]

Some analysts in the loyal-son school argue that Bashar may indeed be more rejectionist in his approach to Syrian foreign policy than his father, perhaps under the influence of Hizballah's secretary general, Hassan Nasrallah.[85] (Of course, the degree to which Hafiz al-Asad's conduct of Syrian foreign policy was influenced by rejectionist ideology concerning Israel and the United States is subject to question, as is discussed in chapter 2.)

Bashar as Neophyte

A third image describes Bashar as a callow and inexperienced leader who is probably not up to the job of being president of Syria. Those who see Bashar through this prism argue that he does not have a real vision— whether reformist or status quo in orientation—for Syria's future or a fully thought-through foreign policy agenda. On both fronts, as a Syrian civil society activist put it, Bashar and his advisers "simply do not know what to do."[86] For proponents of this view, Bashar's inexperience and lack of vision are themselves dangers to regional stability.[87]

Each of these images carries its own implications for U.S. policy; the lack of analytic consensus thus exacerbates the lack of consensus as to the appropriate course for policy. Of course, it is possible to array data points selectively to argue the case for any of the three images. Each of them captures legitimate and important aspects of Bashar's leadership and contemporary Syria's political reality. But none of these images is, in itself, an adequate framework for understanding Syrian politics and policymaking during Bashar al-Asad's presidency. To develop an actionable analytic base for formulating sound U.S. policy, it is necessary to take elements from each of these images and assemble them into a more complicated, nuanced, and multivariable account of Bashar's leadership and the realities of Syrian politics today. This is the task to which the bulk of this book is devoted. From this base, it should be possible at the end to evaluate which of the options available to U.S. policymakers—continuing the present course, shifting to a posture of promoting regime change, or moving to serious carrots-and-sticks engagement—is most likely to promote U.S. policy goals with regard to Syria.

CHAPTER TWO

Hafiz's Legacy,
Bashar's Inheritance

T O UNDERSTAND THE challenges confronting Bashar al-Asad—and to draw the correct implications of such understanding for U.S. policy—it is imperative to review the political and strategic situation that he stepped into in 2000. In other words, before examining Bashar's record as president of Syria and considering future possibilities, it is necessary to understand the achievements, failures, and unfinished business that he took over from his father. Hafiz al-Asad was Syria's longest-ruling post-independence leader, dominating Syrian politics for three decades and, more than any other figure, shaping its current political order and social structures.[1] Thus the regime that Bashar heads is still to a significant degree a regime created by his father. Hafiz al-Asad also did more than anyone else to define Syria's place in the region and its posture toward major international players, including the United States.

For these reasons, this chapter is devoted to an examination of Hafiz al-Asad's political bequest to his son and successor. It first considers the nature of the regime that Hafiz al-Asad created, the challenges that managing this regime would inevitably present to a successor, and the substantive policy legacy of Hafiz's tenure as Syria's president with regard to Syria's economy and internal political situation. It then parses the elder Asad's foreign policy record to develop a picture of the strategic challenges facing his son.

The State That Hafiz Built

Hafiz al-Asad's most basic accomplishment as ruler of Syria was to transform the Syrian political order from a coup-ridden, postcolonial, semi-state into a veritable model of authoritarian stability. In doing this, he established a structure of power in Syria that continues to define fundamental political choices for his son.

Before Asad came to power in 1970, Syrian politics was highly unstable. From 1949, just three years after Syria obtained independence, until Asad came to power in the so-called Corrective or Correctionist Revolution (*al-thawra al-tashihiyya*) in 1970, Syria experienced twenty military-backed coups or coup attempts—an average of almost one a year.[2] Even after the Ba'th Party came to power in a 1963 coup, intense factional infighting continued within Syria's new ruling elite. Two more rounds of power struggles occurred, in 1966 and 1970, involving various leadership factions backed by supporting factions in the military-security establishment, before Asad emerged as Syria's supreme leader.

Once he assumed the top position, Asad definitively reversed the historical trend toward instability. During his presidency, Asad fought a bitter struggle against a Sunni fundamentalist challenge to his rule during 1976–82; his own brother, Rifa't, briefly challenged his authority after the president was temporarily sidelined by a heart attack in 1983. Apart from these episodes, however, Hafiz's tenure was an unprecedented episode of stable leadership politics in modern Syria. Understanding the sources of that stability is critical to assessing the challenges confronting Bashar al-Asad today.

Pillars of Stability

At its foundations, the stability of Asad's regime rested on three pillars. These were his nearly absolute mastery of the instruments of power, his construction of a social base sufficiently broad to reinforce his hold on those instruments, and the establishment of a centralized and highly personalized presidential system supported by a strong cult of personality.

The first and most fundamental pillar of stability was, of course, Asad's successful consolidation and exercise of control over key levers of power. This control was manifested in various ways, including:

— the use of the Ba'th Party as a Leninist-style tool for popular incorporation, along with other mass organizations (Peasant Union, Women's Union, Writers' Union, trade unions and professional associations, and youth organizations);[3]

— further use of the party as a tool for establishing the regime's authority over the state apparatus;[4]

— the use of state agencies and public sector enterprises as employers of last resort for an increasingly state-dependent "new bourgeoisie";[5] and

— the "Ba'thization" of the army—or, alternatively, the crafting of an "army-party symbiosis"[6]—to ensure the support of the armed forces for Syria's post-1963 Ba'thist political order.

Along with the mastery of these key levers of power, Asad cultivated a highly developed and coercive police state apparatus to put down perceived, potential, and real threats to the regime.[7] In contrast to Saddam Hussein, Asad was not psychopathic in his use of repression and violence. He employed such measures in an instrumental way to repel what he saw as threats to his regime (as one former U.S. ambassador to Syria has put it, likening Hafiz al-Asad to Don Corleone of *The Godfather*, the Syrian president's use of force or coercion was always "business, not personal"). And, to be sure, there was over time some degree of mitigation in the draconian severity of the treatment meted out to those who ran afoul of the system.[8] Despite this evolution, the human rights situation in Syria remains poor by any internationally recognized standard, and an ongoing record of brutal repression remains an important and inescapable part of Asad's legacy.

Many of these developments were already under way when Hafiz al-Asad assumed the top spot in Syrian politics in 1970, the groundwork for them having been undertaken following the 1963 coup that brought the Ba'th Party to power. But, once he had eliminated his colleagues cum rivals in the post-1963 order, Asad took these ongoing trends in Syrian politics to new heights of sophistication. Moreover, as Asad consolidated his position after 1970, he used his expanding authority to convert the major levers of power—the Ba'th Party, the armed forces, and the intelligence and security apparatus—into personal instruments.[9]

The second pillar of stability was Asad's consolidation of an alliance of social elements sufficiently broad to support his hold on power.[10] Asad's social strategy was largely derived from Ba'thist ideology, but it had very practical benefits for a regime that could all too easily be criticized as narrowly sectarian—indeed, to some, little more than an Alawi cabal—in its base.[11] The essential features of this strategy included:

—the secularization of political and social life, rooted in the Ba'thist commitment to freedom, to appeal to the spectrum of Syrian minorities who define their identities in religious terms (including Christians, Druze, and Isma'ilis, in addition to Alawis) but not to those minority communities (like the Kurds) who define their identities in national terms;

—a populist economic agenda, rooted in the Ba'thist commitment to socialism, to mobilize "new middle class" or "ex-peasant" elements in Syrian society alongside previously marginalized minorities in support of the regime,[12] and

—land reform in the countryside, resulting in a mix of smallholder plots and state-run collective farms in the agricultural sector, to mobilize a significant proportion of the peasantry.[13]

Thus, the social base of Asad's regime was never purely Alawi, or even strictly speaking an alliance of Alawis and other sectarian minorities in Syrian society.[14] Beyond its minoritarian elements, the regime's base also encompassed rural Sunnis who were not part of the Sunni establishment (itself an alliance of the *ulama*—religious scholars—and notable urban families) or not attracted by the increasingly politicized Islamism of the Syrian Muslim Brotherhood. This constituent base never commanded much legitimacy or even acceptance from the urban Sunni population and had to be consistently reinforced by a coercive police state apparatus and a willingness, on Asad's part, to exercise decisive brutality when needed. Nevertheless, it was sufficiently broad to hold the line against a significant challenge to the regime in the late 1970s and early 1980s by the Muslim Brotherhood, seeking to mobilize Syria's Sunni majority against Asad's secular and, in fundamentalist eyes, "heretical" regime.[15]

During his presidency, Asad made important refinements to the established Ba'thist strategy for widening the regime's social base by appealing to the religious sensibilities and economic interests of parts of the urban Sunni population. In the religious arena, while never departing from a fundamental commitment to secularism, Asad tried over the course of his tenure to curry favor with Syria's Sunnis through a variety of public gestures.[16] In the economic arena, Asad sought to find ways, within the statist parameters of Ba'thist economic policies, to provide some limited openings for elements of the traditional Sunni elite to reestablish some of their economic standing.[17]

He had no intention of genuinely empowering these economic elites or, more broadly, the urban Sunni middle class, but wanted, if possible, to co-opt parts of them.[18]

Asad added a third pillar of regime stability to the already established mix of policies and tactics for preserving and enhancing the stability of Syria's Ba'thist regime. This third pillar, uniquely Asad's in its conceptualization and implementation, was the creation of a centralized and personalized presidency.

Asad did not content himself with occupying the top spot in a notoriously unstable political environment; he recast that environment, creating a strongly centralized system of presidential rule that was consciously modeled on Gamal 'Abd al-Nasir's presidential order in Egypt. This strong presidential system was a fundamental break with Syria's previous political experience. It gave Asad a platform from which to exercise not only his increasingly personal control over the levers of power, but also his virtually absolute authority over all matters of state.

Asad installed himself as president and began laying the groundwork for his regime within a year of ascending to the top spot in Syrian politics; he codified the system in a new constitution in 1973. This constitution (and its successors) nominally empowered a legislative assembly and a coalition between the ruling Ba'th and other "progressive parties" in a so-called National Progressive Front.[19] In reality, though, these entities were not institutions in any politically meaningful sense; real power lay with the president, and there were no effective checks on that power.[20]

Asad reinforced this highly centralized power structure by establishing what became, effectively, a tenured inner circle of his regime, the so-called jama'a (group) or, more pejoratively, shilla (gang).[21] This inner circle included a dozen or so senior diplomatic, military, and intelligence officials, all handpicked by the president and often with personal histories (and, in some cases, family ties) linking them directly to Asad. Together, these officials constituted a reliable informal network for executing Asad's instructions and ensuring central control over critical parts of the government.[22] The reliability of inner circle members was ensured not only through careful selection but also through lavish personal perquisites and lucrative opportunities for corruption, either directly or through family members.[23]

Throughout Asad's presidency, the inner circle was clearly subordinate to him. The president maintained regular and direct contact with members of this informal network, compartmentalizing information and rarely meeting them collectively. One former U.S. ambassador to Syria has described this as a "hub and spokes" system, with the president as hub dealing directly and individually with the spokes and the spokes rarely dealing with one another.

During Asad's tenure, the composition of the inner circle consistently reflected the Alawi–rural Sunni alliance that was the cornerstone of his regime's social base. The three most important members of the inner circle who survived Hafiz and continued to serve under Bashar—the so-called old guard—are all Sunnis from rural or small town backgrounds: Vice President 'Abd al-Halim al-Khaddam, Foreign Minister Faruq al-Shar', and Defense Minister Mustafa Tlas.[24]

Beyond developing a strongly supportive and well-regulated inner circle, Asad bolstered his control over the levers of power by nurturing an unmistakable cult of personality around himself as Syria's leader. This did not perhaps reach the heights associated with classic European fascism or Stalinism in the Soviet Union; it probably was less developed than the personality cult surrounding Nasir in Egypt or Saddam Hussein in Iraq. A distinct cult of personality was nonetheless a pronounced feature of Asad's regime throughout his tenure as president.[25]

Challenges for a Successor

Although Hafiz al-Asad spent considerable effort grooming his eldest surviving son—first Basil and, after Basil's death, Bashar—to succeed him and worked hard to prepare the way for a smooth transition, the regime that Hafiz created was bound to be difficult for a successor to master. These difficulties, in turn, would place constraints on a successor's capacity to take bold policy initiatives if he were so inclined.

At least five potential (and interrelated) problems could be anticipated. These were the institutional immaturity of the Syrian presidency, the failure to develop a succession mechanism that was not completely personalized, potential challenges from within the Asad family, the "authority gap" inevitably attached to a successor, and a policymaking apparatus structured for stasis.

INSTITUTIONAL IMMATURITY. It is a commonplace observation among Syria watchers that Asad's dominance over the military, the security apparatus, the Ba'th Party, and the civilian government left Syrian political institutions—such as the ruling National Progressive Front coalition, the Council of Ministers, and the legislative assembly—enfeebled.[26] But this same observation can be applied to the Syrian presidency itself.

The Syrian presidency under Hafiz al-Asad never developed the substantive capabilities of a modern executive, placing constraints on a successor's capacity to take bold policy initiatives. A former U.S. ambassador to Syria has observed that a visit to the president of Syria in the People's Palace on a high hill overlooking Damascus takes on a kind of "Wizard of Oz" quality. One comes to the entrance of the palace—the Syrian equivalent of the White House or 10 Downing Street (but it is much bigger than either)—and takes a two-to-three minute walk along a single long hallway, ascending several levels of steps to arrive at the doorway to the president's ceremonial office. Along the way, one passes a dozen or more offices, arrayed on both sides of the hallway. One notices security officers and other attendants positioned in or around these offices, but it is impossible to discern that any serious policy work is being done in them. No obvious analogues to the National Security Council, the Council of Economic Advisers, or the Office of Management and Budget are to be seen. The palace seems the seat of a president, but not of a true presidency.[27]

Bashar al-Asad himself appears to have come to a fairly acute understanding of these limitations in the power structure and system of governance he inherited from his father. In a January 17, 2004, interview, Bashar told the author that he does not currently have the capacity, within the presidency or the larger bureaucratic structure of the ministries and other agencies, to develop serious reform initiatives in many key policy areas. Until he can revamp the administrative structure of the presidency and the government as a whole, whatever he might do in critical arenas like economic reform would have, in Bashar's words, an "improvised quality."

PERSONALIZED SUCCESSION. Related to the institutional underdevelopment of the Syrian presidency during Hafiz al-Asad's tenure was a second potential difficulty—the failure to develop a succession mechanism that was not completely personalized. Indeed, in Syria, institutionalization of a selection process for succession became impossible following Rifa't al-Asad's attempted takeover in 1984. Hafiz al-Asad judged that he could not designate as his successor anyone who might potentially pose a threat to his own hold on power. Furthermore the designation of a successor could have prompted other regime figures with independent power bases in the military to make a bid for power rather than remain shut out of any possibility to advance to the highest position of authority in Syria. During the last decade of Hafiz al-Asad's presidency, of course, it became increasingly clear that his aim was to pass power to his oldest son—initially, Basil, and then, following Basil's death in 1994, his oldest surviving son, Bashar.[28] This almost guaranteed that Hafiz's successor would have to legitimate himself, at least initially, as a loyal "keeper of the flame" rather than as a bold reformer.

This imperative would make it hard for a successor to chart a coherent policy course that differed significantly from the established way. One of Bashar's advisers on political and policy matters told the author that the need to be seen as keeping faith with Hafiz's legacy is a bigger constraint on Bashar's ability to push reforms than the risk that the old guard will move against him directly.[29]

FAMILY DYNAMICS. Potential challenges from other members of the Asad family placed yet another constraint on an Asad successor, even if that successor came from within the family. If ever a successor appeared to be flagging in his protection of family interest and the broader stability of the regime, other Asad family members could challenge that successor's legitimacy. After all, the most serious direct challenge to Hafiz al-Asad's authority came from his brother when Hafiz was sidelined by a heart attack. Hafiz's clear suppression of Rifa't's challenge effectively closed the question of national leadership for the balance of the elder Asad's presidency; it also ended any real possibility of another challenge to his authority from within the family. Nevertheless, it was widely assumed in the 1990s that Rifa't could pose a similarly serious challenge to the succession of one of Hafiz's sons.[30] Even though that did not happen, generational succession in family and national leadership has reopened the possibility that Bashar might, under the right conditions, face challenges from others in the family.

Bashar, unsurprisingly, has not spoken publicly on Asad family dynamics. But Western diplomats with direct knowledge of the family have pointed out that Bashar's standing in the family is not guaranteed. Bashar's older sister, Bushra, and her husband Asif Shawkat, the deputy director of Syrian Military Intelligence, are, in one former U.S. ambassador's words, a "power couple" in Damascus, with Bushra's ambitions for her husband and herself widely acknowledged in the Syrian capital. Bashar's younger brother, Mahir, is increasingly notorious for his personal greed and complicity in corruption, as are the Makhlufs—Bashar's uncles, aunts, and cousins on his mother's side. Unavoidably, these realities add layers of complexity to

Bashar's calculations about pushing reform initiatives, particularly administrative transparency and the breaking up of sectoral monopolies, that might impinge on the economic interests of core family members.

QUESTIONABLE AUTHORITY. Any Asad successor would surely suffer an authority gap, perhaps even a "brutality gap," in comparison with his predecessor. The presidential system was initially set up to enhance the authority of Hafiz al-Asad in his role as president. After a certain threshold was achieved in its evolution, the system became effectively grounded in universalized elite acceptance of President Asad's prerogatives. Given this history, there was no way that a successor—whether he came from within the inner circle or from outside, whether from inside or outside the family— could take office with anything remotely comparable to Hafiz al-Asad's personal authority and record of decisive brutality. Inevitably, a successor would face the challenge of trying to take decisions that might be potentially controversial within the inner circle—and perhaps beyond—and to hold the system together without the accumulated gravitas of Asad père.

An important implication of this is that any Asad successor would almost certainly have a less hierarchical relationship with the regime's inner circle, which would also make it difficult for him to chart a new course in domestic or foreign policy. This authority gap would almost certainly be more pronounced for someone from a younger generation than for the incumbent members of the inner circle, without, for example, the kind of generational and experiential socialization that historically has helped to legitimate new presidents in Egypt. In this regard, it is notable that old guard officials are frequently described in colloquial Syrian parlance as "the men Bashar called 'uncle.'" Hafiz's departure was also bound to create a situation in which remaining members of the inner circle and their acolytes in the wider governmental structure would have increased opportunities to constrain presidential initiative. Another of Bashar's advisers told me that, since Hafiz al-Asad's death, roughly half a dozen members of the Syrian cabinet have emerged or been appointed who are genuine representatives of "new thinking." This group's impact, however, is limited by its substantive encirclement by a much larger number of ministers who are entrenched defenders of the status quo.

POLICY STASIS. Finally, any successor inclined toward genuine policy reform, especially in the economic sphere, would be hampered by the policymaking structure that Hafiz al-Asad set up for most domestic issues and the professional socialization of the bureaucrats dealing with those issues. As noted earlier, economic and other domestic issues were generally left to the Council of Ministers to handle. The chances for serious reform initiatives being produced by or surviving a vetting process within the established policy process were therefore poor. While Hafiz al-Asad sometimes appointed genuine technocrats to head key ministries (Muhammad 'Imadi at the Ministry of Economy being a good example), they inevitably operated within guidelines defined by the Ba'th Party and in the broader context of a cabinet overwhelmingly composed of Ba'th Party loyalists and ideologically safe representatives of the other parties in the National Progressive Front and headed by prime ministers generally more interested in balancing the interests of various regime constituencies than in formulating coherent policy. These factors inevitably limited the technocrats' impact.

The tendency toward policy stasis within the Council of Ministers was reinforced from below. The ministerial bureaucracies were populated by legions of mediocre civil servants, entrenched in their positions over the decades of Asad's tenure. Asad's limited liberalization measures, while incorporating parts of the traditional Sunni merchant class (particularly in Damascus) into the regime's social base, also fostered a significant degree of dependence on the state within the private sector.

Bashar al-Asad appears acutely aware of this dynamic. Although Bashar was reluctant to talk about the existence of an old guard early in his presidency, as time went on he began to analyze some of the systemic barriers to change in the Syrian government in terms of an expansive definition of the old guard.[31] In January 2004, for example, Bashar told the author that it was a mistake to think of the old guard as simply two or three older officials occupying senior positions at the top of the Syrian power structure. The old guard should also be viewed as a much broader network of "mediocre" and "fossilized" bureaucrats entrenched in their positions over decades. The old guard also extends to a private sector that to a considerable extent is private in name only; important segments of the so-called private sector in Syria have long relied on special arrangements with various parts of the government for the bulk of their business.[32] This unhealthy partnership of status quo–minded bureaucrats and their preferred allies in the private sector, Bashar noted, is a real obstacle to change.

The Economic Inheritance

These five challenges would inevitably test a successor, especially if that successor were Hafiz al-Asad's son. The elder Asad, however, left Bashar not only a hard-to-manage power structure, but also a substantial legacy of unfinished business on the domestic scene. This is true with regard to both Syria's economic development and its internal politics and social dynamics.

During his entire presidency, Asad never moved beyond limited tactical adjustments, described earlier, to alter the basic framework of state socialism for the Syrian economy. Fundamentally, the elder Asad was blissfully unaware of the economic imperatives captured in Thomas Friedman's image of the "golden handcuffs"—the set of measures (such as currency convertibility, reducing barriers to imports, lowering barriers to foreign investment, privatizing state enterprises, eliminating state subsidies, and fighting corruption) that define the liberalization of formerly closed and statist economies in the era of globalization.[33] Indeed, Asad's fundamental attitude toward globalization was one of ignorance supplemented by vague suspicion. His ignorance of basic economics is reflected in a story related by a U.S. diplomat who visited Syria in 1990. In their conversation, Asad adduced recent reports of the high percentage of taxi drivers in Damascus with professional degrees in engineering and medicine as evidence of Syria's socioeconomic success.[34] Asad had little international experience to sensitize him to the realities of a globalizing economic order. Before becoming president, his overseas experience consisted of stays in Egypt and the Soviet Union for training and service as a fighter pilot and a summer spent in Great Britain largely in seclusion from internecine struggles among the leading figures of Syria's Ba'th regime following the 1963 coup.[35]

The overriding objective of Syrian economic policy during Asad's presidency was to avoid the sort of profound socioeconomic crisis that could threaten the stability of the regime. Asad believed—probably not incorrectly—that an important proximate cause for the outbreak of the Islamic revolt in 1976 had been a precipitous decline in Syria's economic performance and standard of living.[36] For the remainder of his presidency, Asad was determined to avoid a similarly destabilizing downturn in Syria's economic conditions (while also avoiding enriching the Sunni merchant class too much). From this perspective, the near-to-medium term costs of serious structural adjustment seemed decidedly unattractive.

Asad was able to avoid being forced to implement more thoroughgoing reforms in Syria's increasingly outmoded economy in significant measure because of exogenous developments that, at critical points, relieved intensifying pressures for a fundamental rethinking of his regime's basic economic policies.[37] Asad was also helped by a kind of indigenous and informal social safety net in Syria provided, for the most part, by families and, to a lesser extent, by mosques, churches, and other religious institutions. Syria, as even a study highly critical of the human rights situation in the country notes, "is not plagued with the crushing urban poverty found in many Middle Eastern countries; there are virtually no shantytowns around its cities and malnutrition is rare."[38] Somehow the economically stressed are accommodated better in Syrian society than elsewhere in the region, which mitigates the social and political impact of economic underperformance.

Cosseted by these developments, Hafiz al-Asad over the course of his presidency never seriously engaged with the process or substance of economic policy reform and structural adjustment as prescribed in the so-called Washington Consensus. In 1991 Asad accepted a reform of Syria's legal and regulatory environment for foreign investment, codified as Investment Law Number 10. This, however, only chipped away at the margins of state socialism in Syria.[39] Asad also could not turn to the United States for technical expertise, as Syria's designation as a state sponsor of terrorism beginning in 1979 meant that the United States was barred by its own law from providing economic assistance to Damascus. And, during the last decade of Asad's presidency, Syria never developed other international relationships that might have helped it chart a course of serious economic reform, despite Asad's frequent meetings with World Bank president James Wolfensohn during the 1990s.[40]

As a result of this record, Hafiz's successor would face virtually all of the policy challenges posed by a largely unreformed socialist economy in a post–cold war, increasingly globalized international order. Indeed, it is no exaggeration to say that the economy that Bashar inherited from his father was stuck in a central-planning time warp.[41] The public sector remained huge, with grossly inefficient state-owned enterprises employing well over half of the workforce and another 23 percent of the labor force working directly for the government bureaucracy.[42] Private sector initiative and entrepreneurship continued to be stifled by overweening regulation and poor economic conditions. Despite the promulgation of Investment Law

Number 10, foreign investment was negligible because of an inhospitable bureaucratic environment and corruption.[43]

In addition, the economy was dangerously undiversified in its sources of income. During the last decade of Hafiz's presidency, the Syrian economy became increasingly dependent on petroleum, which emerged as the leading sector in Syria's export profile in that period. By the end of the 1990s, the petroleum sector accounted for 20 percent of Syria's total gross domestic product, two-thirds of its exports, and about half of government revenues. Yet, at the time of the transition from Hafiz to Bashar, oil production from Syria's aging fields was in decline, and some analysts anticipated that Syria might return to being a net oil importer in just a few years. [44] Earnings from agriculture, a traditionally important sphere of economic activity and the second largest export sector of the Syrian economy after petroleum, fluctuated considerably based on rainfall and other weather conditions.[45]

Moreover, the Syria that Hafiz al-Asad bequeathed to his son was a textbook example of the nexus of demographic expansion and poor macroeconomic performance that characterizes so many states in the Middle East. The annual population growth rate in Syria, though slowing, is still one of the more rapid rates of population expansion in the world.[46] Almost half the population is under fifteen years of age, creating the classic demographic profile of a "youth bulge," with at least 200,000 new entrants to the labor market in Syria each year.[47] The weak private sector and overstaffed public sector are unable to create enough jobs fast enough to absorb the rapidly burgeoning labor force and stem rising rates of youth unemployment.[48] At the time of the transition from Hafiz to Bashar, international experts estimated that Syria would need to reach and maintain roughly three times the rate of annual real growth in the economy as it was actually achieving to accommodate growth in the labor force and ease unemployment and chronic underemployment.[49] Obviously, such an expansion of economic performance could not be achieved without very significant structural adjustment.

Thus, given the economic situation that Bashar al-Asad inherited, his ability to put Syria on a more positive economic trajectory might be perhaps the greatest policy challenge confronting him. From early in his presidency, starting with his inaugural address, Bashar himself acknowledged the importance of improving Syria's economic performance.[50] More recently, in January 2004, Bashar described for the author his sense that economic reform is the essential foundation for urgently needed social and political reforms in Syria.

But, given the difficulties that Bashar continues to face in managing the power structure he inherited, the task of economic reform and structural adjustment in Syria is more politically daunting than in many other developing countries. Bashar confronts an overriding challenge in balancing the imperatives of economic liberalization in Syria with the imperatives of consolidating and maintaining his power as president.

Politics and Civil Society

In the political and social spheres, the most significant long-term domestic challenge left over from Hafiz al-Asad's presidency is the unresolved sectarian cleavage in Syrian society between the Sunni majority, on the one hand, and the ethnic and religious mosaic of various minority communities, on the other. This unresolved cleavage is an important challenge to Asad's successor for a number of reasons, most immediately because of the widely perceived minoritarian character of the regime. As was seen earlier, Hafiz al-Asad was able to win the backing of other minority communities in Syria beyond his Alawi base; he also won at least the passive support of those rural Sunnis who benefited from Ba'thist economic policies, such as land reform in the countryside that displaced urban Sunni notables from their traditional status as absentee landlords.[51] At various points and in various ways over the course of his presidency, Asad tried to accommodate the interests and sensibilities of urban Sunnis to mitigate their opposition to his regime and co-opt key actors in the Sunni community. These efforts, though, never succeeded in definitively closing the sectarian split in Syrian society.

This reality was demonstrated most dramatically in the Muslim Brotherhood's uprising against the Asad regime in the late 1970s and early 1980s.[52] The brutal suppression of this uprising in the city of Hama in 1982 was the defining moment for the domestic standing of Hafiz al-Asad's presidency. How a contemporary Syrian feels about Hama reveals much about his political orientation; how an outside analyst interprets Hama says much about his view of Syrian political culture and of the Asad regime. In the latter category, Thomas Friedman's observations about Hama remain impressive. He argues that Hama really needs to be interpreted simultaneously in three ways: as the struggle of a particular tribe to fend off a mortal challenge from an alien tribe, yes; as the response of a Middle Eastern autocrat who does not enjoy full legitimacy among his people to a serious threat to his rule, undoubtedly; but also as the reaction of a modernizing politician in a relatively new nation-state trying to stave off retrogressive elements aiming to undermine the construction of a secular political order.[53] While the latter two of Friedman's interpretations say much about the nature of Asad's regime, his "tribal" interpretation captures an inescapable truth about Syrian society.

In this regard, the successful suppression of the Muslim Brotherhood's armed challenge to Asad's regime did not change the basic reality of Syria's sectarian divide. The Brotherhood itself has apparently never recovered organizationally from the blow it suffered at Hama.[54] But the sectarian divide in Syrian society continued. The elder Asad recognized this and kept trying even in the years after his confrontation with the Brotherhood at Hama to assuage Sunni sensitivities.[55] Sectarian divisions were reinforced by ongoing trends in Syrian society, particularly the intensifying "Islamization" of the Sunni majority.[56] Moreover, as urbanization has proceeded since 1982, the balance of urban versus rural Sunnis has shifted in favor of the former, creating a social climate potentially even more conducive than that of the early 1980s to an Islamist resurgence.[57]

The Islamization of Sunni society is not unique to Syria; given Syria's recent history, though, it has special significance there, raising the specter of a resurgence of the Muslim Brotherhood and, prospectively, Islamist rule in Syria. But there are also reasons to argue that genuine political openness in Syria would not automatically mean an assumption of power by the Brotherhood. Civil society activists of a decidedly liberal, non-Islamist persuasion suggest that the alternative, regime-sanctioned Islamist movement founded and run for many years by Grand Mufti Ahmed Kuftaro has made inroads in some parts of Syria that, historically, have been Brotherhood strongholds.[58] In a more open environment, Sunni politics in Syria might display more complexity and nuance than assumptions of reflexive support for the Muslim Brotherhood would predict.

However one might assess the chances for a resurgence of the Muslim Brotherhood, the ongoing Islamization of Syria's Sunnis underlines that ameliorating the sectarian divide through some sort of attenuation of sectarian identity remains the most fundamental social and political challenge facing Bashar al-Asad, and is critically important for successful long-term political liberalization in Syria. The most powerful long-term antidotes to a prospective Islamist resurgence are likely to be, first of all, economic modernization and more effective integration of Syria into the global economy and, second, the development of a robust civil society as a foundation for political liberalization. The economic challenges that Bashar al-Asad inherited from his father were considered earlier. With regard to the development of civil society in Syria, the legacy of Hafiz al-Asad's presidency leaves substantial unfinished business for his successor.

The right of the Syrian population to establish civil society organizations is enshrined in the Syrian Constitution (Article 39), but this is hardly reflected in the reality in Syria under the Asad regime. During Hafiz al-Asad's tenure, a handful of Syrian intellectuals, such as Sadiq al-'Azm and Muhammad 'Aziz Shukri, managed to establish themselves in the 1980s as civil society theorists with some measure of freedom to articulate their views publicly and even develop ties outside the region. [59] The regime, particularly in the early 1990s, flirted with a few largely cosmetic liberalization measures, and some nascent civil society organizations and activists emerged.[60] But the emergence of truly independent political associations was inhibited by the government's use of long-standing emergency powers to crack down on opposition figures. Compared with what the Syrian polity needs as a platform for meaningful political liberalization, civil society in Syria remains woefully underdeveloped.[61] Thus, given the domestic situation that Bashar al-Asad inherited from his father in 2000, the new president's evolving posture toward the development of civil society is another important litmus test for his administration.

The Foreign Policy Record

In his conduct of Syria's foreign affairs over thirty years, Hafiz al-Asad developed a "grand strategy" for his country that still conditions his son's foreign policy choices and options. The elder Asad's approach to foreign policy was a steely mix of ideology and Machiavellian calculation. On the one hand, Asad's formative exposure to Ba'thist ideology conditioned in him a deep attachment to Arab nationalist ideas and narratives.[62] Asad appears to have seen himself as a latter-day Saladin, leading a sanctified Arab struggle against twentieth century Crusaders from Europe, the United States, and Israel.[63]

As Asad's thinking on regional affairs evolved in the years leading up to his political ascendancy in 1970, he seems to have abandoned a passion for pan-Arabism in favor of a pan-Syrian view. The idea of Greater Syria would be an important reference point in his approach to thinking about Syria's posture in the region—his political and strategic aspirations in Lebanon, his attitude toward Israel, and his expectations of other Arab states.[64] As his strategic framework evolved, Asad always retained an acute sense, grounded in his Ba'thist formation, that European colonial treachery had undercut the possibility of Arab unity, whether defined in pan-Arab or pan-Syrian terms, and that the creation of the state of Israel with U.S. and Western backing was a consummate imperialist act.[65]

At the same time, Asad was widely recognized by adversaries and allies alike as a highly intelligent practitioner of power politics who was not likely to let ideology or grandiose ambitions get in the way of the effective pursuit of his regime's interests.[66] The intra-Ba'th power struggle that brought Asad to power in 1970 was, in substance, a struggle between the intensely ideological approach of radical Ba'thists seeking to make Syria the spearhead for a pan-Arab revolution and war of liberation in Palestine and the more realistic inclinations of those, like Asad, who judged that this kind of messianic revisionism had brought about Syria's defeat in the 1967 Arab-Israeli war. Throughout his presidency, in approaching foreign policy decisions, Asad always refracted his ideological vision through a balance-of-power prism.[67]

Asad was, by all accounts, a genuinely strategic thinker, with a consistently held set of long-range policy goals growing out of both his Arab nationalist worldview and his considered assessment of the regional balance of power. Of these goals, the two most important were intertwined, forming the core of Asad's foreign policy agenda: containing what the Syrian leader saw as Israel's hegemonic aspirations in the region and forestalling Syria's diplomatic isolation. Tactically, Asad was generally very cautious in the way he managed the various threads of Syrian foreign policy, but no one doubted that he had carefully integrated these threads into an overall strategy for pursuing his long-range goals.[68]

Containing Israel would be the hallmark of Hafiz al-Asad's foreign policy. Throughout his presidency, Asad cultivated an image as the most stalwart Arab leader in his resistance to Israel. But Asad's resistance was more than just the basis for an image likely to be well received on the Syrian and

Arab streets. Throughout his public life, Asad appears to have held an extremely negative view of Israel, seeing it not only as an imperialist outpost but also as a territorially acquisitive neighbor bent on becoming the dominant power in the region.[69] If that happened, from Asad's perspective, it would mean the end of any prospect for true Arab self-determination. By the time Hafiz al-Asad became leader of Syria, Israel had wrested the Golan Heights from Syrian control in the 1967 war, after many years of cross-border skirmishes and raids, and Asad had effectively given up on whatever youthful aspirations he may have had to reverse the catastrophe of 1948. He understood that the Jewish state was there to stay; but there was still a battle to be fought over the terms on which it stayed.[70]

Related to Asad's perceived imperative to contain Israeli influence in the region was an equally strong imperative to avoid diplomatic marginalization. As noted earlier, Asad was chronically concerned that Syria could become encircled by pro-Western regimes willing to coexist with Israel. In such a scenario, Syria would become isolated and utterly marginal to regional diplomacy. The United States and, by extension, Israel would have no incentive to address Syria's legitimate grievances in the Arab-Israeli arena or accommodate its other regional interests.

Asad integrated the threads of his foreign policy into a disciplined approach to pursuing his two overriding strategic goals. In this carefully elaborated and sustained strategic approach, Asad created a legacy that was bound to be an important point of reference for a successor. It is not an exaggeration to argue that, as Asad integrated the various threads of Syria's foreign policy in pursuit of his long-range strategic goals, he was effectively drafting a "script" for managing Syria's diplomacy and national security, rooted in his thirty years of experience as a national leader, that he would leave for his son. This script reflected not only his sense of the policies that were needed to maintain and enhance Syria's regional and international position, but also his notion of the essential foreign policy parameters that were necessary for preserving the stability of the regime he had created. Analytically, it could be said that the script brought together four major components of Asad's national security strategy and foreign policy: establishing and protecting Syria's position in Lebanon, defining Syria's posture in the Arab-Israeli arena, ensuring Syria's role in the regional balance, and managing Syria's relationship with the United States.

Lebanon

The consolidation of a dominant Syrian position in Lebanon was the first significant foreign policy accomplishment of Hafiz al-Asad's presidency; defending that position would be an important part of the foreign policy script for his successor. As he consolidated Syrian hegemony in Lebanon, the elder Asad came to see the maintenance of that hegemony as critical to pursuit of both his core strategic objectives. Denying Israel the use of Lebanon as a platform for military operations was, from Asad's perspective, essential to any prospects for containing Israeli influence in the region. Similarly, keeping Lebanon closely tied to Syria and depriving it of an independent foreign policy was a vital part of Asad's defense against diplomatic marginalization in the region.

Asad built Syrian hegemony over Lebanon in a long struggle running for a decade and a half, from the mid-1970s until the conclusion of the Ta'if Accord in 1989.[71] This struggle unfolded in three phases. In the first phase, during the mid-1970s, the imperative to contain the spread of confessionally driven instability from Lebanon to Syria (at a time when Asad was in the early stages of his struggle against the Muslim Brotherhood) led the Syrian leader to establish himself as the ultimate arbiter of Lebanese political life. In the aftermath of the 1973 Yom Kippur war, Asad worked assiduously to displace Cairo as the principal external point of reference for Lebanese politicians of various confessional backgrounds.[72] After the Lebanese civil war broke out in 1975, Asad used diplomatic means in an attempt to patch together a compromise that would extinguish the conflict, before intervening militarily in 1976 on behalf of conservative, predominantly Maronite forces. Asad won considerable regional and international endorsement for this initial intervention.[73]

In the second phase, during the late 1970s and early 1980s, Asad had to defend Syria's nascent hegemony against significant challenges from Israel and the United States. After the outbreak of the Lebanese civil war, Israel had begun to intervene in Lebanon—politically and, in 1978, militarily—to quell a mounting security threat from Palestinian paramilitary and terrorist operations originating from southern Lebanon.[74] In response to an emerging alliance between Israel and the Maronite-led Phalange movement, Syria shifted its support from Maronite forces toward Lebanese radicals and the PLO.[75]

The deepening involvement of Israel in Lebanese affairs eventually prompted a showdown between Israel and the United States, on the one hand, and Syria, on the other, for strategic dominance in Lebanon. Intensifying conflict between Phalange forces, now backed by Israel, and Syrian troops and proxy militias prompted Israel to invade Lebanon on a more massive scale in June 1982, in Operation Peace for Galilee.[76] The stated goal of the operation was to end the threat of Palestinian attacks against Israel from Lebanese territory. But, as part of the strategic rationale for its military campaign, Israel, with backing from the United States, also sought to negotiate a separate peace treaty with a Lebanese government to be headed by the Phalangist Bashir Jumayyil, who was elected president by the National Assembly in August 1982.[77] This initiative was to be aided by the introduction of a U.S.-led peacekeeping-cum-stabilization force, called the Multinational Force (MNF); the initial purpose of this force was to provide a security cover for the evacuation of the PLO from Lebanon. The MNF was introduced into Lebanon in August 1982, the same month as Jumayyil's election.[78]

Hafiz al-Asad responded decisively to this challenge to Syria's position in Lebanon. Following their 1982 invasion, Israeli forces in Lebanon were subjected to an increasingly intense paramilitary campaign. Syrian agents assassinated Bashir Jumayyil in September 1982 before he could take office; his brother, Amin, took office as president in his stead (Amin started up peace negotiations with Israel in December 1982). Syrian-backed Druze and Shi'a militias engaged in repeated clashes with the MNF, and in April 1983 Hizballah carried out its first high-profile suicide bombing attack, against the U.S. Embassy in Beirut. On May 17, 1983, Amin Jumayyil signed the Israeli-Lebanese peace treaty. It was never to be ratified. Five months later, on October 23, 1983, the MNF suffered significant casualties in a car bombing attack by Hizballah on U.S. Marine and French paratrooper barracks in Beirut. U.S. forces responded with naval bombardments and air strikes on Syrian positions in the Biqa'a, but Syrian forces were able to down two American warplanes in December 1983.[79]

Having shown that his forces and Lebanese proxies would do whatever was necessary to forestall a strategic defeat in Lebanon, Asad prevailed in his test of mettle with Israel and the United States. After further deterioration in the security situation—in no small part due to Syrian efforts to make the environment maximally uncomfortable for a continuing U.S. presence—

the MNF withdrew in February 1984. The next month, President Jumayyil abrogated the Israeli-Lebanese peace treaty.[80] In June 1985, with U.S. forces and the MNF withdrawn, Israel reduced the size of the security zone it had set up in 1978 in southern Lebanon with the aim of giving the Israel Defense Forces (IDF) a more defensible position. (Israeli forces would stay in this smaller security zone until their unilateral withdrawal in May 2000.)

The abrogation of the Israeli-Lebanese treaty clearly marked Asad's success in defending Syrian hegemony in Lebanon. In the course of this defense, Asad also solidified Syria's role as Lebanon's ultimate arbiter and enforcer.[81] In the third phase of his struggle for Lebanon, Asad sought to consolidate his gains through establishment of a relatively stable Lebanese government that would be closely allied with Syria and by winning legitimation for a continuing Syrian military presence in Lebanon. For the most part, Asad achieved these aims under the terms of the Ta'if Accord (formally, the Charter for Lebanese National Reconciliation), concluded in 1989 under Saudi and Arab League auspices.[82]

As he consolidated and managed Syria's hegemony over Lebanon, Asad wrote the Lebanese portion of his successor's foreign policy script, identifying Syria's fundamental interests in Lebanon as well as the tactical tools for protecting them. Throughout the post-Ta'if period, Asad defined Syrian interests in Lebanon to include defending Syria's western border against a "flanking" attack by Israeli forces, using the south as a platform for pressing Israel to negotiate the return of the Golan Heights, maintaining control over Lebanese foreign policy and the major currents of Lebanese political life, and monitoring Islamic extremists and other sectarian groups operating in the country.[83] (One might also mention, in elaborating Syrian interests, the use of Lebanon as an employment venue for Syrian expatriate workers, the repatriation of remittances from those expatriate workers, and opportunities for corruption on the part of Syrian intelligence and military officers posted there.)

At the same time, Asad developed four principal tools to protect these interests, which he would also bequeath to his successor. The first of these tools was Syria's military deployments in Lebanon.[84] These deployments effectively bar Beirut from pursuing an independent policy on security matters and foreign affairs, prevent the Lebanese government from extending its control over areas of the country deemed vital to Syrian interests (for example, the south), and block reemergence of sectarian conflict.[85]

A second tool for maintaining Syrian hegemony in Lebanon has been the deployment of an extensive apparatus of Syrian intelligence officers throughout the country. For many years under the command of Syrian military intelligence brigadier general Ghazi Kana'an, this apparatus—and its extension, the Lebanese intelligence and security services—allowed the Asad regime to keep tabs on and influence all important aspects and sectors of Lebanese political, economic, and social life.[86]

Third, Asad leveraged his relationship with Hizballah, the only confessional militia to retain its arms after Ta'if, to maximize the strategic value of Syria's hegemony in Lebanon. In the post-Ta'if period, Syria's use of Hizballah as a paramilitary proxy even became regulated through "rules of the game" negotiated both formally and tacitly with Israel.[87]

Finally, the Asad regime took advantage of characteristics of the Lebanese political system that it helped to create at Ta'if to bolster its dominant role as arbiter of Lebanese political life. From early on, Lebanese politicians in the post-Ta'if period understood that, whatever their particular needs were, they could be met only through cooperation with Damascus.[88] In turn, Syria's role as political arbiter gave Asad a platform for playing factions against one another and for managing, at a national level, the balance among competing sectarian groups.[89] Throughout the post-Ta'if period, Syria has carefully orchestrated Lebanon's elections to bolster its divide-and-conquer strategy for maintaining relative balance among competing factions, using techniques including manipulation of electoral districts, candidate lists, and voter rolls and, in some cases, outright falsification of votes to ensure its preferred outcomes.[90]

By the time of Hafiz's death, this formula for preserving and leveraging Syrian hegemony over Lebanon was showing signs of strain. In 2000 a resurgence of anti-Syrian sentiment within the Maronite community produced at times anti-Syrian protests and occasional violence.[91] The imminent return of Rafiq al-Hariri as prime minister would also challenge a new Syrian leader's stewardship of Lebanese affairs; Hariri, a Sunni billionaire who had originally come to the premiership in 1993 with Saudi backing to oversee Lebanon's post-Ta'if economic reconstruction, had a track record of pushing the limits of Lebanese autonomy and independence vis-à-vis the Syrians. With the Israeli withdrawal from the security zone in south Lebanon a month before Asad's passing, the rationale for Hizballah's military activities in the south was coming under increasing international

The Golan Heights

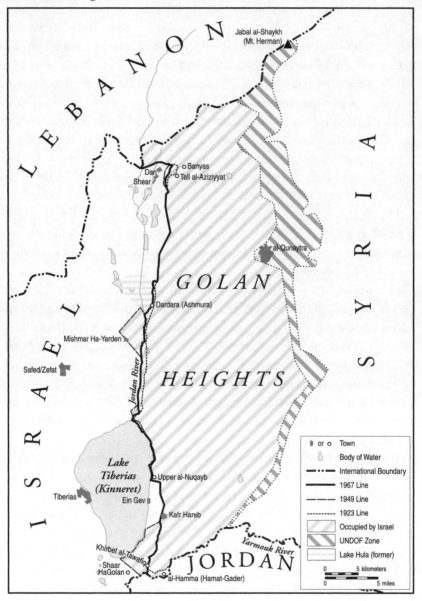

scrutiny and criticism.[92] As chapter 4 shows, adapting to these new Lebanese realities was sure to be a challenge for Bashar al-Asad after he assumed the presidency.

The Arab-Israeli Arena

In the Arab-Israeli arena, Hafiz al-Asad's most significant bequest to his successor was a major evolution in Syria's posture toward a negotiated settlement with Israel. From early in his presidency, Asad recognized that, in all likelihood, return of the Golan could ultimately be achieved only through negotiations.[93] But Asad's views regarding an acceptable strategic framework and format for peace talks evolved in important ways over the course of his tenure. The elder Asad's evolved positions on these issues would be important elements of the foreign policy script he left for his son.

For the first two decades of his presidency, Asad insisted that the only negotiating format in which the Arabs could get an acceptable deal with Israel was a multilateral process aimed at a comprehensive agreement, with the Arab parties negotiating in close coordination with one another.[94] Even after Egypt had dropped out of the equation by concluding a separate peace with Israel, Asad continued to emphasize the importance of a united Arab position for peace talks.[95]

For much of the same period, Asad sought to compel Israel to enter into this sort of negotiation through the actual or threatened use of military force.[96] During these years Asad was prepared to initiate military conflict with Israel (as he did in 1973), viewing the use of force to seize occupied and (if possible) Israeli territory primarily as a means to spark a diplomatic process on terms favorable to Syria. Initially, Asad sought to do this in a military and political alliance with Egyptian President Anwar al-Sadat. After Sadat cut a separate peace with Israel in the 1978 Camp David Accords, Asad sought to develop an alternative posture for pressing Israel militarily, seeking through most of the 1980s to use his ties to the Soviet Union to acquire what Syrian official statements described as "strategic parity" with Israel.

As the 1980s wore on, the unreliability of Soviet military assistance, especially after the ascension of Mikhail Gorbachev to the top of the Soviet leadership, forced Asad to reevaluate this course.[97] Although the rhetoric of strategic parity would linger on to the end of the cold war and the disappearance of the Soviet state, in fact Asad began to shift Syria's strategic posture toward a greater emphasis on "asymmetric" modes of force—principally, the development of nonconventional military options that would provide Damascus with some degree of strategic deterrence against Israel and the increased use of terrorist operations by proxy organizations as a source of tactical leverage in the Arab-Israeli arena.[98] The shift toward asymmetric modes of force meant that Asad was effectively abandoning the initiation of military conflict with Israel as a way of compelling peace negotiations on terms favorable to Syria.[99]

With the end of the cold war and the disappearance of the Soviet Union as a potential strategic or military patron, Asad finally dropped the rhetoric of strategic parity and declared that a negotiated peace with Israel had become Syria's preferred "strategic option" and that peace could, under appropriate conditions, be negotiated on a bilateral basis between Israel and Syria.[100] This was the approach underlying Asad's participation in the October 1991 Madrid peace conference, convened at the initiative of George H. W. Bush's administration in the Gulf War's aftermath to jump-start the Arab-Israeli peace process.

For Asad, "appropriate conditions" for bilateral Israeli-Syrian peace talks meant that negotiations had to be conducted on the basis of internationally recognized "principles" (that is, the substantive elements of United Nations Security Council Resolutions 242 and 338, "land for peace" as codified in the terms of reference for the Madrid conference) and mediated by the United States.[101] These conditions regarding format would be passed along in the foreign policy script for Asad's successor.

Once he navigated the turn in favor of a negotiated bilateral settlement with Israel, Asad moved to establish firm requirements for an acceptable deal. These requirements—which can be distilled to full Israeli withdrawal from occupied Syrian territory within the framework of a comprehensive settlement—also became important elements in the foreign policy script that father would leave to son. Asad's insistence on full withdrawal and comprehensiveness were rooted in his sense of what was necessary to legitimate an agreement among key domestic and regional constituencies and to square a settlement with his status as the last avatar of Arab nationalism.[102] (As the 1990s wore on and Hafiz began to groom first Basil and then Bashar to succeed him, the elder Asad assumed that this would be critical to a smooth transition and long-term regime stability.)[103]

Asad's chief requirement for an Israeli-Syrian peace treaty was an outcome that he could plausibly portray as full Israeli withdrawal from the Golan Heights. Well before there was a serious prospect for bilateral negotiations, Asad had identified return of the Golan as the essential foundation for Israeli-Syrian peace; official Syrian statements from the Madrid conference in October 1991 until the Clinton-Asad summit in April 2000 consistently indicated that full withdrawal remained Asad's most important criterion for an acceptable agreement. Indeed, Syrian statements during these years staked out a stark rhetorical position on the withdrawal issue, making it difficult for Asad or an immediate successor to retreat.

But Asad's insistence on full withdrawal was not simply a declaratory posture. Syrian negotiating behavior clearly reflected the centrality of the withdrawal issue for the Syrian leader. In this regard, the once highly secret but now famous "deposit" by which Israeli prime minister Yitzhak Rabin expressed a willingness to withdraw fully from the Golan if Israeli requirements on postwithdrawal security arrangements and normalization of relations were met became the key to progress in negotiations. Pursuant to the Rabin offer, three "cycles" of Israeli-Syrian negotiations were held in 1994, 1995, and late 1995 and early 1996 (consisting of three separate rounds at the Aspen Institute's Wye River Conference Center).[104] If one examines those negotiations carefully, it seems clear that Asad's degree of confidence that Israel was serious about full withdrawal was directly correlated with his willingness to let Syrian negotiators deal constructively with issues of security and normalization.[105] Even after the Rabin and Peres years, the Rabin deposit continued to be Asad's litmus test of Israeli intentions and seriousness about a peace deal as he negotiated with prime ministers Binyamin Netanyahu and Ehud Barak.[106]

The failure of the Syrian track during Barak's tenure seems a genuinely tragic case of missed opportunities. Barak came into office in mid-1999 eager to do a deal with Syria, giving the Syrian track priority over possible final-status talks with the Palestinians; Asad also seemed particularly interested in concluding an agreement. But Barak was unwilling to endorse, publicly or privately, the Rabin commitment to full withdrawal from the Golan Heights. This severely undermined Asad's confidence, especially during U.S.-mediated discussions in Shepherdstown, West Virginia, between an Israeli delegation headed by Barak and a Syrian delegation headed by Foreign Minister Faruq al-Shar' in January 2000.[107] In the aftermath of the Shepherdstown talks, President Clinton inaccurately conveyed to Asad Barak's willingness to meet Asad's requirements on the withdrawal issue; this inaccuracy may have been reinforced by a follow-up message to the Syrian leader imprecisely conveyed by the Saudi Ambassador to the United States, Prince Bandar bin Sultan.[108] Ultimately, Barak's failure to come through on the withdrawal issue in early 2000—and the failure of the Clinton administration, in the words of a peace team member, to "exercise adult supervision" over Barak on the issue—set the stage for the failure of the April 2000 Clinton-Asad summit in Geneva.[109]

In addition to full withdrawal, the Syrian leader was unrelenting in his insistence that an Israeli-Syrian settlement be comprehensive, with a minimum of phases and a comparatively short timetable for implementation. From the Madrid conference until his death in 2000, Asad consistently rejected suggestions for concluding an initial declaration of principles or an Oslo-like interim accord as a confidence-building measure in anticipation of a final deal.[110] Asad viewed the Oslo approach as highly prejudicial to Arab interests; during the 1990s, chronically missed deadlines in the Palestinian track and the failure of negotiations to engage decisively on final status issues only reinforced his skepticism about incrementalism.[111]

In the end, of course, Asad did not conclude a peace agreement with Israel, the Syrian track having effectively collapsed at the Geneva summit meeting with President Clinton in March 2000, just three months before Asad's death.[112] This outcome would have profound implications for the foreign policy challenges that would confront his successor. In particular, the failure of the Syrian track would significantly complicate Bashar al-Asad's management of Syria's position in the Arab-Israeli arena. On this front, as in Lebanon, shifts in Syria's strategic circumstances at the end of Hafiz's presidency put significant strain on the established policy formula at precisely the moment that a new and untested leader was assuming power.

The Regional Balance

Hafiz al-Asad believed that he could not fulfill his requirements for a settlement with Israel without managing the wider regional balance of power and avoiding diplomatic marginalization.[113] Thus the elder Asad's script provided his son and heir with guidelines and parameters for managing Syria's relations with other important regional players, rooted in the father's historical experience.

Hafiz's efforts to avoid marginalization focused on two tracks. First, he sought to maintain the support of moderate Arab states for Syria's position vis-à-vis Israel. Second, as a hedge against fundamental deterioration in Syria's strategic position, he cultivated bilateral ties with states in the region that were problematic from a U.S. foreign policy perspective.

Over the course of his presidency, Hafiz al-Asad's inter-Arab diplomacy evolved in its tactical orientation, but not in its foundational strategic logic. During the 1980s the Syrian leader was highly motivated to keep other Arab parties from negotiating separate peace treaties with Israel, focusing on Lebanon, Jordan, and the Palestinians. As this proved an increasingly quixotic undertaking, at least with regard to Jordan and the PLO under Arafat, Asad shifted to a different approach in the 1990s, trying to manipulate the regional balance to ensure that his requirements regarding an acceptable Israeli-Syrian peace agreement were supported by other Arab states.[114]

In this context, Asad paid special attention to his ties with Egypt's president, Hosni Mubarak.[115] In the early 1980s Asad had vigorously tried to enforce Egypt's ostracism from the Arab fold.[116] However, as the quality and quantity of Soviet patronage began to decline after Gorbachev's accession as Soviet leader in 1985, Asad realized he would need Egypt as a mainstay in the regional balance. The passage of an Arab League resolution in 1987 allowing member states to restore diplomatic relations with Cairo coincided roughly with the beginning of Asad's embrace of a negotiated peace with Israel as Syria's "strategic option." Calculating that Egyptian support would strengthen his position, Asad sought Mubarak's endorsement of his requirements for an acceptable deal in return for his acceptance of Egypt's return to an inevitably dominant position in the inter-Arab arena. This bargain has been the foundation for Egyptian-Syrian relations since Asad restored diplomatic relations with Cairo in 1989.

At the beginning of the 1990s, Asad also moved to shore up his relations with the Gulf Arab states and, above all, with Saudi Arabia. Asad had been able to win significant financial assistance from Saudi Arabia and other Gulf states in the 1970s, but Syria's support for Iran during the Islamic Republic's war with Iraq had led to the diminishment and then termination of Saudi Arabian support. When assistance from Saudi Arabia and other Gulf states pledged to Syria as a frontline state in the Arab-Israeli conflict expired in 1988, it was not renewed.[117] In that context, as Alasdair Drysdale has pointed out, Iraq's invasion of Kuwait in 1990 "could not have come at a better time from Syria's point of view, since it provided the Asad regime with a perfect opportunity to maneuver its way back to the center of things, cement its relationship with Egypt, ingratiate itself with Saudi Arabia and the Gulf shaykhdoms, and demonstrate its importance both within the region and to the West."[118] The Gulf War not only restored (at least for a few years) the flow of financial assistance from Saudi Arabia to Syria, but it also restored some measure of Saudi-Syrian strategic cooperation.[119]

The revitalization of Syria's alliances with Egypt and Saudi Arabia was an important aspect of Hafiz al-Asad's diplomacy during the last decade of his presidency and an important element of the foreign policy script bequeathed to Bashar. With the demise of the Soviet Union completed by 1991, Islamic extremism again on the rise in the region, and Syria engaged in an unprecedented process of bilateral negotiations with Israel, Asad needed the support of the two leading moderate Arab states. In particular, Asad wanted a better relationship with the United States, from his perspective the only effective restraint on Israeli expansionism and the indispensable intermediary for an acceptable peace agreement. Egypt and, to a lesser degree, Saudi Arabia could help Asad "make the case" for Syria in Washington. Thus, maintaining their support was essential to Asad's strategy for containing Israel and forestalling diplomatic marginalization.

In addition to cultivating ties with moderate Arab states, Asad sought to bolster his regional position by leveraging bilateral relationships with "problem" states. The goal of such relationships was to increase the prospective costs to the United States, Israel, and other regional actors of ignoring or threatening Syria's interests.

Asad's relationship with the Islamic Republic of Iran, started in the early days of the Iran-Iraq war, clearly fit this logic.[120] In any prospective confrontation with Israel, cooperation with Tehran gave Asad at least potentially greater strategic depth.[121] Cooperation with Iran—albeit sometimes strained by diverging interests—was also a significant factor in Asad's strategy for consolidating Syria's hegemonic position in Lebanon during the 1980s.[122] As time went on, Hizballah's anti-Israeli operations in Lebanon served as a focus for further development of Iranian-Syrian relations, particularly after the conclusion of the Ta'if Accord in 1989.[123]

In addition to deepening his ties to Iran during the 1990s, Asad in the latter half of the decade sought progressive relaxation of tensions with Saddam's Iraq. For almost three decades, Syria and Iraq had been at odds, divided by Ba'thist ideological disputes dating back to the 1960s, by Syria's support for Iran during the Iran-Iraq war and its participation in the Gulf War coalition, and by the mutual distrust and antagonism that had grown up between Hafiz al-Asad and Saddam Hussein.[124] With the UN imposition of economic sanctions on Iraq after the Gulf War, Saddam had come to see the value of improving economic and diplomatic relations with Syria, but Asad remained skeptical. After the announcement of the Israeli-Turkish alliance and the election of Israeli prime minister Netanyahu in 1996, however, Asad began to shift Syria's posture toward Iraq, allowing for a resurgence of Syrian-Iraqi trade and, by the end of the decade, undertaking preparations for reopening an oil pipeline between the Kirkuk oil fields in northern Iraq and the Syrian port of Banyas.[125] Additionally, rumors periodically cropped up in the regional press in 1998 and 1999 about the possibility of a diplomatic and strategic entente between the two countries.[126]

By pursuing better ties with Saddam's regime alongside Syria's established ties to Iran, Asad clearly signaled the Clinton administration that he could undercut both legs of the administration's "dual containment" policy. More broadly, Asad's relationships with Iran and Saddam's Iraq also provided a kind of strategic insurance against a complete collapse of the Syrian track of the Middle East peace process or of Syria's relationship with the United States.[127] (At the most extreme end of strategic possibilities, Asad's posture raised the prospect of a "bad boys" alliance consisting of Saddam's Iraq, the Islamic Republic of Iran, and Syria.) Keeping up this kind of strategic insurance would be a signal point in the foreign policy script Bashar received from his father.

At the time of the succession, though, the value of such strategic insurance was becoming subject to question. After September 11, 2001, the potential benefits for Syria of relationships with members of the "axis of evil" would grow even more dubious. Thus, Bashar al-Asad, from fairly early in his presidency, would have to find new ways to manage Syria's regional position, adding another level of challenge to what would prove a problematic foreign policy agenda.

Relations with Washington

Throughout his presidency, Hafiz al-Asad understood that success in achieving his two fundamental strategic objectives was inextricably bound up with his relationship with the United States. Both during and after the cold war, Asad's posture toward Washington swayed between cooperation and confrontation in accordance with his perception of broader regional developments. In the last decade of his presidency, though, the attraction of a strategic realignment toward the United States increased in importance as a driving consideration in his foreign policy calculations. As a consequence, the centrality of Syria's relationship with Washington would be an important feature of the foreign policy script left to Bashar.

During the cold war, the elder Asad adroitly exploited his evolving relationship with the Soviet Union to further his strategic aims while flirting with the United States when that served his interests. Asad knew that Moscow was eager to recruit Syria as a major regional ally in the zero-sum competition with the United States for influence in the Arab world and the Middle East more generally.[128] Asad calculatingly used this Soviet interest to leverage military support from Moscow while periodically signaling to Washington his willingness to turn westward in his own strategic orientation. The Syrian leader's balancing act was intended to ensure that he could maintain a position of strength vis-à-vis his regional adversaries, through either force of arms or diplomatic cover by one of the superpowers. This approach guided Asad in his dealings with the Nixon, Ford, Carter, and Reagan administrations.

Asad's basic approach to the superpowers emerged during the Nixon administration in the diplomacy surrounding the October 1973 war. Senior U.S. diplomats came to Syria for the first time in Asad's tenure in the immediate aftermath of the war. Although Soviet weaponry and technical support had enabled him to launch a surprise attack on Israel, the Syrian leader recognized that his ally could not influence his enemy in postwar negotiations; as a result, Asad accepted U.S. mediation of the postwar disengagement agreement. During Secretary of State Henry Kissinger's shuttle diplomacy, Asad made clear that he sought to improve relations with the United States despite the ongoing conflict with Israel.[129] Asad's discussions with Kissinger helped to pave the way for the conclusion of a separation of forces agreement between Israel and Syria in May 1974 and a visit by President Nixon to Damascus in 1974.[130] The Nixon visit marked a new high in U.S.-Syrian relations in the 1970s, as U.S. aid to Syria resumed and Syria gained greater room to maneuver between the two superpowers.

U.S.-Syrian relations continued to improve after President Gerald R. Ford replaced Nixon; several major agreements for the provision of U.S. assistance to Syria's economy and its agricultural and educational sectors were signed in 1975. Syria's new channel with the United States paid off for Asad in important ways in 1976, providing the Syrian leader critical diplomatic cover for his initial intervention in the Lebanese civil war. Asad feared the conflict in Lebanon was following the pattern of the 1970 Jordan crisis, when Syria had been drawn into battle in defense of Palestinian guerrillas fighting the Jordanian state, only to be hit by Jordanian forces and threatened by Israel, with the United States backing both. As noted earlier, powerful strategic considerations compelled Syrian intervention in the Lebanese civil war, but intervention risked provoking an unwanted confrontation with Israel. The United States shared this concern and initially urged both sides to hold back, while encouraging Syrian diplomatic efforts to forge a compromise among warring Lebanese factions. When those efforts failed, Asad was able to persuade the Ford administration to act as a go-between with Israel and arbitrate the first red-line agreement, effectively providing U.S. and Israeli authorization for Syria's intervention in Lebanon on behalf of the beleaguered Maronites as long as Syrian forces did not enter the southernmost part of the country.[131]

This episode also demonstrated Asad's ability to play Syria's military relationship with the Soviet Union against his burgeoning diplomatic dealings with Washington. Syria's intervention rankled Moscow, which supported the leftist forces in Lebanon, and caused delays in Soviet arms shipments to Damascus. But Asad was able to maintain the U.S. cover he had obtained for his Lebanese intervention while coaxing the Soviets back to his side.[132] Moscow had no choice but to resume arms shipments if it wanted to retain any influence on Syrian foreign policy.

After Jimmy Carter was inaugurated in 1977, Asad welcomed the new administration's recognition of the need for a Palestinian "homeland" and believed that this was a sign of further convergence of U.S. and Syrian interests.[133] But while the Carter administration remained at least rhetorically supportive of the Syrian role in Lebanon, the U.S.-Syrian relationship began to decline during the late 1970s, most significantly because of the U.S. role in brokering the 1978 Camp David Accords. As was noted, Camp David was a major blow to Asad's aspirations for a united Arab front against Israel.

The Syrian leader viewed Egypt's peace treaty with Israel as a betrayal of pan-Arab interests, and his confidence in U.S. diplomatic initiatives was weakened by President Carter's role in midwifing the agreement.[134] Developments in Lebanon also undermined Asad's confidence in U.S. intentions, beginning with Israel's March 1978 invasion of southern Lebanon, at a time when his regime was also coping with the Muslim Brotherhood revolt and restive Lebanese Christian militias spoiling for a fight against Syrian occupation forces. Asad felt surrounded and read into the multiple challenges a U.S. plot, publicly accusing Washington in 1979 of fomenting domestic strife in Syria.[135] To signal his displeasure, as well as boost Syrian military capabilities in a quest for strategic parity with Israel, Asad signed a Treaty of Friendship and Cooperation with the Soviet Union in 1980.[136]

Asad's return to the Soviet fold coincided roughly with the election of President Ronald Reagan, in whose administration regional conflicts such as that in Lebanon and the Levant more broadly were viewed primarily as an arena for cold war competition. On coming to office, the Reagan administration reoriented U.S. policy toward Lebanon, adopting a position that all foreign forces, including Syrian troops, should be removed from Lebanon.[137] Only when Israel downed two Syrian helicopters and Syria responded by moving surface-to-air missile batteries into the Biqa'a in May 1981 did Reagan reengage diplomatically with Damascus.[138] From 1981 to 1983, Philip Habib, Reagan's special envoy to the Middle East, played a central role in U.S. diplomatic maneuvering with Syria, attempting throughout to contain the chaos that was unfolding on the ground in Lebanon. Habib's initial assignment was to cobble together a new red-line agreement. But Asad's perceptions of U.S. intentions darkened with the apparent green light the Reagan administration gave to Israel for its invasion of Lebanon in 1982. Habib was dispatched again to separate Israeli and Syrian forces, but by the time of the envoy's arrival in the region, the Israel Defense Forces had already mounted an offensive against Syrian positions in Lebanon. Syrian forces took a beating, and America's inability or unwillingness to compel Israeli compliance with numerous cease-fires exhausted U.S. credibility in Asad's eyes. U.S. diplomacy brokered the departure of the PLO from Beirut in 1982 but then failed to prevent the massacre of Palestinian civilians in the Sabra and Shatila refugee camps in southern Lebanon after Washington had pledged to guarantee their safety.[139]

As noted earlier, the Reagan administration's decision to push forward with an effort to reconstitute a Maronite-dominated Lebanese state by force and broker a separate peace treaty between Israel and Lebanon was viewed by Hafiz al-Asad as a serious threat to Syrian interests. After winning a strategic victory by forcing the United States to recognize Syrian prerogatives in Lebanon, Asad continued to view Washington with suspicion through the remainder of Reagan's tenure in office. U.S. contacts with Damascus were limited for the most part to terrorism issues. In response to U.S. entreaties, Syria ejected the Abu Nidal organization from its territory when Washington presented evidence of the group's involvement in airplane hijackings.[140] But Reagan's retaliatory air strike against Libya in 1985 and the international fallout from the Hindawi affair raised Asad's concern that the United States was preparing for a similar strike against Syria, resulting in reduced diplomatic contacts and a tense period of mutual wariness.

With the decline and collapse of the Soviet Union at the end of the 1980s, however, Asad recognized that he needed to effect a fundamental strategic realignment toward the United States.[141] Asad's reappraisal coincided roughly with the presidency of George H. W. Bush. Compared with his predecessors, the first president Bush was uniquely receptive to the potential benefits of engaging Syria.[142] And, soon after Bush's inauguration, Asad's suspicions of U.S. intentions toward Syria's position in Lebanon were assuaged somewhat by U.S. acquiescence in the conclusion of the Ta'if Accord in 1989.[143] Thus, the advent of the first Bush administration made it easier for Asad to contemplate a strategic realignment toward the United States.

Asad's first positive step in the process of realignment was his participation in the U.S.-led Gulf War coalition in 1990–91. Damascus was swift to react when Iraqi forces overran Kuwait in August 1990 and responded with relative alacrity to U.S. overtures in the fall of that year to join the emerging international coalition to liberate Kuwait.[144] In return for a Syrian military deployment that contributed Arab legitimacy to the operation, Asad attained a new high in his relations with Washington, in addition to reaping an economic windfall from Gulf states.

Asad's second step toward realignment was his decision to join in a renewed, U.S.-sponsored effort at Arab-Israeli peacemaking. Secure in his mastery over Lebanon and having established a new level of cooperation with the United States, Asad was positioned by 1991 to embark on a diplomatic process meant to return the Golan to Syrian control and establish a final peace with Israel. Syria was the first Arab nation to respond positively to the first president Bush's invitation to the Madrid peace conference. For the last decade of Asad's presidency, the post-Madrid Syrian track of the Middle East peace process was his chief venue for seeking a better relationship with Washington. For Asad, concluding a peace agreement would be the vehicle not only for addressing Syria's strategic concerns about Israel's regional influence, but also for arriving at a new strategic understanding with Washington and for resolving outstanding bilateral differences (on terrorism and weapons of mass destruction, for example). Bilateral Israeli-Syrian talks did not progress very far during the balance of the first Bush administration, but the Syrian track prompted extensive and high-level U.S.-Syrian interaction during both terms of the Clinton administration, particularly after Rabin indicated his contingent willingness to consider complete Israeli withdrawal from the Golan Heights.[145]

In the end, of course, the Syrian track failed to pay off as Asad had anticipated, an outcome that would have profound implications not just for Syria's standing in the Arab-Israeli arena but for its relationship with the United States as well. The collapse of the Syrian track effectively left Damascus and Washington with no alternative avenue for constructive engagement just two months before the transition in Syria's political leadership.[146] This component of Syrian foreign policy would thus become a major challenge for Bashar al-Asad.

CHAPTER THREE

Bashar and the Possibilities of Domestic Reform

A RANGE OF COMPETING images of Bashar as a national leader is at play in current analytic discussions about Syria. The three principal images, described in chapter 1, are of Bashar as closet reformer, loyal son, and neophyte. Each of these images offers a relatively simple and straightforward explanation for policy outcomes during his tenure, and each carries its own implications regarding the most appropriate U.S. policy toward Syria. But, while each image captures some portion of the "truth" about Bashar, none in itself provides a wholly adequate framework for understanding Syrian politics and policymaking under his leadership. To develop an analytic base that is truly "actionable" for those formulating U.S. policy toward Syria, it is necessary to take elements from each of these images and assemble them into a more complicated and nuanced account of Bashar's leadership and the realities of Syrian politics today.

Constructing such a framework requires, above all, a careful examination of Bashar's record in the presidency and his handling of key policy issues. With this in mind, this chapter concentrates on Bashar's approach to internal issues. It opens by looking at Bashar's background and preparation for the presidency, his views about the domestic economic and political challenges confronting Syria, and the steps he has taken to consolidate his position since succeeding his father. Against that backdrop, Bashar's handling of domestic issues is reviewed, with particular reference to questions of economic reform and fostering a more robust civil society in Syria.

The Asad family: Anisa and Hafiz al-Asad flanked by their children, from the left, Majid, Bashar, Basil, Mahir, and Bushra.   (© Corbis Sygma)

The Making of a President

Bashar's background and the process by which he came to the presidency provide essential information for understanding him as a national leader. A review of Bashar's personal and political formation suggests that he is capable of thinking about political and policy issues in a different way from his father, but is reluctant to put himself fundamentally at odds with his father's legacy or regime figures closely associated with that legacy. Such a review also suggests that Bashar is genuinely inclined toward reform in his approach to governance, but did not come to power with a well-elaborated vision for change.

Bashar al-Asad was born in Damascus on September 11, 1965, the third surviving child of Hafiz and Anisa al-Asad and their second son.[1] Bashar grew up with an older sister, Bushra (five years older), and an older brother, Basil (three years older). They would be joined over the years by two other brothers, Mahir and Majid.[2] Syrians who know the family typically describe Bushra as bright, outgoing, and extremely ambitious and Basil as having been dashing and domineering; Bashar, in comparison, seems to have been the polite and slightly ungainly middle child, carving out an identity among his siblings largely by excelling academically.

Bashar was educated in a manner characteristic of children of the Syrian elite during the early years of the Asad regime. He attended the Fraternity School, a well-known institution in Damascus serving the children of the Syrian elite.[3] Syrians who attended school with Bashar and his siblings remember him as the most academically inclined of the Asad boys, quieter and more bookish than either Basil or Mahir.[4]

In looking at Bashar's decisions about his own academic career and professional aspirations, it is important to keep in mind that he was not his father's first choice as the next Asad to hold Syria's presidency. Hafiz al-Asad initially chose his oldest surviving son, Basil, for grooming as a successor, apparently in the early 1990s.[5] The elder Asad made this selection on the basis both of primogeniture and an assessment of the relative suitability of his sons' personalities to the demands of ruling Syria. Basil's anointing left Bashar more or less free to determine his own path in life. In contrast to his brothers, Basil and Mahir, who pursued careers in the Syrian military, Bashar chose to study medicine, matriculating at Damascus University's medical school in 1982.

Bashar's decision is interesting both in terms of what it may indicate about his relationship to his father and what it suggests about Asad family dynamics more broadly. As a young man, Hafiz al-Asad originally wished to study medicine but had to give up this ambition because of a lack of family resources.[6] Bashar's decision to pursue a medical career undoubtedly won him a unique sort of paternal approval. More broadly, as a senior Israeli intelligence official pointed out to the author, Bashar's choice of a medical career reflects a traditional pattern of occupational choice within Semitic families, whether Arab or Jewish: the eldest son prepares to take over the family business (even if that business is ruling a country), the second son enters a learned profession (that is, medicine or law), the third son gets a secure government job (as with Mahir's military career), and the fourth son may turn out as something of a ne'er-do-well (Majid has for years been rumored to suffer from a mix of substance abuse problems and mental illness and may have received treatment for these problems in Germany).

Once Bashar chose to study medicine, the pattern of his university education and medical training was also characteristic of his generation of the children of Syria's elite. He initially studied at Damascus University, receiving his medical degree there in 1988. In contrast to elite offspring from other Arab countries, who commonly begin their university studies outside the region or, in some cases, at the American University of Cairo, children from the top stratum of Syrian society have usually done an initial round of university training in Syria, perhaps supplementing that with a period of postgraduate study in Europe or the United States.[7] Bashar's educational career followed this pattern: after graduating from medical school at Damascus University and fulfilling his military service obligation by working as an army doctor, Bashar went to the United Kingdom in 1992 to begin postgraduate training in ophthalmology—the equivalent of a residency program in the United States—at Western Eye Hospital, part of the St. Mary's group of teaching hospitals in London.[8]

This pattern is noteworthy not least because it delimited Bashar's exposure to the West, both chronologically and substantively, with potentially important implications for his future perspective as a national leader. Not only is Bashar from a younger generation than the members of Hafiz al-Asad's inner circle, but he has had more direct experience in the West than most of them.[9] Bashar's time in London may have encouraged his sense that Syria needed to change in significant ways. Yet in the relatively short time he was there, he focused primarily on his medical studies and not on the political and economic issues that might have enabled him to develop a fully fledged reform agenda.[10] One might reasonably hypothesize from this that Bashar's reformist impulses are probably somewhat attenuated and that he will need a high degree of substantive support to translate them into concrete policies.

Preparing for the Presidency

Bashar's medical education and exposure to the West were abruptly interrupted, and the course of his life radically altered, by the death of his brother Basil in an automobile accident at Damascus International Airport in January 1994.[11] After returning to Damascus for his brother's funeral, Bashar was promptly put in Basil's place to be groomed for the succession. Bashar was never formally designated as Hafiz al-Asad's successor; as we will see, the elder Asad died just before steps of this nature might have been taken. Nevertheless, over what turned out to be a six-and-a-half-year period, the father worked systematically to prepare the son for power.[12]

The process of preparing Bashar for the presidency moved forward on three levels. First, the elder Asad sought to build up Bashar's support within the military and security apparatus. Second, he sought to build up Bashar's standing with the Syrian public. Finally, Hafiz al-Asad worked to familiarize his son with the substantive dimensions of his future role.

Bolstering Bashar's standing within the military and intelligence apparatus was a critical aspect of the grooming process, since it would be impossible for him to accede to the presidency and hold onto the position without at least acceptance and passive support from the armed forces and the security services. It was also an aspect that required special attention. Both Basil and his younger brother Mahir were seen (at least in the public eye and, presumably, within military ranks as well) as men with genuine inclination toward and competence regarding military matters. In contrast, the new heir apparent was comparatively unexposed to this important lever of power.

Part of the effort to build up Bashar's standing with the military focused on developing his meager military credentials; after all, he had left the army as a doctor two years before Basil's death at the relatively junior rank of captain. Shortly after returning to Syria, Bashar was put through the army's course for commanders of tank battalions. He was placed in command of such a unit in November 1994 and was promoted to major in January 1995, a year after Basil's death.[13] In 1996 Bashar enrolled in the command and general staff course at the Higher Military Academy, from which he graduated with honors (some accounts claim he was first in his class) in July 1997.[14] Upon graduation, Bashar was promoted to lieutenant colonel and put in command of the same elite Republican Guard brigade that Basil had commanded. At the beginning of 1999 Bashar was promoted again, to the rank of staff colonel.[15]

Moves to bolster Bashar's personal military credentials were supplemented by regular manifestations of support by the highest-ranking military officers within the elder Asad's inner circle. Within months of his return to Syria, Bashar was appearing at military ceremonies and events with Defense Minister Mustafa Tlas; as early as the November 1994 ceremony for Bashar's installation as a tank battalion commander, Tlas began expressing his positive regard for Bashar as a potential successor to Hafiz al-Asad. As Bashar's military training proceeded, it became publicly known that the deputy chief of staff, Lieutenant General 'Ali Aslan, was also supportive of Bashar's accession to the presidency. In June 1998 it was reported that Bashar, then a lieutenant colonel, presided over a major military exercise alongside Tlas and Aslan.[16] It is difficult to gauge the impact of such measures on attitudes about Bashar's fitness to lead Syria's armed forces among either more rank-and-file members of the officer corps or the public at large. Nevertheless, these measures were signals of Bashar's rise as a potential successor.

To manage whatever doubts about Bashar's suitability to lead that would still be felt within the armed forces at the time of the succession, Hafiz al-Asad also sought to pave the way for his son by shaping leaderships for key military elements that were less likely to question Bashar's credentials and, therefore, more likely to support his accession to the presidency when succession occurred. Initially, the focus was on units traditionally considered essential for regime protection. In 1994 President Asad replaced the long-time chief of the special forces, Major General 'Ali Haydar, after Haydar expressed opposition to a hereditary succession.[17] The following year, the president accepted the resignation of Republican Guard commander Major General 'Adnan Makhluf, a nephew of the elder Asad's wife, after Makhluf had a falling out with Bashar.[18]

Over time, the effort to forge a military leadership that would support Bashar when the time came extended to the highest echelons of the security apparatus. In February 1998 Hafiz al-Asad dismissed his brother Rifa't from the office of second vice president (for national security affairs).[19] Later the same year, President Asad allowed the retirement of his long-time ally and long-serving armed forces chief of staff, Lieutenant General Hikmat Shihabi, replacing him with 'Ali Aslan. While a number of factors may have contributed to Shihabi's retirement, including poor health, knowledgeable Syrians and some foreign observers believed that an overriding reason was his lack of enthusiasm about Bashar as a successor.[20] Similarly, Asad accepted the retirements or otherwise removed a number of long-serving senior officers in the army's higher echelons (that is, division commanders), replacing them with younger officers with connections to the heir apparent or, at least, a sense that their rise was attributable to Bashar's pending accession to the presidency.[21]

A comparable evolution took place in the leadership of Syria's intelligence and security agencies. The longtime head of the General Intelligence Directorate (GID), Major General Bashir Najjar, was replaced by Major General 'Ali Khuri (an Isma'ili) in July 1998; Najjar was subsequently

imprisoned on corruption charges.[22] More significantly, two younger officers considered close to Bashar, Brigadier General Bahjat Sulayman and
Brigadier General Ayyad Mahmud, were placed in charge of the directorate's
internal and external branches, respectively.[23] From these positions Sulayman and Mahmud became increasingly influential within the General Intelligence Directorate, eclipsing their nominal superior, the long-entrenched
deputy director, Major General Muhammad Nassif.

Bashar's brother-in-law, Bushra's husband Asif Shawkat, was installed at
Syrian Military Intelligence in the late 1990s, rising quickly to the rank of
major general and becoming, effectively, the agency's second-in-
command.[24] In February 2000 the long-standing chief of military intelligence, Major General 'Ali Duba, was eased out and replaced with Major
General Hassan Khalil, who was considered more likely than Duba to coordinate his decisions with Shawkat and less likely than Duba to challenge
Bashar on matters of position or policy.[25]

The elder Asad also sought to build up Bashar's standing with the Syrian
public. To some degree, the father sought to do this by linking, in the public eye, the recently departed Basil with the newly prominent Bashar. For a
year after Basil's death, the regime blanketed Syria with representations of
the deceased son bordering on the hagiographic. In January 1995, however,
after a year of mourning, the regime began covering public spaces throughout the country with posters highlighting the new trinity of Hafiz, Basil,
and Bashar—usually described in captions as "our leader, our ideal, and our
hope" (qa'idna, mithalna, amalna), respectively.

But Hafiz also worked to construct Bashar's image in a manner strikingly—perhaps necessarily—different from the way in which Basil's public
image had been crafted. In contrast to the public relations campaign mounted
for Basil in the early 1990s, which emphasized Basil's more charismatic qualities as the "golden knight" of Syria's future (for example, his military prowess
and his accomplishments as a competitive equestrian), the presidency worked
to foster public perceptions of Bashar as someone devoted to the popular
interest.

Most notably, Bashar was made the public face for a carefully orchestrated
anticorruption initiative in the mid- and late 1990s.[26] This initiative was
highly selective, never coming near the dozen or so most important members of the regime or their families, but it allowed Bashar to be seen as someone on the right side of a true "hot button" issue for most ordinary Syrians.

(At times, anticorruption prosecutions were also used to sideline potential sources of opposition to Bashar, as with the arrest of former general intelligence director Najjar.) As an extension of his work as an anticorruption crusader, Bashar was also presented to the public as a kind of all-purpose "ombudsman" for their complaints about state services. He reportedly opened offices in all of Syria's major cities where citizens could come with various grievances against state agencies or requests for assistance.[27]

Bashar—no doubt with his father's acquiescence—seemed to take the lead in establishing another dimension of his public persona, seeking to present himself as someone capable of leading Syria into the twenty-first century. For this, the chief vehicle was Bashar's chairmanship of the Syrian Computer Society, a group of academics and information technology professionals in Damascus. Bashar's brother Basil had been chairman of the society before his death but had been nothing more than a titular head for the organization. Bashar, by contrast, took his role as chairman far more seriously. In particular, as head of the society, Bashar played a prominent role in a highly contested bureaucratic process during the late 1990s that ultimately led to a decision by the Syrian government to allow the Internet into Syria. In this bureaucratic battle, Bashar was cast as the champion of younger academics and businessmen strongly supportive of introducing modern information technology against the resistance of long-entrenched ministers who opposed the Internet as, among other things, a tool of Israeli propaganda.[28] While all of this clearly contained an element of calculated image crafting, it also seemed to evince a genuine commitment on Bashar's part to a freer flow of information in Syria.

Hafiz al-Asad worked, over the course of Bashar's six-year apprenticeship, to familiarize his son with the substantive dimensions of his future role. Bashar settled into an office at the presidential palace not far from his father's and became involved in deliberations on a progressively expanding portfolio of policy issues.

Initially, Bashar's policy tutorials focused on domestic issues. (During the last two years of his apprenticeship, Bashar also became more involved in foreign policy issues, and this aspect of his preparation for the presidency is considered in the following chapter.) In this context, Bashar established a profile as someone interested in questions of economic and, at least to some degree, political reform.[29] In the months preceding Hafiz al-Asad's death in June 2000, the limits of debate over possible economic reforms broadened considerably and even some discussion of possible political reforms was allowed; Bashar was widely considered to be a driving force behind this development.[30] As is discussed later, there seems to have been an element of genuine commitment on Bashar's part to the substance of reform, in addition to a calculated effort to craft a favorable public image.

Bashar's efforts to cultivate an image as someone interested in policy reform intersected nicely with his public profile as an anticorruption proponent in early 2000. During preparations for a cabinet shuffle in March 2000, Bashar was allowed to draw up an initial list of new ministers for consideration by the elder Asad. According to Western diplomats and journalists, Bashar reportedly tried to install reform-minded technocrats in several ministries involved in economic policymaking, but these recommendations were, for the most part, overruled by his father, who appointed a cabinet more comfortable with the status quo.[31] The appointment of a new cabinet, however, resulted in the replacement of the long-serving prime minister Mahmud al-Zu'bi with Mustafa Miru, who would serve as Bashar's first prime minister. Two months later, Bashar engineered Zu'bi's indictment on corruption charges; the former prime minister committed suicide before he could be taken into custody.[32]

Over the course of his apprenticeship, Bashar's own attitude about the new and unforeseen direction of his life appeared to evolve. At the beginning of the grooming process, Bashar seemed decidedly unenthusiastic about his new role; the quality of his performance at public events where he was called upon to speak was frequently lackluster and uncommitted. It was during this phase of his preparation that doubts about his temperamental qualifications to lead Syria were most widely discussed around the Damascus rumor mill. By the late 1990s, though, Bashar seemed to have crossed a psychological Rubicon, internalizing and accepting the reality of his new life; he appeared increasingly interested in his duties and committed to the tasks ahead.

Becoming President

Despite these preparations, at the time of Hafiz al-Asad's death on June 10, 2000, there was an appreciable level of doubt about Bashar's chances for acceding to the presidency and holding on to the position. Some analysts pointed out that the elder Asad had died too soon to complete Bashar's grooming. In particular, Hafiz had delayed designating Bashar as a potential

Bashar al-Asad following the coffin of his father into the mosque of Qurdaha, his father's home village, June 13, 2000.   (Wolfgang Rattay/© Reuters/Corbis)

successor in any formal way, although the elder Asad had scheduled the first Ba'th Party Congress in years, at which it was widely expected that Bashar would be elected a member of the Regional Command. That would have set up Bashar for nomination as a vice president, formally making him his father's successor.[33] Hafiz al-Asad died just days before the party congress was to convene.

Other analysts focused on less formalistic considerations that might impede Bashar's progress, pointing to key players on the Syrian political scene who might be resistant to a generational succession. Scenarios were posited in which Bashar's uncle, Rifa't, might emerge as a rallying point for displaced and, presumably, disaffected members of Hafiz al-Asad's inner circle—senior Alawi "barons" such as 'Ali Duba, the former military intelligence chief; Muhammad al-Khuli, a former chief of Syrian Air Force Intelligence and an air force commander; and 'Ali Haydar, the former special forces commander.[34] Such scenarios assumed that Rifa't, by presenting himself as a proven and more capable defender of Alawi interests than Bashar, would be able to rally sufficient support within the Alawi community and among Alawi officers occupying key commands in the armed forces and security services to push his nephew aside.[35] Other commentators questioned whether Bashar would enjoy sustained support from the remaining members of Hafiz's inner circle or, by extension, from the military and security services.[36]

These doubts notwithstanding, when Hafiz al-Asad died, Bashar's succession went smoothly. The next day, Vice President Khaddam, in his constitutional capacity as the acting president, announced Bashar's appointment as commander of the Syrian armed forces and his promotion to the rank of general (fariq), the most senior military rank, which only Hafiz al-Asad had held.[37] Over the next couple of weeks, Defense Minister Tlas made a number of public statements expressing the security establishment's acceptance of Bashar as its new commander-in-chief.[38] On June 17, Bashar succeeded his father as the secretary-general of the Ba'th party. The National Assembly amended the Syrian constitution, which had specified a minimum age of forty for aspirants to the presidency, to permit the candidacy of the thirty-four-year-old Bashar for his late father's office. In a July 10 referendum, in which virtually the entire Syrian electorate took part, 97.3 percent of the voters affirmed Bashar's candidacy. A week later, on July 17, the new president was inaugurated.

Throughout this process, not a hint of opposition to Bashar was heard from within the Asad family, the inner circle, or the military and security apparatus. Indeed, in the end, there seemed to be a fairly well understood arrangement of mutual convenience between Bashar and the key pillars of Hafiz's regime that facilitated a smooth transition. Bashar obviously needed the cooperation of regime stalwarts and senior officials who controlled key levers of power, as well as their political clout. In return, the top stratum of the leadership needed the legitimacy and modern face that Bashar represented. Furthermore, by agreeing to support Bashar, the inner circle forestalled the possibility of several rapid successions, which might have proved destabilizing.[39] As one commentator put it, the inner circle apparently realized that, if they did not "hang together" at the time of the succession, they might literally end up "hanging separately."[40]

Charting a Course

Of course, once Bashar was in office, the key question became the direction of his inclinations as a national leader. The question was (and is) usually posed in simple, dichotomous terms: Would Bashar seek to embark on a bold, reformist course? Or would he be so caught up in consolidating and maintaining his position that he would be unable to consider significant policy changes?

The question of Bashar's intentions can be posed in such stark terms, but the answer is inevitably more complicated. As noted earlier, an examination of Bashar's personal and political formation suggests that he is genuinely inclined toward reform but does not have a fully elaborated vision for transforming Syria and is reluctant to put himself fundamentally at odds with his father's legacy or figures closely associated with it. A review of Bashar's expressed views on Syria's domestic situation since becoming president and his choice of personal advisers further supports the hypothesis that the younger Asad has a general predilection toward reform and is working out a broad conceptual approach to changing Syria, but still needs help in laying out particular policies and integrating these policies into a comprehensive reform program. Such a review also lends additional support to an assessment that, for both strategic and tactical reasons, the pursuit of reform is a gradual and long-term undertaking for the new president.

Views on Reform

In his early days in office, the new president seemed to want to straddle questions about his basic orientation toward reform, presenting himself as someone seeking to balance change and continuity. In his inaugural address, Bashar noted that his job was simultaneously to "maintain" his late father's approach and "to develop it as well."[41] In February 2001, in his first major interview after becoming president, Bashar underscored his interest in balancing change and continuity: "It is not possible to start any political development in Syria except through the historical position of the country. I said in my inaugural speech that we are not coming to overthrow the reality but to develop it, and the word 'development' means that you are basing yourself on something and moving from it forward and not moving into a vacuum."[42]

Given the highly personalized process by which Bashar had succeeded his father and the new president's "authority gap" upon entering office, it is not surprising that the younger Asad would take such a public stance on reform. But, at a minimum, this approach was bound to disappoint those outside Syria who were investing such hope in Bashar's accession as the dawn of a new day in Syrian politics. Given Bashar's situation, reform was unlikely to come at a pace or with a scope that would satisfy outside expectations. Progress has been slow, subject to setbacks and in some cases even reversals. Thus, as Bashar's presidency has proceeded, there has been an increasing tendency to bemoan the lack of progress and to question Bashar's capacity or ultimate intention to reform Syria.

This questioning of Bashar's reformist credentials is understandable. As becomes clear in examining Bashar's handling of domestic economic and political challenges, he is no proponent of radical change. There has been and will be no "shock therapy" for the Syrian economy on his watch, nor a rapid, wholesale opening of the political process. But Bashar's political reality is more complicated than a simplistic dichotomy of "reformer" and "reactionary" can capture. Although Bashar does not have a thoroughly elaborated vision for transforming Syria, his reformist predilections are arguably more strategic than the skeptical reading that has become increasingly common in the West would imply.

Bashar's approach to reform can be characterized as strategic in both his time frame for achieving change and the phased process he projects. With regard to timing, Bashar clearly takes a long view. In part, this reflects the realities of Bashar's political situation. As an Israeli commentator has noted, "in contrast to 'short-distance runners'—that is, Western leaders caught between the hammer of their term's end and the anvil of criticism from the democratic institutions of their country—Bashar sees time differently, believing himself to be in a long-distance race."[43] Certainly he does not face the constraints of term limits imposed on popularly elected leaders. Not only do the imperatives of consolidating his position in the near-to-medium term incline Bashar toward gradualism; he can plausibly interpret his political situation as one in which he can afford to take a longer-term view.

But Bashar also seems to have a strategic appreciation for the risks of proceeding too rapidly with economic and political reform in a society still characterized by unresolved ethnic and sectarian cleavages, a pronounced trend toward "Islamization" within the Sunni Arab majority, and an under-developed economy. This appreciation gives rise to a model of reform in phases. In his January 17, 2004, conversation with the author, Bashar described reform in Syria as operating on three planes: economic, social, and political. The three planes are not purely sequential—the president acknowledged the necessity of working them simultaneously—but there is a definite sense of priority, with economic reform treated as the foundation for all else and social reform treated to a large degree as an antecedent for political reform.[44] (Of course, Hafiz al-Asad had watched reform processes in the Soviet Union and China and almost certainly favored the phased Chinese approach in his guidance for Bashar. The elder Asad was deeply concerned about the possibility that Syria could disintegrate, as the Soviet Union had under Mikhail Gorbachev, and devolve into a fractious and criminalized state like post-Soviet Russia if simultaneous economic, political, and social reform moved too quickly.)

Economic reform seems to have held primacy in Bashar's thinking since the beginning of his tenure. In his February 2001 interview with *al-Sharq al-Awsat*, Bashar said that his "general vision" for his country could be summed up in a single proposition, "to see Syria more prosperous." In his January 2004 interview with the author, the president noted that Ba'thist ideology no longer matters; his view, as he put it somewhat humorously, is, "if it contributes to prosperity in Syria, we can call it socialism." But Bashar obviously intends to move more slowly with market-oriented reform than the Washington Consensus prescribed by the International Monetary Fund (IMF) and other international financial institutions would consider desirable. Given his assessment of the weakness of Syria's private sector, the president wants to build up a real private sector, able to create jobs, before proceeding with large-scale privatizations, which, he anticipates, will put significant numbers of public sector employees out of work.

Looking further down the road, a more prosperous Syria is, for Bashar, a necessary condition for social and political reform. Not surprisingly, in light of the Asad regime's historic struggle with the Muslim Brotherhood and ongoing Islamization among Syrian Sunnis, for Hafiz's successor social reform means primarily the attenuation of sectarian identities. In turn, the attenuation of sectarian identities is a necessary prelude to political reform. Bashar has been very clear about his determination not to move too quickly on political reform, noting that moving too rapidly to democratize Syria would produce a result like Algeria in the early 1990s, where arguably "premature" elections produced victory by presumably antidemocratic Islamist forces, prompting military intervention and the abrogation of the electoral outcome.[45]

Bashar's Circle

This view of economic, social, and political reform obviously implies a long-term, strategic perspective on transforming Syria. The manner in which Bashar has begun to put together his "own" regime provides additional evidence for an assessment of his leadership that takes seriously his reformist ambitions.

While Bashar was, at the time of the succession, the beneficiary of an arrangement of convenience with key pillars of his late father's regime, this arrangement was by no means assured. At least prospectively, Bashar has from the beginning of his presidency faced opposition from a disparate group of holdovers from the elder Asad's inner circle, ambitious family members, and entrenched bureaucratic, business, and institutional interests—often intertwined—that could resist efforts to change established policies if they perceived those efforts as a threat to their privileges.

Since the beginning of his tenure, Bashar has eschewed confrontation with the power structure bequeathed to him by his father. Instead, Bashar has sought to deal with potential opposition to his attempts to change entrenched policies in other ways. Taken together, these measures could be interpreted as a sustained effort to develop a kind of "alternative regime" alongside the structure of power that Bashar inherited from his father and to use that alternative structure as a basis for an even longer-term strategy of gradually co-opting the established order.[46]

The core of this evolving alternative structure is what might be described as Bashar's personal network. From before his accession to the presidency, Bashar has tried to elaborate his own "inner circle" and, beyond this relatively intimate group, a more dispersed body of supporters. This still fairly loose network appears to consist of at least two strands. The first is a kind of "kitchen cabinet" of individuals who advise Bashar personally from outside of government. The second is individuals with bases outside the Syrian government that Bashar has placed directly into official positions where they can help advance his agenda.

The kitchen cabinet has seemed to focus—for the most part, but not exclusively—on questions of economic policy, affirming Bashar's own identification of the economic arena as his priority for reform. So far, Bashar has used this informal network primarily to balance the influence of the old guard and provide him with alternative sources of information and policy advice. It is possible to identify a number of individuals who have had a hand in shaping Bashar's views on economic reform.

One of the first experts from outside the Syrian government to emerge as a source of advice for the new president was Nabil Sukkar. Sukkar, who earned a Ph.D. in management from Indiana University, is a pro-reform economist who worked for the World Bank for a decade and in the financial sector in London before returning to Syria in 1991 to found a private consulting firm.[47] In the last years of Hafiz al-Asad's presidency, under Bashar's apparent encouragement, Sukkar became the leading publicly tolerated critic of long-standing economic policies. One can readily discern his influence on Bashar's image of the Syrian economy. In Sukkar's view, Syria does not have a national economy in the normal sense of the term. The Syrian economy is a classic *rentier* economy that has survived on aid from the Gulf states and military assistance from the now-defunct Soviet Union.[48] Sukkar's views on policy reform, as expressed in a 2002 interview, also had a significant impact on Bashar's thinking:

> I am opposed to privatization in Syria. This is because no one will buy inefficient, outdated, and loss-making public enterprises except, perhaps, to strip their assets, acquire land, and make shady deals. In the

case of the profit-making state enterprises, privatization could mean a golden opportunity for corruption, cronyism, and the Mafia-style operations that accompany them in almost every instance. The best policy for Syria would be to encourage the emergence of a genuine new private-enterprise sector. This means that the government should let entrepreneurs, whether Syrian or foreign, . . . invest, produce, buy and sell, and thus create a genuine market-based economy. The experience of many countries, from Russia to Algeria, shows that the privatization of state-owned businesses is not a sufficient basis for economic modernization. Why waste money trying to upgrade a public sector that is no longer viable or even relevant?[49]

Another interesting figure to emerge relatively early in Bashar's tenure as a notable member of the new president's circle is Ayman 'Abd al-Nur. An engineer by training, 'Abd al-Nur pursued a private sector career in Syria and developed a relationship with Bashar after the president-to-be had returned to Syria in 1994. Following Bashar's accession to the presidency, 'Abd al-Nur was appointed the new president's personal economics adviser. More recently, he has created a web-based press service, *All4Syria*.[50] Operating with the apparent protection of the presidential palace, the service publishes a daily electronic newsletter reproducing articles on reform in Syria from a variety of sources, as well as providing a forum for original pieces and the exchange of information. The articles frequently include comments from regime critics and opponents in Syria and abroad.

Bashar drew additional members of his informal network from other settings. During the first year of his presidency, he established a so-called "Group of 18" (G-18) advisers to counsel him on economic matters; the members of the G-18 were drawn almost exclusively from the worlds of academia and business. Some G-18 participants appear to have been selected on the basis of their positions in the Syrian establishment and are not inclined toward fundamental change.[51] Other members of the group were chosen because of their international experience and strong support for market-based reform and restructuring. A number of these reform-minded G-18 members developed their own individual relationships to Bashar. In this category, one should place Riyad al-Abrash, a former academic and IMF economist.[52]

Bashar also drew informal advisers from a group of economists and consultants associated with the Syrian-European Business Centre (SEBC).[53] The

SEBC is a European Union project, growing out of the Barcelona process launched by the EU in 1995, to increase the competitiveness of the Syrian private sector in anticipation of Syria's integration into a Euro-Mediterranean Free Trade Area by 2010. Syrian economists and management specialists associated with the SEBC have been active in helping local businesspeople develop entrepreneurial ideas and initiatives. Some of these economists and consultants, such as Samir Seifan, have provided advice to Bashar on economic reform. Like Nabil Sukkar, Seifan runs a private sector consulting firm in Damascus.[54] Seifan was commissioned by Bashar in 2000 to draft a report recommending economic reform measures. This report stimulated significant discussion in official and private sector circles in Damascus about the need for private banks in Syria to provide capital for entrepreneurial development.[55] SEBC associates—including Seifan and Sami al-Khiami—also played important roles on the Syrian team that carried out one of Bashar's more important policy initiatives to date—concluding negotiations with the EU over an association agreement for Syria. Khiami holds a Ph.D. in engineering, was a founder of the Syrian Computer Society, and was an early advocate of the Internet in Syria, which provided a channel for developing a relationship with Bashar before the younger Asad acceded to the presidency. Khiami also has been active as an academic and information technology entrepreneur in Syria. In 2004 Bashar named Khiami Syria's ambassador to the United Kingdom.[56]

An important member of Bashar's personal inner circle is his wife, Asma, whom he married on January 1, 2001, less than a year after becoming president. Bashar's choice of Asma—over his mother's objections—undoubtedly reveals notable things about him. Asma, born in 1976, is the daughter of Dr. Faris al-Akhras, a world-class interventional cardiologist and longtime medical faculty member at the University of London's Kings College.[57] Dr. al-Akhras is a scion of a prominent Sunni family from Homs; thus, Bashar's wife is not only non-Alawi, but from an urban notable background. Asma was born, raised, and educated entirely in the United Kingdom. After graduating from Kings College in computer science in 1996, she went through the executive trainee program at J.P. Morgan and worked as an investment banker at Deutsche Bank. At the time Bashar proposed to her, she had been admitted to Harvard Business School's MBA program.[58] Asma's public role in Syria is discussed further later in the chapter. However, it is clear that, as the most intimate member of Bashar's kitchen cabinet, she brings world-class

Syria's first lady, Asma al-Asad, poses with local women at a ceremony marking International Literacy Day in Homs, September 8, 2004.   (© Khaled al-Hariri/Reuters/Corbis)

training in business and exposure to the highest international standards and practices in global finance and investment to bear in her inputs to her husband's thinking.

The second strand of Bashar's informal network consists of individuals from outside the Syrian government whom he has placed directly into government positions where they can help advance his domestic agenda. In placing these people in government posts, Bashar appears to be developing a stratum of officials in upper-level positions with direct loyalty to him. In this way, he can sidestep the normally time-consuming (and, in the Syrian case, sclerosis-reinforcing) processes of recruitment, socialization, and advancement. The growing number of these individuals suggests that Bashar may in fact be pursuing a kind of "long march" through Syria's institutions. Bashar's aim in pursuing this course would seem to be the establishment of a bureaucratic platform for more robust reform initiatives in the future.

An early example of someone that Bashar took from outside of the Syrian government and installed in an important position is Ghassan al-Rifa'i, who was appointed minister of economy and foreign trade in December

2001. Rifaʻi holds a doctorate in economics from Sussex University in the United Kingdom and worked for thirty years at the World Bank before his ministerial appointment.[59] He is a highly regarded technocrat and is generally considered, by both Syrian and foreign observers, to be an outspoken proponent of economic restructuring in Syria. Rifaʻi had nonetheless said publicly that Syria should not plunge into wholesale privatization of state enterprises, which made him compatible with Bashar's gradualist inclinations on reform.

Other examples of individuals that Bashar has taken from outside the state agencies and placed in relatively important domestic policy positions include:

—The current tourism minister, Saʻdallah Agha al-Qalʻa, a French-trained economist brought in by Bashar to reform the underdeveloped but potentially lucrative tourism sector.

—Mahir al-Mujtahid, whom Bashar appointed to a new position as secretary-general of the presidency of the Council of Ministers (the prime ministry) in late 2003. Mujtahid holds a doctorate in management and is a former member of the Syrian Computer Society's board of directors.

—ʻAli Kanaʻan, who was appointed president of the Industrial Bank of Syria in December 2003. Kanaʻan was a reform-oriented economics professor at Damascus University and an original member of the G-18.[60]

—ʻAbdallah al-Dardari, another Ph.D. economist, who served Bashar as the new president's first chairman of the State Planning Commission. Dardari is now head of the Syrian Economic Society.

—ʻIssam al-Zaʻim, who has served Bashar as minister of state for planning, minister of industry, and, since 2004, chairman of the State Planning Commission. Zaʻim, considered a competent economic technocrat, led the delegation that negotiated Syria's association agreement with the EU.

The members of Bashar's personal network, whether in the kitchen cabinet or in government positions, tend to share several characteristics:

—They tend to be slightly older than Bashar, but at least a generation younger than the old guard; for the most part, members of Bashar's informal network are in their forties and fifties.

—They tend, far more than members of Hafiz al-Asad's inner circle and senior officials of his regime, to have had some measure of Western education and exposure, often more than Bashar experienced.

—They tend to have technocratic expertise, credentials, and experience in areas such as business, economics, and information technology—fields critical to meeting the long-term demands of modernization in Syria.

Bashar seems indifferent to the political pedigrees of the people he draws into his network; in a growing number of cases, he has moved individuals into important government positions even though they are not members of the Ba'th party.[61]

Bashar has had limited success to date in moving "his" people into cabinet positions. In December 2001 Bashar carried out his first cabinet shuffle as president, assigning three of the four economic portfolios to non-Ba'thist technocrats, including Rifa'i as minister of economy and trade. In September 2003 Bashar installed a new cabinet, under a new prime minister, Muhammad Naji al-'Utri. As part of this exercise, Bashar tried to streamline the cabinet, reducing the overall number of seats from thirty-four to thirty by combining functions. Half of the ministers in the cabinet announced in September 2003 were new to their positions, with the new appointees concentrated in ministries dealing with the economy, education, and social services. But defenders of the status quo still outnumbered advocates of change by a considerable margin.[62] Bashar promised at the first meeting of the new cabinet that the ministers' performance would be reviewed after twelve months, with an eye to making further changes. However, in the third cabinet reshuffle of his presidency, in October 2004, Bashar was able to improve the representation of reformers only slightly.[63] (Rifa'i, in fact, left government during this reshuffle, but was replaced by 'Amir Hosni Lotfi, former head of the state-run cotton marketing board and a recognized economic reformer.)

The disposition of the strands of Bashar's informal network over time is likely to be an important indicator of his continuing interest in reform. One could anticipate that, as more senior officials move on, more members of the kitchen cabinet or other informal advisers to the president would take government posts, perhaps even as ministers. For example, Riyad al-Abrash, Samir Seifan, and Nabil Sukkar are frequently discussed among Damascus elites as candidates for finance or trade and economy minister. In addition, one could anticipate that some of the individuals Bashar has placed in second-tier positions might move up to higher levels of authority and responsibility.

Besides building his own network of advisers and supporters, Bashar has taken steps to put people loyal to him in positions of control over important levers of power—a continuation of a trend already under way before Hafiz al-Asad's death. Not surprisingly, a focus of this effort has been the military and security apparatus. Bashar has, to date, probably been able to install more of "his" people in key positions in the intelligence services than in any other segment of the regime's coercive apparatus. As has been seen, even before the succession, new directors and deputies were installed at the General Intelligence Directorate and Syrian Military Intelligence. As Bashar's presidency proceeded, the rising influence of Bahjat Sulayman at general intelligence and Asif Shawkat at military intelligence marked the new president's deepening personal imprint on the leaderships of these agencies.[64] Ghazi Kana'an, an early supporter of Bashar as successor to Hafiz al-Asad, was promoted to major general and brought back from Lebanon in October 2002 to head the Political Security Directorate, which is responsible for uncovering organized political activity in opposition to the regime.[65] In October 2004 Kana'an was promoted again, becoming minister of the interior.

Similar changes have taken place in the armed forces and the Ba'th party. In January 2002 'Ali Aslan retired as chief of staff of the army, to be replaced by his deputy, Hassan Turkmani.[66] Aslan had reportedly resisted Shawkat's efforts to exert control over personnel and assignments in the Syrian military on behalf of the president.[67] Asad has removed or marginalized several senior military and security officials whom he perceived as obstacles to his agenda. In 2002 he removed the army's three long-serving corps commanders, who had been put in their positions and retained past retirement age by his late father, from their posts.[68] Likewise, Bashar has worked over time to place supporters in the Ba'th party's two leadership bodies, the Regional Command and the Central Committee.

Most important, in May 2004 the first of the three most senior old guard officials retired. Mustafa Tlas, the long-serving defense minister, stepped down on his seventy-third birthday, May 12, and was replaced by Hassan Turkmani.[69] (Tlas displayed his penchant for surreal public statements right up to the end of his official service. In a retirement interview for Syrian media, Tlas expressed his "happiness" for having been a "champion of the poor" throughout his career.)[70] Because of the role that Tlas had played in ensuring a smooth transfer of power in 2000, avoiding a major disagreement with the defense minister was an important consideration for Bashar in seeking to maintain an image as someone keeping faith with Hafiz's legacy. If Bashar is, in fact, pursuing a "long-distance runner" strategy to consolidate his position, Tlas's departure is potentially a milestone. (It is noteworthy that, during the summer of 2004, a variety of Arab press stories reported speculation in Damascus about the impending retirement of Vice President Khaddam. By the fall, though, these rumors had stopped, perhaps reflecting a sense among the old guard and security establishment that it was not yet time for the remaining members of Hafiz al-Asad's inner circle to step aside.)

Thus there is considerable evidence, from his own statements and the development of his personal network, that Bashar is committed to a certain set of reformist ideas. Ascribing priority to improving Syria's economic performance and standard of living, Bashar judges that reform, particularly in the economic arena, should proceed in a gradual manner to avoid social disequilibrium. And Bashar obviously favors what some describe as the Chinese model of reform, putting initial emphasis on economic reform and moving more slowly on political reform until a foundation of increased prosperity has been laid.

In this regard, the risks of social fragmentation continue to seem very real from the perspective of the presidential palace. Since the U.S.-led military campaign to unseat Saddam Hussein in Iraq, there has been a resurgence of Kurdish activism in Syria, particularly in the northeast, where Syria's Kurdish population is concentrated and overlaps with Kurdish concentrations in northern Iraq and southeastern Turkey; at times, Kurdish protests have elicited a forceful response from the Syrian security apparatus.[71] The car bomb attack on a building formerly occupied by the United Nations in the Mezzeh neighborhood of Damascus in April 2004—which Syrian security services claim was carried out by Islamic fundamentalists— underscored the risk that an Islamizing Sunni population could be the base for a renewed Islamist challenge to the Asad regime.[72]

From Bashar's point of view, all of these considerations argue for a gradual, evolutionary approach to reform. The next step in understanding Bashar as a national leader is to consider how well he has been able to apply this approach in dealing with Syria's internal economic and political problems.

Confronting Obstacles to Economic Reform

As noted in the previous chapter, Bashar inherited a daunting array of economic problems upon assuming the presidency. Having ruled out IMF-style shock therapy or rapid, wholesale privatization, the new president focused his economic policies on trying to stimulate development of a more entrepreneurial private sector, reducing transactional costs in the local economy, and beginning to lower barriers to interaction with the global economy.

Under this rubric of developing a more robust private sector, Bashar introduced a number of noteworthy changes in the policy framework for Syria's economy during the first year of his tenure. To increase consumer demand, in his first months in office the new president ordered long overdue and much needed salary increases for public sector employees. He also changed relevant rules to allow the introduction of credit cards and private importation of automobiles.[73] Even more significantly, Bashar launched an initiative to permit the establishment of private banks in Syria.[74] This was very much in keeping with recommendations advanced by Samir Seifan and Nabil Sukkar, motivated by a sense that a private financial sector was essential for sustained entrepreneurial development in Syria.[75]

To reduce transactional costs and begin opening up the Syrian economy to global markets, Bashar took a number of other steps early in his tenure. In January 2001 he began reforming Syrian policies governing currency exchange, with the aim of making the Syrian pound fully convertible at a single exchange rate.[76] Once Ghassan al-Rifa'i came on board as minister of economy and trade in the cabinet shuffle at the end of 2001, the former World Bank official assumed a leading role for Bashar in pursuing this goal. The new president also engaged a leading American consulting firm to draw up a proposal for the creation of free trade areas in Syria, similar to those operating in Dubai.[77]

Bashar's track record in translating these ideas and initiatives into concrete results has been decidedly mixed. On a positive note, Rifa'i was able to oversee a significant rationalization of Syrian currency policies before he left office in October 2004. But, in most other areas, reform has lagged. At times, both Samir Seifan and Nabil Sukkar have publicly bemoaned the lack of progress in implementing serious reforms.[78] Implementation has been slow because of the systemic deficits in Syria's governing apparatus and because of structural barriers, most notably those rooted in the Asad regime's legacy of high-level corruption.

Capacity Deficits

The impact of the Syrian system's capacity deficits is felt most acutely in the formulation of economic policy. Potentially positive economic reforms have lagged in part because of deficiencies in the capacity of the Syrian bureaucracy to follow through on particular initiatives.

The saga of introducing private banking in Syria illustrates this phenomenon well. Despite the issuance of decrees by early 2001 permitting the establishment of private banks, the system had not developed the necessary legal and regulatory framework for operation of a private financial sector. As a result, even licensed private banks would not open. It was not until mid-2002 that a money and credit committee was established at the central bank with the power to define monetary policy, including the authority to set interest rates.[79] In 2003 a special commission (including Samir Seifan) was formed to draft implementing regulations for the presidential decrees legalizing private banks; with the promulgation of these regulations, a couple of small private banks opened.[80] But delay and uncertainty have kept a potentially important reform initiative from having anything like the positive impact on Syria's economy that it might have.

These delays were partly caused by bureaucratic inertia, but they also stemmed from a lack of qualified cadres of technocrats within relevant bureaucracies to draw up the necessary laws and regulations for governing a world-class private financial sector. (It is interesting to note that the "radical" new Syrian banking laws were modeled on 1950s-era Lebanese regulations; a regulatory framework that may have been cutting-edge a half-century earlier was the best model the Syrian system could come up with for producing its own rules.) This was a weakness in the Syrian economy that Samir Seifan and others identified early in Bashar's term.[81] Bashar himself recognized this problem with regard to banking reform, noting that any Syrian with the expertise to work in a real private financial sector had probably already left Syria.[82] Banking is not the only sector in which reform has languished because of deficiencies in the capacity of the system to craft and implement initiatives. Movement on the creation of economic zones was hampered by this lack of capacity as well as by resistance within the regime to creating "islands" that could alienate those working outside free trade areas.[83]

More generally, the president, senior officials supportive of change, and forward-looking economists have all come to recognize the lack of technocratic expertise in critical parts of the bureaucracy as a major constraint on reform.[84] Despite Bashar's efforts to recruit individuals with backgrounds as world-class experts, there are simply not enough people with relevant credentials, expertise, and experience to staff serious reform proposals in key areas. Bashar clearly sees himself as constrained by this deficiency and openly acknowledges his need for external support to improve development and implementation of reform initiatives and policies. In his January 17, 2004, interview with the author, when asked where he saw Syria in five years, the president said that depended on how much assistance and expertise would be available from outside Syria during the intervening period.

In addition to inadequate technocratic capacity within particular bureaucracies, Bashar must also deal with dysfunctionality in integrating planning across multiple bureaucracies. As noted earlier, Bashar has come to realize that he does not currently have the capacity to develop and implement reform initiatives in key policy areas or to integrate these in a genuinely strategic fashion. Policy changes such as those discussed above have often seemed ad hoc in character, not part of a coherent plan for systematic reform. Individual ministries have tended to go their own way in formulating policies, even under ministers interested in change. As a consequence, economic reform in Syria under Bashar's leadership has indeed had an "improvised" quality.

In an effort to address this problem, the president has been putting added emphasis on administrative reform as an essential precursor to economic reform. The appointment of Mahir al-Mujtahid, with his background in management, as secretary-general of the Council of Ministers at the end of 2003 was a first step in this direction.[85] In the spring of 2004 Bashar also brought in a new batch of fourteen younger technocrats—several with doctorates from U.S., British, and European universities—to form the nucleus of a policy staff within the presidency; these new officials are charged with monitoring the activities of various ministries and ensuring more effective coordination across bureaucracies.[86] Bashar has sought assistance from the French government in revamping the administrative apparatus of the Syrian presidency and improving the policy planning process across ministries;

both sides intend to have a plan for administrative reform drawn up and ready for implementation by the beginning of 2005.[87] Additionally, France has begun providing training to Syrian bureaucrats through the *Ecole Normale d'Administration* to improve the level of technocratic expertise within the Syrian government.[88]

Structural Barriers

Beyond these capacity limits on Bashar's ability to push policy changes, the president also faces significant structural barriers to more thorough-going reforms. Many of these structural barriers stem from the Asad regime's long record of high-level corruption.

In many cases, Bashar has been unable to break up trade monopolies or introduce competition into key sectors because of the well-established legacy of corruption on the part of his late father's inner circle. The president's desire to avoid impinging on the financial interests of powerful regime figures, for example, has allowed well-connected businessmen to maintain their hold over the retail auto market despite the formal lifting of restrictions on automobile imports; the requirement for foreign manufacturers to use local agents as dealers has been manipulated to allow these businessmen to retain their dominant position in the Syrian market. In some cases, even initiatives that superficially appeared to encourage competition, such as the issuance of a tender for mobile phone licenses in the telecommunications sector, were actually decidedly noncompetitive processes.[89]

Under Bashar's presidency, such corruption continues to involve families of important regime figures. For example, Vice President Khaddam's family developed food processing and restaurant interests in Syria during his years of service to the Asad regimes.[90] Food processing is an area frequently identified by reform-minded businessmen and economists in Syria as a sector in which Syria might have some competitive advantage, but domination of the sector by a small number of powerful players, like the Khaddam family, discourages new entrants.

Former defense minister Tlas's family has developed extensive economic holdings in defense procurement, telecommunications, and the media sector. These holdings are managed through the *Min Ajli Suriya* (On Behalf of Syria) group, known as MAS, headed by Tlas's son, Firas.[91]

In some instances, the corruption extends to Bashar's own family. Most notoriously, the family of Bashar's mother, the Makhlufs, has leveraged its connections to amass a commercial empire, the value of which is estimated to exceed $3 billion.[92] In the process, the Makhlufs have become arguably the single most prominent business family in Syria. The dominant figures in the Makhluf family's business activities are Bashar's uncle (his mother's brother) Muhammad Makhluf and Makhluf's son, Bashar's cousin Rami.

The extent of the Makhlufs' empire is impressive, both in its wealth and in the family's ability to leverage political ties for personal gain.[93]

—The Makhlufs continue to control the Real Estate Bank, one of Syria's state-run banks, giving them privileged access to capital for their business ventures.

—Rami and his brother, 'Ihab, also control the free-trade zones along the Syrian-Lebanese border and the duty-free shops in Syria's airports. Thus, corruption tied to Bashar's family undermines the economic benefit from one of the relatively few liberalization measures carried out by the Asad regime.

—In addition, experts on privatization of telecommunications markets in the region say that the Makhluf brothers effectively own Syriatel, Syria's leading cellular telephone service provider. This has given the family a dominant position in Syria's telecommunications sector, undercutting prospects for significant economic gains from that sector's liberalization.[94]

The regime figures, their family members, and affiliated businessmen who profit from the status quo form a loose coalition that resists economic liberalization measures that would introduce competition into key sectors of the Syrian economy.[95] Even more than deficiencies in technocratic capacity, this antireform coalition has stymied movement on fundamental economic reforms. It certainly imposes limits on Bashar's professed strategy of growing the private sector before radically restructuring state-run enterprises.

Bashar's reluctance to challenge the elements of this coalition in the near-to-medium term is perhaps tactically understandable. It is not clear, however, whether and how Bashar intends to resolve his structural problem over the long run. (To return to the Don Corleone metaphor for the late Hafiz al-Asad, Bashar is in something of the situation of the don's son, Michael: an improbable successor who has promised to make the family enterprise "completely legitimate," but who must operate in an environment that makes transformation exceedingly difficult.)

One strategy that Bashar has pursued in an effort to work around these structural barriers to reform is the use of international economic agreements—particularly an association agreement with the EU—as a lever for impelling greater transparency and spurring policy reform. Negotiations between the EU and Syria over an association agreement started in the mid-1990s, soon after the launch of the Barcelona process, but the process languished in the last years of Hafiz al-Asad's tenure.[96] Upon his accession, Bashar worked to reinvigorate the talks. The new president saw an association agreement as a useful tool for accelerating the pace of change, and he brought in reform-minded economists from outside the Syrian Government to serve on the Syrian delegation conducting negotiations with Brussels. In the aftermath of the Iraq war, as Syria's relations with the United States declined, Bashar used arguments about the strategic importance of developing better relations with Europe to overcome resistance from the old guard to the policy reforms that an EU association agreement would require.[97] Finally, in December 2003 negotiators from Syria and the European Commission reached agreement on what Damascus believed would be the final text, and Bashar made plans to travel to Brussels in March 2004 to sign the accord.[98]

Bashar's efforts to make the association agreement a reality have yet to bear fruit, however, and it remains to be seen whether he will, in the end, have the association agreement to use as a lever for accelerating reforms. In early 2004 the European Council, representing the EU's member governments, declined to sign off on the text agreed to by the commission's negotiators, citing rules adopted by the EU in October 2003 mandating more explicit commitments by association agreement signatories to eliminating weapons of mass destruction.[99] (Britain, Germany, and the Netherlands were particularly insistent on this position.)[100] Discussions between Brussels and Damascus to resolve the impasse stalled in February 2004, and Bashar put off his trip to Brussels.

However, after the Bush administration announced in May 2004 the specific measures with which it was implementing the Syria Accountability Act, the EU announced it would resume negotiations with Damascus with the aim of finalizing the association agreement. Chris Patten, the EU's commissioner for external relations, noted that, while the EU shared America's policy goals for Syria, "we do not share the same tactical approach."[101] Finally, in October 2004, European Commission and Syrian officials initialed a revised text containing slightly tougher language on weapons of mass destruction. By then, though, Damascus was at odds with France over the question of Syrian hegemony in Lebanon, and the EU had taken in ten new member states. As a result of these developments, European diplomats and EU officials say it is not clear how quickly the EU can move to approve the new draft, a necessary step before an association agreement can be signed and go into effect.[102]

Stopgap Measures

Given the improvised quality of policymaking for economic reform and the entrenched structural barriers to implementing reform initiatives, it should not be surprising to outside observers that the course of reform in Bashar's tenure has been fitful and, taken as a whole, slow. In the meantime, Bashar has worked to find stopgap measures to help avert a major deterioration in Syria's economic performance. These "workarounds" have included a dramatic increase in illicit Syrian trade with Iraq in the period preceding Saddam Hussein's overthrow and a concerted effort to expand oil production and attract new foreign investment to this sector of the Syrian economy in the near-to-medium term. (Bashar has also benefited from a reversal of several years of drought in Syria; increased rainfall has permitted significantly improved performance in Syria's agricultural sector since 2003.)

Between his inauguration in July 2000 and the launch of Operation Iraqi Freedom in March 2003, Bashar presided over a massive increase in illicit Syrian trade with Iraq. In November 2000 Bashar authorized the reopening of the main Iraqi-Syrian pipeline running from Iraq's northern oil fields around Kirkuk to the Syrian port of Banyas.[103] Syria and Iraq also began planning construction of another large-capacity pipeline. These actions started a dramatic expansion of Iraqi oil flows to Syria. During 2001–02, Syria imported roughly 200,000 barrels a day of Iraqi oil outside of the United Nations' Oil for Food (OFF) program.[104] The bulk of the oil came through the main Kirkuk-Banyas pipeline; the rest came through a smaller, second pipeline (essentially an offshoot of the Iraqi-Turkish pipeline) and by rail and road transfers. The Iraqi oil was sold to Syria at a heavily discounted rate; Syria then resold the oil internationally at world market prices, pocketing a windfall profit in the process.

Expansion of illicit trade with Iraq proceeded in other sectors as well. In January 2001 Syrian prime minister Miru traveled to Baghdad to sign a trade protocol—effectively a free trade agreement—with Iraq; Syria never submitted the protocol to the UN Sanctions Committee for approval.[105] Under

Syria: Major Oil and Gas Pipelines

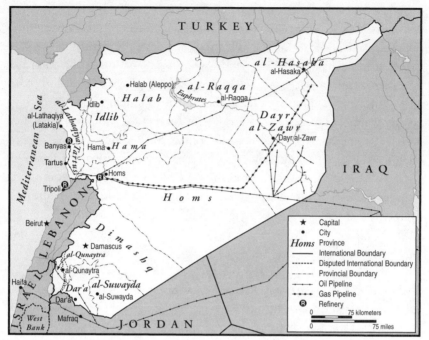

Bashar's leadership, Syria also authorized direct flights between Baghdad and Damascus in violation of UN Security Council resolutions. At its peak, illicit trade with Saddam's regime provided revenues of roughly $2 billion dollars annually for the Syrian economy. This infusion was a much needed stimulus for the economy; the involvement of old guard members and other senior officials in profit-taking from the illicit Iraqi trade also helped ensure the cooperation of key regime figures during an early stage in Bashar's consolidation of power.

Increased oil revenues have been another important economic stopgap for Bashar, even after the fall of Saddam's regime. Over the course of Bashar's presidency, the Syrian economy has benefited from a fairly consistent trend of rising world oil prices. As a result, earnings from oil exports significantly boosted Syria's hard currency reserves during 2003–04.[106]

Given the importance of oil exports and the revenues and foreign exchange earnings they generate for Syria's economy, one of the more pressing economic challenges confronting Bashar has been the prospective depletion of the country's oil reserves. The new president apparently recognized that coping with that depletion and maintaining a relatively steady income stream from oil exports required attracting foreign oil companies, with their capital and advanced technology, to Syria. As a result, the Syrian Oil Ministry has stepped up its efforts to expand foreign participation in the country's upstream sector. In December 2001 the ministry began to offer drilling concessions in five exploratory areas in a tender. In January 2003 Damascus began awarding concessions to a range of foreign oil companies that had participated in the initial tender. In addition to Shell, which was already well established in Syria, concessions were given over the course of the next year and a half to oil companies from Canada, Chile, Croatia, and India, along with several U.S. companies.[107] Damascus put out a tender for additional drilling concessions in fourteen blocks in the spring of 2004.

The Difficult Birth of Civil Society

To the extent that Bashar has pursued social and political reform, his efforts have focused on what might be described as the development of civil society in Syria. Over the long run, the emergence of a more robust civil society is critical to accomplish the attenuation of sectarian identities that is at the heart of Bashar's agenda for social reform. The growth of civil society is also linked to the president's efforts to develop a more entrepreneurial private sector. But, as in the economic sphere, Bashar is interested in gradually developing civil society, not in rapid political liberalization. Like his attitudes regarding economic reform, his gradualist approach to developing civil society reflects both his own preferences and his assessment of the requirements for consolidating his position.

Bashar's attitude toward civil society has been one of the more controversial aspects of his tenure. His posture toward the issue is widely taken as an important indicator of his attitude toward fundamental political reform in Syria; shifts in how this posture is perceived outside Syria account for a good deal of the fluctuation in perception of him as a national leader during the first three years of his presidency.

Mixed Signals

Perhaps because of the successful crafting of Bashar's public image as someone sympathetic to arguments for the freer flow of information and open discussion of current problems, his accession to the presidency spurred considerable anticipation about the possibilities for political liberalization in Syria. During his first year in office, Bashar seemed sympathetic to—indeed, at times, supportive of—the aspirations of those Syrians pushing for greater openness. Shortly after taking office, Bashar acted to reduce the cult of personality that had been built up around the presidency during his father's tenure, ordering the removal from public places of his own picture and banners praising the new president—a development much noticed around Damascus.[108]

Additionally, Bashar began to allow greater freedom of expression and the press in Syria. During his first month in office, he appointed new directors for the official Syrian news agency (the Syrian Arab News Association, or SANA) and state radio and television, as well as new editors-in-chief for the three main state-controlled daily newspapers: *al-Ba'th*, *al-Thawra*, and *Tishrin*. *Al-Thawra*, in particular, would pursue a much more liberal editorial policy under its new editor, Mahmud Salameh. In December 2000 Bashar announced that constituent parties in the National Progressive Front would be permitted to publish their own newspapers; the first began appearing in January 2001. Also in January 2001 the first license for a privately owned, independent newspaper in Syria was issued upon Bashar's authorization; the newspaper, *al-Dommari* (*The Lamplighter*) began publication in February 2001.[109]

Another interesting early indicator of Bashar's reformist inclinations was his treatment of 'Aref Dalilah, a former dean of economics at Damascus University who had been dismissed from his position in 1998 for criticizing then prime minister Mahmud Zu'bi for corruption. In August 2000 Bashar received Dalilah as an honored guest in the presidential palace, restored the former professor to his faculty position, and made him a member of the G-18. In October 2000 *al-Thawra* devoted two full pages to an explication of Dalilah's critique of Ba'thist economics.[110] Dalilah certainly could not have gotten such a public platform for his ideas without Bashar's appointment of a more forward-leaning editor and the perceived cover of the new president's patronage and approval.

Bashar also acted to empower civil society organizations. Within the first year of his tenure, a leading unofficial human rights organization that had been suppressed in the 1990s, the Committees for the Defense of Democratic Freedoms and Human Rights in Syria (*lijan al-difa' 'an huquq al-insan fi suriya*) resumed its public activities.[111] A new human rights organization, the Syrian Human Rights Committee (*al-lajna al-suriya li huquq al-insan*), also emerged, under the leadership of Haytham al-Maleh, a Syrian lawyer and human rights activist who had been imprisoned during the 1980s when Hafiz al-Asad's regime moved to suppress independent professional associations.[112]

Although Bashar never rescinded the state of emergency or lifted martial law imposed in 1963, he took a number of steps to assuage concerns about political detentions and abuse of the criminal justice system. Through his first summer and fall in office, Bashar pardoned and released hundreds of political prisoners, including more than six hundred members of the Muslim Brotherhood.[113] As was noted earlier, Hafiz al-Asad had, from time to time, released selected batches of political prisoners, including Muslim Brotherhood detainees, but Bashar's gesture was unique in its scale and scope. Moreover, Bashar's last amnesty declaration, in November 2000, was reported in official Syrian media with language acknowledging for the first time that the Syrian government had imprisoned people for political reasons.[114] That same month, Bashar went further with such symbolic gestures, carrying through on an order his father had issued shortly before his death to close the notorious Mezzeh prison where many political detainees had been held and issuing a general pardon for nonpolitical prisoners.[115] Bashar issued his own order closing the equally notorious Tadmur (Palmyra) prison the following month.[116]

Yet, at the same time that Bashar was taking these steps, he also appeared to be defining some outer limits for the scope and pace of liberalization. In part, this reflected his own gradualist preferences; it also reflected resistance from entrenched actors in the power structure that Bashar had just inherited. In the early months of Bashar's presidency, there were indications that Vice President Khaddam, the effective leader of the old guard, and the General Intelligence Directorate's General Sulayman—who, despite his loyalty to Bashar, was representative of the security establishment—were displeased by the more liberal bounds for public expression.[117] In August 2000, the new president held a meeting with leaders of the National Progressive Front's six constituent parties at which Bashar decided to postpone introduction of a new political parties law or allowing new parties to join the National Progressive Front.[118]

From Damascus Spring to Damascus Winter

Against this backdrop of mixed signals, the key question, for Syrians and for interested outsiders, was how Bashar would balance his impulse toward liberalization with his interest in regulating the process of change. The course of events during the first two years of his presidency—a period that witnessed the rise and fall of the so-called Damascus Spring—suggested that this balancing act would not be smooth or easy.

Initially, Bashar's accession to the presidency sparked a remarkable flowering of activism on behalf of political reform in Syria. Syrian intellectuals and commentators continue to describe this period as the Damascus Spring, which was marked by the emergence of Syria's first genuine civil society movement (*harakat al-mujtama' al-madani*).[119] Some of the prominent figures in this movement were veteran advocates of political reform, such as Sadiq al-'Azm; others came from a new generation of intellectuals, artists, and political commentators committed to the development of civil society in Syria.

The first widely recognized public manifestation of Syria's renewed civil society movement came in September 2000, just three months after Hafiz al-Asad's death and two months after Bashar's inauguration, when ninety-nine prominent intellectuals, artists, and professionals signed and published a manifesto—the Statement of 99—for increased political participation by all segments of Syrian society.[120] The Statement of 99 argued that administrative, economic, and legal reforms would not accomplish their intended objectives without complementary political reform. Specifically, the authors and signers called first and foremost for "an end to the State of Emergency and martial law in effect since 1963." They also called for an amnesty for all political prisoners, prisoners of conscience, deportees, and exiles. They called as well for the "establishment of a state of law; the granting of public freedoms; the recognition of political and intellectual pluralism, freedom of assembly, the press, and of expression" and an end to all forms of censorship. By promulgating the Statement of 99, the signers put the issue of political reform squarely on the agenda for public discussion. They also sought simultaneously to test and to bolster what they saw as Bashar al-Asad's reformist proclivities. (For text of the Statement of 99 and the subsequent Statement of 1,000, see appendix B.)

These were potentially provocative public demands in the Syrian context, but the ninety-nine signers crafted their statement to minimize the risk of a harsh reaction from the regime. While emphasizing the importance of pluralism, they made no explicit demand for new political parties or for removing the Ba'th party's privileged status; nor did the statement attack Bashar, his legitimacy, or the manner in which he came to power. None of the signatories had significant histories of antiregime activism; many were highly regarded intellectuals and public figures, such as Sadiq al-'Azm and the poet Adonis, who had carved out individualized "public spaces" for themselves and had been tolerated by the regime over many years.[121]

The publication of the Statement of 99 was a catalytic event that sparked a considerable increase in civil society activism in Syria. Informal political forums and discussion groups proliferated in Damascus and other Syrian cities. Some of these groups antedated the Damascus Spring, having originated in the last few years of Hafiz al-Asad's presidency, but the number of these civil society "cells" increased significantly during the last half of 2000. Many of these groups would eventually be loosely organized under the rubric of the Committees for the Revival of Civil Society in Syria (*lijan ihya' al-mujtama' al-madani fi suriya*).[122] Initially, Bashar seemed supportive of these developments. The new president reportedly told security officials who were concerned about these developments, "You have the right to know what these people are doing, but you can't stop them from doing it."[123]

As the movement developed in the months following Bashar's inauguration, two distinct factions emerged. One was a relatively moderate camp, exemplified by the more prominent signers of the Statement of 99. The moderates sought, in effect, a tacit alliance with Bashar and other reform-minded actors in the regime to change the system gradually and from within. To encourage such an alliance, this camp was deliberately self-limiting in its aims, as the text of the Statement of 99 demonstrated.[124]

The other faction was more radical in its aims and tactics, taking the example of civil society activists in Eastern Europe before the collapse of the Soviet bloc as a model for its activities. Rather than seeking to test and challenge Bashar's reformist proclivities, this faction was out to challenge fundamental pillars of the regime, based on an assessment that the system was incapable of reforming itself and had to be confronted directly by a broad-based popular movement. Within this wing, one should include, most prominently, the dissident parliamentarian Riyad Sayf, who was a major player in the proliferation of discussion forums during the early months of Bashar's presidency through his leadership of the National Dialogue Forum. Sayf founded another organization, the Friends of Civil Society (*ansar al-mujtama' al-madani*), in August 2000 and used it as a platform to announce plans for an independent political party, to be called the Party for Social Peace (*hizb al-salam al-ijtima'i*), in January 2001.[125]

One should also include 'Aref Dalilah in the radical camp. Once restored to public life, the economist proved to be not simply another advocate of market-oriented reforms; his agenda was as much political as economic. In October 2000 Dalilah published an editorial in the state-run *al-Thawra* arguing that one-party rule was "no longer effective" and had to change if economic reform were to succeed.[126] Ultimately, Bashar would cut Dalilah adrift as the rehabilitated academic's positions grew too radical for the president to defend. Among the radicals, one should include as well Muhammad Sawwan, a former member of a National Progressive Front constituent party, who launched the Gathering for Democracy and Unity (*al-tajammu' min ajli al-dimuqratiya wa al-wahda*) in early 2001.[127]

The turning point in the Damascus Spring came with the publication of the so-called Statement of 1,000, prepared by civil society activists as a follow-on to the Statement of 99. The drafting of the Statement of 1,000 was reportedly very contentious within the civil society movement, reflecting the movement's bifurcation; the text was leaked prematurely to a Lebanese daily before all 1,000 of the intended signatories had in fact signed on.[128] The published text of the Statement of 1,000 is a significantly more radical document than its predecessor, explicitly calling for an end to the leading role of the Ba'th party in Syria's political life and the creation of a multiparty democracy.

Publication of the Statement of 1,000 prompted the beginnings of a concerted counterattack on the civil society movement by regime hard-liners, later described by civil society activists as the Damascus Winter that ended the Damascus Spring. With the premature publication of the statement, the more radical wing of the civil society movement overplayed its hand, giving regime hard-liners a pretext to crack down.[129] Bashar, in the end, did little to resist this counterattack; indeed, at times, he legitimized it by making public statements cautioning against the excesses of unrestrained activism for reform.[130]

Over the course of 2001 and continuing into 2002, the regime took a number of steps to curtail the activities of the civil society movement and roll back other manifestations of liberalization.[131] In February 2001, for example, the government began shutting down meetings of civil society forums. In May 2001 Mahmud Salameh was dismissed as editor-in-chief of *al-Thawra*.[132] After several months of government pressure and harassment starting in the spring of 2001, *al-Dommari* suspended publication in January 2002.[133] In September 2001 Riyad Sayf and another dissident parliamentarian, Ma'mun al-Homsi, were arrested; they were eventually sentenced to prison terms in the summer of 2002.[134] 'Aref Dalilah was also arrested in September 2001, tried, and sent to jail in 2002 for his advocacy of independent political parties.[135] Several other prominent figures—including officers in the Committees for the Defense of Democratic Freedoms and Human Rights and the Syrian Human Rights Committee—in the civil society movement were likewise arrested, tried, and sentenced to prison, as was the Syrian Communist Party–Political Bureau chief, Riyad al-Turk.[136] In the summer of 2002, arrest warrants were issued for the top leaders of the Syrian Human Rights Committee, forcing the committee to relocate to London, where it continues to operate.[137]

Renewing Gradualist Reform

The suppression of the Damascus Spring remains an important reason for the widespread disappointment with Bashar al-Asad as a potential reformer in Syria's political life. It is frequently argued that, with the turn away from fundamental political change, Bashar implicitly adopted a Chinese model of reform, in which economic modernization would clearly precede political liberalization.[138] From this perspective, the best interpretation that could be offered about Bashar as a potential agent for political reform is that he has tried to position himself in the middle of Syria's political spectrum, as an advocate of evolutionary change in between the extremes of the "continuist" old guard and the civil society movement's radical innovators.[139] This means that no significant changes in the Syrian political system can or will take place in the foreseeable future, although certain improvements in the overall political climate may be felt.

Much in this perspective seems inarguably valid. Certainly, Bashar is unable or unwilling to force a confrontation with the old guard and other elements of the establishment in the way that would be required to bring about a bold and systematic transformation of Syrian politics. But, in subtle ways, Bashar has continued to show an appreciation of the need for the gradual empowerment of civil society alongside the pursuit of economic reform, and he has worked to plant seeds that might one day grow into a genuine reform-oriented civil society network in Syria. Perhaps the most notable of these seeds is Bashar's encouragement of a fledgling movement for nongovernmental organizations (NGOs) in Syria. This approach certainly fits his interest in promoting a more entrepreneurial private sector and increasing the appeal of nonsectarian and nonethnic identities.

For the most part, these new NGOs fit the definition of a GONGO—a government-sponsored NGO. Even today, Syria has no law regulating the activities of NGOs; groups that want to organize private citizens for various types of social activism and advocacy must register under the charities law and seek government approval for their work. Nevertheless, since mid-2003 more than twenty such groups have appeared.[140] Not surprisingly, the groups that have been permitted to organize have agendas that are compatible with Bashar's overall approach to social reform. Some of the groups have a specific issue focus, such as environmental protection or wildlife preservation. Others, though, are explicitly focused on laying the foundations for a more robust and entrepreneurial private sector. In this category, one should include the Fund for the Integrated Rural Development of Syria (FIRDOS), which was founded under the patronage of Asma al-Asad.[141] FIRDOS runs microcredit programs in an expanding swath of rural Syria. Other recently founded NGOs focused on entrepreneurial development are an organization known as Modernizing and Activating Women's Role in Economic Development (MAWRED), which was also started under the patronage of Asma al-Asad, and the Syrian Young Entrepreneurs Association.[142]

In encouraging the development of a fledgling NGO movement, Bashar has drawn on the resources of the Syrian-European Business Centre. Since the crackdown that ended the Damascus Spring, the center's work in supporting entrepreneurial initiatives has extended to the nurturing of NGOs that are focused on developing more effective private sector actors. Since her arrival in Damascus as Syria's first lady, Asma al-Asad has become a high-level champion of the SEBC's activities, providing a direct link for the center and its Syrian associates with the presidential palace.[143]

At the same time that Bashar has encouraged the growth of GONGOs in Syria, there has been an expansion of what might be described as "true"

NGOs—organizations that are not requesting registration with the state under the charities law. While some of these groups fit the model of traditional charities, a number are devoted, in various ways, to cultivating the conditions for more liberal politics in Syria. One example of such an organization is the recently launched *Tharwa* (Wealth) Project, which is devoted to encouraging serious discussion of minority rights issues, surely a critical subject for any prospective process of democratization in Syria.[144]

At the same time that Bashar has sought to use a possible association agreement with the EU as a prospective lever to intensify the pace of economic reform, he seems to have similar ambitions for using such an agreement to facilitate political liberalization in Syria. Syrian civil society activists are cautiously optimistic about the potential social and political benefits of an association agreement between Syria and the EU.[145] In the negotiations between Syria and the EU that produced a draft agreement in December 2003, Damascus accepted explicit language committing it to social and political liberalization. Civil society activists believe that this language could provide the impetus for increasing press and media freedom and for the establishment of political parties outside the NPF.

Another example of Bashar's gradualist approach to the empowerment of civil society is his pursuit of significant reforms in Syrian higher education. Working through the moderately reformist president of Damascus University, Hani al-Murtada, Bashar encouraged the creation of the Syrian Virtual University, intended to connect Syrian students with professors and courses taught at universities around the region, in Europe, and in North America.[146] More strikingly, Bashar has opened the Syrian education system to the establishment of private universities; the first of these, Qalamoun University, began operating in 2003.[147] While many problems remain in Syrian higher education, Bashar's recent initiatives in this sphere reflect an ongoing commitment to the slow expansion of the social space in Syria.[148]

Bashar's approach to the emergence of civil society in Syria since the Damascus Winter would seem to provide another body of evidence that he is committed to a gradualist model of reform. But some observers have questioned whether Bashar and the fledgling civil society movement may be facing another backlash from the old guard, similar to the one that ended the Damascus Spring. From this perspective, the official harassment of artist-entrepreneur and gallery owner Issa Touma during 2004 and the arrest of the intellectual and social critic Nabil Fayyad in September 2004 portend another crackdown by the security apparatus.[149]

Certainly the potential for a backlash from the old guard and security establishment is real. No doubt the old guard was concerned about U.S. and French efforts in the summer and fall of 2004 to ratchet up international pressure on Syria over its military presence and hegemonic position in Lebanon. The security establishment may also have been concerned about an increased diffusion of jihadist sentiment in Syria as a result of U.S. military action in Iraq and about the potential for trouble among Syrian Kurds signaled by the Kurdish riots in northeastern Syria in 2003. These factors may have provided the rationale for official heavy-handedness in the cases of Touma and Fayyad.

But it is not clear that these recent actions have thrown Bashar off his chosen course in a decisive way. Some observers argue that the appointment of Ghazi Kana'an as interior minister is additional evidence that the old guard is reasserting itself. But it would seem just as plausible that Kana'an's appointment reflects Bashar's interest in elevating an internal security boss who can satisfy the imperative to maintain order when Syria's regional position is under pressure, while doing so in a relatively sophisticated manner that may allow the new architecture of civil society to remain in place. In this regard, shortly after Kana'an's appointment, rumors of the impending restructuring of Syria's security and intelligence apparatus began to appear in the Arab press and Syrian opposition publications. According to the oppositionist online daily *Akhbar al-Sharq*, Kana'an planned to force into early retirement "tens" of high-ranking officers in the security and police organs. Those to be dismissed are said to be the holdouts who refuse to go along with the interior minister's bid to unify the security services around Bashar's new reformist line.[150] Another sign of change in the security apparatus was Asif Shawkat's elevation to deputy to Syrian Military Intelligence Director Hassan al-Khalil. Khalil retired in February 2005, paving the way for Shawkat's succession.[151]

Similarly, the same cabinet reshuffle that placed Kana'an at the interior ministry also brought Mehdi Dakhlallah into the government as minister of information. As editor-in-chief of the ruling party daily, *al-Ba'th*, Dakhlallah authored editorials in 2003–04 calling for a reduction in the role and influence of the Ba'th party and championing Bashar's gradualist approach to reform.[152] Dakhlallah ushered in an immediate change in tone in the regime's reaction to criticism, going so far as to appear on a live *al-Jazeera* television program to answer questions posed by Syrian oppositionists living in exile and members of the Lebanese opposition.[153] An even greater surprise was the appearance in the state-run *Tishrin* newspaper of a satirical editorial mocking the security services' treatment of prisoners.[154] Dakhlallah's appointment signaled a continuation of Bashar's efforts to reformulate the role of the Ba'th party in Syrian politics and society, which would be an important stepping-stone toward deeper and more genuine political reform.

At the same time that Bashar was carrying out this cabinet reshuffle, he also took some other small steps toward a still very limited political liberalization. In the summer of 2003, the Ba'th Party announced that it would no longer interfere in the day-to-day running of the country.[155] In October 2004 the National Progressive Front charter was amended to allow new (but still politically tame) parties to come under the Front's umbrella.[156]

It would seem, then, that the jury is still out about Bashar's gradualist approach to internal reform. Given Bashar's professed ambitions and his self-acknowledged constraints, implementation of a gradualist agenda for economic and social modernization is likely to take years—probably a decade or more. But in light of Syria's increasingly problematic strategic situation, it is questionable whether its leader has that kind of time. Even within that time frame, Bashar recognizes that he cannot achieve his policy goals for reforming Syria without a substantial measure of international assistance and support. And, when the old guard and the security establishment feel that Syria's regional position is under pressure, they are likely to react in ways that engender additional resistance within the system to Bashar's gradualist agenda. Thus, perhaps the most overarching challenge facing Bashar is managing Syria's external environment. Bashar's handling of Syria's foreign relations is the focus of the next chapter.

CHAPTER FOUR

Bashar and Syria's Place in the Regional Order

Protecting Syria's place in the regional order has been particularly trying for Bashar during the initial years of his presidency. The first four and a half years of his tenure were a period of tumult and strategic fluctuation unusual even by Middle Eastern standards. Navigating these stormy waters was bound to be a special challenge for a new national leader.

The major threads of Syrian foreign policy are, of course, Lebanon, the Arab-Israeli arena, the regional balance, and relations with the United States. Before examining how Bashar has handled these aspects of Syria's external relations, however, this chapter looks first at Bashar's preparation for handling them in his presidency, including the initial image he sought to project as a fledgling statesman, and the challenging realities he confronted upon assuming office.

Image and Reality

As noted in chapter 2, Hafiz al-Asad left his son a fairly well-elaborated script for handling Syria's external relations, one rooted in the elder Asad's three decades of experience as a national leader and a recognized player in regional affairs. Over the course of his grooming for the presidency, Bashar had been increasingly exposed to and involved in his father's management of Syria's diplomatic and national security posture—in effect, learning the script from the author himself.

It is possible to date the beginning of Bashar's engagement with foreign affairs and national security to a point no later than the end of 1998, when he was given responsibility for day-to-day management of the critical Lebanon file. (Bashar took over this account from Vice President 'Abd al-Halim al-Khaddam, who had been Hafiz al-Asad's point man on the issue for almost twenty years.)[1] Between 1995, when Bashar emerged as a potential successor, and late 1998, his education in Lebanese affairs included meetings with a range of Lebanese political figures, including Hizballah's secretary general Hassan Nasrallah.[2] As Bashar assumed increasing responsibility for the Lebanon file over the course of 1998, he blended his handling of Lebanese issues with his already established anticorruption initiative. A number of the targets of Bashar's campaign had long-standing ties with Lebanese prime minister Rafiq al-Hariri and had grown rich through their dealings with the billionaire politician.[3] Bashar's pursuit of these targets also had the effect of undercutting Hariri, whose removal from power had become a Syrian objective.

Bashar's involvement in other regional issues apparently accelerated during 1999 and the first half of 2000. In February 1999, for example, he traveled to Amman to pay a condolence call on King Abdallah in the wake of King Hussein's death the preceding month.[4] The heir apparent also began occasionally to meet foreign leaders visiting Damascus. There is no indication, however, that Bashar ever assumed a role in Syria's peace process diplomacy before becoming president.[5]

Whereas on the domestic scene Bashar cultivated an image of someone interested in change and reform, when it came to foreign policy, he projected an image of someone who would maintain his father's course on major issues. When he assumed the presidency, Bashar stressed publicly the importance of continuity in Syrian foreign policy. He retained his father's long-serving vice president and foreign minister, both of whom had been directly involved in Hafiz al-Asad's conduct of Syria's external relations. Bashar's inaugural address is striking in that in the first half of the speech dealing with domestic, economic, and political issues, the new president emphasized the necessity of improving Syria's performance and updating outmoded ideas and practices (while admittedly avoiding specifics about how far such updating might go). In the second half of the speech, however, dealing with regional and international affairs, he stressed the strategic, legal, and moral soundness of the policies pursued by his father on major issues such as peace with Israel and Syrian-Lebanese relations and vowed to preserve the "principles of international legitimacy" underlying them.[6]

But, in the period surrounding Bashar's accession, Syria's strategic environment shifted in ways that strained the applicability of Hafiz's script to the challenges confronting the new president. Indeed, since the beginning of his tenure, Bashar has been forced to adapt his father's national security script to rapidly changing circumstances. Throughout his presidency, Bashar has maintained the same broad strategic and foreign policy objectives that his father had but has had to adjust many established tactical approaches. How well Bashar does at making these adjustments is as much a test of his leadership as is his engagement with Syria's many internal problems.

A Changing Strategic Environment

Syria's strategic environment began to shift in important ways even before Bashar succeeded his father. In March 2000, two months before Hafiz al-Asad's death, the Syrian track of the peace process effectively collapsed at the Clinton-Asad summit in Geneva, removing the principal framework for structuring Syria's relations with Israel and the United States. In May 2000, just weeks before the elder Asad died, Israel withdrew its military forces from southern Lebanon.[7] A month after that, in June 2000, the United Nations Security Council certified that Israel had complied with Security Council Resolution 425 by withdrawing completely from Lebanon, undercutting a critical element of traditional Syrian strategy for both the Lebanese and Arab-Israeli arenas.[8] (Syria and Lebanon, of course, claimed that the Israeli withdrawal was incomplete as long as Israeli forces remained in a twenty-five-kilometer square area called the Sheba'a Farms, which Lebanon claimed as part of its historical territory. The Security Council rejected that claim, endorsing Israel's position that this territory was historically Syrian, and thus fell under the purview of UN Security Resolution 242, which governed the Israeli-Syrian conflict, rather than resolution 425.)[9] In September 2000, just three months after Hafiz's death and two months after Bashar's inauguration, the Intifada al-Aqsa erupted, which added layers of challenge and complexity to the new president's handling of Arab-Israeli matters and Syria's regional stance.

Syria's strategic environment was also affected by political changes in the United States and Israel. In January 2001 President George W. Bush took office in the United States. While Bush's arrival was initially viewed positively in many Arab capitals, including Damascus, as the beginning of a return to the policies of President George H. W. Bush, it would soon become apparent that the son's administration had an approach to the region very different from that of either his father's administration or the Clinton administration. Shortly after Bush's inauguration, Ariel Sharon became prime minister of Israel.[10] Sharon's personal history and his strategic outlook posed additional difficulties for Syria's relations with Israel and, by extension, with the United States.

And, of course, a little more than a year after Bashar's inauguration, the September 11, 2001, terrorist attacks and the launch of a U.S.-led global war on terror would have a dramatic impact on Syria's strategic environment. The elevated importance of terror and "rogue regimes" in U.S. foreign policy would heighten tensions between Damascus and Washington over Syria's status as a state sponsor of terrorism that was also pursuing weapons of mass destruction. As the war on terror moved from Afghanistan to Iraq, the Bush administration's military campaign to unseat Saddam Hussein would pose unprecedented challenges to Syria's established strategy for protecting its regional position.

Thus, even though Bashar was inclined to emphasize continuity in Syria's foreign policy to a greater extent than in domestic affairs, events have compelled him to adapt established policy to new circumstances. And, even though Bashar has retained key players in the conduct of Syria's foreign policy from his father's inner circle, the new president has sought to develop an alternative network of advisers to help him make sense of the new circumstances and develop appropriate policy responses.

In developing this alternative advisory network for foreign affairs, Bashar has seemed motivated by an interest in avoiding complete dependence on Foreign Minister Faruq al-Shar' for information and advice. Early in his presidency, Bashar elevated the status of Deputy Foreign Minister Walid al-Mu'allim. A career diplomat, Mu'allim was for many years Hafiz al-Asad's ambassador to the United States, including at the height of the peace process. During his service in Washington, Mu'allim developed a reputation as someone committed to improved relations and greater strategic cooperation between the United States and Syria. He was brought back to Damascus in

1999 and appointed deputy foreign minister in the aftermath of emergency surgery in October 1999 on Shar' for an aortic aneurysm; Mu'allim's return to the Foreign Ministry was, in large part, meant to ease the foreign minister's burden of work. After Bashar's accession to the presidency, Mu'allim became a higher-profile interlocutor on relations with the United States, although his bureaucratic subordination to Shar' limited his direct access to the president. In 2003, following the Iraq war, Bashar retired the other deputy foreign minister, Sulayman Haddad, establishing Mu'allim as the clear number two figure at the Foreign Ministry. Intermittent speculation continues in Damascus that Bashar will retire Shar' and replace him with Mu'allim.

Buthayna Sha'ban has emerged as an even more important adviser to the new president on international affairs. Sha'ban, who earned a Ph.D. in English literature from the University of Leeds and still holds an appointment as an English professor at Damascus University, was for many years the head of foreign media relations at the Foreign Ministry and Hafiz al-Asad's personal translator. After Bashar's accession, she quickly became identified as part of Bashar's personal network and was soon marked as a rival to Shar'. As part of Bashar's ongoing effort to revamp the Syrian bureaucracy, Sha'ban personally oversaw a model, meritocratic recruitment effort to bring a crop of Syria's most talented university students into positions in her department at the Foreign Ministry, the prime minister's office, and the presidency itself.[11] In 2003 Bashar elevated Sha'ban to the cabinet, naming her to the newly created position of minister of expatriates. This role gives Sha'ban ample justification to travel abroad on the president's behalf, and she may be establishing herself as a de facto alternative foreign minister.

One should take note of the recent career of 'Imad Mustafa, currently Syria's ambassador in Washington. Mustafa, who holds a Ph.D. in computer science from the University of Surrey in the United Kingdom, was a professor at Damascus University and became acquainted with Bashar in the late 1990s as a member of the Syrian Computer Society's executive board. During the first year of his presidency, Bashar personally tapped Mustafa to serve as the founding dean of a new information sciences faculty at the university. In early 2003, Bashar—over what well-placed Syrians have described as strong opposition by Shar'—installed Mustafa, who had no experience in the Foreign Ministry, as deputy chief of mission at the Syrian Embassy in Washington, with the clear intention of making Mustafa the next Syrian ambassador to the United States. In August 2003, Bashar recalled the incumbent ambassador, an unimpressive career diplomat, elevating Mustafa to the status of chargé d'affaires. Mustafa ultimately presented his credentials to President Bush as Syria's ambassador to the United States in April 2004.

More recently, Bashar has applied the "Mustafa model" to other key ambassadorial appointments. In 2004 Bashar went outside the Foreign Ministry to name a dozen new ambassadors in important posts, including Sami al-Khiami as Syria's ambassador to the United Kingdom. The new appointees were uniformly individuals with outstanding educational and professional credentials and experience who spoke the language of the posts they were taking. Many, like Khiami, had personal ties to Bashar. Certainly, these appointments broke established norms for ambassadorial assignments in the Syrian system.

But to what extent does the ascent of figures like Mu'allam, Sha'ban, and Mustafa reflect a different course for Syrian foreign policy? In particular, to what extent do these figures have a different sense, relative to the old guard, of how best to protect Syria's position in the region? At a minimum, the leaders of Bashar's alternative advisory network for foreign policy share their leader's sense that Syria needs a better relationship with the United States, for strategic reasons as well as to support progress on internal reform. Certainly, these players are bound, like Bashar, by the broad parameters of Hafiz al-Asad's script. Nevertheless they differ from the old guard in that they are more capable of realizing that Syria's strategic situation has shifted in important ways since Hafiz al-Asad's death and that, to protect Syrian interests, his script had to be adapted to changing circumstances. (In this regard, one could fairly characterize members of the old guard as "strategically autistic" in their seeming inability to recognize how the world changed on September 11, 2001, in ways significant for Syria.)

Thus, there is an appreciable "old guard vs. younger generation" dynamic on foreign policy issues. The real test of Bashar's stewardship of Syria's national security and regional standing is his handling of the four major foreign policy threads—Lebanon, the Arab-Israeli arena, the regional balance, and relations with Washington.

Lebanon

Bashar came to office at a period of striking fluidity in Lebanon's external and internal situation. Externally, many of the aforementioned shifts in

Israel-Lebanon-Syria Triborder Region

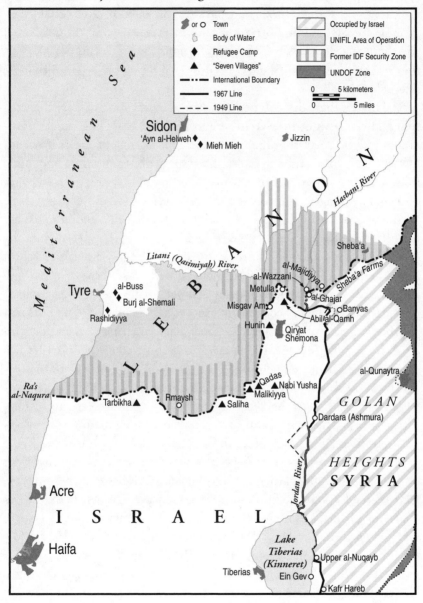

Syria's strategic environment held significant implications for the Syrian position in Lebanon, putting palpable stress on Hafiz al-Asad's established formula for maintaining Syrian hegemony there. Beyond these external environmental shifts, the elder Asad's formula for preserving Syria's position in Lebanon was further stressed by two developments in Lebanese internal politics.

The first of these developments was an intensification of public discussion and criticism of the Syrian role in Lebanon following Israel's withdrawal in June 2000 from the south. Since the signing of the Ta'if Accord in 1989, calls to oust the Syrian military presence came most frequently from within Lebanon's Maronite Christian community, with the newspaper *al-Nahar* serving as the traditional mouthpiece for the expression of Maronite grievances.[12] In the aftermath of the Israeli pullout, Lebanese opposition to the Syrian presence became more vocal, especially among Maronites.[13] This spurred a more intense public discussion of Syria's role in Lebanon than at any time since the signing of the Ta'if Accord.[14]

The second political development that potentially complicated Bashar's management of Syria's Lebanese interests was the return of Rafiq al-Hariri as prime minister of Lebanon in October 2000.[15] During Hariri's first stint in office, starting in 1992, Damascus had become concerned that he was developing his own channels to the United States and other Western powers (most notably France), bypassing the foreign minister and other pro-Syrian officials tied to the Lebanese presidency.[16] Under Syrian pressure, Lebanese president Emile Lahud accepted Hariri's threat-cum-offer of resignation when Lahud took office in December 1998. But Hariri was by no means a spent force in Lebanese politics. Using his status as de facto leader of the opposition in parliament and his considerable personal fortune, Hariri carefully prepared the ground for a political comeback. In this he was helped by the decline of the Lebanese economy under Lahud and Hariri's replacement, Salim al-Huss; Hariri may even have used his personal fortune to precipitate an exchange rate crisis in early 2000 that boosted his political standing. By the August–September 2000 parliamentary elections, Hariri's return as prime minister was all but assured. Bashar and the leadership in Damascus knew that they would have to deal with a powerful personality as prime minister in Beirut, an ambitious political actor not entirely under Syrian control.

Managing the Occupation

Against this backdrop of strategic and political shifts in the Lebanese arena, Bashar had to adapt the foreign policy script for Lebanon to manage the Syrian occupation following the Israeli withdrawal and ensure his country's dominant role in Lebanese politics.[17] As president, Bashar has made adjustments to the approach he inherited from his father. Notably, he has tried to assuage and contain anti-Syrian sentiment in Lebanon while preventing the emergence of any truly independent power center there.[18]

To this end, on a seemingly positive note, Bashar has continued his father's practice of reducing the number of Syrian soldiers stationed in Lebanon. Indeed, Bashar has intensified and accelerated this process, ordering six separate withdrawals of Syrian forces since becoming president.[19] In February 2001, in an interview with the London-based regional daily *al-Sharq al-Awsat*, Bashar defended the Syrian military presence in Lebanon, arguing that Syrian troops were in Lebanon on two missions: to restore "civil peace," in accordance with the mandate Damascus received in the Ta'if Accord; and to respond to the situation of "no peace and no war" with Israel. Neither of those missions had been accomplished, according to Bashar, and he declined to commit to a withdrawal of Syrian forces from Lebanon, even if peace with Israel were achieved.[20] But, by reducing and redeploying Syrian forces in Lebanon, Bashar was able to lower Syria's profile somewhat and minimize the most obvious manifestation of Syrian hegemony for most Lebanese, especially in the Maronite community.[21] At least until 2005 he could also claim that he was making progress in implementing the provisions of the Ta'if Accord dealing with the disposition of Syrian military forces in Lebanon, while fostering an image of allowing the Lebanese a measure of greater autonomy in managing their own affairs.

Bashar sought to bolster this more benign face of Syrian hegemony with other conciliatory moves. In the run-up to the August–September 2000 parliamentary elections in Lebanon, Bashar initiated an intensified dialogue between Syrian officials and Maronite leaders. As a result, the clerical establishment publicly opposed a Christian boycott of the elections, and a number of traditional Maronite politicians who had stayed out of the 1992 and 1996 polls participated in the 2000 elections. Bashar also cut deals with several prominent Maronite opponents of the Syrian occupation, allowing them to return to Lebanon from exile in France in exchange for their silence on political matters (a bargain that lasted only for a short while). In the end, as two critics of the Syrian occupation have written, the new Syrian president "managed to square a very difficult circle: ensuring the election of pro-Syrian elites while cultivating the illusion of a free and fair electoral process."[22] Bashar's highest-profile gesture to Lebanese sensibilities was his state visit to Beirut in March 2002, the first such visit by a Syrian president since Hafiz al-Asad traveled there in 1975.

On closer examination, however, the diminution in Syrian control over Lebanese affairs seems more apparent than real. Bashar has balanced the reduction in Syrian troops with an increase in the number of Syrian intelligence personnel stationed in Lebanon; some Lebanese claim that the number of Syrian intelligence personnel in Lebanon has actually increased during Bashar's presidency.[23] Indeed, during the post-Ta'if period, Syrian Military Intelligence cadres in Lebanon have arguably been more important to the maintenance (or possible expansion) of Syrian dominance there than the presence of Syrian soldiers; in this regard, Bashar's shift in the ratio of overt to covert Syrian operators should not be taken to represent a watering down of his father's determination to remain on top in Lebanon.[24] The expansion of the Syrian intelligence apparatus in Lebanon has been accompanied by what could be interpreted as a more authoritarian posture on the part of the Lebanese security and intelligence services, with a particular focus on radical Maronite elements and Sunni Islamists. This more aggressive stance clearly had Syria's backing.[25]

Playing Politics

Politically, Bashar was intent on containing the influence of Prime Minister Hariri to ensure that the Lebanese leader did not embark on strategic initiatives that could enhance Lebanon's autonomy at Syria's expense. Under Bashar's leadership, the Syrian government employed several tactics for this purpose. First, Bashar facilitated Hizballah's further ascendance on the Lebanese political scene as a counterweight to Hariri.[26] Hizballah's rise reflected, in part, its increased stature in Lebanon and across the region following what was widely perceived in the Arab world as the group's success in driving the Israel Defense Forces off occupied Arab land. But, in contrast to his father's suppression of Hizballah's political status in 1996, following a similar upsurge in the group's popularity in the aftermath of Israel's Oper-

Keychains bearing the likenesses of Bashar al-Asad and Hizballah secretary general Hassan Nasrallah on sale in Damascus in May 2004.   (© Khaled al-Hariri/Reuters/Corbis)

ation Grapes of Wrath, Bashar allowed Hizballah to create its own "Hizbal-lahland" in southern Lebanon following the Israeli withdrawal.[27]

Since the IDF pullout, Hizballah has used its territorial base in the south as a platform for mobilizing popular support not only in that region, but in other parts of Lebanon as well.[28] In its quest for greater political standing, Hizballah has consistently enjoyed the support of the new Syrian president. Bashar apparently calculates that Hizballah's increased popularity makes the group a useful ally in his approach to managing the Lebanese political arena. It also seems evident that Bashar respects what he views as Hassan Nasrallah's leadership qualities and accomplishments.[29] In his February 8, 2001, inter-view with *al-Sharq al-Awsat*, Bashar clearly implied that Hizballah had become part of the Lebanese structure of governance, noting that decisions about continuing attacks against Israeli targets from Lebanese territory after the IDF withdrawal had to be taken "through coordination between the state and its institutions, including the army and the Lebanese resistance"—that is, Hizballah. (Hizballah's political ascendancy was in many ways a complement to Bashar's efforts to alter and regulate the group's paramilitary posture toward Israel and in the region more generally in light of Syria's shifting strategic environment; these efforts are discussed later in the chapter.)

Bashar also sought to undermine Hariri's political standing by bolstering the prime minister's archrival, President Lahud. In the February 2001 interview with *al-Sharq al-Awsat*, Bashar seemed to respond to both Maronite critics of the Syrian presence and to supporters of Prime Minister Hariri by declaring that his partner in Syrian-Lebanese "joint decisionmaking" was Lahud, whom Bashar described as standing at the "top of the pyramid."

Similarly, the Syrian leadership under Bashar undermined Hariri's standing by supporting Lahud in blocking the prime minister's policy initiatives. Since reassuming the prime minister's post, Hariri had sought to implement a renewed program for Lebanon's economic recovery, a program presented in outline to the so-called "Paris II" conference in November 2002.[30] For two years after Paris II, however, Lahud—with Syrian backing—blocked most of Hariri's policy proposals, such as privatizations. (To be sure, Lahud partisans defend the president's actions by pointing to earlier charges of corruption and private profit-taking by Hariri and his associates during the prime minister's earlier service.)

Finally, Bashar did not hesitate to utilize more direct means to rein in Hariri when circumstances warranted. The Syrian president summoned the Lebanese prime minister to Damascus in early 2001, after Hariri's publicly stated willingness to allow former president Jumayyil to return to Lebanon from exile in France put him fundamentally at odds with Syrian preferences. At their meeting, Bashar reportedly delivered a severe reprimand to Hariri, who thereafter did not reiterate the position that had caused such anxiety in the Syrian capital.[31] (Of course, in the end, Bashar struck his own deal with Jumayyil, but the episode underscored the Syrian leader's determination not to let Hariri set the political agenda inside Lebanon.) Similarly, in April 2003, as the U.S. military campaign in Iraq was drawing to a close and Syria perceived a higher risk of U.S. action against its interests in the region, Damascus forced the resignation of the Lebanese cabinet, making sure that the successor body would have an even higher number of unquestionably reliable Syrian proxies to keep the prime minister in check.[32]

The confrontation between Bashar and Hariri came to a head in the fall of 2004, when the Syrian leader supported an extension of Lahud's term as president in defiance of Lebanese constitutional processes. As part of his efforts to assuage anti-Syrian sentiment in Lebanon, Bashar had apparently considered allowing Lahud to be replaced, in accordance with the Lebanese constitution, by another (presumably compliant) Maronite when the presidential term expired in November 2004.[33] But, in the face of increasing international criticism over Syrian hegemony in Lebanon, Bashar—perhaps under pressure from the old guard or the security establishment not to risk Syrian control in Lebanon at a critical moment—opted to stick with Lahud.[34] At Syria's urging, Lebanese authorities amended the constitution in September 2004 to extend Lahud's term in office for three years.

Syria's determinative role in Lahud's extension prompted the UN Security Council to adopt resolution 1559 in September 2004, calling on Damascus to remove its troops from Lebanon and stop its interference in Lebanese affairs (see appendix C). This set in motion a dramatic sequence of events that is still being played out as this book goes to press. In the aftermath of the resolution's passage, the Bush administration considered freezing the assets of Lebanese and Syrian officials until Syrian forces were withdrawn. This, along with his frustration over Lahud's extension, prompted Hariri (who reportedly had extensive financial holdings in the United States) to resign as prime minister in October 2004.[35] He was replaced by Omar Karami.

After his resignation, Hariri entered into discussions with the anti-Syrian opposition bloc in Lebanon's parliament. On February 14, 2005, as he was apparently on the verge of publicly joining the opposition, Hariri was assassinated in Beirut. The assassination sparked a series of anti-Syrian and antigovernment protests on the streets of the Lebanese capital, leading to the resignation of the Karami government later that month.

Thus, Bashar is facing an increasingly serious challenge to maintain Syria's grip on the key levers of power and prevent the emergence of genuinely independent power centers. With or without a direct presence in Lebanon, however, Syria will likely continue to enjoy the support of a considerable swath of Lebanese society for its foreign policy prerogatives. The counterdemonstration on March 8, 2005, called for by Nasrallah and attended by an estimated half million people provides evidence for the demographic weight of Syria's supporters in Lebanon, especially among the Shi'a community. Nonetheless, Bashar's efforts to adapt his father's script to new realities in the Lebanese arena has (as is discussed below) set the stage for increased tension in Syria's relations with the United States and some of its presumptive allies in Europe, especially France.

The Arab-Israeli Arena

The challenge of adapting Hafiz al-Asad's script to changed circumstances was especially acute in the Arab-Israeli arena. When the succession occurred, the Syrian track of the peace process was in hiatus, and the government of Israeli prime minister Ehud Barak was focused on reaching a final-status deal with the Palestinians.[36] Bashar initially seemed to entertain the possibility of resuming negotiations with Barak. But he did not have sufficient time to explore that possibility before developments on the Palestinian track and in Israeli and U.S. politics foreclosed it indefinitely.

Faced with an effective collapse of the Syrian track, Hafiz's script would suggest that the new president continue developing Syria's chemical weapon and ballistic missile capabilities as a strategic deterrent, something that Bashar has done. The script would further suggest the employment of traditional tools, particularly Hizballah operations, to press Israel. Additionally, the script would suggest that Bashar use diplomatic means to signal to Israel and the United States the strategic costs of neglecting Syria's needs and to forestall an erosion of regional and international support for Syria's position on the basis of an acceptable peace settlement.

But, as in the Lebanese arena, new realities in Syria's strategic environment made Bashar's application of Hafiz's script in the Arab-Israeli arena more difficult than either father or son probably had anticipated. This was particularly true with regard to using paramilitary and terrorist proxies to press Israel and managing Arab-Israeli diplomacy in the absence of a meaningful Syrian track.

New Roles for Proxies

The option of escalating Hizballah's anti-Israel operations was complicated by the Israeli withdrawal from southern Lebanon and, after March 2001, the arrival of an Israeli prime minister whose threshold for retaliating against Syrian interests in response to Hizballah provocations was likely to be lower than that of his predecessors. And, as the second intifada heated up, the new Syrian president had to balance the political imperative of support for Palestinian resistance against a heightened risk of being drawn into conflict with Israel. In light of these considerations, Bashar has had to adjust Syria's "indirect support" for Hizballah and the various Palestinian rejectionist groups to which it has ties. Bashar has tried three alternative avenues to maintain the relevance of Syria's ties to terrorist organizations: allowing these groups to continue applying pressure directly to Israel; encouraging them to involve themselves in the intifada; and—with specific reference to Hizballah—building up their military capabilities so that they could serve as a kind of "strategic deterrent" to Israeli military action against Syrian interests.

APPLYING PRESSURE. Initially, Bashar seemed to want to find ways in which Hizballah, in particular, could keep playing its traditional role in Syrian strategy toward Israel—that is, pressing Israel, through the calibrated use of force, to engage politically with Damascus on terms acceptable to the Asad regime. At least prospectively, the Israeli withdrawal from southern Lebanon had devalued Syria's Hizballah card.[37] Bashar apparently calculated that he needed to demonstrate the continuing viability of the threat posed along Israel's northern border by Hizballah fighters who, after the IDF withdrawal, could come right up to the Blue Line demarcating the international border. This concern seemed particularly pressing as Bashar began to doubt the willingness of the outgoing Clinton administration to push for a resumption of Israeli-Syrian negotiations on terms acceptable to Damascus.

Bashar's interest in finding ways to continue playing his Hizballah card intersected with Hizballah's own decision to continue the armed struggle against Israel.[38] In the summer and fall of 2000, Hizballah was feeling triumphant over the Israeli withdrawal, viewing it as a victory for its model of armed resistance.[39] After an internal debate over the group's future course—whether to continue the fight against Israel or give up armed resistance and concentrate on political and social activities—Hizballah's leadership clearly opted for what the group's secretary general Nasrallah described as "completing the liberation."[40]

Thus, in the immediate aftermath of the withdrawal, both Syria and Hizballah calculated that they should continue taking the fight to Israel, and could do so with relative impunity. Some analysts interpret Bashar's willingness to endorse ongoing direct action by Hizballah against Israeli targets as ideologically driven, reflecting both the Syrian president's admiration for Hassan Nasrallah and a less calculating and risk averse approach than that of his late father.[41] Jordanian, Saudi, and other Gulf Arab officials expressed such concerns to U.S. officials, arguing that Bashar's "embrace" of Hizbal-lah's leader and his pan-Arab and pan-Islamic appeal was an indication of the new Syrian leader's lack of judgment.[42]

It is certainly true that Bashar has a genuine admiration for Nasrallah's considerable skills and accomplishments. It is also true that Bashar has spent more time meeting with Nasrallah and other Hizballah officials than his father did. But a close examination of Hizballah's activities since the fall of 2000 suggests that, when using the group in traditional ways proved overly risky, Bashar sought new ways to leverage Hizballah to advance long-established Syrian goals. In pursuing this course, the Syrian leader evinced no interest in precipitating anything approaching full-fledged war between Israel and Syria; indeed, to the contrary, he displayed an awareness of the unacceptable costs such an outcome would impose on Syria and his regime.[43]

Given Bashar's relative newness to the presidency and the seriousness of the challenges confronting him as a result of the shifting strategic environ-ment, it is hardly surprising that the adjustment process has entailed a con-siderable measure of trial and error. In particular, Bashar experienced a steep learning curve in determining whether and how he could continue to use Hizballah's traditional paramilitary activities as a tool to press Israel. Nevertheless, whenever Bashar has gone too far in the operational scope he has afforded Hizballah, he has to date always managed to correct course suf-ficiently and in time to avoid an unwanted level of conflict with Israel.

In the first phase of his learning curve regarding the use of Hizballah, Bashar sought to establish a framework for continued Hizballah operations against Israeli targets in a postwithdrawal environment.[44] But Bashar and Hizballah leaders soon learned that they could not manage the risks of regional and international blowback from the group's operations as easily as they had previously, particularly after Ariel Sharon took office as prime minister of Israel.

In the face of an unexpectedly robust Israeli response to Hizballah provo-cations, including Israeli air strikes on Syrian targets in Lebanon, Bashar sought to reinstate the traditional rules of the game regulating military interactions between Israel and Hizballah.[45] In particular, Syrian officials sought to reaffirm the rules that had grown up around the April 1996 understanding. Israel's attack on the Syrian radar post in Lebanon in April 2001 signaled Sharon's intention to change the old rules, raising the chances of an escalatory spiral between Israel and Syria. Damascus clearly hoped that the United States would prevail on Sharon not to change the rules of the Lebanese game in this way, in order to forestall the risk of escalation to a regional conflict.[46]

Bashar's reaffirmation of the old rules of the game was tested in mid-May 2001 with a Hizballah missile attack on an IDF border post in the Sheba'a Farms area that produced no Israeli casualties. When Israel did not respond, it seemed to confirm an assessment in official Damascus that Sharon had abandoned his effort to define new rules for Israeli-Syrian interaction in the Lebanese theater. But this relatively optimistic view was short lived. Following Hizballah attacks around Sheba'a Farms in late June and July, Sharon responded by ordering the Israeli Air Force to attack another Syrian radar post in the Biqa'a. Concerned about the risk of much larger Israeli retaliation—and, after the September 11, 2001, terrorist attacks in the United States, the risk of being caught on the wrong side of the Bush administration's war on terror—Syria endorsed a Hizballah stand-down in the late summer and early fall of 2001.[47]

In the second phase of Bashar's learning curve, Hizballah leaders and the Syrian president tried again to strike a proper balance between keeping up the fight against Israel and avoiding unwanted escalation. In October 2001 Hizballah resumed limited attacks in the Sheba'a Farms area.[48] From this relatively low base, Hizballah began to ratchet up the level of anti-Israeli operations, to see how far it could go and escape an overly punishing Israeli response.[49]

With the rules of the game still uncertain, Israel, Hizballah, and Syria found themselves in a new escalatory spiral starting in March 2002. Early that month, Hizballah—undoubtedly with Syrian agreement—began sending Palestinian militants across the Blue Line to attack Israeli targets, ostensibly as a way of manifesting solidarity with the ongoing intifada. The group also began to use Palestinian fighters to launch Katyusha rockets into northern Israel. On March 28, a day after the "Passover massacre" in Netanya, Israel launched Operation Defensive Shield, sending IDF formations deep into the West Bank and occupying virtually all major Palestinian population centers. In response, Hizballah launched an unprecedented series of attacks against Sheba'a Farms, conducting fourteen separate operations in the space of two weeks. Israel responded to these provocations largely with artillery fire against Hizballah targets in southern Lebanon, but the odds of a large-scale Israeli military operation into Lebanese territory were unquestionably growing.[50] It was this danger that prompted Secretary of State Colin Powell, on an April 2002 trip to the region to try to restart some sort of political process between Israel and the Palestinians, to make stops in Damascus and Beirut in an effort to break the escalatory spiral between Israel and Syria.

Powell's side trip brought one of the few successes on what was an otherwise frustrating journey for the secretary, and marked an important turning point in the evolution of Hizballah's operational posture toward Israel after the IDF withdrawal.[51] Highlighting for Bashar the potential dangers of a regional conflict for Syrian interests, Powell was able to persuade the Syrian leader to restrain Hizballah's attacks against Israeli targets. Following Powell's meeting with Bashar, Hizballah did not carry out any operations against Israeli interests until five months later, in August 2002, when the group attacked an Israeli military outpost in the Sheba'a Farms area. Since then, Hizballah has settled into a pattern of relatively small-scale attacks, fairly widely spaced in time, against Israeli targets in Sheba'a Farms as well as small-scale retaliation against perceived Israeli provocations across the Blue Line.[52] (Antiaircraft fire by Hizballah against Israeli military aircraft continues to produce occasional casualties in civilian settlements in northern Israel.)

Bashar obviously experienced a noticeable learning curve about the limits of the possible in that specific theater. He has not been able to prevent erosion in the value of Hizballah's paramilitary activities as a source of leverage over Israel. Indeed, Hizballah has been largely stalemated with regard to the political and tactical effect of its operations directly targeting Israeli interests. The stalemate has occurred not only because changing strategic realities in the region raised the risks of escalation, but also because of diminishing support within Lebanon for the group's anti-Israeli operations, as the prospective costs of large-scale retaliation came to be recognized by more and more Lebanese.[53] At the same time, though, Bashar never pushed his tactical experiments with Hizballah beyond a point of no return. In the end, a new, if still tentative, equilibrium was established along Israel's northern border.

It would, of course, be imprudent to discount completely the possibility for deterioration in the security situation along the Blue Line and a further escalatory spiral in the future. The stalemate along the Blue Line is not guaranteed; miscalculation by Hizballah or overreaction by Israel could start another escalatory spiral.[54] As Bashar's learning curve continues, steady U.S. management of the situation is required, including reminders to Bashar about the prospective costs to him and his regime that escalation to a regional conflict would pose.[55]

SUPPORTING THE PALESTINIAN CAUSE. Alongside his less-than-wholly-successful efforts to shore up Hizballah's value as a paramilitary proxy, Bashar has sought to use the group to increase Syria's influence on the Palestinian intifada.[56] Bashar appeared to calculate that raising Syria's profile in the context of the intifada would help him on several fronts: it would burnish his credentials as an Arab nationalist leader, bolster his popular standing, potentially weaken Yasir Arafat's standing as the preeminent Palestinian leader, and increase Syrian influence over Palestinian affairs. (Bashar may have assessed these considerations as being consistent with the script that he inherited from his father.)

Here, too, Bashar's calculations intersected with Hizballah's internal deliberations. In the aftermath of the IDF withdrawal, part of Hizballah's internal debate about its future agenda focused on whether to provide active support to the Palestinian resistance. By early 2001 the group had clearly decided, as Nasrallah himself said later that year, "never to allow the Palestinians to fight alone."[57]

Hizballah's involvement in the Palestinian resistance has taken several forms. Well before the outbreak of the current intifada in September 2000, Hizballah was providing training at camps in Lebanon to Palestinian rejectionists opposed to the Oslo Accords between Israel and the PLO; this activity has apparently increased since late 2000, to include cooperation with Hamas and Palestinian Islamic Jihad. Hizballah also started supplying arms and military equipment to Palestinian rejectionists in the territories; the scope of these activities may be gauged by the scope of smuggling operations that have been thwarted.[58] Most notoriously, Hizballah was involved in the Iranian-sponsored attempt to transport fifty tons of weaponry to Gaza on board the *Karine-A* in January 2002.[59] Hizballah also attempted to smuggle Katyusha rockets to the West Bank through Jordan in early 2002.[60]

Beyond provision of training and supplies, Hizballah has sought to extend its operational reach into the territories and into Israel proper. For example, the group has infiltrated operatives into the West Bank and Gaza to assist Hamas and Islamic Jihad; these operatives have also worked to set up Hizballah's own recruiting network in the territories to enlist young

Palestinians for training at its Lebanese camps, presumably to return as terrorist operatives themselves.[61] Analysts with contacts in Israeli security and intelligence circles claim that Hizballah also has organized a network of rogue Fatah Tanzim elements (a militant suborganization of the PLO's dominant Fatah faction) in the West Bank.[62] In addition, Israeli authorities have uncovered cells of Israeli Arabs recruited by Hizballah for intelligence and terrorist missions.[63]

The "Palestinianization" of Hizballah has been complemented during Bashar's presidency by ongoing Syrian support for Palestinian rejectionists active in the intifada. Syria's posture toward the Palestinian groups to which it has ties is discussed later, but it is worth noting here that Bashar has tried to follow his father's script on this point as well, seeking to derive leverage and enhanced popular standing from continued indirect support for organizations like Hamas and Islamic Jihad while controlling the risks of escalation.

Arguably, however, the Palestinianization of Hizballah and ongoing Syrian ties to rejectionist groups pose bigger escalatory risks than Hizballah operations along the Blue Line. As Israel's air strike in October 2003 against a (probably abandoned) Palestinian rejectionist training camp in Syria following a Hamas suicide bombing attack in Haifa indicates, Syria's association with Palestinian rejectionists has put it under threat of further Israeli military action.[64] If Hizballah were ever implicated in a significant Palestinian terrorist attack in the territories or within Israel proper, the potential for substantial Israeli retaliation against Syria would be great, indeed.

Syria's ongoing support for Palestinian rejectionists does not seem to have advanced its interests during the first four years of Bashar's presidency. These developments may have contributed to an undeniable weakening of Arafat's status but may have imposed costs on Syria's strategic position more generally. Beyond the escalatory risks, Israeli and U.S. perceptions of Syrian support for intensification of the intifada have further undermined prospects of resumption of Israeli-Syrian peace talks. And, as discussed later, those same perceptions have contributed to deterioration in Syria's relationship with the United States. In this regard as well, there has been a devaluation of the terrorist cards Bashar inherited from his father.

Bashar may well be drawing the same conclusion about the value of Syria's ties to Palestinian rejectionists. In September 2004 Khalid Mish'al and Ramadan Shallah, the respective heads of Hamas and Palestinian

Islamic Jihad operations in Damascus, departed Syria ostensibly to investigate alternative places of residence.[65] In the end, both returned to their Syrian safe haven. But the move seemed to signal an exploration by Bashar of the possibility of a reduction in the level of Syrian support for these organizations.

It remains to be seen how Arafat's death in November 2004 may affect Bashar's assessment of the residual value of ties to the groups. The visit by the new PLO chairman Mahmud 'Abbas (also known as Abu Mazen) to Damascus in December 2004, the first meeting in Syria between the head of the PLO and the Syrian regime since 1983, indicated a possible thaw in relations between the mainstream Palestinian movement and the Asad regime. 'Abbas opened the possibility of greater cooperation between Syria and the PLO when he remarked that the Syrians were "very receptive" to a request to upgrade their bilateral relationship.[66] Bashar, however, retains the option of working to undercut a moderate Palestinian leadership if that leadership behaves in ways he perceives as inimical to Syria's interests.

CREATING A STRATEGIC DETERRENT.   One area where Bashar has perhaps been able to increase the value of Hizballah as an adjunct to Syria's national security posture is in the cultivation of Hizballah's paramilitary apparatus in southern Lebanon as a deterrent to a potential Israeli invasion. For many years, Syria's worst-case scenario for Israeli military action against it has been an armored strike up Lebanon's Biqa'a Valley, which turns east, crosses into Syria, and drives toward Damascus. The only potential deterrent to that scenario that Hafiz al-Asad was able to develop was the threatened use of chemical weapons against Israeli targets. This has always been an unsatisfactory deterrent posture, since Syrian officials are well aware of the retaliatory response that Israel is capable of launching.

As the chances for an early resumption of peace negotiations vanished and the risk of military conflict with Israel began to increase in early 2001, Bashar apparently decided to use Hizballah as a supplement to Syria's deterrent posture. By all indications, Bashar agreed to allow Iran to increase dramatically not just the amount of weaponry it was providing to Hizballah through supply flights to Damascus International Airport but also to send more advanced weapons systems. In particular, Iran began to send Hizballah rockets with longer ranges than the Katyusha, including the Fajr-5.[67] The Fajr-5 has a range of forty-five miles, giving it the capability, if launched from southern Lebanon, of hitting any Israeli city north of Haifa.

The expansion of Hizballah's long-range strike capabilities seems directly correlated to Syria's apprehensions about the risk of military conflict with Israel. The shipments, which started in early 2001, intensified after September 11, 2001, when Syria was concerned about being caught on the wrong side of the Bush administration's war on terror. [68] By extension, Bashar was also concerned about the possibility that Sharon might take advantage of a U.S.-led war on terror to conduct his own regional campaign against Israel's neighboring state sponsor.

The buildup of Hizballah's missile arsenals as a part of Syria's deterrent posture certainly complicates the calculations of Israeli planners considering various military options in the Lebanese and Syrian theaters. At the end of 2004, estimates of the number of short- and long-range rockets at Hizballah's disposal in southern Lebanon run from 8,000 to 10,000. [69] Given these numbers and the disposition of Hizballah's rocket arsenal, it is unlikely that Israel has a meaningful "first-strike" capability to remove unilaterally and comprehensively the threat posed to Israeli targets. In that sense, Bashar has probably succeeded in obtaining an added increment of strategic deterrence for his regime. But the purchase of that increment has come at a price—a price denominated in the extra layer of complexity that has been added to the calculations of *all* parties in the Israeli-Lebanese-Syrian triangle, thereby increasing the chances of miscalculation. In addition, the expansion of Hizballah's longer-range strike capabilities has raised the levels of damage that miscalculation would likely produce.

Difficult Diplomacy

Bashar has also sought to defend Syrian interests in the Arab-Israeli arena through diplomatic means. As noted in chapter 2, Hafiz al-Asad defined a negotiated peace with Israel as Syria's preferred "strategic option." The elder Asad left his son not only a well-defined set of parameters for an acceptable peace treaty (full Israeli withdrawal from the Golan Heights, comprehensiveness, and a relatively short period for implementation), but also a clearly enunciated set of conditions for proceeding with negotiations (most important, a reaffirmation of Rabin's contingent commitment to full withdrawal—the so-called deposit).

From the beginning of his presidency, Bashar has presented himself both as committed to continuing the pursuit of a negotiated peace as Syria's preferred strategic option and as bound by his father's parameters for an acceptable deal. In his inaugural address, the new president reaffirmed his commitment to a "just and comprehensive peace" as Syria's "strategic choice" but noted that such a peace would come "not at the expense of our territory nor at the expense of our sovereignty."[70] In his February 8, 2001, interview with *al-Sharq al-Awsat*, Bashar said of his approach to peace, "I have not taken anything out nor have I added anything. President Hafiz al-Asad did not give in, and neither shall we; not today and not in the future." And, in fact, throughout his presidency, Bashar has not departed substantially from the peace process positions he inherited from his father.

But keeping faith with that legacy has generated real challenges for the new national leader. Bashar's management of Syria's diplomatic posture in the Arab-Israeli arena has unfolded in three phases. In the first, he seemed to want to renew negotiations quickly, presumably from the point at which his father had broken them off. In the second phase, Bashar abandoned hope for a near-term resumption of negotiations, opting instead for a vituperative public diplomacy campaign meant to put the onus on Israel for the breakdown of the Syrian track. In the third and current phase, Bashar seems to have returned to an interest in resuming negotiations.

CONTEMPLATING RENEWED NEGOTIATIONS. In the initial months of his tenure, Bashar seemed to entertain the possibility of inducing the Clinton administration to make "one last try" to mediate talks with the Barak government and broker an Israeli-Syrian peace. In his inaugural address, Asad called on the United States "to play its full role as an honest broker and a cosponsor of the peace process," noting that "pressure has to be exerted in order to implement the sources of international legitimacy and all the legitimate rights they dictate for the Lebanese, Syrian, and Palestinian people." In October 2000, on his first trip abroad as president of Syria, Bashar said in Cairo, "For the United States, we feel that President Bill Clinton and the Secretary of State Madeleine Albright have the real intention and willingness to help parties achieve peace, a just and comprehensive peace."[71] Two weeks later, on a trip to Saudi Arabia, Bashar met with Secretary Albright in Riyadh to discuss, among other things, a possible resumption of the Syrian track.

By the time of his meeting with Albright, though, Bashar must already have been considering the likelihood that the Barak government and the Clinton administration were not prepared to resume negotiations with Damascus. This is surely an important part of the context for the launch of

Hizballah's offensive campaign along the Blue Line that same month, an offensive intended, at least in part, to remind Israel of the costs of neglecting Syria's diplomatic interests and needs. As 2000 drew to a close, the same developments on the Palestinian track that prompted Bashar to try to increase Syria's influence over Palestinian affairs also persuaded the new Syrian leader that he could not immediately pick up Syria's peace process diplomacy where his father had left off. Escalating Israeli-Palestinian violence and an upturn in anti-Israeli sentiment throughout the region as the Intifada al-Aqsa intensified complicated any possible renewal of the Syrian track. These considerations soon led the new Syrian president to conclude that it would be politically impossible for him to resume negotiations, even if an Israeli government were willing to proceed on the basis of the Rabin deposit.

That conclusion in turn produced an important shift in Syria's diplomatic posture toward the peace process. The elder Asad's position, as conveyed to U.S. officials by Foreign Minister Shar' in the mid- and late 1990s, was that Arafat had broken Arab solidarity by proceeding with the Oslo process; if Syria could achieve a deal meeting Asad's redlines, the Syrian president would take it, regardless of the status of Israeli-Palestinian negotiations.[72] In contrast, Bashar assessed by early 2001 that he could not return to negotiations with Israel until there had been an improvement in conditions on the Palestinian track. He may also have decided he had an opportunity to reassert Syrian influence over the Palestinian track, a position consistent with his acquiescence in the Palestinianization of Hizballah.

Bashar's position regarding the impossibility of resuming negotiations without some improvement on the Palestinian front was conveyed to Washington and was reflected as well in his public pronouncements. In February 2001, Bashar noted that

> the ultimate goal is a just and comprehensive peace. "Comprehensive" means all the occupied territories: the Golan and Lebanon do not constitute the comprehensive peace and therefore there must be a symmetry between the Syrian and Lebanese tracks on the one hand and the Palestinian track on the other. . . . The word "comprehensive" has a pan-Arab connotation and we insist on comprehensive peace and on cooperation and coordination with the Arabs on other tracks.[73]

When pressed for an explicit statement that Syria would not sign a treaty with Israel before the Palestinians did so, Bashar said, "The issue is not 'to sign or not to sign.' Tracks should move simultaneously. We do not know, they might sign before us. We shall not sign on anything unless we make sure that it serves the region and achieves an enduring peace . . . and peace will not be enduring unless it restores all Arab rights with no exception whatsoever."[74]

A month later, at the March 2001 Arab League summit in Amman, Bashar defined Syria's peace process goals in similar terms: Syria sought a "just and comprehensive peace based on the Madrid terms of reference, withdrawal from the Lebanese, Syrian, and Palestinian territories to the June 4, 1967, lines, the return of East Jerusalem, and the establishment of an independent Palestinian state with Jerusalem as its capital."[75]

Bashar's reluctance to resume peace talks was surely bolstered by the election of Ariel Sharon to replace Ehud Barak as prime minister of Israel and the inauguration of George W. Bush as president of the United States. Sharon had made clear over many years his opposition to full withdrawal from the Golan Heights, making it highly unlikely that as prime minister he would agree to conditions for entering negotiations with Syria that would include reaffirmation of the Rabin deposit. In the United States, the new president Bush—disdainful of his predecessor's vigorous pursuit of Arab-Israeli peace and assessing that he had no opening for successful engagement—initially decided to disengage from the peace process and wait for a more propitious time.[76] Once the Bush administration began to engage more seriously on the Palestinian issue in 2002—through the launching of the "Quartet" (the United States, United Nations, European Union, and Russia), the definition of the Bush administration's approach to Arab-Israeli matters in the president's June 24, 2002, speech, and the drafting of the Middle East Roadmap—it largely left Syria on the sidelines.[77]

PUBLIC DIPLOMACY. As Bashar grew more skeptical of the near-term possibilities for a renewed Syrian track, his focus shifted from prospective negotiations to public diplomacy designed to focus international criticism for the deteriorating regional situation on Israel. In particular, the Syrian president's rhetoric placed ever-greater emphasis on Israel as the chief obstacle to a settlement. In October 2000, on a visit to Cairo, Bashar did not categorically rule out the possibility of an Israeli commitment to resume negotiations: "In peace, there are not balls in courts. But if we have to suppose that there are balls in peace making, we should say that Syria's position on peace is clear, and that Israel has not decided yet whether it wants peace or not."[78]

By the time of the Arab League summit in Amman in March 2001, however, Bashar's rhetoric on Israel's attitude toward peace had hardened: "The Israelis killed Rabin, when they suspected he would offer something for peace; a mere suspicion made them kill him though he was the hero in breaking the Palestinians' bones during the first intifada. Israel does not want to abide by any principles approved by the international community to achieve peace. Israel doesn't have the willingness to achieve real peace." The Syrian leader also became more categorical in his condemnation of Israel's resistance to a settlement acceptable to Damascus: "We were occupied with analyzing the difference between the right and left in Israel. . . . For Arabs there is no right and no left. In Israel, whoever kills 1,000 Arabs is left, and whoever kills 5,000 is right. For us Arabs, all Israelis are right."[79]

At times in late 2000 and the first half of 2001, Bashar's rhetoric about Israel employed formulations that can fairly be described as antisemitic. At the summit of the Organization of the Islamic Conference in Doha in November 2000, for example, Bashar referred to Israel's

> continued attempts at judaising Al Quds through destroying its Islamic and Christian landmarks and through asserting that it is the united and eternal capital of Israel, despite the fact that the Torah talks about the land of Canaan, which is Palestine. The Canaanites were an Arab tribe who built Al Quds three thousand years before Christ. The existence of the Hebrews in Palestine throughout history was only short-lived and distant intervals as a minority amongst native inhabitants of the country. The Israeli arrogance and practices . . . have no connection whatever with the ethics and teachings of any heavenly religion.[80]

Four months later, at the Arab League summit in Amman, Bashar argued that "the reality of Israeli public opinion should be probed; Israel is a racial society and a more racist one than Nazism."[81]

The height of such rhetorical flourishes came at the beginning of May 2001, in the aftermath of the Israeli air strike on a Syrian radar post in Lebanon the preceding month. On an official visit to Spain and in his remarks welcoming Pope John Paul II to Damascus a few days later, Bashar employed the traditional formulation of Jews as Christ-killers, asserting that

> our brethren in Palestine are being murdered and tortured, justice is being violated, and as a result territories in Lebanon, the Golan, and Palestine have been occupied by those who even killed the principle of equality when they claimed that God created a people distinguished above all other peoples. We notice them aggressing against Muslim and Christian Holy Sites in Palestine, violating the sanctuary of *al Aqsa*, of the Church of the Holy Sepulcher in Jerusalem and the Church of the Nativity in Bethlehem. They try to kill all the principles of divine faiths with the same mentality of betraying Jesus Christ and torturing Him, and in the same way that they tried to commit treachery against Prophet Muhammad (peace be upon him).[82]

Under Bashar's leadership, Syria used its seat on the United Nations Security Council, which it took up in January 2002, to further its public diplomacy campaign on Arab-Israeli issues. During the winter and spring of 2002, as Israeli-Palestinian violence intensified, Syria tabled, virtually on a weekly basis, draft Security Council resolutions critical of Israel. Damascus, however, usually resisted compromise on language that would permit Middle East–related resolutions to be adopted by the Security Council, rejecting formulations balancing references to Israeli military actions with references to Palestinian attacks on Israeli civilians. Syria abstained, for example, in the vote of Security Council Resolution 1397 in March 2002.[83] This resolution, adopted with the support of the United States, provided Security Council endorsement for the first time for a two-state solution to the Israeli-Palestinian conflict. Even though the resolution called for the creation of a state of Palestine, Syria objected to provisions calling for an end to "all acts of violence."

Bashar has also used tools of public diplomacy to undermine regional and international support for U.S. peace initiatives that he considers inimical to Syrian interests. As the Bush administration launched its effort to implement its roadmap for a two-state solution to the Israeli-Palestinian conflict in June 2003, Bashar—in keeping with his father's script—stepped up efforts to discredit an approach that effectively ignored Syria. In both public statements and diplomatic representations to American, European, and Arab interlocutors, Syrian officials—including Bashar and Foreign Minister Shar'—conveyed their assessment that the Bush administration was not serious about pursuing the roadmap and that the current diplomatic effort was doomed to fail.[84] By the end of the summer of 2003, the Bush administration's retreat from serious diplomatic activism to advance the roadmap appeared to validate Syrian skepticism for many regional audiences. In 2004 Syria has been similarly critical of Prime Minister Sharon's "Gaza First" initiative and President Bush's assurances to Sharon on final status issues.[85]

RETURN TO NEGOTIATIONS? Since the Iraq war in the spring of 2003, Bashar's rhetoric on resuming peace talks with Israel has shifted to reflect an apparently renewed willingness to enter negotiations. Sorting out what is genuine and what is tactically convenient in Syrian statements on resuming negotiations with Israel is not easy. Would Bashar modify his insistence that talks had to begin on the basis of an effective Israeli reaffirmation of the Rabin deposit? Would he enter talks without prior movement on the Palestinian track? And might he be willing to consider a deal that deviated from his father's redlines for an acceptable settlement?

Bashar's statements bearing on these questions went through something of an evolution following what in Damascus was viewed as the unexpectedly rapid conclusion of the military campaign to unseat Saddam Hussein. In the immediate aftermath of Operation Iraqi Freedom, Bashar and other Syrian officials began stating in various public and media venues that Syria was ready to restart peace talks with Israel; the Syrian president also sent a similar message to Prime Minister Sharon through U.S. representative Tom Lantos (D-Calif.).[86] Sharon responded in late April that he was ready to resume negotiations but that talks should take place "without conditions"— a clear rejection of any reaffirmation of the Rabin deposit.[87]

Later that spring, the Syrian position seemed to evolve even further. After Secretary of Defense Donald Rumsfeld suggested that coercive regime change might be a suitable approach to dealing with Syria and an unproductive visit by Secretary of State Powell to Damascus in early May, Bashar gave an interview to *Newsweek* in which he said that the basis for renewed negotiations between Israel and Syria should be "the Madrid conference" of October 1991.[88] Of course, the Madrid principles have long been part of the terms of reference for any peace negotiations acceptable to Syria. But the Rabin deposit—as much as Syrian diplomats may wish to argue that it was clearly implied in the Madrid principles and the notion of "land for peace"—was a separate and historically later development in the Israeli-Syrian diplomatic record. By identifying Madrid as an acceptable basis for resuming talks without any reference to the Rabin deposit, Bashar was arguably signaling a relaxation in Syrian terms for restarting a diplomatic dialogue. By late summer 2003, however, as it became clear that the Bush administration's initiative with the roadmap had stalled and that U.S. forces were getting bogged down in Iraq, Damascus went back to explicit statements of the established line.

Bashar's expressions of interest in returning to the negotiating table went through a similar cycle several months later. In the aftermath of the Israeli air strike against a Palestinian terrorist training camp in Syria in October 2003, Bashar said in a late November interview with the *New York Times* that the Bush administration should revive negotiations between Israel and Syria, noting that a deal was "80 percent" complete when talks had broken off a few months before Hafiz al-Asad's death.[89] Once again, Bashar advanced a rhetorical formula that some interpreted as suggesting he might not insist on an explicit reaffirmation of the Rabin deposit in order to resume talks. In the *New York Times* interview, Bashar said that "some people say that there are Syrian conditions, and my answer is no; we don't have Syrian conditions." The president noted that "negotiations should be resumed from the point at which they had stopped simply because we have achieved a great deal in these negotiations"; he did not explicitly make resumption at the point where previous talks had left off a requirement for restarting dialogue.

In making these statements, Bashar may have been counting on Prime Minister Sharon to be disinclined to resume talks with Syria and to respond in a way that would let Damascus off the hook. If that were the case, Sharon answered Bashar's expressions of interest in renewed talks in precisely the expected manner. Sharon not only reiterated his insistence that peace talks start from scratch, without any precondition; according to the *Jerusalem Post*, Sharon told his cabinet in late December that Israel would negotiate with Syria only after Syria stopped harboring Palestinian terrorists, allowed for the removal of Hizballah fighters from the Israeli-Lebanese border, and dismantled Hizballah's expanded rocket arsenal.[90] Sharon's spokesman and members of the cabinet made similar public statements.[91] Perhaps more tellingly, on the last day of 2003, Sharon's government announced plans to double the number of Israeli settlements in the occupied Golan Heights over the next three years.[92] Prospects for renewed talks seemed poor.

But Israel soon followed up with an overture of its own. Days after Sharon's government announced its settlement construction plans for the Golan, Israeli president Moshe Katsav, seemingly on his own initiative, publicly invited Bashar to come to Jerusalem for talks without any precondition but in which either party could raise any issue for consideration.[93] Syrian officials and state-controlled media dismissed Katsav's offer as not "serious," and Damascus quickly returned to explicit statements of the established conditions for returning to the negotiating table.[94] By mid-January 2004 Bashar himself was telling visitors that Syria was ready to resume peace talks, but that discussions had to pick up at the point where earlier negotiations had broken off.[95] Subsequent efforts by the Turkish government under Prime Minister Recep Tayyip Erdogan in early 2004 to find a formula for getting Israel and Syria back to the negotiating table also proved unsuccessful.[96]

Throughout 2004, Bashar continued to stress his interest in resuming negotiations, but very much on "his" terms. In October 2004 the Ba'th party Regional Command passed a resolution reaffirming that peace with Israel was Syria's "strategic choice." In November 2004 Bashar held meetings with Egyptian president Mubarak and UN Middle East envoy Terje Roed-Larsen.[97] Media reports coming out of those meetings recapitulated Bashar's self-serving rhetorical flexibility. Reportedly, Bashar was willing to engage in talks without preconditions but insistent that talks resume from where they left off.

All this produced a lively debate within the Israeli national security establishment regarding Bashar's seriousness and the desirability of taking him up on his offer of renewed negotiations. Some major players in the Israeli intelligence community, including the director of military intelligence and others in the senior ranks of the IDF, argued that Bashar is serious and that Israel should explore a resumption of the Syria track.[98] But others, including senior officials close to Prime Minister Sharon and, it would seem, Sharon himself, do not believe that Bashar is able (as the relatively new head of a minority "Alawite" regime) or willing to negotiate seriously. (Some of these Israelis also question whether Hafiz al-Asad's involvement in peace negotiations during the 1990s was strategically serious or merely a tactical charade.) Officials in this latter camp, in many cases, are also reluctant to pay the price that Israel would presumably have to pay to reach a deal with

Syria. So far, at least, Bashar's expressions of interest in resuming peace negotiations have come to naught in terms of a meaningful Israeli response.

It seems doubtful that Bashar would ultimately be willing to relax his insistence on a reaffirmation of the Rabin deposit as the basis for renewed peace talks. Ostensible suggestions that Syria might relax its stance on this issue came only at points of what Damascus perceived as maximum external pressure on the regime over Iraq and terrorism issues. Without exception, the inherited position was restated in short order, as soon as pressure was even minimally relieved.

However, Bashar might be inclined to resume negotiations on acceptable terms even without a measurable improvement in conditions on the Palestinian front. Given the centrality of achieving an acceptable settlement with Israel to the fulfillment of father Hafiz's strategic objectives, it seems probable that Bashar's retreat from the pursuit of a bilateral agreement was a temporary aberration, a function of the low likelihood that the Barak government and Clinton administration would be prepared to push for a Syria deal in their last months in office and of the popular reaction on the Arab street to the outbreak of the Intifada al-Aqsa.[99] At the same time, current political configurations in Israel mean that the parties are unlikely to test this proposition in the foreseeable future. As long as Damascus sticks to its conditions for resuming peace talks, there will be no meaningful reengagement on the Syrian track until political currents shift substantially in Israel and, perhaps, in the United States as well.

From the available evidence, it seems highly likely that Bashar remains bound by the basic parameters defined by his father regarding the terms of an acceptable peace agreement. Nothing in Bashar's rhetoric or behavior since the end of the Iraq war suggests that he is prepared to settle for less than what could be plausibly portrayed as full Israeli withdrawal from the Golan Heights. To the contrary, Bashar has, throughout his presidency, repeatedly stated his adherence to these parameters. Departing from them at this juncture would, indeed, represent a major change in Syrian foreign policy.

Managing the Regional Balance

With the Syrian track in suspension, Hafiz al-Asad's script would indicate that Bashar should engage diplomatically to maintain the support of moderate Arab states for Syria's peace process position. At the same time, Bashar would play the Iraq and Iran cards as a signal to the United States and Israel of the costs of ignoring Syria's diplomatic needs. To be sure, he has worked assiduously to maintain regional and international support for Syria's stance on negotiations with Israel. But the Bush administration's decision to overthrow Saddam Hussein by invading Iraq seriously undercut the Asad regime's "rogue state" option. The political tumoil flowing from Hariri's assasination has also complicated Syria's relations with moderate Arab states.

Protecting Syria's Peace Process Position

As prospects for reengagement on the Syrian track receded in the first year of his presidency, Bashar—very much in keeping with his father's script—worked to prevent erosion of regional and international support for the core elements of Syria's peace process position. The two most important moderate Arab states, Egypt and Saudi Arabia, received Bashar's greatest attention.

Bashar's first three trips abroad as president, in October 2000, were to Egypt, Saudi Arabia, and Jordan. All three trips were undertaken as preparation for the extraordinary Arab League summit in Cairo later that month. Similarly, Bashar hosted President Mubarak of Egypt and King Abdallah of Jordan together in Damascus in March 2001 to prepare for the Arab League summit in Amman later that month (a meeting marking the resumption of "ordinary" summits, which had been suspended since the Gulf War). In both cases, Bashar was able to maintain explicit support for Syria's peace process position in the communiqués issued by these gatherings.

In similar fashion, Syria engaged key states before the March 2002 Arab League summit in Beirut, which took up the peace initiative advanced by Saudi crown prince Abdallah in February 2002.[100] The Beirut summit communiqué included, as the first item in the list of Arab demands on Israel, "full Israeli withdrawal from all the territories occupied since 1967, including the Syrian Golan Heights, to the June 4, 1967, lines as well as the remaining occupied Lebanese territories in the south of Lebanon." This requirement validated not only Syria's most fundamental demand but also its position regarding Sheba'a Farms. Additionally, Bashar and Foreign Minister Shar' worked to ensure that Crown Prince Abdallah's original reference to "normalization" with Israel was modified in the summit communiqué to "normal relations in the context of this comprehensive peace."[101] This change clearly reflected the

In March 2002, before an Arab summit in Beirut, Syrian President Bashar al-Asad and Egyptian President Hosni Mubarak tour the pyramids south of Cairo.   (© Reuters/Corbis)

late Hafiz al-Asad's acceptance of formally normal relations with Israel as part of a peace settlement as well as his resistance to any commitment to extensive peacetime interaction between Israel and Syria. (Bashar's success in achieving his bottom line position also says something about his learning curve as national leader. Bashar first sought to keep the Arab League from endorsing the initiative, and put enormous pressure on Lebanese president Lahud to put up numerous obstacles, including trying to keep a speech by Palestinian leader Arafat from being delivered by Palestinian representatives at the summit. The Saudi delegation, however, led by Abdallah, made clear that it would intervene decisively to ensure the summit's backing for the Saudi peace initiative. In the end, Bashar accepted the inevitability of the initiative's endorsement but worked to make sure that Syrian redlines were respected.)[102]

In July 2003, following a meeting between Bashar and Mubarak in Sharm al-Shaykh, the two leaders issued a communiqué calling on the Quartet to push for peace on the Syrian and Lebanese tracks as well as between Israel and the Palestinians.[103] Damascus also encouraged efforts by the European Union's special envoy for the Middle East at the time, Miguel Moratinos, to advocate a complementary roadmap for the Syrian track within the context of the Quartet.[104]

Bashar has been largely successful in preserving regional and international support for the core elements of his peace process posture. Nevertheless, the fallout from Hariri's assasination has strained his relations with key moderate Arab states, notably Saudi Arabia. Bashar is relying on his Arab League brethren to forestall Security Council action to enforce resolution 1559. But, to give themselves a credible diplomatic position, Arab moderates are requiring him to modify significantly the ways in which Syria protects its interests in Lebanon, under the rubric of implementing the Ta'if accord.

Iraq and Iran

Bashar has also had difficulty playing the Iraq and Iran cards against the United States and Israel. In reality, the post–September 11 war on terror rendered obsolete the portions of father Hafiz's script covering Syria's relations with Iraq and Iran. Bashar's expansion of Syrian economic ties to Iraq was considered in chapter 3; his handling of Syrian diplomacy with Washington before, during, and after the U.S. military campaign to overthrow Saddam is discussed later in this chapter. At this point, it is important to note that in the run-up to the 2003 Iraq war, the increasingly evident determination of the Bush administration to unseat Saddam by force significantly affected Syria's strategic environment. At least part of the impact was the implication of Saddam's prospective overthrow on Syria's relations with Iran.

During the first year and a half of Bashar's presidency, Syria and Iran were able to maintain important levels of strategic cooperation, particularly with regard to Hizballah and southern Lebanon. Just four months into his tenure, in October 2000, Bashar received the Iranian foreign minister in Damascus to discuss the regional situation in light of the outbreak of the new intifada. The initial decision by the Hizballah leadership to continue some sort of paramilitary campaign against Israel following the Israeli withdrawal from Lebanon was backed by Damascus and clearly endorsed by Tehran as well. Bashar himself traveled to Tehran in January 2001 for meetings with President Muhammad Khatami and Supreme Leader Ali Khamenei; two months later, in March, Iranian Foreign Minister Kamal Kharrazi visited Damascus. After April 2001 Bashar's efforts to manage the risks of Israeli blowback to continued Hizballah provocations were, for the most part, backed by Tehran.

However, Syrian relations with Iran experienced strain over the two countries' respective postures toward the U.S.-led military campaign to topple Saddam Hussein. In the aftermath of the September 11, 2001, attacks, Iran—which had its own long-standing grievances against the Taliban cadres ruling Afghanistan—supported the U.S. military campaign to destroy the Taliban regime. Tehran also cooperated with the United States to support creation of the post-Taliban Afghan Interim Authority at the December 2001 Bonn Conference. As the Bush administration turned its attention from Afghanistan to the overthrow of Saddam's regime, Iran projected a similarly supportive posture toward the prospect of removing its western enemy and aspired to play a role in establishing a post-Saddam political order in Iraq. Although, in the end, the Bush administration did not pursue sustained tactical cooperation or coordination with Iran regarding Iraq, Tehran's perspective on regime change there put it at odds with Damascus.[105] With Saddam's overthrow and the divergence of Iranian and Syrian interests regarding U.S. efforts to effect coercive regime change in Iraq, Bashar lost an important hedge in his diplomatic position.

Looking ahead, Iran and Syria might in theory be able to restore some form of strategic cooperation. Regarding developments in post-Saddam Iraq, both states share an interest in preventing the breakup of Iraq along sectarian lines because of the precedent such a development would establish for Kurdish populations in Syria and Iran. Both states were active in the meetings of the "neighbors' group," an informal diplomatic forum for the states bordering Iraq (Turkey, Saudi Arabia, and Kuwait, in addition to Syria and Iran) to discuss developments in post-Saddam Iraq, in 2003 and 2004. Both also took part in the Bush administration's multilateral conference on the future of Iraq in Sharm al-Shaykh in November 2004.[106] But so far nothing much has come of these efforts. Furthermore, as Iran's own relations with the Bush administration have worsened, Iranian diplomats and officials remain suspicious about Bashar's ultimate interest in a strategic realignment toward the United States, which would significantly compromise the Islamic Republic's strategic position in the region.[107] It remains to be seen whether the Bush administration's simultaneous efforts in early 2005 to ratchet up international pressure on Iran over its nuclear activities and on Syria over it position in Lebanon will prompt closer strategic cooperation between Tehran and Damascus.

Relations with Washington

The progressive loss of the hedge that Hafiz al-Asad had created during the last decade of his presidency, along with the absence of Israeli-Syrian negotiations, meant that Bashar had to manage Syria's relations with the United States with significantly fewer assets than his father had enjoyed. Since becoming president, Bashar has repeatedly stated his interest in a better relationship with the United States. Such interest is fully in keeping with father Hafiz's script and in line with any realistic assessment of Syria's strategic needs. Beyond the strategic benefits of successful realignment toward Washington, Bashar sees improved relations with the United States as critical to his long-term ambitions for internal reform.

With significantly diminished diplomatic assets, however, Bashar has been unable not only to achieve closer ties to Washington but to prevent a real decline in bilateral relations. This deterioration represents the most significant failure of Bashar's diplomacy so far and poses his most important foreign policy challenge for the future. This deterioration, and the challenge it engenders, requires examination in the contexts of the regional crisis over Iraq, the post–September 11 war on terror, and more recent U.S.-Syrian tensions over Lebanon.

The Iraq Crisis

Bashar's relations with the Bush administration over Iraq got off to a rocky start well before the United States began to prepare for Operation Iraqi Freedom. During the first year and a quarter of his presidency, Bashar's cultivation of closer economic ties with Iraq overlapped with the Bush administration's initial quest, during its first nine months in office, to reconstitute international sanctions on Saddam's regime. As Syrian-Iraqi economic relations expanded, Damascus soon emerged as far and away the worst violator of UN sanctions on Iraq, both in quantity and quality. Perhaps most troubling from an American perspective, Syria was implicated in the transfer of military and dual-use equipment to Iraq by overland shipment.[108]

Syrian violations of the sanctions regime became a point of diplomatic contention with the United States in February 2001, during Secretary of

State Powell's first visit to Damascus. In a meeting with Bashar, Powell pushed for the Syrian president to place the principal Iraqi-Syrian pipeline under the United Nations Oil-for-Food program. Powell believed that he had received such a commitment from Bashar, but U.S. diplomats attending the meeting report that the Syrian leader only pledged to put a new Iraqi-Syrian pipeline still in the planning stages under Oil-for-Food auspices. The U.S. ambassador to Syria at the time, Ryan Crocker, tried to get to Powell after the meeting to forestall any misunderstanding but was unable to do so before Powell left Damascus.[109] On his plane, the secretary briefed reporters on the apparent breakthrough with Bashar. When Powell subsequently learned that Bashar was not going to place the main Iraqi-Syrian pipeline under U.N. auspices, he interpreted this episode as one in which the president of Syria had lied to him.[110]

The February 2001 meeting between Bashar and Powell made Syrian sanctions violations a provocative issue for the Bush administration. After the administration abandoned its campaign to craft "smart sanctions" on Iraq in the summer of 2001 and, following the September 11 attacks, began to plan for Saddam's overthrow, the interagency process contemplated punitive action against Syria. Consideration was given to countering or interdicting shipments violating the sanctions regime and targeting the main Iraqi-Syrian pipeline though special forces attacks or air strikes to interrupt the oil flow. In the end, however, there was minimal legal justification for such steps and little likelihood of international support for them. Moreover, striking the pipeline might disrupt Iraqi oil flows to Jordan and Turkey, with serious negative economic consequences for each of these two important members of the administration's anti-Saddam coalition. So, in the period before the war, no decision was taken to punish Syria for its sanctions violations.

Beyond these considerations, there was also a sense at the State Department and at upper levels of the National Security Council throughout 2002 that U.S. reaction to Syrian activities contravening U.N. sanctions against Iraq should be subordinated to the broader pursuit of regime change in Iraq. On the question of soliciting Syrian participation in a military campaign, administration officials were predictably divided. State Department participants recalled the benefits of Syrian participation in the Gulf War coalition and argued that Syria could provide important political cover as well as covert support for U.S. military operations in Iraq. Civilians in the Office of the Secretary of Defense were strongly opposed to Syrian partici-

pation, arguing that it was unnecessary and might create a sense of indebtedness to Damascus, which could inhibit an appropriate U.S. response to
Syria's ongoing support for terrorist groups.

Ultimately no decision was taken by the administration on this question
either; the White House chose to defer the most fundamental issues of Syria
policy until after the Iraq war. Up until the start of the war, the administration continued to demand Syria's compliance with the U.N. sanctions regime, with no indication of what negative consequences might befall Syria
if it declined to cooperate or what positive consequences might flow from
support for U.S. objectives.[111]

With no offers of U.S. engagement to counter the benefits of Syria's
ongoing economic partnership with Iraq, and tensions increasing between
Damascus and Washington over terrorism, Bashar went in the opposite
direction from his father regarding Syrian support for U.S. military action
against Iraq. The Syrian president apparently decided in the run-up to the
war that he would do what he could to undermine U.S. chances for success—diplomatically and, if events came to a head, by indirect military
means. He seemed to judge that this approach was the only way he could
seek to fend off the growing threat of a serious U.S. backlash against Syria.

On the diplomatic front, Bashar argued repeatedly during 2002 that coercive regime change in Iraq would result in the deaths of millions of Iraqis
and plunge Iraq and the surrounding countries into chaos.[112] From its seat
on the Security Council, Syria defended Baghdad's interests through much
of 2002. Even Syria's decision in November to join the unanimous vote in
favor of Security Council Resolution 1441, giving Iraq an ultimatum if it
continued to refuse to comply with previous resolutions, was portrayed as
a form of opposition to U.S. military ambitions.[113] Bashar defended Syrian
support for resolution 1441 by arguing that it sought a peaceful way of dealing with the Iraq crisis through a return of inspectors to Iraq; it was the
Bush administration, according to the Syrian president, that was unhappy
with the inspections process and was rushing to war.

In the aftermath of the military success of Operation Iraqi Freedom,
commentators in the United States and Israel cited Bashar's opposition to
the American military campaign in Iraq as evidence of their doubts about
the Syrian leader's strategic orientation and the soundness of his judgment.[114] Certainly it seemed at times in the spring of 2003 that Bashar had
miscalculated in a potentially catastrophic way for his regime. But in the

end, Bashar escaped the direst potential consequences of his misjudgments. In some respects, the difficulties that the United States encountered in trying to stabilize Iraq after the war may have vindicated some of Bashar's initial instincts about the consequences of American military action there. Moreover, given the utter unacceptability, from a Syrian perspective, of the precedent that would be established by a relatively easy U.S. military intervention in Iraq—the forcible overthrow of a secular Arab regime (dominated by an ethnic and sectarian minority group) for failing to acquiesce to U.S. policy goals—Bashar had little choice but to oppose the Bush administration.

Bashar's decision to oppose U.S. military action appears to have been rooted in an assessment that Iraq would become a quagmire for the United States—a Middle Eastern Vietnam. (It was also convenient for Bashar to allow regime heavyweights and their families to continue profiteering from their illicit cross-border activities.) From this perspective, as war approached in late 2002, it made sense to take actions meant to increase the likelihood of military stalemate in Iraq—not least to reduce the chances of U.S. military action against Syria over the near-to-medium term. In keeping with this logic, Syrian shipments of dual-use and military equipment to Iraq continued until the eve of the war. Additionally, as war became imminent in early 2003—and even through the first week of fighting in March—the Syrian government took steps to facilitate the movement of what would come to be known as "foreign fighters" into Iraq.[115] (There is no evidence, however, bearing out claims that Syria took possession of Iraq's WMD stockpiles during the run-up to the war.)

For a few weeks in March and April 2003, it seemed that Bashar's opposition to Operation Iraqi Freedom was a major misjudgment. As it became clear that coalition forces would achieve their military objectives quickly, Syria apparently stopped facilitating the movement of foreign fighters across the Syrian-Iraqi border.[116] Damascus was caught short by the unexpectedly rapid conclusion of the coalition's military campaign. On April 7, when television screens around the world showed images of a large statue of Saddam being pulled down in Baghdad, Syrian television broadcast a documentary on archaeological sites in Syria. Anxiety within the regime was surely increased by Secretary Rumsfeld's statements in March suggesting that Syria might be the next target for a U.S.-led campaign of coercive regime change.[117]

By mid-April, however, it became apparent that the United States had its hands full with the postwar situation in Iraq and was not likely to embark on new military adventures in the region anytime soon. Rumsfeld's comments were contradicted by statements from Secretary of State Powell indicating that the administration had no plans for military action against Syria[118]; this posture was affirmed by President Bush himself.[119] Syria had, at least for the time being, dodged a bullet. Bashar's sense that Iraq would be a quagmire for the United States has proven increasingly defensible as a basis for his decisionmaking in light of the course of events on the ground since the fall of Saddam's regime. Bashar's predictions that the war would result in the deaths of "millions" of Iraqis have not been borne out, but his warnings that "even the United States does not know how a war in Iraq is going to end" and that military action would plunge Iraq and the region into "uncertainty" seem retrospectively very much on point.[120]

Following Saddam's removal, Washington and Damascus both faced the question of whether they could come to a mutually beneficial understanding about Iraq's future course and how to put the region on a more stable geopolitical footing. The United States was confronting increasingly serious challenges in postconflict stabilization; Bashar's regime had important interests at stake in the evolution of post-Saddam Iraq—interests rooted in Hafiz al-Asad's long-standing strategic objective of avoiding Syria's marginalization in the region and preserving Iraq as a source of economic benefit.

To protect these interests, Bashar sought ways to influence the shape of postwar Iraq. As noted earlier, Syria was an eager participant in several meetings of the foreign ministers of Iraq's neighbors, even hosting one of the meetings.[121] However, without U.S. endorsement of a regional diplomatic forum for discussion of Iraq-related issues, it was highly unlikely that these countries on their own could establish an effective mechanism for promoting common interests in a post-Saddam environment. The Bush administration finally convened a multilateral conference on the future of Iraq in November 2004, a year and a half after the military campaign ended, but the gathering did not seem to provide any impetus toward greater U.S.-Syrian cooperation.

The United States has made limited efforts to encourage bilateral cooperation with Syria over Iraq, all narrowly focused on tactical issues such as control of the Iraqi-Syrian border and the return of official Iraqi assets from Syria. In the absence of an overarching strategic framework for cooperation, it has proven difficult to sustain tactical engagement on individual issues.

Local U.S. commanders, for example, made noteworthy efforts to engage Syria on the border issue. During the summer and fall of 2003, U.S. military commanders in the field took issue with claims by civilian officials in the Office of the Secretary of Defense that Syria was continuing to help foreign fighters cross into Iraq.[122] One U.S. commander, General David Petraeus of the 101st Airborne Division, who had responsibility for a large portion of northern Iraq, worked out his own arrangement with Syrian authorities. In return for allowing Syrian businessmen to reestablish trade routes into Iraq, local Syrian officials coordinated border control efforts with officers of the 101st Airborne and provided the division's sector of northern Iraq with daily electricity.[123] U.S. officials also noted publicly in the fall of 2003 that Syria was doing more to control its border with Iraq.[124]

This upturn in U.S.-Syrian cooperation over border security was short lived. Throughout 2003, the Office of the Secretary of Defense resisted such cooperation, overruling proposals to engage the Syrians in a coordinated campaign to control traffic across the Iraqi-Syrian border.[125] By the spring of 2004, as the security situation in Iraq deteriorated and U.S. casualties there mounted, officials in Washington were once again citing Syria as a source of the foreign fighters battling coalition forces and demanding that the Syrian government "do more."[126]

Possibilities for the restoration of some measure of U.S.-Syrian cooperation over the border issue were reopened by the visit of interim Iraqi prime minister Iyad Allawi to Damascus in July 2004. Allawi came back from his visit convinced that he could do business with Bashar, and encouraged the Bush administration to make a more serious effort to reengage Bashar on border security.[127] (Indeed, according to U.S. officials, Allawi was relatively more optimistic about the possibilities for establishing a cooperative relationship with Syria than with Iran.)

The encouragement of America's handpicked man in Baghdad was hard for Washington hard-liners to resist, and the Bush administration followed up on Allawi's visit to Damascus with two high-level trips to Syria. On the first of these trips, Assistant Secretary of State William Burns returned to Damascus in September 2004, this time accompanied by Assistant Secretary of Defense Peter Rodman. The two met with Bashar and other senior Syrian officials in what were described as productive discussions on the terms for U.S.-Syrian military cooperation on the Iraqi-Syrian border. Days later, at a meeting on the margins of the UN General Assembly meeting in New York, Foreign Minister Shar' reaffirmed to Secretary of State Powell Syria's commitment on controlling the border. Shar' also pledged action to stanch the flow of money across the border intended to finance insurgent activity in Iraq.

The results of the Burns-Rodman mission were mixed. On the one hand, U.S. officials say that the Syrians have taken steps to improve physical security along the Iraqi-Syrian border (such as placing new berms at key crossing points and replacing worn-out barbed wire). On the other hand, Syrian officials have reportedly been slow to move against former officials of Saddam's regime that the Bush administration believes are in Syria. Syrian officials say (and U.S. officials acknowledge) that the expansion of military-to-military cooperation along this border also has been hampered by the slow response of Iraq's interim government on initiatives such as joint patrols along the border.

The Burns-Rodman mission was followed in January 2005 by a visit from the outgoing deputy secretary of state, Richard Armitage, to Damascus. At this meeting, according to officials on both sides, the Syrians were exhorted to take a more proactive stance against former Iraqi elements in Syria. The United States, for its part, pledged to follow up with the Iraqi government to encourage faster progress on military-to-military cooperation along the border.

Not surprisingly, different elements of the Bush administration have evaluated Syria's performance in contradictory ways.

—In early December 2004, senior U.S. military officials told the *Wall Street Journal* that Syria was making a serious effort to control the border.[128] The Syrian regime received praise for increasing the number of border guards, building new checkpoints to prevent infiltration, making "hundreds of arrests at the border," and using its security services "to go after guys," according to a senior U.S. military officer in the field. Another U.S. official cited Syria's arrest—at the request of the United States—of a former Iraqi military officer residing in Syria, who was suspected of directing the insurgency.

—By contrast, civilian Pentagon officials continue to charge that the Iraqi insurgency is receiving funds and manpower through Syria. Rumsfeld said in an interview in early December that Syria's (and Iran's) meddling in

Iraq "is killing Americans." After the United States retook the insurgent stronghold of Fallujah in Iraq in November 2004, a global positioning signal receiver was reportedly discovered in a bomb factory; it was said to have "contained waypoints originating in Western Syria." U.S. officials touted this as evidence of the involvement of Syria-based Iraqi Ba'thists in directing the insurgency.[129]

The truth probably lies in between these two divergent assessments. It seems clear that Syria has taken some steps to improve its posture on security along its border with Iraq. At the same time, it seems equally clear that Damascus has not been doing all that it could to prevent the flow of people, money, and equipment across the border. In sum, while Bashar opposed the U.S. military intervention in Iraq, he seems willing to "make a deal" with the United States regarding post-Saddam stabilization there. As U.S. pressure on Syria's position in Lebanon has increased, Damascus has shown itself willing to be even more forthcoming about what it is prepared to put on the table, as evidenced by the Syrian role in effecting the turnover of Saddam's half-brother and a number of other former regime officials to the new Iraqi government in February 2005.

A similarly unsatisfying pattern has played out regarding the return of official Iraqi assets from Syria. In September 2003 a team from the Treasury Department went to Damascus to help identify official Iraqi funds that had been transferred to Syrian banks before Saddam's downfall. The officials reported that they received excellent cooperation from Syrian counterparts, and administration spokesmen noted publicly that Syria was behaving more positively on the issue.[130] But here, too, the upturn in U.S.-Syrian cooperation was short-lived in the absence of an overarching framework for U.S.-Syrian coordination on Iraq's future or for improving bilateral relations more generally. Despite its cooperation with the Treasury Department investigators, by the end of 2004 Syria had not returned any of the assets identified by those investigators to Baghdad. In fact, the Syrian government had used some of the funds to pay claims by Syrians who had done business in Iraq before the war, much to the dismay of U.S. officials.[131] Following the Burns-Rodman visit to Damascus in September 2004, a team of Treasury Department investigators returned to Damascus. It was made clear to the Syrians that if Damascus did not return the assets to Iraq within six months, the administration was prepared to cite the Commercial Bank of Syria as a "primary money-laundering concern" under the

Patriot Act, effectively cutting off Syria from international financial transactions. It remains to be seen if the Syrian regime will become more forthcoming on the issue.

The War on Terror

The inability to establish and sustain meaningful U.S.-Syrian cooperation over Iraq has been an important factor in the deterioration in U.S.-Syrian relations during Bashar's presidency. Perhaps even more determinative, however, is Syria's problematic standing in the global war on terror.

After the September 11, 2001, terrorist attacks, Syria's status as a state sponsor of terror pursuing weapons of mass destruction put Bashar at odds with the Bush administration. To keep Syria from ending up fundamentally on the wrong side of the war on terror, Bashar within weeks of the attacks offered to share intelligence on al-Qaeda and related Sunni extremist groups with the United States. As administration officials subsequently acknowledged publicly, this offer prompted the establishment of an intelligence-sharing channel between the Central Intelligence Agency and Syrian Military Intelligence, which had not been in contact since the first Gulf War.[132]

The intelligence channel moved ahead until the eve of the Iraq war, periodically raising speculation about a broader rapprochement between Washington and Damascus. As Seymour Hersh reported in the *New Yorker*, the information Syrian Military Intelligence provided exceeded the CIA's expectations in quantity and quality.[133] At times, the information generated actionable leads, allowing the CIA and allied security services to thwart what administration officials described as operations that would have resulted in the deaths of Americans.[134] President Bush, in his communications with Bashar, whether by letter or phone, always acknowledged Syria's cooperation with the United States against al-Qaeda.

Continuation of the channel, however, was always a controversial issue within the Bush administration. Neoconservatives in the Office of the Secretary of Defense and the Office of the Vice President opposed accepting Syrian help, arguing that it might create a sense of indebtedness to Damascus and inhibit an appropriate American response to a state sponsor of terrorism. Defense Department officials, in fact, argued that any form of engagement with a state sponsor was a concession that threatened the integrity of the administration's global war on terror. As a result of this internal disagreement, the administration's engagement with Damascus remained limited to intelligence sharing against al-Qaeda.

While Damascus was cooperating with the United States against al-Qaeda, its own indirect involvement with terrorist activity was proving increasingly problematic for Syria's standing in Washington. This was true both in the context of the global war on terror and in the context of an increasingly violent intifada. Over the course of 2002, the Bush administration had reiterated demands that Bashar close Palestinian rejectionist facilities in Syria, expel key rejectionist leaders, assist in shutting down Hizballah's terrorist leadership in Lebanon, and block further transshipment of Iranian military equipment to Hizballah fighters via Damascus. These demands were conveyed personally to Bashar during Secretary Powell's April visit to Damascus, Assistant Secretary of State Burns's visit in October (at which Burns delivered a letter from President Bush to Bashar making these points), and another visit by Burns in January 2003.

Bashar wanted to use intelligence sharing against al-Qaeda to leverage broader cooperation with the United States and indicated his understanding that Syria would have to modify its stance toward terrorist organizations to which it maintained ties. He also indicated that establishing a more cooperative strategic relationship with the United States was a matter of some sensitivity for him within his regime. In his October 2002 meeting with Assistant Secretary Burns, for example, Bashar expressed interest in using the intelligence-sharing channel to address more contentious bilateral issues, such as Iraq and terrorism, noting that what came to him through the intelligence channel came "unfiltered."[135] However, the divisions within the administration over the advisability of engaging Syria thwarted a serious test of this offer. On the terrorism front, as with Iraq, the administration deferred fundamental questions of Syria policy until after the Iraq war.

Once the Iraq war was over, Syria's support for terrorism became the highest-priority item on the U.S. agenda with Bashar. But the administration was still unable to decide on a coherent strategy for pursuing its objectives in Damascus. In the weeks following Saddam's overthrow, coercive regime change had been put aside as a near-term policy option for Syria. But neoconservative elements in the administration continued to oppose contingent offers of strategic, political, or economic benefits to a state sponsor like Syria in return for the cessation of its involvement in terrorism; such a carrots-and-sticks approach would be, they argued, a reward for bad behavior. The only alternative left was reiteration of long-standing U.S. demands that Syria sever its ties to terrorists, backed by intermittently escalating pressure on Bashar to comply.

This has remained the Bush administration's basic orientation toward Syria since the spring of 2003. In May 2003 Secretary Powell returned to Damascus with talking points heavily focused on U.S. demands that Syria roll back its terrorist ties. But Powell had little to put on the table to induce significant changes in Syrian behavior. Predictably, the secretary accomplished nothing of importance in his exchange with the Syrian leader. A subsequent visit to Damascus by Assistant Secretary Burns in August 2003 was no more fruitful. As the administration grew more frustrated with continued Syrian intransigence on Iraq and terrorism, it shifted its position in the fall of 2003 and dropped its opposition to the Syria Accountability and Lebanese Sovereignty Restoration Act, which President Bush signed into law in December. The administration began to implement the new law in May 2004, imposing new sanctions on Syria. At the end of the year, the administration was considering imposing additional sanctions on Syria that would further circumscribe the ability of U.S. companies to do business there.

Despite the lack of any appreciable success in getting Syria to modify its problematic behaviors, particularly regarding terrorism, the administration continues to resist a strategy of conditional engagement with Damascus. Pressed on this point in February 2004, a member of the National Security Council staff said to the author, "Of course we're not going to negotiate with Syria over that. They should stop those activities because it's the right thing to do."

Lebanon as Pressure Point

As the Bush administration sought new ways to increase pressure on Damascus, it found its way back to an old policy idea—using Lebanese sovereignty as a way of threatening what Syrian leaders perceive as vital interests. Hard-line elements in the administration, including Secretary Rumsfeld and younger neoconservative advocates in the Office of the Secretary of Defense and the Office of the Vice President, were intrigued by the idea of using Lebanon as a pressure point against Damascus from the beginning of Bush's tenure. But the administration lacked a partner on the Security Council willing to support a resolution condemning the Syrian occupation of Lebanon. By the summer of 2004, however, French president Jacques

Chirac had become sufficiently angered at Bashar's handling of Lebanese prime minister Hariri that France shifted its position and agreed to cosponsor, with the United States, a strongly worded Security Council resolution. In particular, the increasingly obvious Syrian meddling in Lebanese wrangling over President Lahud's possible extension in office prompted a tougher French position.

President Chirac's government had long opposed an extension for Lahud and had supported the Maronite patriarch, Cardinal Sfayr, and other Maronite leaders in their opposition to such a step.[136] When it became clear that Lahud would get the extension, Chirac wanted to mobilize international criticism of the move and quickly won U.S. backing for what would become Security Council Resolution 1559.

The passage of resolution 1559 was a significant diplomatic defeat for Bashar. Not only did Syria's longtime ally, France, support the measure, but China, Russia, and the council's only Arab member, Algeria, all abstained. Since the resolution was passed, France and the United States have cooperated to establish a timetable for regular reports by the secretary general on the resolution's implementation. In the aftermath of Hariri's assasination in February 2005, the reelected Bush administration decided to use the issue not simply to compel the withdrawal of Syrian forces from Lebanon, but also to weaken Syria's strategic position.

Since the end of the Iraq war, Bashar has grown increasingly frustrated by what he sees as the Bush administration's unwillingness to strike a strategic bargain with Syria. According to Bashar and other senior Syrian officials, U.S. officials do not seek to negotiate important issues with Damascus. Rather, they repeat long-standing demands and expect compliance without any discussion of a quid pro quo.[137] Bashar presents himself as unable, under these circumstances, to do much to satisfy Washington or build a better bilateral relationship. As the Syrian president himself told the author in January 2004, Syria is "a state, not a charity. If it is going to give something up, it must know what it will get in return."

Thus, Bashar has been unsuccessful in his efforts to prevent a substantial deterioration in Syria's relations with the United States. Since the end of the Iraq war, Bashar has sought ways to compensate for the lack of positive engagement with Washington. The decision to conclude an association agreement with the European Union, discussed in chapter 3, had a strategic dimension in addition to its internal economic and political aspects. In January 2004 Bashar traveled to Turkey in an effort to give Syria's burgeoning economic relationship with its northern neighbor a strategic cast; in particular, the Syrian leader is interested in using Turkey—a NATO member and close ally of the United States—as an intermediary to the Bush administration.[138] State visits to China in June 2004 and Russia in January 2005 further expanded and solidified Bashar's trade network and political alliances.

But the absence of positive engagement with Washington remains Bashar's biggest diplomatic liability. This deficit is a drag on Syria's regional standing and handicaps any strategy for its internal reform. The question of U.S.-Syrian relations during Bashar's tenure must now be explored from the perspective of U.S. foreign policy.

CHAPTER FIVE

Options and Recommendations for U.S. Policy

O VER THE COURSE of successive administrations, Democratic and Republican, the United States has defined an ambitious policy agenda toward Syria. Currently, U.S. objectives include preventing Syria from interfering with U.S. goals in Iraq, ending Syria's support for Palestinian terrorist groups and Lebanese Hizballah while restoring its cooperation against al-Qaeda, stopping Syrian WMD programs, and ending the Syrian occupation of Lebanon. It is a logical extension of the Bush administration's emphasis on promoting economic and political liberalization in the greater Middle East that the United States should encourage reform in Syria without sparking social instability there, so as to limit Syria's potential as a source of militant Islamism. Although no Israeli-Syrian peace talks have been held since 2000, the United States continues to have a strong interest in encouraging an eventual negotiated peace between Israel and Syria; such an agreement would be valuable in itself and as an essential part of a comprehensive Arab-Israeli peace.

Notwithstanding the importance of these objectives, the Bush administration has failed to develop a genuine policy toward Syria, if by "policy" one means an integrated series of public positions, diplomatic initiatives, and other measures (including, perhaps, the actual or threatened use of force, either overtly or covertly), all rooted in a strategy for persuading Syria to change its problematic behaviors and cooperate in the pursuit of

U.S. goals. The administration has yet to resolve its internal differences over Syria policy, leaving it with an ineffective "neither fish nor fowl" posture. During its first term in office, the administration was able to agree only on a laundry list of complaints about Syria's lack of cooperation with U.S. goals in Iraq, support for terror, and pursuit of weapons of mass destruction, which it reiterated in largely unproductive diplomatic exchanges with Damascus. Although the administration was able to coordinate effectively with France and other members of the Security Council to win passage of Security Council Resolution 1559 in September 2004, the Bush team eschewed for the most part any serious or sustained effort to coordinate policy toward Syria with the European Union or other important international players.

The Bush administration's lack of a serious policy toward Syria should be viewed in historical perspective. For almost a decade, from the Madrid conference in 1991 until 2000, successive Republican and Democratic administrations thought about engaging Syria primarily in the context of the Syrian track of the Arab-Israeli peace process. In this approach, outstanding bilateral differences were to be resolved as part of a peace settlement between Israel and Syria. For example, it was generally understood that, as part of such a settlement, Syria would have no need for and would sever its ties to Palestinian rejectionists and disarm Hizballah fighters in southern Lebanon. Similarly, Syria's WMD programs would be put into a less threatening and ultimately more solvable context. But of course, the peace treaty between Israel and Syria that U.S. mediators worked so hard to facilitate never came. Moreover, as has already been noted at several points, in a six-month period in 2000, the underpinnings of the U.S. approach to the Syrian track and the management of the U.S.-Syrian relationship disappeared with the collapse of the Syrian track, the Israeli withdrawal from southern Lebanon, Hafiz al-Asad's death, and the outbreak of the Intifada al-Aqsa.

As a result of these events, the Bush administration came to office with no inherited operational framework for policy toward Syria. As President Bush enters his second term, the United States still lacks a framework for dealing effectively with Syria in the absence of a Syrian track of the peace process. Consequently the Bush administration has had little success in getting Syria to modify its problematic behaviors or in cultivating a more constructive relationship with the Asad regime, despite letters and phone calls to Bashar from President Bush, personal meetings with Colin Powell during his tenure as Bush's secretary of state, and visits by other senior administration officials. This policy vacuum is deleterious to U.S. interests and needs to be corrected if the administration is to formulate and sustain a more coherent strategy for the war on terror and for pursuing its agenda in the broader Middle East.

Strategic Underpinnings

What would optimal U.S. policy toward Syria look like? Logically, one can identify four alternative strategic options for U.S. policy toward Syria: increasing sanctions and other forms of pressure, pursuing coercive regime change in Damascus, restarting the Syrian track of the Middle East peace process, and conditional engagement with the Asad regime outside of the peace process. Each of these strategies has its proponents among American foreign policy elites. Each also has its own historical record in U.S. policy, either with particular reference to Syria or to other cases.

Increasing Pressure

To the extent that current U.S. policy toward Syria reflects an underlying strategy, that strategy would seem to be one of trying to change Syrian behavior by increasing pressure on Damascus through additional unilateral sanctions and critical rhetoric. This is certainly the logic of the Syria Accountability and Lebanese Sovereignty Restoration Act (SALSA), which the Bush administration began to implement in May 2004.[1] Some members of Congress would like to impose still more sanctions on Syria.[2] In this regard, the administration is taking preparatory steps to impose additional sanctions under SALSA that would effectively shut down the operations of U.S. companies in Syria and, as noted in chapter 4, is also considering imposing sanctions on the Syrian financial sector under the Patriot Act. The withdrawal of the U.S. ambassador to Damascus could also be considered effectively a sanction.

For their proponents, additional sanctions have a symbolic value in conveying American displeasure with troublesome Syrian behaviors. Unfortunately, little in the historical record suggests that unilateral sanctions contribute significantly to the modification of those behaviors.

Imposing pressure on Syria through unilateral sanctions has a long and essentially unproductive record as a U.S. policy tool. Syria has been designated a state sponsor of terrorism since the state sponsors list was first published in 1979, subject to the automatic imposition of several unilateral sanctions, including prohibitions on the sale or transfer of military items, restrictions on the transfer of dual-use items, a ban on U.S. assistance to designated governments, and mandatory U.S. opposition to the extension of support by international financial institutions to designated countries.

Twenty-five years of this approach do not seem to have affected Syrian behavior or strategic and tactical calculations appreciably. In 1986, under pressure from the Reagan administration following the Hindawi affair, the U.S. oil company that had initially developed Syria's oil fields, Pecten International, was compelled to divest its holdings in Syria; the holdings passed to Shell, establishing the Anglo-Dutch firm as the biggest foreign oil company operating in Syria. As a senior Shell executive has put it, U.S. divestiture did nothing to stymie Syrian oil production or press Syria's economy; it only provided a non-U.S. company with what has proven to be a very profitable business opportunity.

To argue that imposing additional unilateral sanctions, whether under the Syria Accountability Act or some other measure, will in itself be more effective in the future, one has to explain why a twenty-five-year record of policy failure should not be taken as a predictor of the likely consequences of doing more of the same. The only circumstance under which sanctions might work to change a problematic regime's negative behavior is when the sanctions are multilateral in scope.[3] But, in the Syrian case, European states, Japan, Russia, China, and other major players in the world economy are not prepared to join the United States in sanctioning the Asad regime over terrorism or weapons of mass destruction, and it is not clear how far these actors would go to press Damascus over Syrian hegemony in Lebanon.

In this regard, the European Union's decision to resume talks with Damascus over an association agreement in the immediate aftermath of the Bush administration's decision to implement the Syria Accountability Act suggests that resort to unilateral sanctions will only reduce the chances for coordinating the positions of the EU and other major international actors with U.S. policy goals toward Syria. When pressed on the point during an on-the-record question-and-answer session in October 2004, Stephen

Hadley, then the deputy national security adviser, could only note that U.S. and European policies toward Syria were characterized by "imperfect coordination." [4]

Coercive Regime Change

In the context of the global war on terror, another U.S. approach that has emerged for dealing with problem states is the threatened or actual pursuit of coercive regime change. Since the September 11 attacks, coercive regime change through direct military action has become the centerpiece of the Bush administration's approach to the war on terror. The United States used military force to topple problematic regimes in Afghanistan in 2001 and Iraq in 2003. More recently, the administration has claimed that the perceived threat of being the next target for coercive regime change—a perception generated by U.S. military action to unseat Saddam Hussein in Iraq—drove Libyan leader Mu'ammar al-Qadhafi's decision to give up his WMD programs and renounce terrorism.[5]

Even before the September 11 attacks, neoconservative foreign policy advocates were interested in the possibility of pursuing coercive regime change in Syria. In 1996, a group of American neoconservatives, including Douglas Feith and Richard Perle, published a report making recommendations to then-incoming Israeli prime minister Binyamin Netanyahu regarding Israeli national security policy, including using military force for purposes of "weakening, containing, and even rolling back Syria."[6] The report was drafted by foreign policy analyst David Wurmser, who in subsequent works made clear his preference for creating political orders based on tribal and familial lines in place of strong secular regimes in both Iraq and Syria.[7]

Feith and Perle came to hold positions of influence in the Pentagon in the Bush administration's first term; Wurmser served as a staffer to Under Secretary of State John Bolton and at the end of 2004 was a Middle East adviser on Vice President Dick Cheney's staff. It is thus not surprising that the Office of the Secretary of Defense became the principal agent advocating a coercive regime change strategy toward Damascus, supported by the Office of the Vice President. In April 2003, Deputy Secretary of Defense Paul Wolfowitz was the first senior administration official to suggest that the United States might take military action against Syria, citing reports that the Asad regime was harboring senior Iraqi leaders and WMD following the launch of Operation Iraqi Freedom to justify his declaration, "There's got to be a change in Syria."[8] Wolfowitz's statement helped prepare the ground for Secretary Rumsfeld's remarks later that month. Although the Bush White House has not opted to pursue regime change in Damascus, neoconservative advocates inside and outside the administration continue to look at Syria as a prospective target.

Although coercive regime change through direct military action offers the attraction of allowing the United States to seize the initiative toward a problematic state with policy instruments of unequaled effectiveness, it is not an all-purpose option. In some situations, as in Afghanistan under the Taliban, the use of force may be unavoidable and thus eminently justified on strategic and moral grounds. It is by no means clear, however, that overthrowing the Asad regime is the only way to achieve U.S. policy goals toward Syria; indeed, Bashar's interest in engagement strongly suggests that the United States could achieve its objectives more efficiently through hard-nosed diplomacy than by armed invasion.

Moreover, ongoing commitments in Iraq make it doubtful that the United States has a serious option to launch "Operation Syrian Freedom" anytime soon. Notwithstanding its superpower status, the United States does not have the resources, either material or political, to resolve its differences with every problematic state around the world in this way in a time frame that is meaningful for the global war on terror. Logistically and operationally, the U.S. military has come under increasingly severe strain because of ongoing requirements in Afghanistan and Iraq.[9] The Pentagon is already unable to field sufficient forces to complete the job in those theaters and meet its commitments in other hot spots, such as the Korean Peninsula.[10] The United States simply does not have enough military assets at its disposal for an extended series of campaigns to topple troublesome regimes across the greater Middle East.[11] Over time, this state of affairs has become increasingly clear to regional observers, diminishing whatever diplomatic utility the implicit threat of additional campaigns of coercive regime change might have had.

Politically, it is doubtful that the United States can maintain the international legitimacy of a global war on terror in the absence of strategic alternatives to coercive regime change.[12] In the aftermath of the September 11 attacks, the United States had the support of virtually the entire international community for a military campaign to unseat the Taliban in Afghanistan and for other actions to eliminate the threat of further attacks by al-Qaeda.[13] By shifting its focus to Iraq, where the justification for urgent forcible regime change was perceived in many quarters as less clear-cut, the Bush administration lost a significant measure of that support.[14] Further resort by the United States to coercive regime change in countries such as Syria where other options are not widely perceived to be either nonexistent or exhausted would almost certainly further reduce international support for the war on terror. Especially in the Arab and Muslim worlds, the risk of popular blowback against the United States would increase.

In the case of Syria, one would also have to consider the strong likelihood of postconflict difficulties on a scale comparable to those confronted by U.S. and allied forces in Iraq. Syrian society is at least as complicated as Iraqi society, with similar tendencies toward fragmentation along ethnic and sectarian lines. And the Iraq experience suggests that the U.S. government has a long way to go before Americans should be confident in its ability to anticipate the most likely difficulties in such challenging environments and plan effectively for postwar stabilization.[15]

Given the prospective problems associated with pursuing coercive regime change in Syria through direct military action, some have suggested relying on external opposition elements to sweep away the Asad regime. A group of legislators are preparing a so-called Syria-Lebanon Liberation Act, modeled on the Iraq Liberation Act, to encourage such a strategy. There is, to be sure, a loose Syrian external opposition movement, consisting of exiled Muslim Brotherhood figures and secular opponents of the Asad regime in various European locales (mostly London and Paris). And in 2002, a Syrian-American activist, Farid Ghadry, launched the Reform Party of Syria, putting it forward as the core of a more vital external opposition to the Syrian regime.[16]

Historically, however, a strategy of relying on an external opposition to bring about political change in authoritarian regimes has an unbroken record of failure as a guide for U.S. policy. The work of Miami-based Cuban exiles has done very little to improve the political situation in Cuba or the lives of ordinary Cubans. The exile strategy for regime change did not work in Iraq, either; direct foreign intervention was required to meet that goal.

(Moreover, since the fall of Saddam's regime, the coalition's overreliance on returning exiles has arguably been one of the factors creating a risk of strategic failure for the United States in Iraq.)

Similarly, the Syrian expatriate opposition movement would seem to be an inadequate base for changing the political environment inside Syria. There is no evidence that exiled secular oppositionists have much of a following inside Syria; indigenous civil society activists eschew association with the exiles, preferring not to put their own standing within Syria in question. The one exception to this is the Kurdish Yakiti Party, which has developed an affiliation with the Reform Party of Syria. However, given the risks of regional fallout from Kurdish separatist ambitions in a politically unsettled environment, the United States should be exceedingly cautious before opting to play the "Kurdish card" in Syria. In the near term, such an approach would at a minimum complicate U.S. relations with important regional players like Turkey and Iran in return for uncertain gains. In the longer term, such an approach could raise the risks of the dismemberment of multiethnic states in the heart of the Middle East, fomenting further regional instability.

In addition, even if an external opposition were somehow able to destabilize the Asad regime, the experience of Afghanistan and Iraq strongly suggests that making a smooth transition to a new political order will not be easy. Indeed, given the fractiousness inherent in Syrian society, the most likely political outcome in the near term would be chaos. And the most likely alternative to emerge from that chaos would be a heavily Islamist state, hardly an advance for U.S. interests.

Finally, some neoconservative advocates argue that the Bush adminstration's current campaign to increase international pressure on Syria to withdraw from Lebanon should be broadened into a campaign to bring down the Asad regime. All the caveats about the desirability of coercive regime change, whether through direct military action or external opposition activity, would, of course, apply to this scenario as well. Beyond these concerns, there is also the risk that a precipitous Syrian withdrawal from Lebanon could contribute to a reemergence of sectarian conflict there, particularly if a new government in Beirut pushed too quickly on the issue of disarming Hizballah (in keeping with the requirement in resolution 1559 that all Lebanese militias be disbanded and disarmed). Alternatively, any new political order in Beirut purporting to represent all elements of Lebanese society would have to include Hizballah—which, to say the least, would not be a clear gain for U.S. interests.

Restarting the Syrian Track

Among those inclined toward more constructive ways of dealing with Damascus, a number of analysts have focused on the importance of restarting a meaningful Syrian track of the Middle East peace process. Given the long experience of Israeli-Syrian negotiations in the 1990s, some have argued that renewal of the Syrian track is the best way for Washington to encourage the Asad regime to take a more conciliatory and cooperative posture toward U.S. concerns.[17] Others have suggested that, given the central importance of a return of the Golan Heights to Syrian control for both Hafiz and Bashar al-Asad, restarting negotiations toward that end is effectively the only way to engage the Asad regime.[18]

These arguments are not unsound. Certainly, the prospect of U.S. activism in the peace process was a key factor in winning Syrian support for the first Gulf War coalition. During the 1990s the Syrian track was the framework for structuring the U.S.-Syrian relationship more broadly; it would be difficult to argue that the relationship was not in better shape in those years than today. Resumption of the Syrian track would allow a U.S. administration to put differences with Damascus over terrorism and weapons of mass destruction into a more politically manageable framework; it could also make it easier for the United States and Syria to cooperate on issues outside the Arab-Israeli arena, such as Iraq.

Moreover, if a renewed Syrian track bore fruit, the benefits would be undeniable. A treaty with Syria is essential for Israel to complete the "circle of peace," to use Shimon Peres's phrase, with its Arab neighbors. Peace with Syria would also eliminate Hizballah's terrorist threat to Israeli security and remove Iran's forward base in Lebanon.

Given all these advantages, restarting peace negotiations between Israel and Syria would clearly serve U.S. interests. As noted earlier, the Bush administration has paid far less attention to the Syrian track than to the Palestinian issue. The benefits of Israeli-Syrian peace for Israeli and U.S. interests should prompt the administration to overcome its first-term reluctance to lean forward on a possible resumption of the Syrian track. Nevertheless, the reality is that political conditions in both Syria and Israel will make it hard to bring the two parties back to the negotiating table any time soon.

On the Syrian side, it seems unlikely—based on the analysis presented in the preceding chapter—that Bashar would agree to a resumption of talks without some sort of Israeli reaffirmation of the Rabin deposit. It seems even more improbable that Bashar would conclude an agreement that did not meet his late father's conditions for an acceptable settlement.

On the Israeli side, however, it is exceedingly unlikely—given current political configurations in Israel and the tensions that have accumulated between Israel and Syria since 2000—that there will be an Israeli government willing to meet Syrian conditions for resuming and concluding peace talks in the near term. If Prime Minister Sharon remains in office, even in coalition with Labor, the chances that the government would reaffirm the Rabin deposit as the basis for renewed negotiations with Syria seem low indeed. Martin Indyk has constructed a scenario in which, after carrying out his Gaza disengagement initiative in 2005, Sharon opts for resuming negotiations with Syria if only to deflect pressure to repeat in the West Bank what he had just completed in Gaza.[19] While Sharon seems eminently capable of making that sort of complicated tactical calculation, no evidence exists to indicate that he would be willing under any conceivable circumstances to pay the price that Syria would require for a peace agreement. Sharon has shown no interest in the arguments of those in Israel's intelligence community and senior ranks of the IDF who favor such a course.

Conditional Engagement

In light of the difficulties in restarting the Syrian track under existing circumstances, the last strategic option for dealing with Syria is for the United States to engage Damascus without waiting for progress in the peace process. This would represent something of a historical departure in U.S. policy toward Syria, since the United States has yet to develop a framework for constructively engaging Damascus apart from the Syrian track.

What does a strategy of conditional engagement look like? Fundamentally, it is a strategy for modifying the behavior of problematic regimes through hard-nosed, carrots-and-sticks engagement. The essence of conditional engagement is to contrast the benefits of cooperation with the likely costs of noncooperation—in other words, to tell rogue leaders what is in it for them if they change their behavior and to make sure they understand what will happen to them if they do not.

Although the United States has yet to try a strategy of conditional engagement with Syria, Washington has pursued this strategy successfully with other regimes:

—Conditional engagement, started before the September 11 attacks, helped to get Sudan out of the terrorism business and on the road toward a settlement of its civil war; the country's regression into the horrors of Darfur does not fundamentally undercut the significance of these counterterrorism achievements.[20]

—Conditional engagement, started with British support during the Clinton administration and picked up by the Bush administration before the September 11 attacks, was also key to getting Libya to meet its obligations pursuant to the Lockerbie/Pan Am 103 case as defined in United Nations Security Council resolutions, removing the main barrier to U.S.-Libyan discussion of bilateral differences.[21]

In both these cases, the United States defined a clear quid pro quo—the lifting of multilateral sanctions—for specified positive changes in Sudanese and Libyan behavior regarding terrorism.

The logic of conditional engagement also contributed to Libya's decision to abandon its WMD programs. Throughout the diplomatic dialogue with Tripoli over the Lockerbie case, U.S. representatives made clear that there would be no fundamental improvement of bilateral relations, including a lifting of U.S. sanctions, until U.S. concerns about Libyan WMD programs were addressed.[22] On both Lockerbie and WMD issues, the United States employed a classic carrots-and-sticks approach with Tripoli, making clear that no progress was possible until U.S. concerns were definitively addressed, but also making clear the benefits that would accrue to Libya from cooperation. Washington is continuing this approach by declining to remove Libya from the list of state sponsors of terror until Tripoli institutionalizes a counterterrorism dialogue with the United States and satisfactorily addresses questions regarding its alleged involvement in a plot to assassinate Saudi crown prince Abdallah.

Unfortunately, the Bush administration has been unwilling to extend this approach to other state sponsors of terror. In fact, the administration decided soon after September 11, 2001, that, as a matter of policy, it would not offer or define potential carrots for inducing state sponsors to change their problematic behaviors.[23] This basic posture has also characterized Bush policies toward Iran and North Korea over their nuclear activities. If U.S. diplomatic engagement with Sudan and Libya had not begun before the September 11 attacks, it is far from clear that the administration would have been willing to begin this kind of diplomatic process with either state.

Would such a strategy work with regard to Syria the way it has worked to move Sudan in a positive direction on terrorism and to induce Libya to meet its international obligations in the Pan Am 103 case and renounce weapons of mass destruction? Or is Syria more analogous to Afghanistan under the Taliban or Iraq under Saddam Hussein—an irredeemable regime, incapable of modifying its behavior, regardless of the incentives and disincentives put in front of it? The answers to these questions lie in an assessment of Bashar al-Asad as national leader.

Based on the analysis developed in preceding chapters of Bashar's background, his views on reform, and his handling of domestic and foreign policy issues since assuming the presidency, it would seem that the Syrian president is, for U.S. purposes, "engageable." On the positive side of the ledger, Bashar has demonstrated some reformist impulses. He is not an ideological fanatic like Mullah Muhammad Omar or violent thug like Saddam Hussein. Bashar has made it clear that Syria needs to modernize, but he does not have a fully elaborated vision for reform and lacks the technocratic capacity to develop such a vision. He has also made clear his view that Syria's long-term interests would be served by better relations with the United States—in part because of his need for external assistance and support to push reform at home. Bashar has frequently expressed to American and other foreign visitors his interest in an authoritative dialogue with the United States, something that has not been available to him with the Bush administration. Bashar envisions, in this kind of dialogue, that both sides would put their various concerns on the table and would negotiate to put together a strategic "package." When asked what concerns he would raise, Bashar notes three items: a return of the Golan Heights, a constructive relationship with whatever post-Saddam political structure emerges in Iraq, and a robust bilateral relationship with the United States to help him obtain the expertise and other resources he needs to advance Syria's internal reform.

On the negative side of the ledger, Bashar's reformist impulses have been constrained by a still powerful old guard, by security service and familial networks that benefit from the status quo, and by the imperative to be perceived as keeping faith with his father's legacy. Bashar can fall into strident

Ba'thist, anti-American rhetoric, and he is still trying to follow and adapt the strategic script he received from his father. But this script affords an opportunity for engaging Bashar as well as for putting limits on his flexibility; the script acknowledges the desirability for Syria of a better relationship with the United States while making a strategic breakthrough dependent on meeting conditions rooted in the tensions of Syrian domestic politics.

What all of this suggests is that Bashar could be a suitable subject for diplomatic engagement if engagement provides him with a clear roadmap to the desired goal and empowers him to move in that direction. To engage Bashar successfully, it is not enough to complain about problematic Syrian behaviors. Instead, the United States must give Bashar explicit and specific targets for reversing those behaviors. And engagement must be backed by a set of policy tools that would impose costs for continued noncompliance with U.S. requirements but also promise significant benefits in the event of cooperation—in other words, carrots and sticks.

But is it possible to engage Bashar outside a renewed Syrian track? Again, the answer would seem to be a qualified "yes." Based on his sharply negative assessment of Prime Minister Sharon's intentions regarding Syria, Bashar has frequently expressed pessimism about the chances for a resumption of talks or conclusion of an agreement while Sharon is in office. In early 2004, when asked whether it would be possible to "bracket" the issue of the Golan Heights to avoid having the possibilities for improved U.S.-Syrian ties held hostage to a peace process that is not likely to be very active in the near term, Bashar replied in the affirmative. With regard to the Golan's return, Bashar said, "we don't need our land back tomorrow or next week"; Syrians know that "it will come back to us" eventually. All that Bashar needs from Washington on the peace process to be able to work on other parts of a U.S.-Syrian strategic package is, by his own statement, "some words, some rhetoric."

Putting Together a Package

It is very much in the interest of the United States to explore this kind of strategic package with Syria, rooting such exploration in the logic of conditional engagement. To do this, the United States will need to sort out its priorities among its various policy objectives toward Syria. Given the ongoing U.S. commitment to postwar stabilization in Iraq and the precedence of the global war on terror for America's post–September 11 foreign policy, eliciting Syrian cooperation with U.S. goals in Iraq and getting Syria out of the terrorism business should be the top priorities. U.S. policymakers should link the pursuit of ending Syria's involvement in terrorism with initiatives to strengthen the capacity of Bashar and reform-minded members of his regime to undertake internal reforms.

Other U.S. policy objectives are either less pressing in the current environment or less immediately attainable in a manner supportive of the broad range of U.S. goals in the region. For example, the solution to the WMD problem is inevitably bound up with the achievement of peace between Israel and Syria. It is also unlikely that the problem of Syria's standing in Lebanon will be resolved through negotiation among various power centers in Lebanon and Syria, almost certainly mediated by regional and international actors; complete resolution will only be achieved over time. The retrenchment of Syrian hegemony in Lebanon will also need to be implemented carefully to avoid a reemergence of sectarian conflict and violence. Israeli prime minister Sharon's national security adviser Giora Eiland recently echoed long-standing Israeli concerns that an overly precipitous Syrian withdrawal from Lebanon would pose a threat to Israeli security.[24]

Iraq

In Iraq the United States and a new Iraqi government would benefit from sustained and more far-reaching coordination with Syria on problems of border security; in the longer run, Syrian endorsement would give a post-Saddam political order greater perceived legitimacy among Iraqis and the region. To win greater Syrian cooperation with these U.S. goals, Syria must be offered prospective accommodation of its legitimate interests in post-Saddam Iraq, if Damascus proves to have helped the United States and other international and regional partners tackle the security and political problems there.

To be maximally effective, this accommodation should have both economic and strategic components. In the economic sphere, appropriate carrots to induce greater Syrian cooperation could include facilitation of Syrian-Iraqi trade and Syrian participation in Iraqi reconstruction. In the strategic sphere, Washington should indicate openness to dialogue with Damascus on Syria's diplomatic and political interests in Iraq. Such a dialogue could be launched under the rubric of a regional "contact group" for Iraq—including Iraq's neighbors along with, perhaps, the permanent members of the Security Council—but could then be taken into a freestanding bilateral channel. (The multilateral conference on Iraq's future held in Sharm al-Shaykh in November 2004 could in theory serve as the starting point for establishing a contact group framework for Iraq, but it is not clear how assiduously the Bush administration will follow up on the meeting.) Alternatively, the United States could simply start a bilateral dialogue on Iraq with Damascus.

To be sure, within the Bush administration, the State Department has been relatively forward-leaning in pushing for some kind of dialogue with Damascus regarding Iraq. But the idea has been resisted by harder-line elements in the interagency process, and the Syrians have yet to receive a clear signal from the administration as to what they could expect in return for greater cooperation with U.S. goals there. The possibility of an incipient "strategic dialogue" with the United States would be attractive to the Asad regime. As noted earlier, the regime has a long-standing and chronic fear of regional marginalization. Following the 1991 Persian Gulf War, Syria's principal forum for having its regional interests considered by the United States was the Syrian track of the Middle East peace process. In the aftermath of Saddam's overthrow, U.S. willingness to begin talking with Bashar about Syria's regional interests, with an initial focus on Iraq, would be an appropriate carrot for improving Syrian behavior. Among other things, it would allow Bashar to demonstrate to other powerful players in the regime that Syrian interests are better served by cooperation with the United States than by continued resistance to U.S. objectives. Over time, as Syrian behavior improved, a U.S.-Syrian strategic dialogue could be broadened to encompass other subjects of mutual interest, reinforcing this positive dynamic.

Of course, for a conditional engagement strategy to be complete, it must have sticks as well as carrots. In the case of Syria, the definition of sticks probably needs to go beyond the withholding of potential carrots to include the imposition of negative consequences. If Syria were not willing to increase and sustain its cooperation with U.S. objectives in Iraq, the most suitable negative consequence for the United States to impose would be to declare publicly its intention to send U.S. military forces into Syrian territory at will in pursuit of insurgent cadres, and to publicly announce each time it had done so.

Terrorism

In the context of the global war on terror, getting Damascus out of the terrorism business is perhaps the most important near-to-medium-term U.S. policy objective toward Syria. Currently, Syria's status as a state sponsor of terror is the single biggest impediment to any sustained improvement in U.S.-Syrian relations.

In light of these considerations, the United States should adopt a new approach to managing Syria's designation as a state sponsor of terrorism. In the 1990s the United States made Syria's removal from the state sponsors list contingent on a peace treaty with Israel that never came. In the current environment, it should now tie removal to changes in Syria's relations with terrorists. Specifically, the United States should indicate it would be pre-pared to take Syria off the state sponsors list provided the Asad regime expelled terrorists from its territory, renewed counterterrorist cooperation with the United States against al-Qaeda, and broadened that cooperation to include rolling back Syria's own terrorist links. Many readers may assume that this is already U.S. policy, and at least some U.S. diplomats will suggest that it is. But the fact of the matter is that the United States has never made such an offer to the Asad regime. Indeed, during the Clinton administra-tion, the policy was that Syria would be removed from the state sponsors list only in the context of a peace agreement with Israel. Since the Bush admin-istration has been in office, it has declined to offer the Syrians the kind of roadmap for getting off the list advocated here.

Again, sticks need to accompany the carrots. On the terrorism issue, the United States should indicate that in its view, the old rules of the game cov-ering Syria's ties to terrorist groups and paramilitary proxies no longer apply. That means, first of all, that Syria cannot rely on Washington to restrain Israeli responses to terrorist provocations in quite the same way as in the past. While the United States clearly does not want to see escalating conflict along Israel's northern border or Israeli reoccupation of southern Lebanon, it may have a more tolerant posture toward Israeli retaliatory strikes against not only Syrian targets in Lebanon but also targets inside Syria. (The international nonresponse to Israeli air strikes inside Syria in November 2003 provides something of a precedent that the United States could build on in making its diplomatic representations to Damascus.)

As the United States defines a new approach to handling Syria's status as a state sponsor of terrorism, Syria's prospective removal from the list should be tied explicitly to initiatives to strengthen Bashar's capacity for undertaking significant internal reform. It should be made clear to Damascus that taking Syria off the list would allow American economic aid to flow to the country for the first time in decades and substantially increase assistance from international financial institutions. Even though Syria's delisting as a state sponsor would be offered as a quid pro quo for Damascus effectively getting out of the terrorism business, the resulting opportunities to encourage significant internal reform would make this a "win-win" proposition for U.S. policy. Washington should also coordinate the provision of aid and assistance with the EU's efforts to promote economic and political reform under an association agreement with Syria to maximize the potential gains. EU officials and officials of various European governments indicate that they would welcome such an approach.

Linking Syria's delisting as a state sponsor of terror with measures to bolster Bashar's standing to carry out more sweeping internal changes would give a more strategic cast to the notion of promoting reform in Middle Eastern states as part of the war on terror. The Bush administration has defined the promotion of fundamental political and economic transformation in the Middle East as a vital strategic objective in the war on terror, but it has not defined a high-level strategy for pursuing this objective. The lack of a strategy for promoting internal reform is particularly true with regard to states like Iran and Syria, with which the United States has strained bilateral relations.[25] The administration has proposed a pair of initiatives—the Middle East Partnership Initiative and the Middle East Trade Initiative—to encourage transformation within and among regional states.[26] Neither will apply in a substantial way to problem states like Syria. The partnership initiative is essentially a compilation of already existing democracy-promotion and social reform programs; its funds cannot be spent in problem states like Syria.[27] The trade initiative, too, is aimed almost entirely at states with which the United States already has some kind of strategic cooperation or, at least, a positive bilateral relationship; state sponsors of terror like Iran and Syria are deliberately excluded.[28]

To lend further support to Syrian reform efforts, the United States should modify other aspects of its current policy to strengthen Bashar's hand against those inside Syria resisting positive change. History would suggest that refusing to engage with either the Syrian regime or civil society actors through provision of official assistance is counterproductive to the goal of encouraging greater openness, economic reform, and political liberalization. A strategy of simultaneously engaging authoritarian regimes in the early stages of reform and civil society actors has had an impressive record of success, particularly in the former Soviet bloc and Latin America. This should be the model for U.S. policy toward Syria under Bashar al-Asad.

To that end, the United States should modify current provisions of its emerging initiatives for promoting economic and political reform in the greater Middle East to permit greater engagement with both regime and civil society in Syria. Two specific changes are in order. First, the United States should stop blocking Syria's application to begin the process of accession to the World Trade Organization. Like implementation of an EU association agreement, the WTO accession process holds the potential of helping Bashar overcome at least some of the deep-rooted impediments slowing or blocking economic reform in Syria. Second, the United States should permit official funds to flow to NGOs in Syria, even before diplomatic engagement might succeed in getting Syria out of the terrorism business. The NGO movement in Syria is perhaps the most hopeful channel for promoting social and political reform in Syria, and merits U.S. support. Again, the logic of carrots and sticks should apply. As the United States stepped up its support for NGOs in Syria, any effort by the regime in Damascus to constrain the activities of these groups should be the occasion for formal diplomatic protest and perhaps even public criticism along the lines of the Bush administration's posture regarding Egypt's detention of civil society activist Sa'd Eddin Ibrahim in 2001–02.

Completing the "Circle of Peace"

As noted, other issues of concern to the United States—including Syria's pursuit of weapons of mass destruction and its ongoing occupation of Lebanon—are likely to be resolved only in the context of an Israeli-Syrian peace settlement. Given an assessment that a resumption of Israeli-Syrian peace talks is not likely in the near term, what should the United States do to manage these issues in the meantime? Such consideration is also bound up with the matter of the U.S. declaratory posture regarding an Israeli-Syrian peace agreement.

As noted above, Bashar believes that he needs rhetorical cover from the United States regarding the Syrian track in order to move ahead and deal with Washington on other issues. As it is in the U.S. interest to explore a strategic package with Syria focusing on Iraq, terrorism, and the promotion of internal reform, it is also in the U.S. interest to offer such rhetorical cover, consistent with Washington's traditional role as sponsor of the peace process and with Israeli security interests.

There are two possible vehicles for providing Bashar cover for moving ahead on other issues in the absence of concrete progress on the return of the Golan Heights to Syrian control. First, the United States could indicate bilaterally to Damascus that it understands Syrian requirements for peace with Israel and is open to working for an agreement meeting those requirements, as long as Israeli requirements for a settlement are also addressed. Alternatively, the United States could endorse more fully than it has so far the 2002 Arab League peace initiative, while noting that final boundaries between Israel and its Arab neighbors remain, ultimately, subjects for negotiations among the parties.[29] Such a posture would, among other things, convey to Damascus that the United States understands an Israeli-Syrian agreement returning significantly less than all of the Golan Heights to Syrian control is not diplomatically feasible for Syria and the other Arab states. (The two approaches, of course, are not mutually exclusive.)

Would either or both of these approaches provide sufficient cover for Bashar to respond constructively to a U.S. strategy of conditional engagement? The chances would seem relatively good. As noted in the previous chapter, the value of Syria's ties to anti-Israeli terrorist groups has already declined in ways that Bashar appears to appreciate. In that context, U.S. adoption of either or both of the positions described above would send an important signal to Bashar that giving up Syria's terrorist cards would not compromise his chances of an acceptable peace agreement down the road. In fact, such a U.S. position would allow Bashar to argue within the regime and publicly that cooperation with Washington on terrorism would bring Syria closer to its goal of regaining the Golan.

In return for such an understanding with the United States, Bashar should be asked to acknowledge at least privately that as part of an overall Israeli-

Syrian settlement, questions regarding Syria's weapons of mass destruction and its presence in Lebanon would need to be addressed definitively.

These are the elements of a U.S.-Syrian strategic package rooted in a realistic assessment of on-the-ground political realities in Syria. By working toward such a package, the United States could improve its situation in Iraq, make appreciable gains in the war on terror, and accelerate the pace of internal reform in Syria. In the process, Washington could also lay the foundations for an eventual Israeli-Syrian peace and establish predicate conditions for dealing with Syria's WMD programs and the gradual normalization of its relationship with Lebanon. At a time when the U.S. position is under severe challenge in the Middle East, it would be truly disappointing if the American body politic were unable to muster the wherewithal for proceeding with policies so manifestly in the U.S. interest.

Chronology of Bashar al-Asad's Presidency

June 2000 to December 2004

2000

June 10 Hafiz al-Asad dies of heart failure at age sixty-nine. Vice President 'Abd al-Halim al-Khaddam becomes acting president. The Ba'th regional command promotes Bashar al-Asad to general, appoints him commander-in-chief of the armed forces, and nominates him for president. Parliament votes unanimously to amend Article 82 of the Syrian constitution, lowering the age requirement for president from forty to thirty-four, Bashar's age.

June 13 Rifa't al-Asad, exiled brother and erstwhile challenger to Hafiz, calls Bashar's ascension "a knife in the back of the Syrian nation" and later suggests that he himself is a more qualified standard-bearer. (*al-Jazeera*, 6/12/00; Zisser, "Does Bashar al-Asad Rule Syria?")

June 14 U.S. secretary of state Madeleine Albright meets with Bashar in Damascus and declares him eager to renew efforts for peace. (NYT, 6/14/00)

June 17 The ninth Ba'th Party general congress selects Bashar as its secretary general and nominates him for president. A new ninety-member central committee and a twenty-one-member national command council are elected. (AP, 6/17/00; AFP, 6/20/00)

June 26 Foreign banks are permitted to operate in five new free-trade zones: Adra, Aleppo, Damascus, Latakia, and Tartus. (*al-Thawra*, 6/26/00)

June 27 Parliament unanimously elects Bashar president of the republic.

July 3 Prime Minister Mustafa Miru announces an emergency plan to alleviate unemployment in Syria. (AFP, 7/4/00)

Note: A source key may be found at the end of the timeline.

July 7 Syria revokes its thirty-year ban on private automobile imports. (AFP, 7/8/00)

July 10 Bashar is elected president in a national referendum, winning 97.29 percent of the vote. (AP, 7/11/00)

July 17 Bashar orders the state media to refrain from using terms such as "immortal president" to describe the late Hafiz al-Asad and to curtail the use of magnification, glorification, or exaggeration in general in the state-run news. He also orders the removal of street signs and posters bearing his own image. (*Tishrin,* 7/17/00)

July 17 In his inaugural address, Bashar calls for serious economic reform—namely, a greater role for the private sector. He also supports the modernization of laws and administrative reform, rejects Western democracy as a suitable model for political development in Syria, and pledges his commitment to a peaceful recovery of the occupied Golan Heights.

July 22 Bashar decrees the establishment of Internet technology departments at the four Syrian public universities. (AFP, 7/22/00)

July 26 Riyad al-Turk, first secretary of the Syrian Communist Party, publishes an article in the Arab press proclaiming that "Syria cannot remain a kingdom of silence," criticizing the hereditary succession of Bashar, and calling for democracy in Syria. (*al-Quds al-'Arabi,* 7/2/00)

July 27 Thirty members of the Syrian Muslim Brotherhood are released from prison. (AP, 7/27/00)

July 27 'Ali 'Abd al-Karim is appointed the new director of the Syrian Arab News Agency (SANA), and new editors are appointed to the official newspapers *al-Thawra* (Mahmud Salameh) and *Tishrin* (Khalaf Mohammed al-Jaraf). (AFP, 7/27/00)

August 5 In a meeting with the leadership of the ruling National Progressive Front, Bashar considers proposals for "modernizing" and "developing" the party, including changing the political party law, loosening restrictions on the press, and reevaluating the emergency law. (*al-Sharq al-Awsat,* 8/5/00)

August 8 Syria grants permission to three foreign banks—Société Générale Libano-Européenne de Banque, Fransabank, and the Banque Européenne pour le Moyen-Orient—to operate in special free-trade zones. (AFP, 8/8/00)

August 26 Bashar raises civil servant salaries by 25 percent, the first such raise in six years. (AP, 8/26/00)

September 27 Syrian intellectuals issue the Statement of 99 in the London-based Arabic newspaper *al-Hayat,* calling for an end to the state of emergency, amnesty for political prisoners, rule of law, freedom of speech and the press, a more liberal climate for public life, and open political participation.

September 28 The al-Aqsa Intifada erupts in the wake of Ariel Sharon's visit to the Temple Mount/al-Haram al-Sharif.

October 1 Breaking with tradition, the state-owned *al-Thawra* publishes a stinging critique of rampant corruption and nepotism in the state bureaucracy, directly faulting the policies of past governments. Author 'Aref Dalilah, former dean of the economics department at Damascus University, writes that "social and economic development had been frozen for 20 years." (AFP, 10/2/00)

October 3 Bashar holds his first press conference with the international media at the conclusion of a state visit to Egypt, with Egyptian president Hosni Mubarak at his side. (*al-Quds al-'Arabi,* 10/4/00)

October 18 Bashar, meeting with U.S. secretary of state Madeleine Albright in Riyadh, rebuffs her suggestion for a new Syrian-Israeli peace initiative, on the grounds that Syria will not negotiate during the Palestinian intifada. (*Mideast Mirror,* 12/22/00)

October 22 At the Arab Summit in Cairo, Bashar delivers a stern rebuke to the Israeli military for its attempt to crush the intifada by force of arms but calls for a peaceful end to conflict. (NYT, 10/22/00)

November Iraq begins pumping oil through the Kirkuk pipeline to the Syrian oil terminal at Banyas, reportedly at a rate of 150,000 barrels a day, violating the UN sanctions on Saddam Hussein's regime. This is the first time the pipeline has been used since it was closed in 1982. (*Oil Daily,* 11/22/00)

November 15 On the thirtieth anniversary of the revolution that brought his father to power, Bashar signs an amnesty freeing approximately 600 Syrian and Lebanese prisoners, out of an estimated political prisoner population of 1,500. The pardon covers criminal and certain political offenses committed before November 16, 2000, and includes a reduction of prison sentences for economic crimes. Bashar presents the bill to parliament for approval, breaking with Hafiz's tradition of issuing decrees without the consultation of the parliament. The bill is also the first public acknowledgment that political prisoners are being held by the regime. (AP, 11/16/00; Zisser, "A False Spring in Damascus")

November 19 Bashar decrees that al-Mezzeh prison will be transformed into a hospital. (AP, 11/21/00)

November 29 The ruling Ba'th Party grants publishing rights to the other National Progressive Front parties and permission for them to recruit members. (UPI, 11/29/00; *al-Hayat,* 12/1/00)

December 1 The state budget, presented to the Syrian parliament on October 30, is signed into law before the start of the fiscal year for the first time in a decade. The $7.7 billion budget is a 10 percent increase over the previous year's budget. (Arabicnews.com, 9/26/00; *Tishrin* 12/1/00)

December 2 The Ba'th Party approves a decision to permit the establishment of private banks and to open a securities exchange market. (SANA, 12/2/00)

December 5 The Ba'th national leadership announces the end of the appointment of party leaders. Henceforth, party leaders will be elected by party members, and the leadership will also be subject to votes of no confidence. The first party vote is set for January 20, 2001. (*al-Hayat*, 12/5/00)

December 11 Syrian authorities hand over to Lebanese authorities forty-six Lebanese and eight Palestinian prisoners charged with politically motivated crimes. Several days later, Lebanese prosecutor general 'Adnan 'Addum releases a list of ninety-three Lebanese prisoners remaining in jail in Syria for criminal offenses and declares the issue of Lebanese in Syrian jails closed, over the protest of family associations and human rights groups in Lebanon. (AP, 12/11/00; AFP, 12/15/00)

December 15 Syria signs a $1 billion memorandum of understanding with Lebanon and Egypt to build an undersea pipeline for natural gas from el-Arish in Sinai to the northern Lebanon city of Tripoli. From Tripoli, overland pipelines will branch off to Syria, Jordan, Turkey, and Europe. (AP, 12/15/00)

December 17 The Committees for the Defense of Human Rights in Syria, led by Aktham Nu'aysa, issues a public call for amnesty for the remaining political prisoners in Syrian jails, the abolition of secret trials, and permission for all exiles to return. (NYT, 12/17/00)

December 23 Syria appoints a new ambassador to Jordan, filling a post that had been vacant since Syria recalled its ambassador during a 1993 dispute over the draft peace accord between Israel and Jordan. (AP, 12/24/00)

December 25 The Syrian Savings Bank becomes the first institution in the country to offer credit cards. (AFP, 12/25/00)

2001

January 1 Bashar weds Asma Akhras, twenty-five-year-old daughter of a Syrian cardiologist practicing in London, in a secret New Year's Day ceremony in Damascus.

January 4 *Sawt al-Sha'b* (*Voice of the People*), the newspaper of the Bakdash wing of the Syrian Communist Party in the National Progressive Front, becomes the first paper not controlled by the regime to be published in Syria since 1963. (AP, 1/5/01)

January 7 The Statement of 1,000 is published with the signatures of 1,000 intellectuals. The new document, more radical in its agenda than the Statement of 99, establishes the Committees for the Revival of the Civil Society as a coordinating body for the new political forums around the country and to facilitate the finding of solutions to Syria's problems. (*al-watha'iq al-sadirat 'an al-hay'at al-ta'sisiyya, lijan ihya' al-mujtama' al-madani fi suria*, Damascus, undated).

January 16 Syria announces that it has extensive diamond reserves, larger than those it discovered in 1983, and invites private companies to make bids on developing the mines. (MEED, 1/26/01)

January 18 The Syrian Telecommunications Establishment awards build-operate-transfer contracts to Syriatel (a subsidiary of the Egyptian mobile phone company Orascom) and Lebanon's Investcom to build a network to cover 90 percent of the country and offer services to up to 1.7 million subscribers. (MEED, 2/2/01)

January 19 Muhammad Sawwan announces the formation of the Gathering for Democracy and Unity (*al-tajammu' min ajli al-dimuqratiya wa al-wahda*), a "permanent democratic forum" to tackle issues such as corruption, patriotism, and nationalism. (*al-Safir*, 1/19/01)

January 20 Syria amends its exchange rate laws to permit the Commercial Bank of Syria to conduct limited foreign exchange rate transactions at the free market rate for the dollar for the first time in forty years. The move is seen as an important first step toward a unified market rate that will simplify foreign transactions. (MEED, 2/2/01)

January 25 Riyad Sayf, an independent member of parliament, announces his intention to form a political party called the Party of Social Peace (*hizb al-salam al-ijtima'i*). (*al-Hayat*, 1/26/01)

January 29 Syrian information minister 'Adnan 'Omran, commenting on the reformist discussion salons that have sprouted up since Bashar took power, says "we respect the opinions of others so long as they fall under the constitution and are founded on responsibility and a commitment toward the country and unity. What goes beyond the law is forbidden." He also alleges that civil society activists are often in the pay of foreign governments. On the state of emergency, 'Omran says, "Martial law exists, but it is frozen and is not applied." (AFP, 1/29/01)

January 30 Unidentified assailants assault writer and civil society forum organizer Nabil Sulayman in Latakia, in what many observers identify as the first incident in a state-led counterattack against civil society activists. (George, *Syria*, p. 48)

January 31 Syria and Iraq sign an agreement to set up a free trade zone between them, which goes into effect on April 1, 2001. (AFP, 1/31/01)

February 6 The Ba'th Party leadership decides to permit the establishment of private universities. (SANA, 2/6/01) Four are eventually authorized in a series of decrees in 2003: the Arts and Sciences Private University in Aleppo, Qalamoun Private University in Deir Attih, Maamoun Sciences and Technology University in Qamishli, and the Union Private University in Raqqa. (SR, 10/03)

February 8 In his first extensive interview with the press, Bashar tells *al-Sharq al-Awsat* that opening the Syrian government to new political parties is a possibility but refuses to set forth a timetable. He also announces that he is willing to "continue negotiations" with Israel but says that there must be prior guarantees that Syria will return to its 1967 borders with the conclusion of a peace agreement. Bashar accuses reformists who have spoken out in the foreign press of being "an elite group" that misrepresents itself as the voice of the majority. (*al-Sharq al-Awsat*, 2/8/01)

February 15 The Arab Socialist Union party of the National Progressive Front publishes the second nonofficial newspaper in Syria, *al-Wahdawi* (*The Unionist*). (AFP, 2/15/01)

February 17 The Ba'th Party explains that it has sent members of its Regional Command Council throughout the country to explain the political situation to the party rank and file and Syrian citizens. One Ba'th official explains that the initiative is intended to activate the role of the party and explain the accomplishments of the National Progressive Front to counter the negative rhetoric that has been generated in reformist salons. (*al-Sharq al-Awsat*, 2/17/01)

February 17 Syrian security services begin demanding that salons submit an application for a license before they open their doors to private discussions. Permission is contingent on each salon's registering the name of the owner and site of the forum, as well as submitting to the authorities the names of the salon's participants and the text of the lectures to be given, due fifteen days in advance of any scheduled meeting. (UPI, 2/17/01; *al-Hayat*, 2/20/01)

February 21 A Ba'th Party official says that the civil society activists in Syria "misunderstood President al-Asad's investiture speech last July" and "went beyond the red lines and the national and pan-Arab constants. They could have played a major role if they had not tampered with the fundamental issues [questioning the leading role of the Ba'th]." Vice President 'Abd al-Halim al-Khaddam echoes the criticism, saying that the discussion forums cross "red lines, which are society's security and stability." (*al-Hayat*, 2/21/01; AFP, 2/22/01)

February 21 Riyad Sayf openly defies the ban on unlicensed political discussion forums by holding a gathering at his home. (AFP, 2/22/01)

February 26 Syrian cartoonist 'Ali Firzat, famed throughout the Arab world, publishes the first issue of *al-Dommari* (*The Lamplighter*), a magazine featuring satire, cartoons, and social commentary. The magazine is the first privately owned, independent newspaper not affiliated with a political party published in Syria since 1963. (AP, 2/26/01)

February 27 Bashar decrees a new copyright law protecting authors from "all forms of plagiarism, distortion, or any breach." (SANA, 2/27/01)

March 14 Egypt's President Hosni Mubarak and Jordan's King Abdallah arrive in Damascus for talks and to celebrate the extension of their shared electricity grid to Syria. The grid is to be connected to Turkey and Lebanon in the future. (AP, 3/14/01)

March 21 The parliament endorses a new law on banking secrecy, in a step toward reestablishing private banks in Syria. (UPI, 3/19/01)

March 27 At the Arab Summit in Amman, Jordan, Asad lambastes Israeli society as "more racist than Nazism itself," accuses the Israeli public of ruining the peace process, and calls for peace on the basis of full acceptance of Palestinian, Lebanese, and Syrian territorial demands. (Jordan TV Channel 1, 3/27/01)

March 29 The Syrian parliament authorizes the operations of private banks in Syria. Foreign investors are permitted as long as Syrians own 51 percent of the shares of any private bank. (AP, 3/29/01)

April Syria and the European Union (EU) sign an agreement for a National Indicative Programme designed to support economic development, institutional strengthening, industrial modernization, and trade liberalization. The program, funded by grants from the EU, will progress in several stages of targeted projects led by EU experts who will focus on specific areas in need of reform and will lead toward the goal of integration into a Euro-Med Free Trade Area. (SR, 12/02)

April 10 The officially banned but tolerated Committees for the Defense of Human Rights in Syria issues its annual report in Damascus, estimating that 800 political prisoners remain behind bars in Syrian jails. (AFP, 4/10/01)

April 11 Defense Minister Mustafa Tlas tells Abu Dhabi satellite television that he has "evidence" proving that the intellectuals who signed the Statement of 1,000 are agents of American intelligence. Tlas also asserts that the absence of any mention of the Arab-Israeli conflict in the petition proves that its signatories are in the pay of the enemy. (*al-Quds al-'Arabi*, 4/12/01)

April 15 After a Hizballah attack on an Israeli tank in the disputed Sheba'a Farms area kills one soldier, Israeli warplanes strike a Syrian radar post in central Lebanon, killing two Syrian soldiers and injuring five. (AP 4/15/01; AFP, 4/16/01)

May Bashar issues a decree increasing civilian and military state employee salaries by 20 percent and pensioners' allowances by 15 percent. (SR, 11/02)

May 3 From exile in London, the Syrian Muslim Brotherhood issues a draft of a Covenant of National Honor for Political Activity (*mithaq sharaf watani lil-'amal al-siyasi*), calling for a modern and democratic state, a national dialogue, and a rejection of political violence. (*al-Hayat*, 5/4/01)

May 5 Nizar Nayyuf, journalist and secretary general of the Committees for the Defense of Democratic Freedoms and Human Rights in Syria, is released from prison after serving nine years of a ten-year sentence for membership in an outlawed organization and the dissemination of false information. Nayyuf immediately embarks on a hunger strike to protest his continuing house arrest and the ban on his travel outside the country for medical treatment. (AFP, 5/7/01)

May 6 Pope John Paul II visits Damascus and becomes the first pontiff to enter a mosque. He also meets with Syrian grand mufti Shaykh Ahmed Kuftaro to discuss Christian-Muslim understanding. Asad delivers a speech in the pope's presence in which he derides Jews as the enemy of Christians and Muslims, holding them responsible for "betraying" and "torturing" Jesus Christ. The speech is widely denounced in the foreign media. (AP, 5/6/01; SANA, 5/5/01; NYT, 5/7/01)

May 8 Mahmud Salameh is dismissed from his post as editor-in-chief of *al-Thawra*. (*Mideast Mirror*, 5/30/01)

May 11 Lebanon signs an agreement to buy gas from Syria, to be delivered via a pipeline to be constructed between the two countries. The $13 million pipeline will be linked to the gas pipeline network connecting Syria to Jordan and Egypt, which was completed on March 14, and later will be extended to Turkey. (AFP, 5/12/01)

May 13 The Faysal wing of the Syrian Communist Party, a constituent party of the National Progressive Front, publishes *al-Nur* (*The Light*), the fourth non-regime-sanctioned party newspaper in Syria. (AFP, 5/13/01)

June 14 Syrian troops begin their first major withdrawal in Lebanon since Bashar took power. At least 6,000 soldiers turn over their positions in greater Beirut to the Lebanese Army; most of the Syrian soldiers return home, the rest are redeployed in the Biqa'a Valley. Approximately 20,000 Syrian soldiers continue to occupy Lebanon after the pullout. (NYT, 6/20/01; CSM, 6/21/01)

June 24 *Al-Iqtisadiyya*, Syria's second independent newspaper and first economic journal, publishes its first issue. (AFP, 6/23/01)

August 9 After declaring a hunger strike to protest charges directed at him by regime security services, Ma'mun al-Homsi, an independent member of parliament, speaks out against martial law, the absence of free political expression, and the economic monopoly of regime strongmen and their children. Two days later he is arrested and jailed on charges of defying state orders, insulting the government, and evading taxes. (AFP, 8/9/01)

September 2 Riyad al-Turk, a Communist Party leader who was formerly imprisoned for seventeen years under the Hafiz al-Asad regime, is arrested after he stridently criticizes policies under Hafiz during a public symposium in Damascus. Al-Turk said that political, economic, and social stagnation in Syria were a consequence of the course set by the elder Asad. (AP, 9/2/01)

September 11 Terrorists hijack four planes in the United States and crash three of them into the World Trade Center towers and the Pentagon, killing nearly 3,000 people. Asad responds with a call for "global mutual help" to eradicate terrorism and protect human rights. *Al-Ba'th* runs a headline on September 12 that reads: "Black Tuesday in United States, Syria Condemns Destructive Attacks." (AFP, 9/12/01; NYT, 9/13/01)

September 23 Bashar issues a decree reaffirming private publishing rights "within the framework of the law" but banning articles that reveal information damaging to national security or unity. The decree criminalizes the publication of "falsehoods" and "fabricated reports," and imposes heavy fines or imprisonment, or both, for violators.(AP, 9/23/01; Human Rights Watch, *World Report 2002: Syria*)

October The Reform Party of Syria, a group of "secular, peace-committed American-Syrians, Euro-Syrians, and native Syrians" led by Washington-area businessman Farid Ghadry, is founded. The party calls for U.S.-led pressure on the current Syrian regime to create a "New Syria" that "embraces real democratic and economic reforms." (http://reformsyria.org)

October 8 Syria is unanimously elected to a two-year term as nonpermanent member of the United Nations Security Council. Syria's nomination for an Asian seat on the Council is supported by 160 nations with no opposition from the United States. Israel is the only UN member to express its disapproval. *Al-Ba'th* calls Syria's election "a triumph." Syria's term of service begins in January 2002, and it serves as president of the Security Council in June 2002 and August 2003. (AP, 10/8/01, 10/9/01)

October 11 In response to a question about the U.S. response to countries such as Syria who do not cooperate satisfactorily in the war on terror, U.S. deputy secretary of state Richard Armitage says: "The consequences might be whatever the coalition finds worthy and it runs the gamut from isolation to financial investigation, all the way up through possibly military action." President Bush makes a more conciliatory statement later in the day: "The Syrians have talked to us about how they can help in the war against terrorism. We take that seriously and we'll give them an opportunity to do so." Armitage's statement prompts a protest by the Syrian Foreign Ministry, which summons U.S. ambassador to Syria Ted Kattouf for an explanation. (*Daily Telegraph*, 10/13/01)

October 29 Ahead of the November 9–13 World Trade Organization (WTO) meeting in Qatar, Syria announces its intention to formally apply for admission to the organization. The WTO confirmed receipt of the application on November 13. (AP, 10/29/01, 11/13/01)

November 25 Bashar issues his second sweeping amnesty, releasing at least 122 political prisoners, mainly Islamists. (AFP, 11/25/01)

November 30 Syria passes its 2002 government budget, amounting to $7.66 billion, a 10 percent increase over the 2001 budget. (SyriaLive.net, 11/30/01)

December 6 Bashar's wife, Asma, gives birth to their first child, Hafiz. (AP, 12/6/01)

December 8 Bashar signs into law a plan to create a new agency to combat unemployment, which will "diversify the structure of the economic and services sectors and absorb new arrivals on the job market." Prime Minister Mustafa Miru says the five-year plan will cost $1 billion and create 440,000 jobs. (SR, 12/01)

December 13 The imminent closure of the infamous Tadmur prison in Palmyra is announced. The order does not appear to have been carried out by the end of 2004. (*Gulf News*, 12/13/01; Zisser, "A False Spring")

December 13 In Bashar's first cabinet reshuffle, eighteen of the thirty-three appointed ministers are new faces, the number of Ba'thist ministers is reduced to nineteen from twenty-six, and the key ministries of finance, economy, transportation, tourism, and agriculture have new occupants. Mustafa Miru remains prime minister. (AP 12/13/01; *al-Hayat*, 12/14/01)

2002

January 22 Hassan Turkmani assumes the post of Army chief of staff from 'Ali Aslan, who retires from service at age seventy-two. (Syrian Arab TV, 1/22/02)

January 30 The Council of Ministers approves a draft decree exempting radio stations "confined to music programs and commercials" from the restrictions on private broadcasting. The new regulations are issued as a law on August 21, 2002, but the first private radio station (al-Madina FM) is not launched until February 2005. (*al-Ba'th*, 1/30/02; SANA, 8/21/02; *al-Sharq al-Awsat*, 2/2/05)

February 1 Foreign Minister Faruq al-Shar' rejects an Israeli offer to resume peace negotiations with no conditions because it would signify "the non-application of the principles of peace and a return to square zero." (*al-Safir*, 2/1/02)

February 12 A Jordanian newspaper reports that Defense Minister Mustafa Tlas submitted his resignation to Asad and will retire in July 2002 at age seventy. (*al-Dustur*, 2/12/02)

February 17 Saudi crown prince Abdallah tells Thomas Friedman of the *New York Times* about the land-for-peace proposal he intends to present at the Arab Summit in Beirut in March, prompting widespread discussion and speculation in the media. (NYT, 2/17/02)

March 3 Asad visits Beirut to discuss the upcoming Arab Summit with Lebanese president Emile Lahud. The visit is the first to Lebanon by a Syrian head of state since Hafiz al-Asad traveled to the Lebanese border town of Chtaura in 1975. The elder Asad never visited Beirut. (Tele-Liban TV, 3/3/02)

March 6 After meeting with Crown Prince Abdallah in Saudi Arabia, Bashar "expressed satisfaction," despite some reservations, at the land-for-peace proposal the Saudi prince is to unveil at the Arab Summit in Beirut. (AP, 3/6/02)

March 27–28 In Beirut, Syria joins in the unanimous Arab Summit endorsement of Saudi crown prince Abdallah's initiative toward a "just and comprehensive peace" with Israel. In his address to the summit, Asad calls for the formation of a committee of representatives from Arab countries concerned with the peace process who will explain the initiative to the UN and the EU. He also calls for Arab states to sever relations with Israel and continue to support the intifada "materially and morally." (Tele-Liban TV, 3/27/02; WP, 3/29/01)

April 3 Syria announces the second major withdrawal of its troops from Lebanon. An unspecified number pull out of central Lebanon toward the Biqa'a Valley and back into Syria. (AP, 4/3/02)

April 16 U.S. secretary of state Colin Powell, on a trip to the Middle East, adds an unscheduled stop in Damascus to his itinerary and meets privately with Asad. The visit followed a series of cross-border attacks launched against Israel from Lebanon by Hizballah and Palestinian militants and a heavy Hizballah bombardment of Israeli positions in the Sheba'a Farms area on

April 10. Asad rejects Sharon's proposal for a new Arab-Israeli summit when Powell raises the issue in Damascus. (NYT, 4/16/02; AP, 4/16/02; CSM, 4/17/02)

April 20 Prime Minister Mustafa Miru fires 'Ali 'Abd al-Karim from the directorship of SANA, replacing him with Ghazi al-Dib. Al-Karim is given an advisory position in the Ministry of Information. Fayiz Sayigh is appointed head of Syrian radio and television. (AFP, 4/22/02)

April 21–23 First lady Asma al-Asad hosts a three-day conference on Arab women's role in economic development. The conference, organized by the industrial businesswomen committee of the Damascus Chamber of Industry, is attended by more than 250 businesswomen from at least fourteen Arab countries. (MidEastWeb.com, 4/2/02; ArabicNews.com, 4/23/02)

April 28 Asad decrees the formation of a new Ministry of Expatriate Affairs to "activate the role of Syrian expatriates and communities in bolstering the relationship between their mother country and the countries in which they reside." (SANA, 4/28/02)

May 15 By presidential decree, Defense Minister Mustafa Tlas has his term of service extended two extra years beyond the retirement age of seventy. (AFP, 5/15/02)

May 24 In a sign of growing cooperation between the leadership of Syria and Iraq, the Syrian Information Ministry issues a ban on the "printing, circulation, and distribution" of Iraqi opposition newspapers in Syria. (*al-Hayat*, 5/24/02)

June The Ministry of the Economy announces a $200 million plan to upgrade services and assist in the development of the Commercial Bank of Syria. (SR, 11/02)

June 2 Syrian satellite television begins broadcasting a fifteen-minute daily news bulletin in Hebrew aimed at "revealing the truth to the Israelis." (AFP, 6/2/02)

June 3-4 Javier Solana, foreign policy chief of the EU, meets with Asad in Damascus and tells him "the time is ripe for an initiative of a political nature." (AFP, 6/3/02) The following day, U.S. assistant secretary of state William Burns meets with Asad and reports that "Syria will support an effort based on UN Security Council resolutions relating to the Israeli-Arab conflict and on the principle of land-for-peace." Burns receives only a lukewarm reception from Asad to his proposal for a new peace conference. (AFP, 6/4/02)

July 22 Syria's third independent weekly, a self-described "political, economic, cultural, and general affairs magazine," publishes its first issue. *Abiad wa Aswad* (*White and Black*) was granted a license on April 28 and is owned by

Mohammad Bilal Turkmani, son of Hassan Turkmani, who became defense minister in 2004. (AFP, 7/22/02)

July 22 The Committee of the Parents of the Lebanese Disappeared or Detained in Syria makes a public visit to Syrian interior minister 'Ali Hammud in Damascus to present him with a list of 176 Lebanese believed to be held or "disappeared" by the Syrian authorities. The minister tells them that he needs three months before he can issue a response. When the organization tries to visit Damascus on November 2 to receive his reply, the convoy is turned back at the Syrian border and told to take up the issue with Lebanese authorities. (Human Rights Watch, *World Report 2003: Syria*)

August 23–25 The Syrian Muslim Brotherhood presides over a conference with other Syrian exile opposition parties to draw up a final version of a "national covenant" to define a cooperative nonviolent political program. (*Mideast Mirror*, 8/30/02)

October 8 Damascus hosts a two-day pan-Arab conference of various local and foreign organizations calling for the lifting of the embargo on Iraq. Despite the presence of 800 personalities from many Arab states and the rest of the world, the conference does not include official representation by the Syrian government. (Radio Monte Carlo, 10/8/02)

October 8 The Ministry of the Economy authorizes the purchase and exchange of foreign currency for noncommercial purposes, at exchange rates set by the Syrian Commercial Bank. Syrians are henceforth permitted to obtain up to $20,000 in foreign currency for medical treatment abroad or travel expenses incurred while undertaking the Hajj to Mecca. (MENA, 10/8/02)

October 9 Ghazi Kana'an, commander of the Syrian *mukhabarat* (intelligence services) in Lebanon since 1982, is promoted to head the political security directorate in Damascus. Rustom Ghazaleh, previously serving as head of Syrian intelligence in Beirut, replaces him. (AFP, 10/9/02)

October 22 Asad tells visiting U.S. assistant secretary of state William Burns: "The United States does not seem able to understand events in the Middle East, and that is dangerous." (SR, 11/02)

October 22 Bashar issues a decree increasing private sector wages and salaries by 20 percent. (AP, 10/22/02)

October 23 Reporters Without Borders, the France-based press freedom advocate, issues country rankings for the first time; Syria ranks a lowly 126 out of 139 surveyed countries. (SR, 11/02)

November Russia abandons plans to sell advanced SA-8 surface-to-air missiles to Syria. Israeli prime minister Ariel Sharon tells his government the deal collapsed because of pressure he put on the Russians during his recent visit to Moscow. The United States also reportedly lobbied the Russians to cancel the deal. (SR, 11/02)

November The Commercial Bank of Syria announces the opening of six new branches across the country. (SR, 11/02)

November 8 Syria votes "yes" on UN Security Council Resolution 1441, calling on Iraq to relinquish weapons of mass destruction and permit the reentry of UN weapons inspectors. Syrian officials explain that they believe the resolution will help avert a military attack. (SR, 11/02; AFP, 11/17/02)

November 16 A presidential pardon reportedly prompted by humanitarian concerns frees Riyad al-Turk, who had been sentenced to thirty years in prison in June 2002 for "attempting to change the constitution." (AP, 11/16/02)

December The Syrian parliament passes the 2003 government budget, amounting to $9.13 billion, an 18 percent increase over the 2002 budget. (*al-Hayat*, 12/2/02; SR, 12/02)

December 15 Following an unauthorized December 10 demonstration in front of the parliament building, two central committee members of the unlicensed Kurdish political party Yakti are arrested. The protestors had demanded a meeting with the interior minister to discuss improving the situation of Syrian Kurds. (AP, 12/19/02)

December 16-18 Bashar makes the first-ever state visit by a Syrian leader to the United Kingdom. (AP, 12/17/02; SR, 12/02, 1/03)

December 23 Syrian military security services arrest Ibrahim Hamidi, prominent journalist and Damascus bureau chief for the London-based Arabic daily *al-Hayat*, on charges of publishing "false news." Hamidi had written a story on Syria's preparations to receive Iraqi refugees in the event the United States went to war against Saddam Hussein's regime. Hamidi is eventually released on May 25, 2003. (*al-Hayat*, 12/20/02; AP, 12/27/02; SR, 1/03)

December 24 Israeli prime minister Ariel Sharon announces in a televised address that he has evidence Iraq may have moved weapons of mass destruction into Syria. Syria calls the charges "ridiculous." (*Jerusalem Post*, 12/25/02, 12/26/02)

2003

January Minister of the Economy Ghassan al-Rifa'i officially announces that Syria's gross domestic product grew at an annual rate of 3.35 percent in 2002. (SR, 1/03)

January Syria's first magazine on information and communication technologies, *The Numeric*, is launched, after having been authorized on July 20, 2002. (SR, 1/03)

January 8 An American delegation from the Baker Institute for Public Policy, including former U.S. ambassador to Syria Edward Djerejian and U.S. senator Arlen Specter, meets with a Syrian delegation in Damascus for informal discussion of U.S.-Syria ties, the war on terror, and Middle East peace. The first meeting between the groups took place in May 2002 at Rice University in Houston, Texas. (AP, 1/8/03)

January 15 The Ba'th Party sets new conditions for its candidates in the parliamentary elections scheduled for March 2. Each candidate must now have been an active member in the Ba'th Party for at least ten years, to have played a key role in the party for five years, and to have a college degree unless he is a worker or peasant, in which case he should have at least a secondary school certificate. Under existing Syrian constitutional and electoral law, peasants are to compose at least half of the total parliament, regardless of their party affiliation. (ArabicNews.com, 1/18/03)

January 26 The election campaign for parliamentary candidates begins. More than 10,000 candidates compete for 250 positions on the Syrian People's Assembly (parliament) scheduled for March 2. The last parliamentary elections were in 1998. As was the case in the previous election, 167 candidates are on the joint list offered by the National Progressive Front, most of them from the Ba'th Party. All 167 NPF candidates had won posts in 1998, including 135 Ba'thists. (ArabicNews.com, 2/28/03)

January 28 Asad decrees a law to regulate new free-trade zones within the country, opening investment to all service, industrial, and trade activities. (SR, 2/03)

February 1 A three-day conference on "Women in Education" opens in Damascus, under the patronage of first lady Asma al-Asad. Six first ladies from Arab states attend the conference, intended to help Arab women "broaden their horizons." (AP, 2/1/03)

February 4 Bashar issues a decree establishing the Syrian Gas Company, which will assume control of all aspects of the natural gas industry in Syria from the state-owned Syrian Petroleum Company and which will be attached to the Ministry of Oil and Mineral Resources. (SR, 2/03)

February 19–25 During the third major Syrian troop withdrawal from Lebanon, the number of occupation troops drops from 20,000 to about 16,000. (AP 2/20/03)

March 1 The Arab states meet in Sharm al-Shaykh, Egypt, for what turns into a heated and divisive Arab Summit. The summit refuses to discuss a proposal to ask Saddam Hussein to relinquish power, compromising instead on a resolution calling for diplomatic efforts to avoid war. Syria suggests a resolution—unadopted—calling on Arab countries with U.S. military bases to deny permission for their use in an attack on Iraq. (AFP, 3/1/03)

March 2–3 Syria holds its first parliamentary elections since Bashar took power; the National Progressive Front wins 167 of 250 seats, and the rest are taken by independents. Two-thirds of all those elected are newcomers to the parliament. (SR, 3/03)

March 4 Syria and Egypt join the "Arab committee" initially consisting of Bahrain, Lebanon, Tunisia, and the Arab League Secretary General. The committee, empowered at the Arab Summit in Sharm al-Shaykh on March 1, is to market Arab League resolutions backing a diplomatic solution to the Iraq crisis to Iraq and the permanent members of the UN Security Council. (MENA, 3/4/03)

March 19 The U.S.-led coalition launches Operation Iraqi Freedom. Within days, the Kirkuk-Banyas oil pipeline is reportedly blown up by U.S. forces, cutting off the estimated 150,000–200,000 barrel-a-day flow into Syria from Iraq. (*al-Ra'i al-'am al-Kuwaytiyya*, 4/2/03; *Petroleum Intelligence Weekly*, 10/18/04)

March 27 Syrian mufti Shaykh Ahmed Kuftaro publicly calls for the Arab world to "use all means possible to thwart the aggression, including martyr operations against the belligerent American, British and Zionist invaders" in Iraq. (AFP, 3/27/03)

March 27 In an interview with *al-Safir*, Bashar al-Asad lashes out against the U.S. war in Iraq, saying Americans "removed their masks and said that they wanted oil and that they wanted to redraw the map of the region in accordance with Israeli interests" but warns that although they can conquer it, "the U.S. and Britain are incapable of controlling all of Iraq." (*al-Safir*, 3/27/03)

March 28 U.S. secretary of defense Donald Rumsfeld publicly states that he has information Syria is providing military assistance, including "night vision goggles" to Iraq. Rumsfeld says that if this assistance continues, the United States will consider Syria to be committing "hostile acts." Syrian Foreign Ministry spokeswoman Buthayna Sha'ban calls the charges "absolutely unfounded and irresponsible." (AP, 3/29/03)

March 30 Foreign Minister Faruq al-Shar' tells the Syrian parliament that "Syria has a national interest in the expulsion of the invaders from Iraq."

Concurrently, U.S. secretary of state Colin Powell says Syria "faces a critical choice" and "bears the responsibility for its choices and for the consequences." (AFP, 3/31/03; WP, 4/2/03)

April A new Credit and Monetary Council chaired by the governor of the Syrian central bank is formed. One of its first acts is to permit the reestablishment of private banks in Syria, after a forty-year monopoly by the state banking services. The applications of three banking consortiums for licenses are immediately approved. (SR, 5/03, 1/04)

April The Ministry of Education announces its intention to replace military khakis with new pink, blue, and grey uniforms beginning with the next school year. The ministry says it will remove the military training module from the national curriculum and may also remove components of Ba'thist teachings and some of the religious requirements. (*Middle East International,* 5/16/03)

April 13 U.S. secretary of defense Donald Rumsfeld charges that "busloads" of Syrian fighters are entering Iraq with "hundreds of thousands of dollars" and leaflets offering rewards for the killing of American soldiers. President Bush demands Syria's "cooperation," and says "there are chemical arms in Syria," but does not directly accuse Syria of taking in Iraqi chemical weapons. (NYT, 4/14/03)

April 21 After the United States repeatedly accuses Syria of facilitating the travel of foreign fighters into Iraq, Syrian foreign minister Faruq al-Shar' announces that the borders are completely closed. President Bush praises the move. (AP 4/21/03)

April 23 One hundred and twenty members of Syrian opposition groups, from inside the country and among the exile community, publish a petition in the opposition newspaper *Akhbar al-Sharq* calling for democratic reforms in order to stave off an invasion by the United States. The United States, it says "has never dared occupy a country where there exists minimal harmony between those who govern and those who are governed. . . . The war against Iraq demonstrated the inability of the single party and of the security apparatus to defend national independence, sovereignty and dignity. . . . People living under oppression cannot protect and defend their country." (*Akhbar al-Sharq,* 4/23/03)

April 30 The U.S. State Department releases "A Performance-Based Roadmap to a Permanent Two-State Solution to the Israeli-Palestinian Conflict" under the auspices of the Quartet (the United States, United Nations, European Union, and Russia). Mention is made of a Syrian-Israeli peace settlement, but the roadmap does not provide concrete steps toward a final agreement on this track. In an interview with Kuwait's *al-Anbaa*, Asad complains that "we do not know what is the relation of Syria and Lebanon to the stages [of the roadmap] that were put on it." (NYT, 5/1/03; *al-Anbaa*, 5/26/03)

May The Syrian government publishes the final draft of an economic reform program setting benchmarks and targets for the next five years, with the aim of achieving an economic growth rate of 6 percent by the end of this period. The final draft is agreed upon a year after the government published its first draft of the program in the press and invited open debate and contributions from local and foreign economic experts. (SR, 6/03)

May Operating licenses are granted to two private universities and four private newspapers. (*Middle East International*, 5/16/03)

May Syria's Judiciary Higher Council, the highest judiciary authority in the country, meets for the first time in decades. President Asad tells the council that it should be able to act in an "independent manner." (SR, 1/04)

May The Credit and Monetary Council cuts interest rates for the first time since 1981. Deposit rates come down by 1 percent, credit rates by 1.5 percent. (SR, 1/04)

May 3 U.S. secretary of state Colin Powell meets Asad in Damascus. Afterward, Powell says that a U.S. war with Syria is "not on the table," and that he obtained a Syrian promise to close the Damascus offices of Palestinian Islamic Jihad and Hamas. (*International Herald Tribune*, 5/3/03)

May 17 A petition signed by 287 Syrian intellectuals and professionals—among them active Syrian Ba'thists—is sent to President Asad, calling on him to open a comprehensive national dialogue and undertake "sweeping national reforms." The petition demands amnesty for political prisoners, an end to emergency laws, and a scaling back of the security apparatus, to prepare the country to counter U.S. plans for the region. (*Akhbar al-Sharq*, 6/1/03)

May 25 Three private banks are granted operating licenses. Their applications had been approved one month previously. (AP, 5/25/03).

June The Syrian Ministry of Industry signs a memorandum of understanding with the Egyptian al-Wahab Group, establishing Syria's first vehicle assembly plant. The plant will manufacture 600 thirty-passenger minibuses a year. (SR, 6/03)

June 15 The Ba'th Party pledges to remove itself from day-to-day management of the country, issuing a public statement calling on "the comrades and the party institutions to be entirely distant from daily executive work." (SR, 1/04)

June 18 U.S. forces in northern Iraq penetrate the Syrian border in an attack on a suspicious convoy headed out of Iraq; dozens are killed and wounded. Five

Syrian border guards are injured and held for ten days before their release. The convoy, originally suspected of transporting Iraqi fugitives, appears to have consisted of fuel smugglers. (*New Yorker,* 7/28/03)

July The United Nations Development Program issues its annual *Human Rights Development Report* on world economic and social development. Syria is ranked 110 out of 175 countries, down from 97 in 2001. (SR, 7/03)

July 8 The ban on conducting transactions in foreign currency, which imposed heavy jail terms on violators, is abolished. The ban had been in place since 1986. (SR, 7/03)

July 20 The Syrian Oil Ministry announces that U.S. oil company Veritas has won a contract to explore for oil off the Mediterranean coast of Syria, beating out British, Canadian, and Norwegian competitors. (SANA, 7/20/03)

September Buthayna Sha'ban of the Syrian Foreign Ministry announces the establishment of a new bureau within the ministry charged with communicating Syria's message to the world. Seventy-one of 1,300 applicants were hired, and 50 will be appointed to various government ministries. (*Mideast Mirror,* 9/16/03)

September The European Investment Bank signs a pledge to provide $40 million in funding to small and medium-size enterprises in Syria, through a fund management unit aimed at long-term investments. (SR, 1/04)

September 9 Bashar issues a decree setting up the Agency for Combating Money Laundering to build upon the incipient regulatory framework for private banking in the country. (SR, 10/03)

September 20 A new cabinet is sworn in. Muhammad Naji al-'Utri replaces Mustafa Miru as prime minister after Miru's resignation. The four deputy prime minister posts are abolished, the total number of ministries is reduced from thirty-five to thirty, and seventeen of the appointees are newcomers to the cabinet. (SR, 10/03)

September 26 The Coalition Provisional Authority in Iraq announces that 123 of 248 "foreign fighters" that have been captured in Iraq by coalition forces thus far are Syrian. (NYT, 9/27/03)

October Syria is elected chairman of the Middle East Committee of the World Tourism Organization. (SR, 1/04)

October In a sign of the regime's intention to slowly divest the state of its industrial monopoly, the minister of industry announces that the state will open up to public-private partnerships four industrial sectors in which it has no stake. (SR, 1/04)

October Syria hosts a delegation of Iraqi Sunnis calling themselves the Central Council of the Shaykhs of Iraqi and Arab Clans. In early November, Syria hosts an Arab nationalist party called the National Unity Movement for Reform (*harakat al-wahda al-wataniyya lil-islah*). Both organizations pledge their rejection of the appointed interim government and the occupation of Iraq by the coalition authorities. (*Middle East Intelligence Bulletin,* 11/03)

October 5 Israel launches its first airstrike inside Syria since the 1973 war, bombing the 'Ayn al-Sahib camp outside of Damascus, causing no casualties. Israel claims the site was an Islamic Jihad camp; Syria denies that it is in use. In response, Syria seeks a UN resolution condemning the Israeli action. (AP, 10/06/03)

October 23–25 Damascus hosts the EU-Mashrek business fair, bringing more than 200 European businessmen to meet their counterparts from Lebanon, Syria, and Jordan, to discuss potential joint projects in tourism, textiles, information technology, food and beverages, and construction sectors. (SR, 10/03)

November In a sign of the increasingly repressive climate for journalism in Syria, Reporters Without Borders ranks Syria 155 out of 166 countries in its second annual index, down from 126 out of 139 surveyed countries in the previous index. (SR, 11/03)

November Passenger train service between Aleppo and the northern Iraqi city of Mosul resumes for the first time since the outbreak of the Iraq war in March. (SR, 1/04)

November A new income tax law is passed, cutting rates for individuals and companies across the board. (SR, 1/04)

November In an encounter kept secret until 2004, Israeli prime minister Ariel Sharon rebuffs a U.S. envoy's suggestion that he renew peace negotiations with Syria. (AP, 9/14/04)

November 1–2 Foreign ministers from the six countries bordering Iraq plus Egypt meet in Damascus to discuss the continuing conflict. The delegates pledge support for the Interim Governing Council (IGC) "in carrying out its transitional responsibilities until the formation of an elected and fully representative Iraqi government," and condemn attacks on civilians, UN forces, and humanitarian organizations. The communiqué does not address its position on attacks on coalition troops. Syria refuses to issue an invitation to IGC foreign minister Hoshyar Zibari, arguing that this might imply recognition of the IGC. Under threat of a boycott of the meeting by U.S.-allied Arab countries, Syria permits Kuwait to send the invitation, but Zibari refuses to attend because the invitation is extended only at the last minute. (AP, 11/02/03; AFP 11/03/03)

November 11 The Syria Accountability and Lebanese Sovereignty Restoration Act of 2003 is passed by an overwhelming 89–4 vote in the U.S. Senate. (*Washington Times,* 11/12/03)

November 12–18 The Syrian Democratic Coalition, a grouping of expatriate and banned Syrian political parties led by the Reform Party of Syria, holds its first conference, a closed-door meeting in Washington, intended to consolidate the democratic opposition to the existing Syrian regime. (www.reform-syria.org)

November 14–16 Indian prime minister Atal Behari Vajpayee visits Damascus, the first Indian premier to visit since 1988. The two countries pledge a united stance against terrorism in the context of international law and call for a greater UN role in Iraq. (AP, 11/16/03)

November 15 A new income tax law is enacted in Syria. Among the 126 articles in the new law are provisions for fighting tax evasion, an across-the-board lowering of corporate income tax rates, and detailed provisions remedying the ambiguities of the previous tax system. (SR, 12/03)

November 20 The Syria Accountability Act passes the U.S. House of Representatives by a 408–8 vote. (AP, 11/20/03)

December 1 In an interview with the *New York Times,* Asad calls for the resumption of peace negotiations with Israel; Israeli foreign minister Silvan Shalom responds that "talk is not enough" and demands that Syria first cut off its support for Palestinian militants and Hizballah. (NYT, 12/1/03; AP, 12/2/03)

December 3 The Credit and Monetary Council again cuts interest rates, only eight months after cutting them for the first time since 1981. The ill-advised cuts prompt a run on withdrawals, causing the council to push rates back up again to stem the outflow. (SR, 2/01, 3/04)

December 8 Prime Minister Naji al-'Utri announces the impending merger of two of the three major Syrian newspapers. Tishrin Press and Publishing Organisation and al-Wahda Press will combine, and the *Tishrin* and *al-Thawra* newspapers will become one. The new company (approved by the Cabinet on November 30, 2004, but still awaiting presidential approval as of early 2005) will be called al-Wahda Institute for Press, Printing, and Publishing. (SR, 12/03; AP, 11/30/04)

December 10 European Union representatives complete their negotiations with their Syrian counterparts in Damascus, reaching agreement on a Euro-Mediterranean Association Agreement between the EU and Syria. The process began with the Barcelona Declaration of 1995, which initiated negotiations between twelve Mediterranean countries and the EU toward the establishment of a Euro-Med Free Trade Area by 2010. Upon announcing the completion of the negotiations, Syria and the EU announce that the agreement will be signed in early 2004, pending ratification by the EU national parliaments and Syria. The signing is postponed when several EU nations, led by the United Kingdom, push for an amendment to make the document's clause on weapons of mass destruction more restrictive. (AFP, 12/10/03; SR, 4/04)

December 12 The Syria Accountability Act is signed into law by President Bush. (NYT, 12/14/03)

2004

January Durayd Dergham replaces Tarek Sarraj as director general of the Commercial Bank of Syria, the third official to hold the post in less than two years. (SR, 1/04)

January The Syrian parliament passes the 2004 government budget, amounting to $9.77 billion, an increase of 7 percent over the 2003 budget. For the first time, the budget figures are issued with a deficit line, in a move toward greater transparency. (SR, 1/04, 2/04)

January 6–8 Asad conducts the first-ever visit to Turkey by a Syrian head of state, inaugurating a new era of cooperation. Agreements on expanding trade and travel between the countries are signed, and discussions begin for a joint free-trade agreement between the two states. (*al-Ba'th,* 1/8/04; SR, 1/04)

January 12 Israeli president Moshe Katsav invites Bashar to visit Jerusalem to discuss negotiations for a final peace; Syria rejects the invitation as a trick to avoid serious negotiations. (*Ha'aretz,* 1/13/04)

January 13 The Syrian Young Entrepreneurs Association, a nonprofit organization backed by Asma al-Asad and the Syrian European Business Center, is launched. (SR, 2/04)

January 15–19 The Syrian Democratic Coalition holds the second conference of its constituent parties in Brussels, Belgium. The closed-door meeting aims to enlarge the membership of the coalition and to push the Asad regime to institute reforms. (www.reformsyria.org)

January 19 In an interview with *al-Sharq al-Awsat,* Asad says that the United States has not provided evidence of even one infiltrator from Syria into Iraq, while granting that it is impossible for him to ensure that nobody can sneak across, equating the situation to the U.S. border with Mexico. (*al-Sharq al-Awsat,* 1/19/04)

January 25 Syria, Lebanon, Jordan, and Egypt sign an agreement to implement the second of a three-phase project for an Arab gas pipeline that will link the four countries. The third stage, on which construction is expected to begin in 2005, will connect the gas pipeline from Jordan to Lebanon and Banyas in Syria. (SR, 1/04)

February General Adib Qassem replaces General Ahmed 'Ali as the head of the 16,000 strong Syrian Army contingent in Lebanon. (SR, 2/04)

February The National Progressive Front expands to include a ninth constituent party, the Arab Democratic Union, led by Ghassan Ahmed 'Othman. (SR, 2/04)

February 5 Over a period of days, the regime releases at least 120 political prisoners, mainly from Islamist parties and the Iraqi wing of the Ba'th Party. (al-Bawaba, 2/5/04)

February 9 King Abdallah of Jordan joins Asad in laying the foundation for the al-Wahda (Unity) Dam on the Yarmouk River that forms a border between their countries. Jordan will receive water for irrigation and Syria will use the electricity the dam generates. The dam was originally planned in 1953 and blueprints were finalized in 1986, but the project was delayed repeatedly for lack of funding and political reasons. (SR, 2/04)

February 11 The National Administration Institute, a graduate school offering two-year degrees in advanced managerial training for public sector employees, opens for its inaugural semester. The institute is patterned after the French *Ecole National d'Administration* and has on its faculty many French experts and academics. (SR, 2/04)

February 15 Asad issues a decree abolishing the Economic Security Courts that had been in place since 1977. The extrajudicial courts had been used to deprive those accused of committing economic crimes of constitutional safeguards. (SR, 2/04)

February 16 At the end of a joint Syrian-Iranian Economic Commission meeting, the parties announce that Iran Khodro, Iran's largest car manufacturer, will open a 5,000 car-a-year factory on the outskirts of Damascus in a Syria-Iran partnership. Construction of the plant—Syria's first foray into car manufacturing—begins on October 27. (SR, 3/04, 11/04)

February 17 'Imad Mustafa is sworn in as the new Syrian ambassador to the United States. (AP, 2/17/04)

March The Credit and Monetary Council authorizes private banks to sell currency on the market, a right previously reserved solely for the Commercial Bank of Syria. (SR, 2/04)

March 8 Human rights activists protest outside the Syrian parliament on the forty-first anniversary of the Ba'th Party's accession to power, demanding political and civil reforms and a lifting of the state of emergency. Ninety-eight people—including a few dozen protestors, journalists, and passers-by—are arrested but released later in the day. The U.S. State Department issues a strong diplomatic protest when one of its diplomats is detained for several hours after being picked up by security forces while monitoring the demonstration. (AP, 3/8/04; AFP, 3/10/04)

March 12 A riot breaks out in the predominantly Kurdish northeastern Syrian city of Qamishli, ignited by a clash between rival Kurdish and Arab soccer fans at a local stadium. Kurdish enclaves across the country soon erupt in protest and violence. At least twenty-five people are killed, many wounded, and hundreds jailed before the security services quell the unrest. A month after the riots, Defense Minister Mustafa Tlas is reported to have told the major Syrian Kurdish parties that 30,000 Kurds (and their offspring) deprived of their citizenship in the 1960s will recover it—an estimated total of 100,000 stateless individuals. (NYT, 3/25/04; SR, 3/04)

March 14 In an interview with *al-Hayat*, President Asad says that he is committed to reform, but that the road is long. He also acknowledges that "there will come a day when I will not be president." (*al-Hayat*, 3/14/04)

March 25–26 A meeting of EU foreign ministers in Brussels ends with the parties failing to reach a solution on Syria's opposition to the weapons of mass destruction provisions in its Euro-Mediterranean Association Agreement. The signing of the agreement is indefinitely postponed. (SR, 4/04)

April The Syrian Ministry of Oil and Mineral Resources announces that a joint Canadian-U.K.-U.S. consortium has been awarded an $800 million contract to develop extensive gas fields around Palmyra, beating out competitors from France and Japan. (SR, 4/04)

April 5 Syrian oil minister Ibrahim Haddad upgrades the estimate for Syria's future oil production. He says experts predict that the country will produce 300,000 barrels of oil daily for at least twenty years beyond 2012, the former estimated date of resource exhaustion. (*Elaph*, 4/5/04)

April 22 Aktham Nu'aysa, head of the Committees for the Defense of Democratic Liberties and Human Rights in Syria, is arrested and charged with "publishing false information that distorts the image of the state." He is released four months later reportedly for humanitarian reasons. (SR, 4/04; *RPS News*, 8/16/04)

April 25 Ghazi al-Dib is replaced by 'Adnan Mahmud as director general of SANA. (SANA, 4/25/04)

April 27 A mysterious armed attack on a former United Nations building takes place in the upscale Mezzeh district of Damascus. According to a later SANA report on the incident, the attack was perpetrated by a small fundamentalist group, led by a Syrian from al-Qunaytra province. The report also says the ringleader was an arms trafficker who had committed financial misdeeds in his hometown of Khan al-Shaykh and had fought alongside Islamist insurgents in Iraq. Two attackers, a policeman, and a woman passerby are killed in the attack. (SANA, 5/15/04)

May 11 President Bush issues an executive order implementing selected provisions of the Syria Accountability Act. The mostly symbolic law prohibits export of almost all items to Syria, bans flights between the United States and Syria, freezes the assets of Syrians with ties to terrorism, weapons of mass destruction, or the occupation of Lebanon, and orders American financial institutions to cut ties to the Commercial Bank of Syria. Prime Minister Naji al-'Utri immediately declares the sanctions "unjust and unjustified" and says they "will not have any affect on Syria." (NYT, 5/1//04; *al-Ra'i al-'am al-Kuwaytiyya*, 5/12/04)

May 11 President Asad decrees a 20 percent rise in civil servant salaries, the third such increase since he came to power. (SR, 5/04)

May 12 Defense Minister Mustafa Tlas retires on his seventy-third birthday, after thirty-two years in his post. Army chief of staff Hassan Turkmani, age sixty-nine, succeeds him. General 'Ali Habib takes over Turkmani's post. (AFP, 5/13/04)

May 13 Asad holds a rare press conference with American reporters in Damascus. Playing down the impact of the new U.S. sanctions, he stresses Syria's commitment to "dialogue." (AP, 5/13/04)

May 27 Prime Minister Naji al-'Utri and head of the State Planning Commission Abdallah al-Dardari announce that Syria has ended the expansion of its public sector and will now focus on reorganization and consolidation, as well as support for the private sector. (SR, 6/04)

June The National Progressive Front announces that its eight constituent parties have amended the charter that has guided the ruling coalition for thirty-two years and submitted the changes to President Asad for ratification. Most significantly, the NPF replaces the clause on "no peace or negotiations with the Zionist state" with a call for negotiations based on international resolutions, the land-for-peace formula, and the Madrid discussions. (*al-Sharq al-Awsat*, 6/15/04; SR, 7/04)

June 3 Syrian Military Intelligence informs Kurdish leaders that the activities of all unlicensed Kurdish parties are henceforth "banned." (AP, 6/3/04)

June 13 Syria signs a free-trade agreement with the Gulf Cooperation Council. (MENA, 6/13/03)

June 17 A Syrian government official announces the appointment and reassignment of at least a dozen ambassadors to key countries. Many of the new ambassadors are considered "technocratic" partisans of Bashar. (*al-Hayat*, 6/17/04)

June 20 "Radio Free Syria" (*sawt al-suriya al-hurr*), a "pro-democracy, grass-roots" station reaching most of the Arab world, is launched by the Reform Party of Syria. (www.radiofreesyria.org)

June 21 Scores of protestors gather at Arnous Square in Damascus for a sit-in called by eleven Syrian pro-democracy and human rights groups to mark "Syrian Political Prisoner Day." Riot police break up the protest, but, uncharacteristically, no arrests are made. (AP, 6/21/04)

June 21–24 President Asad embarks on the first visit by a Syrian head of state to China since the countries established diplomatic relations in 1956. In his remarks to the Chinese press, Asad praises China's development path and stresses the two countries' close relations, as well as his hope for greater coordination in the future. Seventy-five Syrian businessmen accompany the delegation, and cooperation agreements in a number of fields are signed. Asad provokes a controversy by leaving twelve hours before his scheduled departure, skipping a trip to Shanghai. Although Syrian officials claim personal reasons for the truncated visit, Asad may have been avoiding a possible meeting with Israeli deputy prime minister Ehud Olmert, already in Shanghai for a business conference. (AFP, 6/20/04; Chu Ming Wei TV, 6/22/04; SR, 7/04)

July A diplomatic crisis between Jordan and Syria erupts over problems along their disputed border region, after Jordanian security services arrest a number of arms smugglers bringing weapons from the Syrian side, and Syria impounds five Jordanian trucks and detains their Jordanian drivers, claiming they are carrying Israeli goods with forged documents. Without holding the Syrian government complicit, Jordan accuses elements of the Syrian security services of facilitating the infiltration of an alleged al-Qaeda cell that intended to bomb the Jordanian Intelligence Ministry in March, before the plot was thwarted by Jordanian security. In the ensuing months, Jordan begins to push the issue of their undemarcated border to the forefront, demanding that Syria return 125 kilometers of land it has occupied since the 1970s. (*al-Sharq al-Awsat*, 7/7/04; *al-Hayat*, 7/8/04; SANA, 7/29/04; *Daily Star*, 10/1/04)

July In an unpublicized but widely noticed move, Syria's state-run media are ordered to stop referring to members of the Ba'th Party as "comrade" (*rafiq*) and instead to use "Mr." (*sayyid*). The directive applies to SANA, *Tishrin*, and *al-Thawra*, while the party daily *al-Ba'th* continues to use the old designations. (*al-Hayat*, 7/7/04)

July The Syrian Ministry of Higher Education, in coordination with UNDP-Damascus and UNESCO, launches the Syrian Higher Education and Research Network, a project to connect Syrian universities via an intra/internet infrastructure and link them to the world research community. (SR, 7/04)

July 4–5 Asad visits Iran, accompanied by Vice President 'Abd al-Halim al-Khaddam and Foreign Minister Faruq al-Shar'. It is the president's third state visit to Iran and the first since the transfer of power to the fledging Iraqi government under Interim Prime Minister Iyad Allawi. (al-Bawaba, 7/4/04; SANA, 7/5/04)

July 15 The Syrian government grants the first operating license to an Islamic bank in Syria. The Qatar-Syria Islamic Bank is a joint project between the Syrian industrial conglomerate, the Daaboul Group, and the Qatar International Islamic Bank. (*al-Bayan*, 7/15/04)

July 15 President Asad issues a partial amnesty for prisoners serving sentences for economic and other minor crimes on the occasion of the fourth anniversary of his coming to power. Twenty-eight Islamist political prisoners—including many long-term detainees—are also released, along with some of the Kurds detained in the March 2004 riots. (ArabicNews.com, 7/21/04)

July 26 Iraqi interim prime minister Iyad Allawi visits Damascus and has a "fruitful and constructive" discussion with Asad. Border security issues dominate the discussion, and Syria expresses a willingness to resolve the issue of former Iraqi regime funds held in Syrian banks, but hints that it would not release the funds until "occupation forces" leave Iraq. Iraqi officials claim $800 million, but Syrian officials and private businessmen produce counterclaims for business conducted with Iraq prior to the toppling of the Saddam Hussein regime. Numerous trade and transport cooperation agreements are signed, as is a swap of Iraqi crude for Syrian oil products. Foreign Minister Faruq al-Shar' announces in a press conference with Arab media that the Iraqi government has a "legitimate aspect" deriving from the United Nations, and that Syria will "give it a chance." (*al-Safir*, 7/27/04; *al-Ba'th*, 7/27/04; *Oxford Business Group*, 7/27/04)

July 28 The European Union and Syria make the surprise announcement of a compromise on the language of the weapons of mass destruction clause in Syria's association agreement with the EU, apparently ending a seven-month deadlock. Each side claims a diplomatic victory. The agreement will not go into effect until the final text is signed by both parties. (*Daily Star*, 7/28/04)

August Human rights organizations in Syria report that over a period of two weeks, 251 political prisoners, many of them members of the Muslim Brotherhood, are released from prison. Several long-term detainees are released, including 'Imad Shiha of the banned Arab Communist Organization, who had been behind bars since 1975. (AFP, 8/4/04)

August 13 Lieutenant General Moshe Yaalon, chief of staff of the Israeli Army, says in an interview that Israel could safely give up the Golan Heights without compromising its security. (NYT, 8/14/04)

August 19 Syria confirms its accession to the UN Convention against Torture. (Amnesty International, 9/23/04)

August 27 For the first time, two Syrian newspapers (*Tishrin* and *al-Ba'th*) print news items that differ in content from the reports issued by the official news agency SANA. Both newspapers' stories present additional information and expand the context of the report issued by SANA. (*al-Ra'i al-'am al-Kuwaytiyya*, 8/27/04)

August 28 After Asad calls top Lebanese leaders to Damascus to discuss the Lebanese presidential election scheduled for November 2004, the Lebanese cabinet meets and agrees to amend the constitution to grant Lebanese president Emile Lahud a three-year extension. (UPI, 8/28/04; *Financial Times*, 8/30/04)

September Syria's ranking in the annual UN *Human Development Report* improves slightly, with most indicators remaining stable. Syria ranked 106 out of 177 countries, up from 110 the year before. (SR, 8/04, 9/04)

September The Central Bureau of Statistics conducts a nationwide census, which shows that the Syrian population has reached 17.79 million. The rate of population growth for the last decade has slowed to 2.58 percent, down from the 1981–94 rate of 3.3 percent. (SR, 12/04)

September 1 Shaykh Ahmed Kuftaro, grand mufti of Syria since 1964, dies at age eighty-nine. Some 50,000 people join his funeral procession. (SANA, 9/2/04)

September 1 After a suicide bombing kills sixteen in the Negev city of Beersheba, Israel threatens Syria with retaliation for allowing Hamas, the organization that claimed the attack, to operate in Damascus. (NYT, 9/1/04)

September 2 The UN Security Council, led by the United States and France, passes Resolution 1559, calling for "a free and fair electoral process" in Lebanon and the withdrawal of "all remaining foreign forces," and demanding a thirty-day review of progress toward these ends. The compromise resolution does not name Syria directly. (AP 9/2/04)

September 4 The leadership of Hamas is reported to have left Damascus under Syrian pressure. (*al-Sharq al-Awsat*, 9/4/04)

September 11 U.S. assistant secretary of state William Burns meets with Asad in Damascus to discuss Syria's interference in the Lebanese elections, the prospect of renewed peace negotiations with Israel, and U.S.-Syrian military cooperation on policing the Iraqi border. American military and security officials joined the delegation and met with their Syrian counterparts to discuss better border cooperation. (AFP, 9/11/04; AP, 9/12/04)

September 13 A measure is introduced in the U.S. House of Representatives to support the Syrian political opposition forces in order to "bring freedom and democracy to the people of Syria" and to end the Syrian occupation of Lebanon. (House Concurrent Resolution 363, 9/13/04).

September 13 The six Arab states of the Gulf Cooperation Council join Jordan in support for Resolution 1559, calling on Syria to respect the decision of the United Nations and comply with the provisions for withdrawal from Lebanon. (AP, 9/13/04)

September 20 The speaker of the Palestinian Legislative Council, Rawhi Fattuh, visits the speaker of the Syrian parliament, Mahmud al-Abrash, in Damascus. The meeting marks the first visit by an official Palestinian Authority delegation to Syria since 1996. A *Jerusalem Post* report on October 17 quotes a Palestinian official as saying: "We are closer than ever to restoring normal relations with Syria." The official cites a new willingness on the part of Damascus to host Palestinian officials and increased communications between Yasir Arafat and Asad. (SANA, 9/20/04; SR, 10/04; *Jerusalem Post*, 10/17/04)

September 21 Syria begins a "comprehensive redeployment" in Lebanon. It is the fifth major redeployment of Syrian troops in Lebanon since Bashar took power. Some 3,000 soldiers are removed from Lebanon over several days, leaving approximately 15,000 stationed mainly in the eastern Biqa'a Valley. (AP, 9/28/04)

September 25 Iraq announces it will be the fifth country to join the Arab Gas Pipeline project. The pipeline originates in Egypt and is already bringing gas into Jordan. Construction for the Syria and Lebanon leg of the network is scheduled to begin in 2005, and Iraq will be brought into the system at a later date. The network will eventually be extended to Turkey and Europe. (AP, 9/25/04)

September 26 Rifa't al-Asad, brother of Hafiz and one-time vice-president and challenger for rule of Syria, reportedly returns from exile to Syria. (*Akhbar al-Sharq*, 9/26/04)

September 26 An official in the Palestinian militant organization Hamas is killed in a car bombing at his residence in Damascus. The assassination comes after repeated warnings by Israeli officials that they will target Palestinian terrorists wherever they reside. (NYT, 9/27/04)

October Syria enters into talks with the European Free Trade Association (EFTA), the largest grouping of European countries outside the EU. The negotiations are expected to lead to the signing of a free-trade agreement between the EFTA and Syria. (SR, 10/04)

October As a consequence of the Syria Accountability Act ban on U.S. financial dealings with the Commercial Bank of Syria, Western Union cuts off its contract with the bank in Syria. Western Union expands its network to deal with several newly established private banks in Syria, whereas it had previously dealt solely with the government bank. (SR, 10/04)

October The Amman-based Arab Bank receives approval to become the fifth licensed private bank in Syria. The bank, which has a large regional presence, previously had a branch in Syria, but it was nationalized in the early 1960s. (SR, 10/04)

October 1 UN secretary general Kofi Annan issues his report on UN Security Council Resolution 1559. Annan singles out the Syrian military by name as "the only significant foreign forces deployed in Lebanon." The report also cites Syria's admission of "a substantial presence of non-uniformed military intelligence officials" in Lebanon and acknowledges the Syrian and Lebanese argument that further withdrawals of Syrian troops are dependent on "the security situation in Lebanon and the region and through the joint military committee established pursuant to the Taif Agreement." Annan concludes that he "cannot certify that [the] requirements [set forth in UNSCR 1559] have been met."

October 4 Asad reshuffles his cabinet, naming former Lebanon security chief Ghazi Kana'an the new interior minister, and Mehdi Dakhlallah, reformist Ba'thist and editor-in-chief of the party newspaper *al-Ba'th*, the new minister of information. Eight ministries in all are reshuffled, but Prime Minster Naji al-'Utri retains his position. (*al-Safir* 10/5/04)

October 9 Asad delivers a defiant speech aired on Syrian television at the inauguration of the Syrian Expatriates Conference, accusing the United Nations of "double standards" for acquiescing to the U.S.-France-led Resolution 1559. He says that recent events threaten to return "Lebanon back to the atmosphere of the 1980s" and calls the resolution a "flagrant interference in the affairs of Lebanon." Asad also denies "Syrian hegemony" in Lebanon and says Syria is "in the heart of a volcano," but he affirms his nation's commitment to "a just peace, based on UN resolutions and the land-for-peace principle." (Syrian TV, 10/9/04)

October 11 The opposition newsletter *Akhbar al-Sharq* reports that Asad promised newly appointed interior minister Ghazi Kanaʿan that he would be permitted to unite the various security and intelligence services under his sole command. Later in the month the same sources report that the "restructuring" of the Syrian *mukhabarat* is taking place "bit by bit," citing the interior ministry's resumption of effective control of the political security department as a first step. The sources also posit that the unification of the security services under the interior ministry was a tacit demand made by the European Union as a quid pro quo for the signing of the EU-Syria Association Agreement. (*Akhbar al-Sharq*, 10/11/04, 10/18/04; *Elaph*, 10/23/04)

October 12 Iraqi diplomatic sources rule out a resumption of diplomatic ties with Damascus until after the Iraqi elections scheduled for January 2005, citing "political and procedural reasons." Because it was Iraq who severed ties with Syria in 1979, it is necessary for the Iraqi government to petition Syria to resume normal relations, a process that will take several months, according to the sources. (*al-Hayat*, 10/12/04)

October 13 The state-run daily *al-Thawra* publishes an editorial encouraging journalists to break free of the tradition of uncritical reportage. Author Asʿad Abbud writes: "Report the news boldly and transparently. Abandon the usual style. President Bashar al-Asad is planning to open the doors for you." (*al-Thawra*, 10/13/04)

October 13 The ruling National Progressive Front coalition, now consisting of nine parties led by the Baʿth, amends its charter for the first time since 1972. Among other revisions, the expression "no peace and no negotiation with the Zionist state" is stricken from the charter and replaced with a call for "peace based on international legitimacy, United Nations resolutions, the return of the refugees, and the setting up of an independent [Palestinian] state whose capital is Jerusalem." (*Akhbar al-Sharq*, 10/13/04; *al-Hayat*, 10/14/04)

October 14 A two-week meeting of the Syrian-Jordanian Security Commission ends without reaching a final solution to their long-running border dispute. Both sides agree that "demographic difficulties" make a solution difficult to formulate "overnight," but say they remain committed to respecting the rights and interests of scattered Syrian and Jordanian families residing along the official border. The parties agree that the 1923 border drawn by France and Britain will be reinstated in full, which obliges Syria to return 125 square kilometers of territory and Jordan 2.5. In November, a joint commission appeared to reach a final agreement on a permanent border demarcation. In return for the annexation by Syria of Jordanian territory that has been populated by Syrian farmers, Syria will swap an equivalent amount of uninhabited territory in a neighboring region. (*al-Safir*, 10/14/04; *al-Dustur*, 10/15/04; SANA, 11/23/04; *al-'Arab al-Yom*, 10/24/04)

October 19 The European Union and Syria initial the text of their association agreement, making Syria the last Mediterranean country since the "Barcelona Process" was launched in 1995 to finalize an agreement to set up a "Euro-Mediterranean" zone of free-trade by 2010. The agreement must still be formally signed by the two parties and ratified by each EU member country's parliament before it becomes law. A special clause will allow the agreement to go into effect as soon as it is officially signed, which is expected to happen in January 2005. The agreement is welcomed by the party mouthpiece *al-Ba'th*: "By signing the partnership with Europe, Syria confirms the EU's role in settling problems of development in the region and of policy linked to the Israeli-Arab conflict." (AFP, 10/19/04; SR, 11/04)

October 20 The UN Security Council unanimously issues a Presidential Statement reaffirming Resolution 1559's call for Syria to withdraw from Lebanon and requesting semiannual reports on compliance by the two countries. Like 1559, the statement does not mention Syria by name. (*Daily Star*, 10/20/04)

October 24 Syrian officials open a registry to track citizens of the Golan city of Qunaytra—depopulated since the 1967 war—in preparation for an effort to repopulate and rebuild the town. Officials say the project is a sign that they have no intention of resorting to military means to recover the Israeli-occupied Golan. (*Ha'aretz*, 10/24/04)

October 27 U.S. under secretary of state John Bolton, the top U.S. envoy for arms control, names Syria, Iran, and North Korea "states of proliferation concern." Speaking in Japan while on a trip to observe multinational exercises as part of the Proliferation Security Initiative, Bolton says partners in the initiative "should be ready to scrutinize shipments going to or from such states or terrorist groups." (AP, 10/27/04)

November Another state-controlled economic sector is opened to gradual liberalization as Lebanon's UFA Assurances becomes the first licensed private insurance carrier to operate in Syria in forty years. Although many private foreign insurance carriers operate in Syria without license or regulation, the state-owned Syrian Insurance Company was previously the sole legitimate carrier. (SR, 11/1/04)

November The head of Syria's General Free Trade Zones authority announces plans to build thirteen new duty-free markets at Syria's border posts. The authority has already granted operating licenses to six individual Syrian investors and a Turkish-Syrian company. Before this decision, all duty-free markets in Syria had been operated by one company (RAMAK), owned by Bashar's cousin Rami Makhluf. (SR, 11/1/04)

November 4 Bashar orders 50 percent bonuses on one month's salary to be paid to civil servants in celebration of 'Eid al-Fitr, the end of the Ramadan holy month. (AP, 11/4/04)

November 8 Iraqi foreign minister Hoshyar Zibari says that Syria has agreed to restore full diplomatic relations with Iraq. He also reports that Syria has accommodated Iraqi requests on coordinating border security. (al-Sharqiyya TV Iraq, 11/8/04)

November 20 Asif Shawkat is elevated to second-in-command of Syrian Military Intelligence (SMI). Shawkat will reportedly take over the position of his superior, SMI director Hassan al-Khalil, upon al-Khalil's retirement in 2005. (*Akhbar al-Sharq*, 11/20/04)

November 30 A delegation claiming to represent seventy Iraqi parties backing a boycott of the Iraqi elections scheduled for January 30 leaves for Damascus, its first stop in a tour of Arab states. The delegation intends to drum up international support for its position and includes Muthanna Harith al-Dari of the Association of Muslim Scholars and the spokesman of Moqtada al-Sadr in Baghdad. (*al-Hayat*, 11/30/04)

November 30 Supporters of the Lebanese government and Syria rally in Beirut against UN Resolution 1559. The Lebanese branch of the Syrian Ba'th party organized the rally, with the backing of the Lebanese government and Hizballah, to counter the image that Syria's presence in Lebanon is opposed by the Lebanese public. The organizers aimed to bring 1 million of Lebanon's 3.5 million people to the streets, but only an estimated tens of thousands join the demonstration. (*Financial Times*, 12/1/04)

December Syria's 2005 draft budget figures are released, showing a 2.2 percent increase from the 2004 budget, to $9.2 billion. (SR, 12/1/04)

December Syria settles its Soviet-era debt with Slovakia and the Czech Republic (previously united as the Soviet bloc country Czechoslovakia). Syria will make a one-time payment of $150 million, approximately 9 percent of the $1.6 billion it owed, in return for debt forgiveness on the remaining balance. (SR, 12/1/04)

December 1 Israel declines Syria's latest offer to resume peace negotiations, publicized the previous week by UN Middle East envoy Terje Roed-Larsen. Israeli Foreign Minister Silvan Shalom tells the press that Israel will not establish contacts with the Syrians until Syria drops its support for Hamas and Hizballah. (AFP, 12/1/04)

December 2 A leaked Israeli government report by National Security Council chief Giora Eiland to Prime Minister Ariel Sharon argues that Israel's interests would not be served by a Syrian withdrawal from Lebanon. Eiland warns that such a pullout could lead to a "warming up" of the situation in the occupied Golan. (*Daily Star*, 12/2/04)

December 5 Tens of thousands gather at the residence of Walid Jumblatt, the most prominent Druze member in the Lebanese parliament, to show their support for his opposition stance and his steadfast call for a Syrian withdrawal from Lebanon. Jumblatt opposed the extension of Lebanese president Emile Lahud's presidential term in September and blamed Syria for imposing its will on the Lebanese government. (*Daily Star*, 12/6/04)

December 7 The Syrian government releases 112 political prisoners, the first such release in three years. Haytham al-Maleh of the Syrian Human Rights Association welcomes the move but calls on the regime to release what he estimates are 320 remaining political detainees. (AP, 12/8/04)

December 8 A global positioning signal receiver discovered in a bomb factory in the former Iraqi insurgent stronghold of Fallujah is reported to have "contained waypoints originating in Western Syria." U.S. officials say this discovery indicates that Iraqi Ba'thists based in Syria have a greater role in directing the insurgency than was previously assumed. (WP, 12/8/04)

December 10 A U.S. Central Command official tells al-Arabiyya television that Syria has undertaken "significant work in terms of building barricades and exchanging intelligence information . . . to tighten control along the Syrian-Iraqi border." However, Syria has not been cooperative enough in rooting out "facilitators" of the Iraqi insurgency residing in Syria. (al-Arabiyya TV, 12/10/04)

December 14 Syria accuses Israel of responsibility for a car bomb that targeted a Hamas member residing in Damascus. The intended target escaped unharmed, but a passerby was wounded. (*Ha'aretz*, 12/14/04)

December 17 Jamil al-Asad, Hafiz al-Asad's youngest brother, dies at age seventy-one in a hospital in Paris. In recent years, he had led the national security committee in the Syrian parliament, but he had not played a significant political role. (*Los Angeles Times*, 12/17/04)

December 18 For the first time since its occupation of the country in 1976, Syria withdraws intelligence contingents from positions in Lebanon. Although no numbers are given, security detachments are removed from Beirut International Airport, the southern suburbs of Beirut, and the northern coastal city of al-Batrun. (*al-Nahar*, 12/19/04)

December 22 Syria and Turkey sign a free-trade agreement during Turkish prime minister Recep Tayyip Erdogan's first visit to Damascus, building on a rapprochement that began with Bashar's historic visit to Turkey in January 2004. (SR, 1/1/05)

December 23 The Iraqi ambassador to Syria tells the press that interim Iraqi prime minister Iyad Allawi informed the Syrian government that photographs of the leader of the insurgent group Jaysh Mohammed standing with a Syrian official were found in the former insurgent stronghold in Fallujah. (CSM, 12/23/04)

December 24 Israeli and Syrian officials agree to allow Druze inhabitants of the occupied Golan to sell their apple crops in Syria. Israeli foreign minister Silvan Shalom says that the agreement comes in the context of mutual confidence-building measures between the two sides. Opposition to the trade had previously come from the Israeli side. (*Jerusalem Post*, 12/24/04)

December 29 Ahead of a visit by U.S. officials to Damascus scheduled for January 2, the Syrian government reportedly returns $3.5 million to the Iraqi government. The funds are paid out from those held by the former regime of Saddam Hussein in Syrian banks. (*al-Hayat*, 12/29/04)

December 30 A state security court sentences twenty-two Syrians charged with plotting the April 27 attacks in the Mezzeh district of Damascus. Two are sentenced to death and two others are given life terms with hard labor; the remainder receive terms of between one and twenty years in jail. One of those condemned to death, Ahmed Shlash Hassan, explains his motivation: "I was trying to respond to the aggression against Muslims of oppressive states like Israel, the United States and all other infidel countries." (AFP, 12/30/04)

Sources

English-language newspapers and news agencies

Associated Press (AP)

International Herald Tribune

Agence France-Presse (AFP)

Jerusalem Post

Christian Science Monitor (CSM)

Los Angeles Times

Daily Star, Beirut

New York Times (NYT)

Daily Telegraph, London

Oil Daily, New York

Financial Times, London

United Press International (UPI)

Gulf News, United Arab Emirates

Washington Post (WP)

Ha'aretz, Tel Aviv

Washington Times

English-language bulletins, digests, magazines, books, and web publications

Al-Bawaba,Amman, Jordan
  (www.albawaba.com)

Amnesty International, London
  (www.amnesty.org)

ArabicNews.com, U.S.

Alan George, *Syria, Neither Bread Nor Freedom* (London: Zed Books, 2003)

Human Rights Watch, New York
  (www.hrw.org)

Middle East Economic Digest, London
  (MEED, www.meed.com)

Middle East Intelligence Bulletin, published by the United States Committee for a Free Lebanon and Middle East Forum, New York
  (www.meib.org)

Middle East International, London
  (www.meionline.com)

Middle East News Agency, Cairo
  (MENA, www.mena.org.eg)

Mideast Mirror, London
  (www.mideastmirror.com)

MidEastWeb.com, Israel

New Yorker (www.newyorker.com)

Oxford Business Group, London
  (www.oxfordbusinessgroup.com)

Petroleum Intelligence Weekly, New York (www.energyintel.com)

RPS News, published by the Reform Party of Syria, Washington, D.C. (www.reformsyria.org)

SyriaLive.net, Ontario and Syria

Syria Report, published by the Middle East Information and Communication Agency, Paris (SR, www.syria-report.com)

Eyal Zisser, "A False Spring in Damascus," *Orient* 44, no. 1 (2003)

Eyal Zisser, "Does Bashar al-Asad Rule Syria?" *Middle East Quarterly,* Winter 2003.

Arabic-language newspapers and news agencies

Damascus
  al-Ba'th
  al-Thawra
  Tishrin
  Syrian Arab News Agency (SANA)
Amman
  al-Dustur
  al-'Arab al-Yom
Beirut
  al-Safir
  al-Nahar

London
  Akhbar al-Sharq
  al-Hayat
  al-Quds al-'Arabi
  al-Sharq al-Awsat
  Elaph (based in Surrey)
Gulf States
  al-Ra'i al-'am al-Kuwaytiyya (Kuwait)
  al-Anbaa (Kuwait)
  al-Jazeera (Qatar)
  al-Bayan (United Arab Emirates)

Various foreign radio and television broadcasts obtained in translation from Lexis-Nexis.

The Statement of 99
and the Statement of 1,000

The Statement of 99
Published on September 27, 2000

*The Statement of 99 was the first widely recognized public manifestation of Syria's
nascent civil society movement after the death of Hafiz al-Asad in June 2000.
Published in September of that year, just two months after Bashar al-Asad's inauguration as president, its signatories include prominent intellectuals, artists, and
professionals. The Statement of 99 argues passionately for long overdue administrative, economic, and legal reforms. Although it contends that political reforms
are a necessary complement to revive the nation, it does not criticize directly either
Bashar or the Ba'th Party's leadership of the government. The Statement of 99
marked the blooming of the "Damascus Spring," a season of relaxed regime restrictions on free expression and criticism.*

Democracy and human rights today constitute a common humanitarian language, gathering peoples and uniting their hopes for a better future. And even
if some major countries use these to promote their policies and interests, interaction among peoples need not result in domination and political dictation. It
was permitted to our people in the past, and it will be permitted to them in the
future, to be influenced by the experiences of others, and to add to their own

Note: The source for The Statement of 99 is *al-Hayat*, September 27, 2000. Translated
text used with permission of Zed Books (spelling conventions have been Americanized).
Extract from Alan George, *Syria: Neither Bread Nor Freedom* (London: Zed Books, 2003).
All rights reserved to publisher.

contribution, thereby developing their distinctiveness without being closed-in themselves.

Syria today enters the twenty-first century in urgent need for all its citizens to join forces to face the challenges posed by peace, modernization and the opening-up to the outside world. And for this our people are invited more than ever before to participate in the construction of Syria's present and future.

From this objective need, and from concern for our national unity, believing that the future of our country cannot be built by its offspring, being citizens in a republican system where everybody has the right to freedom of opinion and of expression, we, the undersigned, call upon the authorities to accede to the following demands:

—an end to the State of Emergency and martial law in effect in Syria since 1963

—an amnesty for all political prisoners and prisoners of conscience and those who are pursued because of their political ideas and allowing the return of all deportees and exiled citizens

—the establishment of a state of law; the granting of public freedoms; the recognition of political and intellectual pluralism, freedom of assembly, the press and of expression

—the liberation of public life from the [restrictive] laws, constraints and [various] forms of censorship imposed on it, such that citizens would be allowed to express their various interests within a framework of social harmony, peaceful competition and an institutional structure that would enable all to participate in the country's development and prosperity

No reform, be it economic, administrative or legal, will achieve tranquility and stability in the country unless fully accompanied by the desired political reform, which alone can steer our society towards safe shores.

Signatories

1. Abdul Hadi Abbas (lawyer and writer)
2. Abdul Mu'in al-Mallouhi (member of the Arabic Language Academy)
3. Antoun al-Maqdisi (writer and thinker)
4. Burhan Ghalyoun (writer and thinker)
5. Sadiq Jalal al-Azm (writer and thinker)
6. Michel Kilo (writer)
7. Tayeb Tayzini (writer and thinker)
8. Abdul Rahman Mounif (novelist)
9. Adonis (poet)
10. Burhan Bukhari (researcher)

11. Hanna Aboud (writer)
12. Omar Amiralay (cinematographer)
13. Khalid Taja (actor)
14. Bassam Kousa (actor)
15. Naila al-Atrash (theater producter)
16. Abdullah Hannah (researcher/historian)
17. Samir Suaifan (economist)
18. Faisal Darraj (researcher)
19. Haidar Haidar (novelist)
20. Nazih Abu 'Afsh (poet)
21. Hasan M. Yousef (novelist/journalist)
22. Usama Muhammad (cinematographer)
23. Nabil Suleiman (novelist/critic)
24. Abdul Razzak 'Eid (researcher/critic)
25. Jad al-Karim Jaba'i (writer/researcher)
26. Abdul Latif Abdul Hamid (cinematographer)
27. Samir Zikra (cinematographer)
28. Ahmad Mu'allah (artist)
29. Fares al-Hellou (actor)
30. Ihsan Abbas (researcher)
31. Hanan Kassab Hassan (university professor)
32. Mamdouh Azzam (novelist)
33. Adel Mahmoud (poet)
34. Hazem al-Azmeh (physician and university professor)
35. Burhan Zraik (lawyer)
36. Muhammad Ra'adoun (lawyer)
37. Yasser Sari (lawyer)
38. Yousef Salman (translator)
39. Hind Midani (cinematographer)
40. Munzir Masri (poet/artist)
41. Ahmad Mu'aitah (university professor)
42. Wafiq Slaitin (university professor)
43. Mujab al-Imam (university professor)
44. Munzir Halloum (university professor)
45. Malik Suleiman (university professor)
46. Sarab Jamal al-Atassi (researcher)
47. Toufiq Haroun (lawyer)
48. Issam Suleiman (physician)
49. Joseph Lahham (lawyer)
50. Attiyah Massouh (researcher)
51. Radwan Kadmani (university professor)
52. Nizar Sabour (artist)
53. Shouaib Tlaimat (university professor)
54. Hassan Sami Youssef (cinematographer/writer)
55. Waha ar-Raheb (cinematographer/actress)
56. Hamid Mer'i (economic consultant)
57. Rif'at as-Sioufi (engineer)
58. Muwafaq Nirbiya (writer)
59. Suheil Shabat (university professor)
60. Jamal Shuhaid (university professor)
61. Omar Koch (writer)
62. Raymond Butros (cinematographer)

63. Antoinette Azriyeh (cinematographer)
64. Najib Nussair (critic/writer)
65. May Skaff (actress)
66. Nidal ad-Dibs (cinematographer)
67. Farah Jukhdar (architect)
68. Akram Katreeb (poet)
69. Lukman Dabraki (poet)
70. Hikmat Shatta (architect)
71. Muhammad Najati Tayyara (researcher)
72. Najmeddine as-Samman (novelist)
73. Ali as-Saleh (economist/researcher)
74. Sabah al-Hallak (researcher)
75. Nawal al-Yazji (researcher)
76. Muhammad Karsaly (cinematographer)
77. Sawsan Zakzak (researcher)
78. Shawki Baghdadi (poet)
79. Bashar Zarkan (musician)
80. Fayez Sarah (journalist)
81. Muhammad al-Fahd (journalist/poet)
82. Muhammad Berri La'awani (theater producer)
83. Najat Amoudi (educator)
84. Adel Zakkar (physician/poet)
85. Mustafa Khodr (poet)
86. Muhammad Sayed Rassas (writer)
87. Kassem Azzawi (poet)
88. Muhammad Hamdan (writer)
89. Nabil al-Yafi (researcher)
90. Tamim Mun'im (lawyer)
91. Ibrahim Hakim (lawyer)
92. Anwar al-Bunni (lawyer)
93. Khalil Ma'atouk (lawyer)
94. Ali al-Jundi (poet)
95. Ali Kanaan (poet)
96. Muhammad Kamal al-Khatib (researcher)
97. Mamdouh Adwan (poet)
98. Muhammad Malass (cinematographer)
99. Muhammad Ali al-Atassi (journalist)

The Statement of 1,000 or Basic Document
Released to the Arab Press on January 9, 2001

The Statement of 1,000 was a follow-up to the Statement of 99, but the reform pre-scription it was to advocate was heatedly debated by the civil activists who drafted it. The document was leaked to the Lebanese press before all the intended signato-ries had approved the final text. Reprising the call for reforms of the Statement of 99, but couched in loftier rhetoric, the Statement of 1,000 goes far beyond previ-ous demands with its call for the replacement of one-party rule by a multiparty democracy. Its publication was one of the triggers that prompted the "Damascus Winter" crackdown on civil society activists by the regime.

Syria needs today, more than ever before, an objective reflection to draw lessons from the last decades and to shape its future, following the deterioration of its social, political, economic and cultural conditions, and in response to the chal-lenges of globalization and economic integration and the challenges of the Arab-Israeli conflict that our people and nation must confront and whose dan-gers they must repel.

Arising from a sincere faith in our country, in our people and in their cre-ative capacities and vitality, and keen to interact positively with all serious ini-tiatives for reform, [we assert that] it is vital today to establish a comprehensive dialogue between all citizens and all social classes and political forces, intellec-tuals and producers and creative people, in order to encourage the development of civil society—a society based on individual freedom, human rights and citi-zenship; and the establishment of a state of justice and rights, a state for all its people, without favor or exception, in which all can take pride. Our country today needs the efforts of all our citizens to revive civil society, whose weakness, and the attempts to weaken it, over the last decades deprived the country's de-velopment and construction process of crucial national capacities that were unable to participate in it actively and positively.

Ambiguity surrounding the meaning of civil society, resulting from multiple democratic experiments in ancient and modern history, negates neither its exis-tence in our country nor its halting progression into a modern society which produced a vibrant culture, a free press, associations, political parties, trade unions and constitutional legitimacy and a peaceful transfer of power. These made Syria one of the least backward—if not the most advanced—of Arab countries.

This path enhanced our society's national cohesion, until the sudden arrival of that interruption based on 'revolutionary legitimacy' rather than constitutional legitimacy. Marginalizing civil society involved disregarding the state, the individual and his position, painting the state with one party, one color and one opinion. It involved creating a state for one part of a society, a part which did not acknowledge its particularity but portrayed itself as representing the people and as 'leading the state and society.' Citizenship was reduced to the narrow concept of belonging to one party and to personal loyalty. This part of society considered the rest of the population as a mere herd. The wealth of the state and of its institutions, the country's resources and those of the institutions of civil society, became like feudal estates that were distributed to followers and loyalists. Patronage replaced law; gifts and favors replaced rights; and personal interests replaced the general interest. Society was desecrated, its wealth plundered and its destiny commandeered by those who became symbols of oppression. Every citizen became a suspect, if not actually considered guilty, to be apprehended at will. The regime treated people not only as a neglected mass, subject to its will, but also as minor, incompetent and under suspicion. The government went so far as to accuse people of treason whenever they took the smallest initiative to express their opinion or demand their rights. It should be mentioned that marginalizing civil society led to marginalizing the state itself, underlining the organic relationship between them as neither exists without the other. Civil society constitutes the very substance of the modern state, while the state is civil society's political expression. Together, they constitute the democratic system of government.

Our society, with its national revolutions against colonialism and its political movement against political oppression; and which revealed its patriotic and nationalist spirit, eager for liberation and progress; which has been patient and has given many martyrs and sacrifices for freedom and justice, is still capable of rebuilding its social and political life; of rebuilding its economy and culture according to the requirements of modernity and development. It is still capable of joining the march of scientific and technological progress, and can overcome the relationships and structures that produce tyranny and that are intimately linked to the imperialism and national fragmentation that were their cause.

The consequences of coups against political democracy in the name of socialism are now plain. With the collapse of the Soviet model and its East European and Third World extensions, the impossibility of building socialism or establishing social democracy without political democracy became obvious. The Soviet experience also demonstrated the fragility of a state that does not draw its legitimacy from civil society, and of an authority that does not draw its legitimacy from the people. Equally plain is the inadequacy of viewing the people as mere subjects of 'revolutionary will,' and of denying the social, cultural and political diversity of a society and the different interests of each of its component parts. The Soviet experience underlined the consequences of denying that rule of law—as a judicial expression of public order and of the essence of the state itself, as well as expression of all that is common between all citizens and social groups—is an historic compromise between all those interests and diverse groups that should be the basis for genuine national unity.

It is this historic compromise which creates constitutions and laws that are in line with the development of society, which itself is affected by the pace of global development. Constitutions are therefore usually modified, changed and improved according to the needs of that development. The concept of civil society in the world to which we belong—geographically at least—that was revived in the 1970s, represented, and still represents, the reality of societal existence, the latter being defined by the transition of mankind from Nature to society, that is, to human construction and civil politics, to use the expression of [the medieval Arab historian] Ibn Khaldoun. From this concept arose an array of concepts leading to a 'social covenant' as opposed to the 'divine right' claimed by dictators, kings and emperors. The development of this social covenant is nothing more that the political counterpart of the triumph of reason which placed the human being at the center of human knowledge. Modern societies and modern thinking gave rise to the modern civil state that guarantees freedom of belief and religious practice and unrestrained thought—all within the framework of acknowledging, in practice, a freedom defined by law, conditioned by responsibility and crowned by the creative initiative, love of knowledge and [the spirit of] working with and for the wider group.

For all these reasons there is a great need today to revive societal and social institutions free of domination by the executive authority and by the security apparatus, which usurped full powers. These institutions should also be free of all traditional forms of social ties, relationships and structures, such as those of tribalism and sectarianism, in order to re-establish politics in society as its primary free, conscious and constructive activity, and to achieve the crucial balance between society and state, co-ordinating their activities and thus achieving liberty, equality and justice. National unity is thus bolstered, as is the dignity and sovereignty of the state. The rule of law becomes the final arbiter for all.

Only in civil society can a comprehensive national dialogue characterized by freedom of expression and speech and respect for diverse opinions be conducted, in order to encourage mass participation for the benefit of all the people. No social or political group has the right to decide by itself where the country's national interests lie, and what means should be pursued to achieve those interests. All groups—including the present ruling power—must make their opinions, ideas and programs known to the people for discussion and dialogue. No dialogue is possible without freedom of opinion and expression, free political parties and trade unions, a free press, free social organizations and a legislature that genuinely and effectively represents the people.

No reform is possible without a comprehensive national dialogue because dialogue always produces new facts that are relevant to all. The logic of dialogue negates that of holding a monopoly on truth, patriotism, or any other monopoly. That is why we are calling for the adoption of the principle of dialogue, constructive criticism and peaceful development to resolve all disagreements through compromise and understanding. This is one of the most important characteristics and advantages of civil society.

The vitality of civil society is strikingly manifested in the establishment of voluntary, independent, non-governmental organizations based on democratic choice, whose objective is the establishment of justice and the rule of law that ensures civil rights and protects general liberties. That is why we believe that in defending civil society we defend the state and the authority holding power in that state.

For economic reforms and anti-corruption measures to succeed, they must be preceded and accompanied by a comprehensive package of political and constitutional reforms. Otherwise these reforms will not achieve their objectives. The economic and anti-corruption reform process therefore must develop into a permanent legal mechanism that stimulates public participation and encourages a continuous monitoring of state institutions as well as the private sector. All this should be done in an atmosphere of transparency that offers all social groups and forces and political parties the opportunity to participate effectively in the processes of planning, preparation, implementation and correction. It will also enable them to identify mistakes, waste and corruption promptly, as well as enabling the judicial system and supervisory bodies to call miscreants to account. Partial and selective measures will not lead to reform.

Our philosophy and practice consider that:

—human beings are aims unto themselves

—freedom, dignity, welfare and happiness are the purpose of development and progress

—national unity and the general interest are yardsticks for all policies and practices

—all citizens are equal before the law, since inequality always creates those who are privileged and those who are deprived of all rights, thus sowing the seeds of discrimination and disunity and degrading social relations to sub-political levels

The foundations of our philosophy and practice are that:

—the correct practice of politics is that based on patriotic, national and human interest rather than on private interests

—national achievements are attributable to the people, not to individuals

—social groups and political parties are defined by the entire national social entity

—the people are the sources of all powers

We therefore believe that political reform is the necessary and only way out of the current state of stagnation and decline, and the only way of extricating the general administration from its chronic torpor. We believe, furthermore, that the following must be implemented urgently as necessary preludes to political reform:

1. Abrogation of the Emergency Law now in force. Martial law regulations, emergency courts and all similar measures must be cancelled forthwith, and all injustices they caused over the years remedied. Political prisoners must be released, and the situation of those deprived of civil and labor rights by special courts and laws must be rectified. Exiles must be allowed to return.

2. Political freedoms—especially freedom of opinion and expression—must be allowed. Civil and political life must be overseen by democratic legislation regulating activities of political parties, associations and non-governmental organizations—especially the trade unions which, through their conversion into state institutions, have lost partly or entirely the very reasons for their establishment.

3. Reinstatement of the publications law ensuring freedom of the press that was annulled by the State of Emergency.

4. Enactment of a democratic election law to regulate elections at all levels in a way that ensures all segments of society are represented fairly, and the electoral process should be subjected to the supervision of an independent judiciary. The parliament elected as the result of this process will be a genuine legislative and

supervisory institution, truly representing the will of the people, acting as the highest authoritative reference for all and symbolizing the people's membership in the country and their positive participation in deciding how it is governed. The wholeness of the state is never expressed more clearly than by the legislative institution and by the independence and integrity of the judiciary.

5. Independence and integrity of the judiciary with laws applied equally to rulers and ruled.

6. Ensuring that citizens are accorded their full economic rights, most of which are stated in the Constitution. The most important of their constitutionally guaranteed rights are (i) a fair share of national wealth and income; (ii) suitable employment and a life of dignity; and (iii) protecting the right of future generations of their fair share of the country's wealth and to a clean environment. Economic and social development are senseless if they are not aimed at erasing injustice, humanizing conditions of work and life and countering unemployment and poverty.

7. Insisting that the parties affiliated to the Progressive National Front (PNF) truly represent the most vibrant forces in Syrian society; that they by themselves today fill the vacuum of Syrian politics; and that the country needs nothing more than the reinvigoration of the PNF will serve only to perpetuate further the social and economic stagnation and political paralysis. It is imperative to review the relationship of the PNF with the government, to reconsider the concept of 'the leading party in society and the state,' and to review any other concept that excludes the people from political life.

8. Abolition of legal discrimination against women.

Stemming from a desire to participate constructively in the process of social development and reform, we call for the establishment of committees for reviving civil society in all sectors of Syrian life as a continuation and development of the concept of the 'friends of civil society.' From a sense of national responsibility and independence, we hope that these committees will play their part in overcoming the negativity and demoralization, and [enabling Syria to] emerge from the stagnation that doubles our backwardness in relation to the pace of international development. Through these committees, we hope to take the step to a free, independent and democratic society that takes part in laying the foundations for a renaissance that will ensure a better future for the Arab nation.

UN Security Council Resolution 1559

Adopted by the Security Council at its 5028th meeting, on 2 September 2004

The Security Council,

Recalling all its previous resolutions on Lebanon, in particular resolutions 425 (1978) and 426 (1978) of 19 March 1978, resolution 520 (1982) of 17 September 1982, and resolution 1553 (2004) of 29 July 2004 as well as the statements of its President on the situation in Lebanon, in particular the statement of 18 June 2000 (S/PRST/2000/21),

Reiterating its strong support for the territorial integrity, sovereignty and political independence of Lebanon within its internationally recognized borders,

Noting the determination of Lebanon to ensure the withdrawal of all non-Lebanese forces from Lebanon,

Gravely concerned at the continued presence of armed militias in Lebanon, which prevent the Lebanese Government from exercising its full sovereignty over all Lebanese territory,

Reaffirming the importance of the extension of the control of the Government of Lebanon over all Lebanese territory,

Mindful of the upcoming Lebanese presidential elections and underlining the importance of free and fair elections according to Lebanese constitutional rules devised without foreign interference or influence,

1. *Reaffirms* its call for the strict respect of the sovereignty, territorial integrity, unity, and political independence of Lebanon under the sole and exclusive authority of the Government of Lebanon throughout Lebanon;

2. *Calls upon* all remaining foreign forces to withdraw from Lebanon;

3. *Calls for* the disbanding and disarmament of all Lebanese and non-Lebanese militias;

4. *Supports* the extension of the control of the Government of Lebanon over-all Lebanese territory;

5. *Declares* its support for a free and fair electoral process in Lebanon's upcoming presidential election conducted according to Lebanese constitutional rules devised without foreign interference or influence;

6. *Calls upon* all parties concerned to cooperate fully and urgently with the Security Council for the full implementation of this and all relevant resolutions concerning the restoration of the territorial integrity, full sovereignty, and political independence of Lebanon;

7. *Requests* that the Secretary-General report to the Security Council within thirty days on the implementation by the parties of this resolution and decides to remain actively seized of the matter.

Notes

Chapter One

1. This figure is the July 2004 estimate recorded in the *CIA World Factbook* (www.cia.gov/cia/publications/factbook/geos/sy.html). According to the same source, seven of the twenty-two states in the Arab League have larger populations than Syria. The Syrian Central Bureau of Statistics issued a preliminary figure of 17.793 million after its September 2004 census; see *The Syria Report*, December 2004.

2. Indeed, the phrase "fragile mosaic" was used by CIA Syria expert Martha Kessler in 1987 in the title of her open-source monograph, *Syria: Fragile Mosaic of Power* (Washington: National Defense University Press, 1987).

3. Figures are derived from the 2004 *CIA World Factbook*; the Bureau of Near Eastern Affairs, *Background Note: Syria* (www.state.gov/r/pa/ei/bgn/3580.htm); Economist Intelligence Unit, *Syria: Country Profile 2003*, p. 14; and Eyal Zisser, *Asad's Legacy: Syria in Transition* (New York University Press, 2001), p. 5.

4. While the bulk of Syrian Kurds are Sunni Muslims, a small number are Alawis.

5. These data are from the *CIA World Factbook* (2004).

6. See, for example, relevant citations in the *Encyclopedia of the Orient* (www.lexicorient.com) and the *Wikipedia Encyclopedia* (http://en.wikipedia.org/).

7. There are eleven officially recognized Christian sects in Syria; the 10 percent aggregate figure is taken from the 2003 *CIA World Factbook*.

8. In an oft-quoted passage, the wife of the British consul in Damascus in the early 1870s described intercommunal relations in Syria in terms that would maintain their applicability through much of the twentieth century, and that still have some resonance even today: "They hate one another. The Sunnis excommunicate the Shias and both hate the Druze; all detest the Alawis; the Maronites do not love anybody but themselves and are duly abhorred by all; the Greek Orthodox abominate the Greek Catholics and the Latins; all despise the Jews." See Isabel Burton, *The Inner Life of Syria, Palestine, and the Holy Land* (London: Henry S. King, 1875), pp. 105-06.

9. For a historical overview, see Moshe Ma'oz, *Asad, the Sphinx of Damascus: A Political Biography* (New York: Grove Weidenfeld, 1988), chapter 1.

10. For a classic scholarly discussion of this problem in the Arab context, see Michael Hudson, *Arab Politics: The Search for Legitimacy* (Yale University Press, 1977), especially chapter 3. For more generalized discussion, see Joel Migdal, *Strong Societies and Weak States: State-Society Relations and State Capabilities in the Third World* (Princeton University Press, 1988). For a discussion of state formation in Syria from a comparative perspective adducing other Middle Eastern cases, see Lisa Anderson, "The State in the Middle East and North Africa," *Comparative Politics* 20, no. 1 (October 1987). For a discussion of the problems in defining national identity in Syria, see Yahya Sadowski, "The Evolution of Political Identity in Syria," in *Identity and Foreign Policy in the Middle East,* edited by Shibley Telhami and Michael Barnett (Cornell University Press, 2002).

11. The formation of the modern state of Syria had its beginnings in the Arab revolt that began in June 1916 when Sharif Husayn bin Ali, Emir of Mecca and patriarch of the Hashemites, the ruling family of what is today Jordan, launched a military campaign against the Ottoman Turkish rulers of the Arabian Peninsula and the Levant. Husayn's campaign was conducted with the guidance of a British liaison officer, T. E. Lawrence (Lawrence of Arabia); the British sought to use the Arab revolt to undermine the interests of the Ottoman Empire, which had allied itself with the Central Powers at the outbreak of World War I. At the end of World War I, Arab forces under the command of Husayn's sons, Abdallah and Faysal, controlled large portions of the Arabian peninsula and the Levant, including Damascus. Faysal set up an independent Arab government based in Damascus, but, in 1919, the Paris Peace Conference refused to recognize it. In 1920, the General Syrian Congress, meeting in Damascus, elected Faysal king of Syria. That same year, the League of Nations awarded mandates for political control of the Levant to Britain and France. The British mandate covered what is today Israel, Jordan, and the Palestinian territories; Britain also received a mandate for what is today Iraq. The French mandate covered what is today Lebanon and Syria. In November 1920, French troops took Damascus by force and removed Faysal from his Syrian throne, thereby ending the Arab revolt. The best account of the Great Power diplomacy surrounding the Ottoman Empire's dissolution following World War I is David Fromkin, *A Peace to End All Peace: The Fall of the Ottoman Empire and the Creation of the Modern Middle East* (New York: Carlton Books Limited, 1989). As Hinnebusch describes the impact of this experience on Syrian perceptions, "In the wake of the 1917 Arab revolt, Syrians expected the creation of an independent Arab state in historic Syria (Bilad Al-Sham) linked to a wider Arab federation. Instead, betraying their promises to the Arabs, the Western powers subjugated the Arab East, dismembered historic Syria into four ministates, Syria, Jordan, Lebanon, and Palestine, and sponsored the colonization and establishment of the state of Israel in Palestine. In time, Syria gained political independence, but its separation from Jordan, Lebanon, and the Arab world proved irreversible; Israel became a formidable enemy on Syria's doorstep and a permanent obstacle to its nationalist aspirations." Raymond Hinnebusch, "Revisionist Dreams, Realist Strategies: The Foreign Policy of Syria," in *The Foreign Policies of Arab States: The Challenge of Change,* edited by Bahgat Korany and Ali E. Hillal Dessouki, 2d ed. (Boulder, Colo.: Westview Press, 1991), p. 374.

12. The definitive historical treatment of this idea is Daniel Pipes, *Greater Syria: The History of an Ambition* (Oxford University Press, 1990).

13. On this general point, see Robert Jackson, *Quasi-States: Sovereignty, International Relations, and the Third World* (Cambridge University Press, 1990). Michael Hudson, in his classic study of the "legitimacy shortage" in Arab politics, adduces the challenge of developing legitimate authority "within state structures whose boundaries are inherently incompatible with those of the nation" as a unique and important feature of the legitimacy problem in the Arab world; see Hudson, *Arab Politics,* pp. 5–7.

14. The best studies of the period remain Patrick Seale, *The Struggle for Syria: A Study of Post-War Arab Politics, 1945–1958* (Oxford University Press, 1965); and Malcolm Kerr, *The Arab Cold War: Gamal 'Abd al-Nasir and his Rivals, 1958–1970* (Oxford University Press, 1971).

15. The designation of *salafi* applies generally to Islamic movements that glorify the "pristine Islam of the pious ancestors" (*al-salaf al-salih*) and advocate a return to the puritanical Islamic state based on the Islam of the first three generations of Muslims. Many strands of Islamic thought sharing these traits can be said to be salafi (such as the Wahhabi movement in Saudi Arabia). A movement of "scriptural fundamentalism," salafism does not by nature call for violent opposition to existing governments, but, yoked to political movements of varying stripes, it has since the early twentieth century become a rallying cry for antiregime Islamists in a number of Arab countries. The Society of Muslim Brothers originated in Egypt in the 1920s under founder Hassan al-Banna as a salafi movement opposed to British rule. Although the Islamic opposition that coalesced against the rule of Hafiz al-Asad in the 1970s contained many (and often competing) ideologies, it was widely referred to as the "Muslim Brothers" and sought the replacement of the Ba'thist regime with a salafi-inspired Islamic state. See Seale, *Asad: The Struggle for the Middle East,* pp. 320–23; Said Amir Arjomand, "Unity and Diversity in Islamic Fundamentalism," in *Fundamentalisms,* edited by Martin E. Marty and R. Scott Appleby (University of Chicago Press, 1995), pp. 179–230. For a brief description of salafism, see the definition at (globalsecurity.org). A detailed and sympathetic description of the Syrian Muslim Brotherhood can be found in Umar F. Abd-Allah, *The Islamic Struggle in Syria* (Berkeley, Calif.: Mizan Press, 1983).

16. The Syrian Muslim Brotherhood was founded in the 1930s by Syrian students returning from study in Egypt, where they encountered the work of Hassan al-Banna, founder of the original Muslim Brotherhood in Egypt. Beginning in the 1960s, the ideas of another Egyptian Islamist, Sayid Qutb, were critical in prompting the Syrian Muslim Brotherhood to reject the Syrian regime's Ba'thist and pan-Arab ideology.

17. All figures are rounded from the 2004 *CIA World Factbook.* By comparison, per capita GDP in Saudi Arabia is $11,800; in the United Arab Emirates, $23,200; and in Kuwait, $19,000.

18. For information on Syria's oil and gas resources, see the Energy Information Administration, Department of Energy, "Country Analysis Briefs: Syria," April 2004: (www.eia.doe.gov/emeu/cabs/syria.html).

19. For example, the 1978 Camp David Accords proposed that the principles set forth in it be adopted for final peace agreements between all of Israel's neighbors, specifically naming Syria.

20. The Arab peace initiative adopted at the 2002 Arab summit in Beirut proposed a final settlement between Israel and the Arab countries and includes as its first enumerated point an Israeli withdrawal from the Golan Heights in return for peace with Syria.

21. For an overview of U.S. diplomatic initiatives with Syria in the context of Arab-Israeli peacemaking through the 1991 Madrid conference, see relevant portions of William Quandt, *Peace Process: American Diplomacy and the Arab-Israeli Conflict since 1967* (Brookings and University of California Press, 1993).

22. On Kissinger's diplomatic efforts to secure a two-front cease-fire in the 1973 October (Yom Kippur) War, as well as his successful bid to pry Egyptian president Anwar al-Sadat away from Syria in the postwar diplomacy, see Henry Kissinger, *Years of Upheaval* (Boston: Little, Brown, 1982). For an assessment of how these efforts were interpreted by Asad, see Patrick Seale, *Asad of Syria: The Struggle for the Middle East* (London: I.B. Tauris, 1988; University of California Press, 1989), pp. 226–66.

23. Carter administration officials have blamed Asad for this turn of events, arguing that the Syrian leader withdrew from Arab-Israeli diplomacy to "sit by the road and observe events"; see the introduction by Cyrus Vance, Carter's secretary of state, to Alasdair Drysdale and Raymond Hinnebusch, *Syria and the Middle East Peace Process* (New York: Council on Foreign Relations, 1991), p. viii. See also Jimmy Carter, *Keeping Faith: Memoirs of a President* (New York: Bantam Books, 1982), pp. 273–429. For a look at the Carter years through the prism of Asad's strategic framework, see Seale, *Asad of Syria*, pp. 290–315.

24. For further discussion, see Nimrod Novik, *Encounter with Reality: Reagan and the Middle East (The First Term)* (Boulder, Colo.: Westview for the Jaffee Center for Strategic Studies, Tel Aviv University, 1986).

25. The jointly issued U.S.-Soviet invitation to the 1991 Madrid peace conference—which inaugurated separate negotiating tracks between Israel and its neighbors—listed Syria as the second invitee, after Israel, granting it pride of place as first-mentioned Arab state to stress the importance of its participation. Secretary of State James Baker, commenting on preparations for Madrid, wrote, "There was no way to move a comprehensive Mideast peace process forward without the active involvement of Syria." See Baker (with Thomas DeFrank), *The Politics of Diplomacy: Revolution, War, and Peace, 1989–1992* (New York: G. P. Putnam, 1995), p. 296.

26. For overviews of Israeli-Syrian negotiations brokered by the Clinton administration, see Itamar Rabinovich, *The Brink of Peace: The Israeli-Syrian Negotiations* (Princeton University Press, 1999); Helena Cobban, *The Israeli-Syrian Peace Talks: 1991–1996 and Beyond* (Washington: United States Institute of Peace, 2000); and Dennis Ross, *The Missing Peace: The Inside Story of the Fight for Middle East Peace* (New York: Farrar, Strauss, and Giroux, 2004).

27. Historically, Syria's pivotal strategic importance for the region has been documented in Seale, *The Struggle for Syria*, and Kerr, *The Arab Cold War*.

28. See, for example, Michael Barnett, *Dialogues in Arab Politics: Negotiations in Regional Order* (Columbia University Press, 1998); and Avraham Sela, *The Decline of the Arab-Israeli Conflict: Middle East Politics and the Quest for Regional Order* (State University of New York Press, 1997).

29. For example, Syria has never been able to reverse the separate peace treaties with Israel that Egypt and Jordan signed in 1979 and 1994, respectively; however, at the extraordinary Arab League summits in 1996 and in 2000, Syria was able to compel consensus that existing ties between various Arab states and Israel would not be expanded. Syrian opposition also was an important factor prompting an embarrassing withdrawal of Arab participants from a 1997 Middle East economic conference in Qatar; the conference was part of the multilateral track of the Arab-Israeli peace process. In the same

context, Syrian pressure probably contributed to decisions by Tunisia to roll back its trade ties with Israel and by Egypt and Jordan not to maintain effective ambassadorial representation in Israel.

30. For example, Secretary of State Warren Christopher recorded his assessment, at the beginning of the Clinton administration, that "for the United States, an Israeli-Syrian agreement would not only remove a major threat to Israel, but would improve the American strategic position in the region as well. On taking office, I had approved a dual-containment policy as to Iran and Iraq, but hoped to find a way to improve relations with Syria, the third country in the northern tier of Arab states. Nothing would have furthered that goal better than reconciliation between Israel and Syria." See Christopher, *Chances of a Lifetime: A Memoir* (New York: Scribner, 2001), pp. 218–19.

31. On this point, see Drysdale and Hinnebusch, *Syria and the Middle East Peace Process*, especially chapters 4 and 5.

32. On the regional background to the Camp David talks, see Kenneth Stein, *Heroic Diplomacy: Sadat, Kissinger, Carter, Begin, and the Quest for Arab-Israeli Peace* (London: Routledge, 1999), especially chapters 4–7.

33. For an interesting and historically grounded discussion of Syria's objectives in dealing with the Palestinian issue, see Aaron Miller, *The Arab States and the Palestine Question: Between Ideology and Self-Interest,* The Washington Papers 120 (New York: Praeger for the Center for Strategic and International Studies, 1986), chapter 4. On Syrian objectives vis-à-vis Jordan, see Drysdale and Hinnebusch, *Syria and the Middle East Peace Process,* pp. 68–72.

34. In this context, it is worth noting that during the first two decades of Asad's presidency, the Soviet Union was principally important to Syria as its leading military supplier and source of military assistance, as well as an important strategic point of reference.

35. For further discussion, see Novik, *Encounter with Reality.*

36. On the origins of the Syrian-Iranian alliance, see, among others, Hussein Agha and Ahmad Khalidi, *Syria and Iran: Rivalry and Cooperation* (London: Pinter for the Royal Institute of International Affairs, 1995); and Anoushiravan Ehteshami and Raymond Hinnebusch, *Syria and Iran: Middle Powers in a Penetrated Regional System* (London: Routledge, 1997).

37. For discussion, see Robert Danin, "An Iraqi-Syrian Entente? Prospects and Implications," Policywatch 253 (Washington: Washington Institute for Near East Policy, June 11, 1997). On threats to the Clinton administation's dual-containment strategy, see Thomas Friedman, "Pay Attention," *New York Times,* September 1, 1997.

38. Alan Sipress, "U.S. Favors Easing Iraq Sanctions; On Mideast Tour, Powell Outlines Plan to Focus Efforts against Military," *Washington Post,* February 27, 2001; Alan Sipress and Colum Lynch, "U.S. Avoids Confronting Syrians on Iraqi Oil," *Washington Post,* February 14, 2002.

39. The terrorism list was created by the Export Administration Act of 1979, Title 22 of the United States Code, Section 2656f. Under this act, the State Department is required to issue an annual report to Congress on countries and groups classified as terrorist. States falling under this rubric are those that support terrorist organizations politically, materially, or financially, or that fail to cooperate in counterterrorism efforts. Along with Libya and Iraq, Syria was included on the initial list of state sponsors issued by the State Department in 1979 and has retained its state sponsor designation in all subsequent annual reports.

40. This was the so-called National Salvation Front; participating groups included George Habash's Popular Front for the Liberation of Palestine, Ahmad Jibril's Popular Front for the Liberation of Palestine-General Command, Fatah dissidents under Abu Musa, and Nayif Hawatmeh's Democratic Front for the Liberation of Palestine, which broke away from the Popular Front for the Liberation of Palestine in 1969. For background on anti-PLO Palestinian radicals, see Helena Cobban, *The Palestinian Liberation Organisation: People, Power, and Politics* (Cambridge University Press, 1984), especially chapter 7; and Barry Rubin, *Revolution until Victory? The Politics and History of the PLO* (Harvard University Press, 1994), chapters 4 and 8. For descriptions of the links between various secular Palestinian rejectionists and Syria, see Kenneth Katzman, *Terrorism: Near Eastern Groups and State Sponsors, 2001* (Washington: Congressional Research Service, 2001) and Gary Gambill, "Sponsoring Terrorism: Syria and the PFLP-GC," *Middle East Intelligence Bulletin* 4 (September 2002).

41. Hizballah was responsible for the car bombing of the U.S. Embassy in Beirut in 1983, the car bombing of the U.S. Marine and French paratrooper barracks in Beirut in 1983, and the bombing of the U.S. Embassy annex in Beirut in 1984. Hizballah was founded in 1982 by Lebanese Shi'a clerics in response to the Israeli invasion. Inspired by the revolutionary ideology of Iran's Ayatollah Khomeini, Hizballah defined its goals as resistance to the Israeli occupation and, ultimately, the creation of an Islamic state in Lebanon. On Hizballah's origins, structure, ideology, and activities, see, among others, Hala Jaber, *Hezbollah: Born with a Vengeance* (Columbia University Press, 1997); Martin Kramer, "The Moral Logic of Hizballah," in *Origins of Terrorism: Psychologies, Theologies, and States of Mind,* edited by Walter Reich (Cambridge University Press, 1990); Martin Kramer, "The Calculus of Jihad," in *Fundamentalisms and the State: Remaking Politics, Economics, and Militance,* edited by Martin Marty and R. S. Appleby, *The Fundamentalism Project,* vol. 3 (University of Chicago Press, 1993); and Shimon Shapira, "The Origins of Hizballah," *Jerusalem Quarterly,* no. 46 (Spring 1988). For a description of Syria's evolving ties to the organization, see Gary Gambill and Ziad Abdelnour, "Hezbollah: Between Tehran and Damascus," *Middle East Intelligence Bulletin* 4 (February 2002).

42. Seale, *Asad of Syria,* p. 477.

43. See, for example, the 2003 edition of the State Department's *Patterns of Global Terrorism,* issued in April 2004: (www.state.gov/s/ct/rls/pgtrpt/).

44. In a similar manner, Damascus provided safe haven for a number of years to Kurdistan Workers Party (PKK, in its Kurdish acronym) cadres in northern Syria as a way of pressing Ankara in an ongoing dispute between Syria and Turkey over water sharing from the Euphrates River. In this case, however, Hafiz al-Asad was unable in the end to manage the risk of regional blowback. Facing a credible threat of Turkish military intervention in 1998, Asad shut down PKK bases on Syrian territory and expelled the group's chief, Abdullah Öcalan, which led eventually to Öcalan's capture by Turkish authorities.

45. For details, see Gambill, "Sponsoring Terrorism: Syria and the PFLP-GC."

46. Hamas (the name is both the Arabic word for "zeal" and an acronym for the group's full name in Arabic, Movement of the Islamic Resistance) was founded in 1988 by Palestinian Islamists associated with the Muslim Brotherhood movement in Gaza. It has maintained an office in Damascus since 1991. Originally, Hamas's chief external supporters were Iran and Jordan. After Jordan signed its 1994 peace treaty with Israel, however, Hamas relocated its so-called Military Committee to Damascus in 1995. A further

crackdown on its activities in Jordan prompted Hamas to move its Political Bureau to Damascus in 1999; although the Political Bureau was not officially reopened in Damascus, Hamas officials associated with the Political Bureau continue to live in or work out of Damascus. Palestine Islamic Jihad grew up around a group of Palestinian students in Cairo in the 1970s, most notably Fathi Shiqaqi (whose brother, Khalil, is a prominent scholar and analyst of Palestinian politics and public opinion). Inspired by the Islamic Revolution in Iran, several Palestinian Islamist factions in the late 1970s and early 1980s took the name Islamic Jihad, but it was Shiqaqi's group that emerged as a prominent rejectionist player in the late 1980s and 1990s. After being expelled from Egypt in the aftermath of the Sadat assassination, Shiqaqi returned to Gaza to establish his Islamic Jihad movement formally in 1981. Israel expelled Shiqaqi to Lebanon in 1988, and he reestablished Islamic Jihad's headquarters in Damascus in 1989. Shiqaqi was assassinated by Israeli agents in Malta in 1995; the leadership of Islamic Jihad was taken over by Ramadan Shallah, who remains resident and active in Damascus. For background on Hamas and Islamic Jihad, see Shaul Mishal and Avraham Sela, *The Palestinian Hamas: Vision, Violence, and Coexistence* (Columbia University Press, 2000); Ziad Abu-Amr, *Islamic Fundamentalism in the West Bank and Gaza: Muslim Brotherhood and Islamic Jihad* (Indiana University Press, 1994); Meir Hatina and Martin Kramer, *Islam and Salvation in Palestine: The Islamic Jihad Movement,* Dayan Center Papers 127 (Syracuse University Press, 2001); and Meir Litvack, "The Palestine Islamic Jihad: Background Information," Tel Aviv Notes 56 (Jaffee Center for Strategic Studies, November 28, 2002). For discussion of Syria's links to these groups, see Gary Gambill, "Sponsoring Terrorism: Syria and Hamas," *Middle East Intelligence Bulletin* 4, no. 10 (October 2002); and Matthew Levitt, "Sponsoring Terrorism: Syria and Islamic Jihad," *Middle East Intelligence Bulletin* 4, no. 11–12 (November–December 2002).

47. The State Department's *Patterns of Global Terrorism 2001* acknowledged Syria's policy of preventing these groups from attacking Western targets.

48. On Hafiz al-Asad's tactical use of Hizballah, see Michael Eisenstadt, "Hizballah Operations: Past Patterns, Future Prospects," Policywatch 197 (Washington: Washington Institute for Near East Policy, May 7, 1996); Frederic Hof, "Syria and Israel: Keeping the Peace in Lebanon," *Middle East Policy* 4, no. 4 (October 1996); and Katzman, *Terrorism.*

49. On Bashar al-Asad's tactical use of Hizballah, see Daniel Sobelman, *New Rules of the Game: Israel and Hizbollah after the Withdrawal from Lebanon,* Jaffee Center for Strategic Studies Memorandum 69 (Tel Aviv University, January 2004), especially pp. 46–48 and chapter 5.

50. For analyses making this point at different historical junctures in Syria's relationship with Hizballah, see, among others, Eisenstadt, "Hizballah's Operations"; and Mark Heller, "The Arab-Israeli Arena," in *The Middle East Strategic Balance, 2002–2003,* edited by Ephraim Kam and Yiftah Shapir (Tel Aviv University, Jaffee Center for Strategic Studies, 2003), p. 122.

51. See *Patterns of Global Terrorism* (2001). Official U.S. government reports and Katzman, *Terrorism,* make clear that Hizballah has, from time to time, exceeded the limits that Syria has placed on its activities by conducting surveillance on U.S. targets in Beirut.

52. Hizballah's *infitah* (opening up) or "Lebanonization" began in 1992, when the group decided to participate in parliamentary elections for the first time. The Hizballah-led "Loyalty to the Resistance Bloc" won twelve mandates for the 128-member National

Assembly in 1992 (eight Hizballah members plus four Shi'ite allies), nine in the 1996 elections (seven plus two), and twelve in 2000 (nine plus three). For discussion, see, among others, Magnus Ranstorp, "The Strategy and Tactics of Hizballah's Current 'Lebanonization Process,'" *Mediterranean Politics* 3, no. 1 (Spring 1998); Augustus Richard Norton, "Hizballah: From Radicalism to Pragmatism?" *Middle East Policy* (January 1998); and Augustus Richard Norton, *Hizballah of Lebanon: Extremist Ideals vs. Mundane Politics* (New York: Council of Foreign Relations, 1999); see also Zisser, *Asad's Legacy,* pp. 147–48; and Sobelman, *New Rules of the Game,* pp. 19–24.

53. U.S. Department of Defense, *Proliferation: Threat and Response* (January 2001), pp. 42–43. For a recent overview of Syria's WMD capabilities, see Eyal Zisser, "Syria and the Question of WMD," *MERIA Journal* 8, no. 3 (September 2004).

54. For an overview of Syria's nuclear program, see Shai Feldman, *Nuclear Weapons and Arms Control in the Middle East* (MIT Press for the Center for Science and International Affairs, Harvard University, 1997), pp. 67–68. For analysis of Syria's decisionmaking with regard to the possible acquisition of nuclear weapons, see Ellen Laipson, "Syria: Can the Myth Be Maintained without Nukes?" in *The Nuclear Tipping Point: Why States Reconsider Their Nuclear Choices,* edited by Kurt M. Campbell, Robert J. Einhorn, and Mitchell B. Reiss (Brookings Institution Press, 2004). The uncovering of the A. Q. Khan network for proliferation of nuclear technology in 2004 sparked renewed speculation that Syria is pursuing a nuclear weapons program. However, as recently as July 2004, Mohammed al-Baradei, director general of the International Atomic Energy Agency (IAEA), said publicly, "We have no information that Syria is involved in any prohibited nuclear activity."

55. U.S. officials publicly acknowledged information on production of chemical warfare agents and munitions in the 1980s; see, for example, the 1989 testimony by William Webster, then-director of central intelligence, as cited on the Federation of American Scientists' website, (www.fas.org/nuke/guide/syria/).

56. See the overview of Syria's chemical warfare program, "Syria's SCUDs and Chemical Weapons," at the Center for Nonproliferation Studies/Monterey Institute of International Studies website (http://cns.miis.edu/research/wmdme/syrscud.htm).

57. See, among others, successive editions of the U.S. Central Intelligence Agency's biannual "Acquisition of Technology Relating to Weapons of Mass Destruction and Advanced Conventional Munitions" report to Congress; Joseph Cirincione, Jon Wolfsthal, and Miriam Rajkumar, *Deadly Arsenals: Tracking Weapons of Mass Destruction* (Washington: Carnegie Endowment for International Peace, 2002), pp. 11–12; and Kam and Shapir, *The Middle East Strategic Balance,* p. 252, table 17.

58 See "Syria: Weapons of Mass Destruction Capabilities and Programs" at the Center for Nonproliferation Studies/Monterey Institute of International Studies website (http://cns.miis.edu/research/wmdme/syria.htm).

59. See Michael Eisenstadt, "Arming for Peace? Syria's Elusive Quest for 'Strategic Parity,'" Policy Paper 31 (Washington: Washington Institute for Near East Policy, 1992), pp. 51–52.

60. See Kam and Shapir, *The Middle East Strategic Balance,* p. 252, table 17; and Center for Nonproliferation Studies, "Syria: Weapons of Mass Destruction Capabilities and Programs." The maximum range of a SCUD-B is 300 kilometers; of a SCUD-C, 500 kilometers; and of a SCUD-D, 700 kilometers.

61. See the statement by Robert Walpole, national intelligence officer for strategic and nuclear programs, to the hearing on the National Intelligence Estimate of Foreign Missile Development and the Ballistic Missile Threat through 2015, before the Senate Subcommittee on International Security, Proliferation, and Federal Services, March 11, 2002, and the testimony of Director of Central Intelligence George Tenet, "The Worldwide Threat 2004: Challenges in a Changing Global Context," to the Senate Select Committee on Intelligence, February 24, 2004.

62. On the Reagan administration's ill-fated engagement in and subsequent withdrawal from Lebanon, see Lou Cannon, *President Reagan: The Role of a Lifetime* (New York: Perseus Books, 2000), chapter 15, and William Quandt, "Reagan's Lebanon Policy: Trial and Error," *Middle East Journal* 28, no. 2 (Spring 1984).

63. For discussion of the trade-offs in formulating U.S. policy toward Lebanon, see the hearing on U.S. Policy toward Lebanon, House Committee on International Relations, June 25, 1997, and the Special Policy Forum Report by Habib Malik and Graeme Bannerman, "Lebanon, the Peace Process, and U.S. Policy," Washington Institute for Near East Policy, Policywatch 265 (August 25, 1997); see also Habib Malik, *Between Damascus and Jerusalem: Lebanon and Middle East Peace* (Washington: Washington Institute for Near East Policy, 1997; rev. 2d ed, 2000); and Gary Gambill, "US Mideast Policy and the Syrian Occupation of Lebanon," *Middle East Intelligence Bulletin* 3, no. 3 (March 2001).

64. For representative specimens of the range of arguments, see Jim Hoagland, "Time to Squeeze Syria," *Washington Post,* September 16, 2004; and Martha Kessler, "Danger in Pushing Syria Out of Lebanon: Western Diplomatic Initiatives Could Go Horribly Awry," *Los Angeles Times,* November 1, 2004.

65. For a discussion of Syria's designation by the U.S. government as a major producing and transit country for illegal narcotics and its eventual removal from the official U.S. list of such states, see Hillary Mann, "Removing Syria from the Narcotics List—A Signal to Damascus?" Washington Institute for Near East Policy, Policywatch 277 (November 10, 1997).

66. Raymond Tanter, for example, includes Syria in his roster of rogue states in *Rogue Regimes: Terrorism and Proliferation* (New York: St. Martin's Press, rev., 1999).

67. As for any country on the list, designation as a state sponsor of terror imposes four main sets of U.S. government sanctions on Syria: a ban on arms-related exports and sales; controls over exports of dual-use items; prohibitions on economic assistance; and what State Department reports describe as "miscellaneous" financial restrictions (most notably, a legally mandated requirement that the United States oppose loans to terrorist-list countries by the World Bank and other international financial institutions, denial of tax credits to U.S. persons and companies for income earned in such countries, and denial of duty-free treatment for goods exported to the United States from these countries). It is interesting that the Taliban regime in Afghanistan, which was never cited formally as a state sponsor of terror, was subjected to comprehensive trade sanctions. For additional general discussion, see U.S. Department of State, *Patterns of Global Terrorism*; Katzman, *Terrorism*; and Paul Pillar, *Terrorism and U.S. Foreign Policy* (Brookings, 2001), pp. 158 and 169–73. For more detailed discussion of the application of U.S. sanctions against Syria, see Tanter, *Rogue Regimes,* pp. 187–89.

68. The Clinton administration, for example, omitted Syria from its first-term list of "backlash states"; see Anthony Lake, "Confronting Backlash States," *Foreign Affairs* 73,

no. 2 (March/April 1994), 45–6. Even President Bush, in the immediate aftermath of the September 11 attacks, left Syria out of the "axis of evil" he described in his January 2002 State of the Union address; the members of the axis were Iran, Iraq (then still under Saddam Hussein's rule), and North Korea.

69. For recent statements of U.S. policy concerns about Syria, see the testimony of John Bolton, undersecretary of state for arms control and international security affairs, before the House International Relations Committee, September 16, 2003, as well as the testimony of Ambassador William Burns, assistant secretary of state for Near Eastern affairs, and Ambassador Cofer Black, special coordinator for counterterrorism, before the Senate Foreign Relations Committee, October 30, 2003.

70. President Bush described Syria as having allied itself with "international terrorism" in a speech to the National Endowment for Democracy, November 6, 2003; earlier that year, on April 14, White House spokesman Ari Fleischer and Secretary of Defense Donald Rumsfeld both cited CIA reports that Syria was known to possess stocks of chemical weapons and was continuing to develop more lethal varieties.

71. In the National Endowment of Democracy speech, President Bush compared Syria with Iraq as a dictatorship that had brought "torture, misery, oppression, and ruin" to its people.

72. See Clifford Krauss, "U.S. Welcomes Thaw in Relations with 'Pragmatic' Syria," *New York Times*, January 2, 2002. Bush administration officials have publicly acknowledged U.S.-Syrian intelligence cooperation against al Qaeda and related Sunni extremist groups.

73. Personal communications by State Department officials with the author.

74. Barbara Slavin, "U.S. Warns Syria; Next Step Uncertain," *USA Today*, September 17, 2003; and Sonni Efran, "Syria Courts a Cool U.S. amid Threat of Sanctions," *Los Angeles Times*, February 17, 2004. This was also the author's observation during his service as senior director for Middle East initiatives at the National Security Council between February 2002 and March 2003.

75. See Gary Gambill, "Syria's Foreign Relations: Iraq," *Middle East Intelligence Bulletin* 3, no. 3 (March 2001); Gary Gambill, "Syria Rearms Iraq," *Middle East Intelligence Bulletin* 4, no. 9 (September 2002); Sean Loughlin, "Defense Secretary Cites 'Hostile Acts,'" CNN, March 29, 2003; and Hans Greimel, "Foreign Fighters Remain Threat in Iraq," Associated Press, April 15, 2003.

76. Personal communications by U.S. officials with the author.

77. The House of Representatives passed a version of the bill on October 15, 2003, and the Senate passed an amended version on November 11, 2003. Both houses adopted the conference report on the bill on November 20, 2003.

78. See Christopher Marquis, "Bush Imposes Sanctions on Syria, Citing Terrorism," *New York Times*, May 12, 2004. President Bush announced the implementation of the Syrian Accountability and Lebanese Sovereignty Restoration Act (SAA or SALSA) sanctions on May 11, 2004. In addition to the mandatory ban on the export of dual-use items to Syria, the president also chose to implement a ban on all American exports except food and medicine, a prohibition on flights between Syria and the United States, and the freezing of certain Syrian assets in the United States. Significantly, Bush chose not to employ some of the harsher options from the basket of sanctions proposed by the SAA, such as a strict ban on the travel of Syrian diplomatic personnel in the United States, a prohibition on investment by U.S. companies in Syria, and a downgrading of U.S.-Syrian

diplomatic contacts. White House Press Office, "Implementing the Syria Accountability and Lebanese Sovereignty Restoration Act of 2003," May 11, 2004.

79. On Bashar's upbringing and exposure to the West, see the profile by Susan Sachs, "Man in the News: The Shy Young Doctor at Syria's Helm: Bashar al-Asad," *New York Times*, June 14, 2000. An adulatory portrait of Bashar published shortly before his father's death described him as "soft-spoken and congenial, a fan of Faith Hill and Phil Collins tunes downloaded to a Walkman-like digital music player"; see Howard Schneider, "Syria Advances Cautiously into the Online Age: Asad's Son Promoting Change," *Washington Post*, April 27, 2000.

80. King Abdallah of Jordan, for example, described himself and Bashar at the time of the succession as exemplars of a new, "Internet generation" of Arab leaders who would take the Arab world into the twenty-first century. A U.S. delegation led by Secretary of State Madeleine Albright returned from the first official U.S. visit to the new Syrian president impressed with his modernist line and his stated interest in continuing the peace process; see Jane Perlez, "Albright Finds Syria's New Leader Willing to Pursue Talks," *New York Times*, June 14, 2000. Several Israeli governmental figures were also cautiously optimistic about the change of leadership bringing new hope to the region; see Deborah Sontag, "With the Loss of an Old Foe, Israelis See a Cloud Lifted," *New York Times*, June 12, 2000. For news analyses at the outset of Bashar's presidency that focused on his reformist tendencies, see, among others, Susan Sachs, "Transition in Syria: Syrians See in the Heir Possibility of Progress," *New York Times*, June 11, 2000, and "He Made It!" *Economist*, July 22, 2000. According to a report on Bashar's early days in office, the new president's "favorite watchwords" were "modernization and technology"; see Andrew Borowiec, "Asad Seen as Agent of Economic Change; Shows Move toward 'Political Flexibility,'" *Washington Times*, November 22, 2000. Another report described him as an "avid technocrat"; see Scott Peterson, "The Grooming of Syria's Bashar al-Asad," *Christian Science Monitor*, June 13, 2000. For an assessment comparing Bashar to another young leader—Kim Jong Il—who was groomed for succession by his father, see Elaine Sciolino, "If Dad Was a Dictator, Just Try Being Mr. Nice Guy," *New York Times*, June 18, 2000. For a comparative discussion of generational change in Syria, Jordan, and Morocco, see Dan Ephron, "Mideast's Young Rulers Face Barriers to Reform," *Washington Times*, June 21, 2000, and David Plotz, "The Arab Brat Pack: They're Young, They're Sexy, and They're Running Dad's Country," *Slate*, June 16, 2000.

81. The first book-length study of Bashar's presidency to date focuses on his failures, so far, as a reformer; see Alan George, *Syria: Neither Bread Nor Freedom* (London: Zed Books, 2003). To be sure, some analysts dissented from the initial optimism about Bashar at the beginning of his presidency. Helena Cobban, for example, pooh-poohed the idea that Bashar was a Western-oriented leader on par with Jordan's King Abdallah; see "Syria's New Asad No Sure Thing," *Christian Science Monitor*, June 28, 2000. John Daniszewski reported on Syrians' unhappiness with their new leader; "In Syria, Not Everyone Is Charmed by Asad's Heir: Dissenters Question the Untested Son's March to Power, They Also Doubt That Life Will Improve," *Los Angeles Times*, July 7, 2000. Writing at the end of Bashar's first year in office, Yossi Baidatz described the conflicting views of Bashar's leadership that were already emerging in discussions of his presidency as the "Mr. Bashar/Dr. Asad" dichotomy. The former is a "clumsy young man divorced from the Syrian-Lebanese reality"; the latter is "a promising young leader with a Western education leaning toward modernization and technological progress." See Baidatz, "Bashar's

First Year: From Ophthalmology to a National Vision," Washington Institute for Near East Policy, Research Memorandum 41 (July 2001).

82. See George, *Syria*; and Claude Salhani, "Syria at the Crossroads," *Middle East Policy* 10, no. 3 (Fall 2003).

83. See Alan Makovsky, "Syria under Bashar al-Asad: The Domestic Scene and the 'Chinese Model' of Reform," Washington Institute for Near East Policy, Policywatch 512 (January 17, 2001). Eyal Zisser also promotes this view, when he describes a new president hemmed in by the Old Guard at whose pleasure he serves, inescapably wedded to the political system he inherited from his father; see Zisser, "Does Bashar al-Asad Rule Syria?" *Middle East Quarterly* 10, no. 1 (Winter 2003); and Zisser, "Bashar of Arabia," *Wall Street Journal*, September 2, 2003. For an analysis of the dangers Bashar would face were he to reform the inherited political spoils system, see Roula Khalaf, "Opposition to the War Has Cost the Damascus Regime Dear," *Financial Times*, August 26, 2003.

84. See Gary Gambill, "Asad's Desperate Diplomacy," *Middle East Intelligence Bulletin* 6, no. 1 (January 2004), in which the notion of a powerful Old Guard restricting Bashar's policy choices is rejected and Bashar is described as an independent actor.

85. See, for example, the testimony of Patrick Clawson of the Washington Institute for Near East Policy before the Senate Foreign Relations Committee, October 30, 2003.

86. Personal communication with the author.

87. Analyses promoting elements of this model can be found in: Gambill, "Asad's Desperate Diplomacy"; Chris Suellentrop, "Bashar Asad: The Evil Moron Who's Running Syria," *Slate*, April 16, 2003; Marc Ginsberg, "Bashing Bashar," *Weekly Standard*, April 28, 2003; Max Abrahms, "When Rogues Defy Reason: Bashar's Syria," *Middle East Quarterly* 10, no. 4 (Fall 2003); Zisser, "Bashar of Arabia"; and Zisser "Syria and the War in Iraq," *MERIA Journal* 7, no. 2 (June 2003).

Chapter Two

1. On Asad's rise to power and his first decade and a half as president, see two classic biographies: Moshe Ma'oz, *Asad, the Sphinx of Damascus: A Political Biography* (New York: Grove Weidenfeld, 1988); and Patrick Seale, *Asad of Syria: The Struggle for the Middle East* (London: I. B. Tauris, 1988; University of California Press, 1989). See also Lucien Bitterlin, *Hafez El Asad: le parcours d'un combattant* (Paris: Éditions du Jaguar, 1986). For an account and assessment of the last decade of Asad's presidency, see Eyal Zisser, *Asad's Legacy: Syria in Transition* (New York University Press, 2001).

2. For detailed discussion, see Patrick Seale, *The Struggle for Syria: A Study of Post-War Arab Politics, 1945–1958* (Oxford University Press, 1965); and Nikolaos Van Dam, *The Struggle for Power in Syria: Politics and Society under Asad and the Ba'th Party* (London: I. B. Tauris, 1996), pp. 15–74; this work is a revised and updated version of Van Dam's earlier *The Struggle for Power in Syria: Sectarianism, Regionalism and Tribalism in Politics* (London: Croom Helm, 1979; 2d ed., 1981).

3. For analysis of the expansion of membership in the Ba'th Party and party-affiliated mass organizations after 1963, see two works by Raymond Hinnebusch: *Authoritarian Power and State Formation in Ba'thist Syria: Army, Party, and Peasant* (Boulder, Colo.: Westview Press, 1990); and *Syria: Revolution from Above* (London: Routledge, 2001), pp. 47–64.

4. For discussion, see Hinnebusch, *Syria*, pp. 80–83.

5. Ibid., pp. 89–93.

6. The phrase is from Itamar Rabinovich, *Syria under the B'ath, 1963–66: The Army-Party Symbiosis* (Jerusalem: Israel Universities Press, 1972).

7. The best appraisal of Asad's use of repression during the first two decades of his presidency remains Middle East Watch, *Syria Unmasked: The Suppression of Human Rights by the Asad Regime* (Yale University Press for Human Rights Watch Books, 1991). For more recent assessments, see successive editions of Human Rights Watch's regional reports on the Middle East and of the Department of State's annual "Country Reports on Human Rights Practices" for Syria.

8. Syrian intellectuals and civil society activists have described to the author what they see as an evolution in the nature of the Syrian police state during the last decade of Asad's presidency: whereas during the 1970s and 1980s, the security apparatus actively came looking for actual or potential regime opponents, by the 1990s one had to cross a certain threshold of public defiance or protest before the security organs would take notice. A reform-minded Syrian intellectual described a similar evolution in the treatment of political prisoners, saying that twenty years earlier the police came in the middle of the night to take someone away and that person was never seen again. Today, according to my interlocutor, a person targeted by the security apparatus for political offenses is arrested under normal criminal procedures and receives a trial with benefit of counsel, but probably has a corrupt judge who accepts bogus evidence fabricated by the state, leading to the defendant's conviction. Once convicted, the political prisoner serves his sentence in a regular prison, where his family is able to visit him, and he is likely be released within the prescribed term of his sentence. None of the author's interlocutors found the current situation acceptable.

9. Under Asad's leadership, the Ba'th Party continued to serve as a tool for political recruitment to incorporate an expanding constituency supportive of the regime. Over the course of his presidency, however, the party became less a source of ideas and policy proposals—historically, its other traditional function since independence, including the 1963–70 period—and more an instrument for enforcing Asad's personal control throughout the government's ministerial structure, in the various provinces, and in key economic and occupational sectors. For additional discussion, see Hinnebusch, *Syria*, pp. 80–85. These developments had specific consequences for economic policy deliberations during Asad's presidency, as party dominance effectively ensured consensus within the bureaucracy for a largely statist economic order; see Volker Perthes, *The Political Economy of Syria under Asad* (London: I. B. Tauris, 1998), pp. 41–53 and 229–30. Asad inherited a military that was already largely "Ba'thized," but that still reflected the cleavages that had characterized leadership dynamics within the post-1963 regime. In this regard, "Ba'thization" of the armed forces after 1963 had effectively nurtured military politics parallel to and mirroring the factional struggles within the party, reinforcing the historically praetorian tendencies of the Syrian military. Asad worked to neutralize these tendencies by careful manipulation of personnel assignments and promotions. He supplemented this process by creating elite units dedicated to regime protection, such as the Republican Guard and the so-called Defense Companies (*saraya al-difa'*) under the command of his brother, Rifa't; after Rifa't's challenge to the president's authority in 1983–84, the Defense Companies were broken up, many of its personnel were shifted into the Republican Guard or the Special Forces, and the Republican Guard assumed primary responsibility for the regime protection mission. For more on Asad's handling of the mil-

itary and his confrontation with Rifaʿt, see Seale, *Asad of Syria*, pp. 421–40; Maʿoz, *Asad, the Sphinx of Damascus*, pp. 169–70; and Van Dam, *The Struggle for Power in Syria*, pp. 118–23. Asad manipulated the leaderships of the various intelligence and security agencies to prevent any one of them from becoming a platform for a potential rival and to ensure that each agency kept an eye on the others as well as the opposition. On this point, see Perthes, *The Political Economy of Syria under Asad*, pp. 153–54.

10. The argument that Asad's regime successfully entrenched itself in Syrian society is developed more fully in Hinnebusch, *Authoritarian Power and State Formation in Baʿthist Syria*; see also Zisser, *Asad's Legacy*, pp. 18–24.

11. The Baʿth motto was, and is, a simple trifecta: unity (*wahda*), freedom (*hurriyya*), and socialism (*ishtirakiyya*). Unity effectively defined the Baʿth external orientation, expressing a commitment to a single Arab nation (*umma ʿarabiyya*). Organizationally, this commitment was reflected in a structure embracing Baʿth parties in several Arab states in a single national command (*qiyada qawmiyya*); each of these individual parties was identified in the overall structure as a subordinate regional command (*qiyada qutriyya*). Freedom and socialism essentially defined the Baʿth program for unseating Syria's established power structure, secularizing Syrian politics, and remaking Syria's economy and social order. On the origins of the Baʿth movement and the development of the party in Syria, see John Devlin, *The Baʿth Party: A History from Its Origins to 1966* (Stanford, Calif.: Hoover Institution Press, 1976). There is, to be sure, a school that interprets Asad's presidency as a narrow, sectarian regime, rooted in and more or less limited to Asad's own Alawi community, with a few Sunni retainers as window dressing. This was one of the principal tenets of the Sunni Islamist critique of the regime within Syria; for a Western scholar espousing this perspective, see Daniel Pipes, *Syria beyond the Peace Process* (Washington: Washington Institute for Near East Policy, 1996). It is certainly true that Alawis are a distinct minority in Syria: in postindependence Syria, demographers have generally estimated that Alawis constitute no more than 15 percent of the population; by comparison, Sunnis are generally estimated to be 65–70 percent of the population. Against this backdrop, the role of Alawis, particularly Alawis from Asad's tribe, the Kalbiyya, has been grossly disproportionate in Syria's leadership since the 1963 Baʿthist coup. It is also true that the Asad regime's most serious domestic weakness has always been its poor standing within the majority Sunni community. Nevertheless, for reasons that are explored later, interpreting Asad's regime exclusively or even primarily as an Alawi cabal seems an overly simplistic and misleading view of the dynamics of authoritarian rule in Syria.

12. The foundations of the Baʿthist economic model included the nationalization of private companies above a certain size and state ownership of the "commanding heights" of the economy.

13. In this regard, a prominent Syrian technocrat said in conversation with the author that the Asad regime could be described, for much of its history, as a "countryside regime," with a social base among rural Syrians of various confessional backgrounds and a more problematic standing among urban Syrians. For scholarly assessments of Baʿthist land reform in Syria, see Raymond Hinnebusch, *Peasant and Bureaucracy in Baʿthist Syria: The Political Economy of Rural Development* (Boulder, Colo.: Westview Press, 1989); and Perthes, *The Political Economy of Syria under Asad*.

14. While some segments of the Alawi community have clearly benefited from their connection to the Asad regime, it is arguable whether the Alawi community as a whole

has gained disproportionate material benefits from the regime. Visits to villages in the traditional rural Alawi heartland suggest that much of this area remains underdeveloped in comparison with other rural areas of Syria. Given the disproportionate material benefits that have accrued to relatively narrow segments of the Alawi community and of other communities that have close connections to the ruling elite, a prominent civil society advocate from an urban Sunni background suggested to me that the Asad regime is more accurately described as a "special interest regime" rather than an Alawi regime.

15. The failure of the Islamist revolt stemmed not only from the willingness of Asad and his senior commanders to apply whatever force was necessary to put down Islamist uprisings, most notably at Hama in February 1982, but also from differences among Muslim Brotherhood factions in various Syrian cities, which the regime exploited, and from the Brotherhood's inability to make much of an inroad among rural Sunnis, which kept localized uprisings in individual cities from spreading across the country.

16. In the initial years of his presidency, Asad frequently prayed at Sunni mosques, made a pilgrimage to Mecca, and sought religious legitimacy for himself and his fellow Alawis through the issuance of a *fatwa* from the Lebanese Shi'a leader Musa al-Sadr recognizing Alawis as Shi'a and, hence, full-fledged Muslims; see Ma'oz, *Asad, the Sphinx of Damascus*, p. 151, and Zisser, *Asad's Legacy*, pp. 8–9. After the struggle against the Muslim Brotherhood's revolt was finally won, Asad tried again to accommodate Sunni sensitivities. In the 1990s Asad allowed the non-*salafi*, *sufi*-influenced grand mufti of Damascus, Ahmed Kuftaro, to organize a nationwide campaign of Islamic education to increase religious observation and piety. At the same time, there was a palpable relaxation in the regime's posture toward *salafi* elements within Syria's Islamist circles, manifested in the release of many imprisoned Muslim Brotherhood activists and the officially permitted return to Syria of several exiled Brotherhood leaders; see Zisser, *Asad's Legacy*, pp. 196–203.

17. By the time Asad seized power in 1970, seven years of Ba'thist rule in Syria had already ingrained what Hinnebusch (*Syria*, p. 60) has described as "an ideological preference for etatist solutions, deep distrust of private capital and a residual populism." Asad never fundamentally challenged these ideological preferences, but at times during his presidency, he moderated some of the more ideologically hard-edged aspects of Ba'thist economic policy.

18. During the "six good years" (1970–76) at the start of his presidency, Asad reduced state controls over foreign trade and imports in a limited *infitah* (opening), without undercutting the dominant economic role of the state. See Hinnebusch, *Syria*, pp. 89–90; Ma'oz, *Asad, the Sphinx of Damascus*, pp. 74–82; and Perthes, *The Political Economy of Syria under Asad*, pp. 49–53. These measures helped to restore some vitality to the traditionally Sunni-dominated private sector, which, together with weather conducive to increased agricultural production, helped to fuel Syria's positive economic performance in this period. Additionally, early in his tenure, Asad purged the rhetoric of class warfare from government and Ba'th Party statements as part of an effort to court urban Sunni notables. See Ma'oz, *Asad, the Sphinx of Damascus*, pp. 74–82; Zisser, *Asad's Legacy*, pp. 8–10; and Itamar Rabinovich, "Stability and Change in Syria," in *The Politics of Change in the Middle East*, edited by Robert Satloff (Boulder, Colo.: Westview Press for the Washington Institute for Near East Policy, 1993), pp. 12–14. On Sunni businessmen who profited from the curtailment of regime-sanctioned class warfare, see Volker Perthes, "A Look at the Syrian Upper Class: The Bourgeoisie and the Ba'ath," *Middle East*

Report, 170 (May/June 1991): 31–37. For similar reasons, at the end of the 1980s, as shortages of indigenously produced consumer goods became endemic in Syria, Asad endorsed a second *infitah*, allowing private businessmen to use foreign exchange earned by exports to import staple foods and other essential consumer goods. This arrangement tended to work to the benefit of established Sunni merchant families and helped raise living standards for most middle-class Syrians, including Sunnis. See Perthes, *The Political Economy of Syria under Asad*, pp. 53–62.

19. The 1973 constitution was adopted in a referendum on March 12, 1973, and took effect the following day. It was amended on three occasions: March 29, 1980; July 3, 1991; and June 11, 2000. The last amendment, adopted immediately after the death of Hafiz al-Asad, lowered the age requirement for the president from forty years to thirty-four in order to legalize Bashar's succession. The Constitution of the Syrian Arab Republic and its amendments are posted in English and Arabic on the official website of the Syrian parliament (syria-people-counsel.org/english/const/). At its inception the National Progressive Front (NPF, also known by its French acronym PNF) comprised the Ba'th Party, the Syrian Communist Party, the Arab Socialist Union (Nasirist), the Movement of Socialist Unionists (a faction that broke from the Ba'th Party in 1961), and the Arab Socialist Movement (a faction that broke from the Ba'th Party in 1964). On the history and development of the individual parties, see Hashem 'Othman, *al-Ahzab al-Siyasiyya fi Suriyya (Political Parties in Syria)*, (Beirut: Riad El-Rayyes Books, 2001).

20. Ma'oz, *Asad, the Sphinx of Damascus*, p. 50; Hinnebusch, *Syria*, p. 78.

21. The concept of the *jama'a* is attributed to Michel Seurat. See Eberhard Kienle, *Entre jamaa et classe: Le pouvoir politique en Syrie*, Ethnizität und Gesellschaft, Occasional Papers 31 (Berlin: Das Arabische Buch, 1992).

22. Rabinovich, "Stability and Change in Syria," p. 13.

23. For discussion, see David Lesch, "Is Syria Ready for Peace? Obstacles to Integration into the Global Economy," *Middle East Policy* 6, no. 3 (February 1999).

24. Vice-President 'Abd al-Halim al-Khaddam, for example, comes from a poor Sunni family in Banyas, a Mediterranean coastal town. Born in 1932, Khaddam was a friend of Hafiz al-Asad from their high school days, when the two met as members of Syria's national student union. Khaddam began his career as a lawyer in Damascus and moved into political life after the Ba'th Party took power in 1963. Khaddam served as minister of economy and foreign trade in 1969–70; after Hafiz al-Asad came to power, he appointed his friend foreign minister in 1970 and elevated him to the Ba'th Party's Regional Command in 1971. Khaddam served as foreign minister until 1984, when he was named first vice president (for foreign affairs) following Rifa't al-Asad's challenge to Hafiz's hold on power. On Khaddam's background and career, see Seale, *Asad of Syria*, p. 37; Bitterlin, *Le parcours d'un combattant*; and Daniel Nassif, "Dossier: Abdul Halim Khaddam," *Middle East Intelligence Bulletin* 2, no. 2 (February 2000). Foreign Minister Faruq al-Shar' comes from a modest Sunni family in Dar'a in rural southern Syria. Born in 1938, Shar' studied English literature at Damascus University. He began his career with Syrian Air Lines, holding executive positions in the Middle East and Europe. While running the airline's regional office in London, he earned a graduate degree in international law from the University of London in 1972. He was recruited by Foreign Minister Khaddam to serve as Syria's ambassador to Italy in 1976. He returned to Damascus in 1980 to serve as deputy foreign minister under Khaddam from 1980 until Khaddam's promotion to vice president in 1984; Shar' then moved up to the foreign minister's post.

Defense Minister Mustafa Tlas was born in 1932 to a Sunni family in the village of Rastan, near the city of Homs. Following a path in many ways identical to the young Hafiz al-Asad, Tlas joined the Ba'th Party as a teenager in 1947 and matriculated at the new Syrian Air Force Academy in 1952, where he and Asad met and became lifelong friends. The two served together as fighter pilots in Egypt during the period of the United Arab Republic. According to Seale (*Asad of Syria*, pp. 68–69), when Asad was incarcerated in Egypt in 1961 after the breakup of the UAR, he relied on Tlas to get his wife and infant daughter Bushra back to Syria safely. This episode gave Tlas an unusually personal bond with Asad, and the Syrian president kept Tlas as part of his inner circle even when his friend's embarrassingly outlandish and spurious comments about Jewish conspiracies and the ancestry of various Arab leaders might have warranted his sidelining. Tlas has been a member of the Ba'th Party's Regional Command since 1969 and served as defense mnister until his retirement in May 2004. For more on his background and career, see "Dossier: Lt. Gen. Mustafa Tlass," *Middle East Intelligence Bulletin* 2, no. 6 (1 July 2000) and his retirement announcement on *SANA*, May 11, 2004 .

25. For discussion, see Ma'oz, *Asad, the Sphinx of Damascus*, pp. 42–45; Seale, *Asad of Syria*, pp. 339–40; and Lisa Wedeen, *Ambiguities of Domination: Politics, Symbols, and Rhetoric in Contemporary Syria* (University of Chicago Press, 1999).

26. See, for example, Hinnebusch, *Syria*, p. 113.

27. This absence of the substantive apparatus of a modern presidency stems from the peculiarities of Hafiz al-Asad's presidential agenda. Focused on the high politics of Syria's national security and foreign relations and on assuring his regime's stability, Asad evinced little interest in the substance of most domestic policy areas. These details were left to the various ministries, operating for the most part under the guidance of the Ba'th Party; for more detailed discussion, see Hinnebusch, *Syria*, pp. 80–85. Asad's forays into economic liberalization were ad hoc and tactical in nature, not fundamental strategic choices. In pursuing limited liberalization measures, he tended to devolve a circumscribed authority to individual technocrats who had earned his confidence, rather than develop the staff apparatus he would have needed to oversee more systematic reforms. (An example of such a figure would be the long-serving non-Ba'thist minister of economy, Ibrahim al-'Imadi, who helped implement both the liberalization measures of the 1970s and the second *infitah* of the late 1980s and early 1990s.) In addition, Asad's "hub and spokes" management style for dealing with the inner circle on matters of high politics also militated against the development of a modern presidential staff apparatus.

28. On succession preparations, see Zisser, *Asad's Legacy*, pp. 153–78.

29. For a discussion of Bashar's efforts, since the beginning of his presidency, to present himself as a representative of continuity as well as change, see Yossi Baidatz, "Bashar's First Year: From Ophthalmology to a National Vision," Policy Focus 41 (Washington: Washington Institute for Near East Policy, July 2001), pp. 17–24.

30. In October 1999, Syrian security forces attacked supporters of Rifa't in the area around Latakia, ostensibly to signal the regime's determination to thwart any attempt by Rifa't to thwart his nephew's accession to the presidency. See "Rifaat Assad and the Syrian Political Crisis," *Middle East Intelligence Bulletin* 1, no. 10 (October 1999).

31. In a 2001 interview with the Arab press, Bashar took issue with the use of the term *old guard* by journalists: "Concerning the old guard, I was asked this question before. I said the old guard is a media term. What do we mean by it? What do we mean by old? Do

we mean old in terms of age? Do we mean by it a person with long service? Or is he a person with a closed mind, in the sense that he is old in his mentality? There are many interpretations. I see that there are persons who are for modernization, and persons who are against modernization, and vice versa. Some young people and new appointees are against modernization. Therefore, this term is inaccurate." Syrian Arab Republic Radio (Damascus), June 28, 2001.

32. In similar fashion, a prominent Syrian civil society advocate described to the author the stultifying effect of a long-established and "corrupt" private sector that lives off the state budget. Younger Syrian businessmen, interested in fostering a climate more conducive to genuine entrepreneurship in their country, speak of an "Old Guard private sector" based on alliances with bureaucrats and officials.

33. The phrase comes from Thomas Friedman's *The Lexus and the Olive Tree* (New York: Farrar, Straus and Giroux, 1999), pp. 86–92.

34. Similarly, Dennis Ross, who spent more time than any other U.S. official interacting with Asad during the last decade of his presidency, has said that his personal understanding of economic theory is minimal, but that in conversations with the Syrian president about economic issues, Ross typically emerged feeling "like a Nobel laureate."

35. Seale, *Asad of Syria*, pp. 100–102.

36. After Asad came to power in 1970, Islamist uprisings occurred in several Syrian cities: in Damascus in 1972, in Damascus and Hama in 1973, and in Aleppo and Hama in 1975. These uprisings were relatively easily contained. It was not until the economic downturn of 1976 that the Muslim Brotherhood was able to mobilize and sustain a more generalized revolt against Asad's regime.

37. During the 1970s, for example, Syria received significant infusions of cash in the form of aid and loans from Arab oil producers as well as from international donors and lenders; remittances from Syrian workers in foreign oil sectors also became an important source of foreign exchange. At the end of the 1980s, Syria benefited from an expansion of its own production and export of petroleum. Although Syria remains relatively small as an oil producer compared to other Middle Eastern countries, the petroleum sector would become increasingly important to the Syrian economy during the last decade of Hafiz al-Asad's presidency. This was especially true with regard to Syria's balance of payments; the infusion of foreign exchange from oil exports effectively allowed Asad to avoid the sort of crisis that might have forced a more thoroughgoing reconsideration of basic economic policies; see Zisser, *Asad's Legacy*, p. 62. In the aftermath of the Persian Gulf War, Syria received more than $2 billion in new aid from oil-producing Arab states for Syrian participation in the coalition that expelled Iraqi forces from Kuwait; see Perthes, *The Political Economy of Syria under Asad*, pp. 29–31. In recent years, financial assistance to Syria from Saudi Arabia and other Gulf States has dwindled.

38. Middle East Watch, *Syria Unmasked*, p. 1.

39. Sylvia Pölling, "Investment Law No. 10: Which Future for the Private Sector?" in *Contemporary Syria: Liberalization between Cold War and Cold Peace*, edited by Eberhard Kienle (London: I.B.Tauris, 1994), pp. 14–25; Perthes, *The Political Economy of Syria under Asad*, pp. 58–59.

40. The author is grateful to Martin Indyk for this point. At least part of the reason for Asad's failure to engage seriously with international institutions may have been his awareness that under U.S. law successive American administrations were obliged to vote

against Syria in both the International Monetary Fund and the World Bank because of Syria's designation as a state sponsor of terrorism.

41. On the economy Bashar inherited, see Volker Perthes, "The Political Economy of the Syrian Succession," *Survival* 43, no. 1 (Spring 2001).

42. The figures on state enterprises and numbers of bureaucrats come from the Syrian State Planning Organization.

43. Pölling, "Investment Law No. 10"; Zisser, *Asad's Legacy*, pp. 188–90; Economist Intelligence Unit, *Syria: Country Profile 2000*, pp. 15–16 (www.eiu.com); Hisham Melhem, "Syria between Two Transitions," *Middle East Report*, no. 203 (Spring 1997): pp. 2–7.

44. Perthes, "The Political Economy of the Syrian Succession."

45. On the importance of the agricultural sector and yearly fluctuations in yield due to weather conditions, see Economist Intelligence Unit, *Syria: Country Profile 2003*, pp. 30–33, and World Bank, *Syrian Arab Republic: Country Brief* (Washington: October 2001).

46. Statistics on population growth in Syria are variously estimated by different sources. According to one source, Syria held the record for natural population growth during the mid-1990s (3.3–3.5 percent); see Zisser, *Asad's Legacy*, pp. 191–92. *The Economist* gives a lower average for the 1998–2003 period: 2.6 percent a year; see Economist Intelligence Unit, *Syria: Country Profile 2003*, pp. 14, 53). The United Nations puts the average population growth in Syria between 1975 and 2001 at 3.1 percent and estimates a 2.2 percent yearly increase between 2001 to 2015; see United Nations Development Programme, "Human Development Indicators: Demographic Trends: Syrian Arab Republic," *United Nations Human Development Report 2003* (Oxford University Press, 2003), p. 252.

47. Perthes estimates 200,000–250,000 new entrants in the labor market yearly; see Perthes, "The Political Economy of the Syrian Succession." The "youth bulge" is a demographic phenomenon in which the subset of young people—usually defined as those under age twenty-four—is much larger than any other age group in the population of a given country. The Middle East as a whole is experiencing this demographic challenge, which will only become more pronounced over the next fifty years. Syria will not be among the countries most affected by the youth bulge, but it will still suffer "major new strains on the social infrastructure including educational facilities, social services, housing, and employment needs, which, if unmet, lead to predictable social instability, volatility, and radicalization." For a comprehensive report on the "youth bulge" and its effects, see Graham Fuller, "The Youth Factor: The New Demographics of the Middle East and the Implications for U.S. Policy," Brookings Project on U.S. Policy toward the Islamic World, Analysis Paper 3 (Washington: Saban Center for Middle East Policy at the Brookings Institution, June 2003).

48. The Syrian government estimated that its 2011 workforce would reach 7.21 million out of a population of 25 million. To attain a workforce that size, it would have to create approximately 300,000 new jobs a year for a decade, whereas the government and the private sector were able to create only 80,000 jobs a year at a maximum in the late 1990s. Unemployment was officially listed at 11.2 percent in late 2002, but unofficial estimates put it as high as 30 percent; the *CIA World Factbook* puts it at 20 percent in 2003, while the Economist Intelligence Unit believes that the figure may approach 25 percent if underemployment is also factored in. The majority of the new entrants to the workforce—

200,000 to 350,000 a year—will not find employment at the current rate of job creation and will continue to add to the unemployment ranks, especially as almost 50 percent of the population was under age fourteen in 2000 and 40 percent under age fifteen in 2003. Unemployment figures and new entrants to the workforce are most likely underestimated, as they do not take into consideration an increase in female participation in the workforce. On these figures, see Zisser, *Asad's Legacy*, pp. 1913; Perthes, "The Political Economy of the Syrian Succession"; *CIA World Factbook*; Economist Intelligence Unit, *Syria: Country Profile* (2000 and 2003 editions); Euro-Med Partnership, *Syria: Country Strategy Paper 2002–2006,* December 2001, p. 9 (http:europe.eu.int/comm/external_relations/syria/csp/index.htm); and Alan George, *Syria: Neither Bread Nor Freedom* (London: Zed Books, 2003), p. 163.

49. The World Bank estimates Syria will have to achieve 5 percent growth in gross domestic product to "improve the welfare of its people," whereas the 2000 rate of growth was only 1.5 percent. The EU, in its Euro-Med Partnership assessment, estimates that Syria will need 6 percent growth to absorb new entrants to the workforce and maintain an acceptable quality of life. See World Bank, *Syrian Arab Republic: Country Brief*; Economist Intelligence Unit, *Syria: Country Profile 2003*, p. 14; and Euro-Med Partnership, *Syria: Country Strategy Paper 2002–2006*, p. 10.

50. Bashar stated in his inaugural address that "it is important to take steady, yet gradual, steps towards introducing economic changes through modernizing laws, removing bureaucratic obstacles to the flow of domestic and foreign investments, mobilizing public and private capital, and activating the private sector and giving it better business opportunities"; see "Bashar al-Asad Sworn In," Syrian Arab TV (Damascus), July 17, 2000.

51. The author has been struck, in conversation with Syrian Christians, by their degree of acceptance of Hafiz al-Asad's regime; when pressed, Christian interlocutors uniformly attribute their support for the Asad regime to a sense that the regime protected Christians and other minorities from the prospect of Sunni fundamentalist rule.

52. Seale, *Asad of Syria*, pp. 316–38; Ma'oz, *Asad, the Sphinx of Damascus*, pp. 149–63.

53. See the chapter "Hama Rules" in Thomas Friedman, *From Beirut to Jerusalem* (New York: Farrar, Straus and Giroux, 1989), pp. 76–105.

54. Zisser, *Asad's Legacy*, pp. 196–203. Aging remnants of the Brotherhood are scattered in exile in various European cities and in Jordan. The group appears to have preserved some limited covert organizational capabilities in Syria but has not mounted a true public challenge to the regime for more than twenty years. The opposition showed signs of resurgence in the wake of the collapse of authoritarian regimes in Eastern Europe and public opposition to Syria's participation in the first Gulf War coalition. These challenges, limited for the most part to the distribution of antigovernment leaflets and rumored public protests against the war, soon faded. See Rabinovich, "Stability and Change in Syria," p. 18.

55. In the early 1990s Asad considered establishing a regime-sponsored moderate Islamic party but "evidently feared that it could appropriate the potent banner of Islam, make the Baath party appear un-Islamic and become a channel of real opposition." See Raymond Hinnebusch, "Syria: The Politics of Peace and Regime Survival," *Middle East Policy* 3, no. 4 (1995): 83.

56. The Islamization of Syrian Sunnis has received greater media attention recently; see, for example, Neil MacFarquhar, "Syria, Long Ruthlessly Secular, Sees Fervent Islamic Resurgence," *New York Times*, October 24, 2003. But the phenomenon is not new.

Indeed, any foreign observer traveling to Syria regularly over the last decade or so could not help but be struck by the increase in overt manifestations of Islamic piety among Syrian Sunnis; see, for example, Robert Satloff, "Anxious Days for Syria," *Jerusalem Report*, July 16, 1992.

57. The United Nations Population Division estimates that Syria was 46.7 percent urban in 1980, reached 51.4 percent urbanization in 2000, and is on a pace to become more than 60 percent urban by 2020. The Economist Intelligence Unit estimated in 2003 that 75 percent of the population lives in or around Syria's six largest cities. UN Population Division, *World Population Prospects: The 2002 Revision Population Database*, UN Population Database (esa.un.org/unpp/), and Economist Intelligence Unit, *Syria: Country Profile 2003*, p.14.

58. Personal communications with the author. Kuftaro died on September 1, 2004, at the age of eighty-nine. Biographical details on his life and work can be found at (www. kuftaro.org/English/biography.htm). Kuftaro's movement, the Abu al-Nur Islamic Foundation (named after the Damascus mosque in which it is based), sponsors educational programs, a language institute, charity, and missionary work. Although sanctioned by the regime, the foundation is independent from the governmental religious establishment under the Ministry of Religious Endowments (*wizarat al-awqaf*). Salah al-Din Kuftaro, son of the founder, has taken over management of the foundation since his father's death. The foundation's website is located at (www.abunour.net/english/index.html). For more information on the Syrian religious establishment, see Paul Heck, "Religious Renewal in Syria: The Case of Muhammad al-Habash," *Islam and Christian-Muslim Relations* 15, no. 2 (2004).

59. Sadiq al-'Azm, for more than three decades a professor of philosophy at Damascus University, has been throughout his career an advocate of secular modernization and ultimately, despite his Marxist orientation, a variant of democratic liberalism as the only viable path for the Arab world's future. Trained in the West, principally at Yale, he has written scathing critiques of various illiberal alternatives that have manifested themselves in the postindependence political experience of Arab societies. In 1968 he published *naqd al-thati ba'd al-hazima* (Self-Criticism after the Defeat), a devastating indictment of the revolutionary socialism of "progressive" Ba'thist or Nasirist regimes. The following year, he published *naqd al-fikr al-dini* (Critique of Religious Thought), one of the earliest critiques of political Islamism. For publishing these works, he lost his professorship at the American University of Beirut and returned to his native Syria, where he has made his subsequent career. In the Syrian context, 'Azm has been a leading theorist and advocate of civil society and its importance to the modernization of traditional Arab societies. For further discussion of 'Azm's career and significance, see two works by Fouad Ajami: *The Arab Predicament: Arab Political Thought and Practice since 1967* (Cambridge University Press, 1981), pp. 30–37, 141–9; and *The Dream Palace of the Arabs: A Generation's Odyssey* (New York: Pantheon, 1998), pp. 142–4. Muhammad 'Aziz Shukri was professor of international law and, intermittently, dean of the law faculty at Damascus University for almost forty years. Since 2003 he has been the founding dean of the international relations faculty at Qalamoun University, Syria's new private university. Trained initially at Damascus University, he earned graduate legal degrees at the University of Virginia and Columbia University before returning to Damascus University to pursue an academic career. He has long been an advocate of academic freedom and institutional autonomy for Syrian universities, which has sometimes put him at

odds with political authorities in Syria. Balanced against this, his public defense of the conceptual underpinnings of Syrian foreign policy and public diplomacy has made him in some ways a useful figure for the Asad regime. See, for example, Shukri's *International Terrorism: A Legal Critique* (Brattleboro, Vt.: Aman Books, 1991).

60. Raymond Hinnebusch, "State, Civil Society, and Political Change in Syria," in *Civil Society in the Middle East,* edited by Augustus Richard Norton, vol. 1 (New York: E.J. Brill, 1995), pp. 214–42.

61. Despite the constitutional right to establish civil society organizations in Syria, the growth of these organizations has been inhibited by the government's use of long-standing emergency powers to crack down on opposition figures and the emergence of independent political parties. See the essay "Syria: State-Civil Society Relations," Programme on Governance in the Arab Region, United Nations Development Programme (www. pogar.org/countries/syria/civil.htm). See also George, *Syria.*

62. As Hinnebusch describes this background, "Syria's foreign policy is ultimately rooted in the historical frustration of Syrian nationalist aspirations by Western imperialism. . . . The resulting powerful brew of anti-imperialist, anti-Zionist, pan-Arab, and pan-Syrian sentiment has imparted an enduring revisionist and irredentist thrust to Syrian foreign policy." Raymond Hinnebusch, "Revisionist Dreams, Realist Strategies," in *The Foreign Policies of Arab States: The Challenge of Change,* edited by Bahgat Korany and Ali E. Hillal Dessouki, 2d ed. (Boulder, Colo.: Westview Press, 1991), p. 374.

63. Asad kept an enormous painting of Saladin's victory over the Crusaders at Hittin in his presidential office and would often regale foreign diplomats and visiting officials with extended narratives on Middle Eastern history, usually starting with Saladin's defeat of the Crusaders and recapture of Jerusalem. Asad frequently equated Israel with the Crusader states and the forces of imperialism in his rhetoric: "It is not a struggle between Arabs and Jews . . . we do not hate Judaism as a religion but we hate Zionism as a colonialist invading movement"; and "Israel's age . . . is only one-sixth of the period of the Crusaders' dominion in our country." Ma'oz, *Asad, the Sphinx of Damascus,* pp. 85, 104.

64. There is some historical irony in this. During Asad's youth, the Ba'th Party, which Asad joined as a teenager, was an ardent champion of pan-Arab unity. The party's great competitor for adherents among young men from the margins of Syrian society at the time was the organization later known as the Syrian Social Nationalist Party, or SSNP, which advocated pan-Syrian unity based on the concept of Greater Syria.

65. Ma'oz, *Asad, the Sphinx of Damascus,* pp. 45–48.

66. The late Israeli prime minister Yitzhak Rabin, for example, told U.S. officials at various points in his tenure that Asad was, in his judgment, the most intelligent and strategically astute Arab leader. Former U.S. president Bill Clinton concurred, remarking: "Of all the Middle East leaders that I have met, I don't think anyone is smarter—as far as IQ is concerned—than President Assad. The man is brilliant." David Makovsky, "Clinton: Asad Is Brilliant, But He May Have Lost His Chance to Get Back the Golan," *Jerusalem Post,* June 19, 1996.

67. As Hinnebusch ("Revisionist Dreams, Realist Strategies," pp. 374–75) notes, Asad, "while no less stamped by Syria's grievances and dreams [than his predecessors], was prepared to chart a more realistic course matching Syrian objectives and means. He scaled down Syria's objectives, focusing them on recovery of the occupied territories, defense of the Syrian state, and enhancement of its stature in the Arab world; he also greatly upgraded Syrian capabilities."

68. Indeed, during the days of the post-Madrid Palestinian and Syrian tracks of the Middle East peace process, members of the Clinton administration's peace team used to quip that while Palestinian leader Yasir Arafat was "all tactics and no strategy," Asad, by comparison, was "all strategy and no tactics."

69. Ma'oz, *Asad, the Sphinx of Damascus*, pp. 45–48.

70. See, for example, Asad's statements in a 1974 interview: "We hope and endeavor for the kind of real peace in the Middle East that will enable us to get on with all phases of our development—economic, educational, technological and cultural. That will only happen after a complete withdrawal and a solution of Palestinian rights. Peace is only possible after these grievances have been removed. . . . I think that it is within our capability to find in U.N. resolutions at least a guide to a lasting solution of this key problem [the Palestinian issue]. We shall support any decision taken by the PLO. I would imagine that what the PLO decides will not exceed the spirit of U.N. resolutions. And these do not call for the dismantling of Israel." Arnaud de Borchgrave, "Hafiz Asad: A Just Peace Can Survive," *Newsweek*, June 10, 1974, pp. 10–11.

71. Asad's struggle to wrest control of Lebanon from Israel, the Palestinians, and various Lebanese factions is recounted in Reuven Avi-Ran, *The Syrian Involvement in Lebanon since 1975* (Boulder, Colo.: Westview Press, 1991).

72. As Itamar Rabinovich notes in *The War for Lebanon, 1970–1985* (Cornell University Press, 1985), pp. 36–37, "Syria had both political and security concerns in Lebanon. Lebanon, as an open political society, was a threat to the closed political society of Syria. And Lebanon could be used militarily by Israel to outflank Syria's defenses or by Syria to open a new front against Israel. But Syria's leaders also fitted Lebanon into a larger design, intended to capitalize on Egypt's declining position in the Arab world and to develop an independent power base for Syria that was to rely on its military strength and the extension of Syrian influence over the immediate environment: Jordan, Lebanon, and with the Palestinians. As the PLO's principal base as well as the center for several Arab political parties and movements, Lebanese territory was vital to a regime with Pan-Arab ambitions."

73. The Syrian leader calculated that, unless he put down the radical Islamist and Palestinian elements seeking to topple the Lebanese state, the unrest could spread into Syria. It was in this regard that Asad observed, "It is difficult to draw a line between Lebanon's security in its broadest sense and Syria's security"; for discussion, see Adeed Dawisha, "The Motives of Syria's Involvement in Lebanon," *Middle East Journal* 38, no. 2 (Spring 1984). At conferences with Lebanese, Palestinian, and Syrian representatives in Cairo and Riyadh in the fall of 1976, the two most important Arab states, Egypt and Saudi Arabia, effectively endorsed Syrian intervention. The United States, under both the Ford and Carter administrations, did so as well and worked to manage the risks of direct Israeli-Syrian confrontation. Most notably, in 1976, Israel and Syria reached their first "red-line" agreement, under which Israel recognized Syria's sway in Lebanon in return for Syrian commitments not to pose a direct military threat to Israel from the Israeli-Lebanese border area.

74. The removal of the Palestine Liberation Organization to Lebanon from Jordan in 1970 and the outbreak of civil war in 1975 had created a destabilizing security vacuum in many parts of Lebanon, including the southern portion bordering Israel. Syrian commitments, under the 1976 red-line agreement, to keep its forces out of the Israeli-Lebanese border area had the effect of attracting PLO paramilitary cadres to the area, set-

ting up a daily threat of Palestinian artillery and terrorist attacks against northern Israel from southern Lebanon in addition to the risk of a takeover in Beirut by the PLO and radical Lebanese Muslim elements. Soon, southern Lebanon had become the principal staging area for Palestinian operations against Israeli interests. This prompted Israel to launch its "Operation Litani" in March 1978, during which the Israel Defense Forces carved out a contiguous security zone under its control in the south of Lebanon. For more detailed assessment and discussion, see Rabinovich, *The War for Lebanon*, pp. 89–110. As the security situation along its northern border deteriorated, Israel intensified its involvement in Lebanon during the late 1970s, developing an increasingly close alliance with dominant elements of the Lebanese Maronite community. The expansion of Israel's role in Lebanese affairs coincided with the ascendance of the Phalange movement (linked to the Jumayyil family) over its rivals for political primacy among Lebanese Maronites (particularly the Franjiyyah family). Ze'ev Schiff and Ehud Ya'ari, *Israel's Lebanon War*, translated and edited by Ina Friedman (New York: Simon and Schuster, 1984), pp. 18–30.

75. See Rabinovich, *The War for Lebanon*, pp. 110–11.

76. For further discussion, see Schiff and Ya'ari, *Israel's Lebanon War*, and Sheila Ryan, "Israel's Invasion of Lebanon: Background to the Crisis," *Journal of Palestine Studies* 11, no. 4, and 12, no. 1 (Summer/Fall 1982).

77. For additional analysis, see Rabinovich, *The War for Lebanon*, pp. 111–53.

78. The Multinational Force (MNF) landed in Beirut on August 21, 1982, and departed on September 10 after the completion of its mission to oversee the evacuation of PLO fighters from Beirut. After Bashir Jumayyil's assassination on September 14 and the ensuing massacre of Palestinians in the Sabra and Shatila refugee camps, the MNF returned on September 29, with the U.S. contingent encamping at the Beirut International Airport until its withdrawal offshore in February 1984.

79. For further details, see Alasdair Drysdale and Raymond Hinnebusch, *Syria and the Middle East Peace Process* (New York: Council on Foreign Relations Press, 1991), p. 192.

80. For additional discussion, see Dilip Hiro, *Lebanon: Fire and Embers: A History of the Lebanese Civil War* (New York: St. Martin's Press, 1992), pp. 94–110.

81. In his interventions, Asad was always prepared to use force, even terrorist violence, not only against his adversaries at a given moment but also against his ostensible allies, so as to leave no doubt about Syrian dominance. In 1987, for example, Asad ordered Syrian troops into West Beirut to assert Syrian authority over Hizballah and other militias who had usurped control there, killing twenty-four Hizballah members at the organization's headquarters in Basta; see William H. Harris, *Faces of Lebanon: Sects, Wars, and Global Extensions* (Princeton, N.J.: Markus Wiener Publishers, 1997), p. 214.

82. The Ta'if Accord was meant to redress the political imbalances that had fueled Lebanon's fifteen-year civil war and end the stranglehold of sectarian militias over the country. The elements of the accord were worked into the Lebanese Constitution, providing a new set of rules to govern Lebanese political life. The accord, for example, created political parity in the parliament, where Christians had once held a six-to-five advantage. Similarly, it forced the president, traditionally a Maronite, to share executive authority with a Sunni prime minister. The accord also legitimated the Syrian military presence in Lebanon and gave Damascus a major role in Lebanese security affairs. The accord did not call explicitly for a withdrawal of Syrian forces from all Lebanese territory; rather, it mandated a redeployment of Syrian forces to the Biqa'a, supposedly two

years after the accord was ratified; the size and disposition of Syrian forces remaining in Lebanon was then to be negotiated between the two governments. The terms give Syria an important voice in deciding the size and disposition of its forces in Lebanon once redeployment is completed. United Nations Security Council Resolution 520 (1982), however, does envision the withdrawal of all "non-Lebanese" forces from Lebanon. On Ta'if, see Harris, *Faces of Lebanon*, pp. 243–78; for textual commentary on the accord, see Joseph Maila, *The Document of National Understanding: A Commentary* (Oxford: Centre for Lebanese Studies, 1992).

83. On the multifaceted Syrian interest in Lebanon, see, among others, Dawisha, "The Motives of Syria's Involvement in Lebanon"; Volker Perthes, "Syria's Involvement in Lebanon," *Middle East Report* 27, no. 2 (Spring 1997); Raymond Hinnebusch, "Pax Syriana? The Origins, Causes, and Consequences of Syria's Role in Lebanon," *Mediterranean Politics* 3, no. 1 (Spring 1998); Zisser, *Asad's Legacy*, pp. 129–51; Daniel Pipes and Ziad Abdelnour, co-chairs, "Syrian Motives for Lebanon's Occupation," Report of the Lebanon Study Group, Middle East Forum, May 2000 (www.meforum.org); and Gary Gambill, "The Syrian Occupation of Lebanon," *Middle East Forum Wires*, May 13, 2003.

84. At its height, when the Ta'if Accord was signed in 1989, the Syrian military presence in Lebanon numbered roughly 35,000 troops; by the time of Hafiz's death in 2000, this figure had come down to roughly 25,000, according to U.S. government estimates. See, for example, U.S. Department of State, "Lebanon: Country Report on Human Rights Practices, 2000." Syrian troop deployments had stabilized at this level by the mid-1990s, according to official U.S. estimates. See, for example, the State Department's "Lebanon Report of Human Rights Practices for 1997." Unofficial estimates, however, usually put the number of Syrian troops deployed in Lebanon during the 1990s at approximately 35,000 throughout the decade; see, for example, Ziad Abdelnour and Gary Gambill, "Syria's Fourth Redeployment from Lebanon," *Middle East Intelligence Bulletin* 5, no. 7 (July 2003). Traditionally, regular Syrian forces have been concentrated in the eastern and northern parts of the country; even after the signing of the Ta'if Accord, Asad refused to redeploy all but a few Syrian troops to the Biqa'a, as called for in the accord, citing the Lebanese government's inability to implement other parts of the agreement, most notably those provisions calling for an end to Israel's occupation of the security zone extending northward from the Israeli-Lebanese border. See Baidatz, *Bashar's First Year*, pp. 33–42, and Abdelnour and Gambill, "Syria's Fourth Redeployment from Lebanon."

85. Zisser, *Asad's Legacy*, pp. 141–49.

86. Ibid. See also George Emile Irani, "Religious Movements and Politics in Postwar Lebanon," *CSIS Briefing Notes on Islam, Society, and Politics* 1, no. 2 (July 1998).

87. In effect, Asad sought understandings governing Hizballah's operations against Israel Defense Forces targets in Israel's self-declared "security zone" in southern Lebanon. As Rabinovich has pointed out, such "rules of the game" are analogous to earlier sets of understandings between Israel and Syria to regulate their military interaction in Lebanon, through the so-called red-line agreements; see Rabinovich, "Southern Lebanon: Area of Confidence Building or Confrontation?" paper presented at a U.S. Department of State conference on "Syria's Foreign Policy: Looking Beyond the Gulf Crisis," Washington (June 20, 1991). From the Syrian leader's perspective, the purpose of such rules was to allow Hizballah to carry out operations against Israeli forces in the occupied security zone in southern Lebanon while seeking to lower the risks of military

escalation. In July 1993 Hizballah exceeded the usual scope of its operations against elements of the Israel Defense Forces in the security zone, launching Katyusha rockets into Israel proper, allegedly because IDF artillery rounds had struck Lebanese villages north of the zone. Israel responded with Operation Accountability—a series of air raids on Syrian artillery positions in the Biqa'a and the expulsion of thousands of Lebanese civilians from southern Lebanon. Israel and Lebanon became parties to an informal agreement ending Hizballah rocket attacks into northern Israel in exchange for an end to the Israeli air strikes; effectively, Syria and Hizballah were parties to the agreement as well. In April 1996, after a similar escalatory spiral between IDF elements in the zone and Hizballah cadres in southern Lebanon, Israel launched Operation Grapes of Wrath, which included a sizable incursion of Israeli ground forces north of the zone. Ultimately, Israel and Syria, with U.S. and French mediation, agreed to a set of more formal understandings, including the creation of the Israel-Lebanon Monitoring Group (ILMG). The understanding, a written but unsigned document between the parties, prohibited Hizballah, Israel, and Israel's proxy South Lebanon Army from targeting civilians, while reaffirming the right of self-defense for the combatant parties. The ILMG, formed to monitor the understanding and hear claims of violations, included civilian representatives from the United States and France and military representatives from Syria, Lebanon, and Israel. Although the ILMG had no enforcement mechanism, it dampened the impact of the conflict on civilians by sorting out responsibility for violations and urging calm and the avoidance of escalation when violence flared up. For an assessment, see Adam Frey, "The Israel-Lebanon Monitoring Group: An Operational Review," Research Note 3 (Washington: Washington Institute for Near East Policy, September 1997).

88. The carefully balanced political system established under the Ta'if Accord frequently produces gridlock in decisionmaking that requires Syrian intervention to break. Asad consistently sought to reinforce the tendency of Lebanese political actors to seek outside help in resolving their disagreements by cultivating a "finger-in-every-pie" array of contacts across the Lebanese political spectrum. For discussion, see Zisser, *Asad's Legacy*, p. 145. For the text of the Treaty of Brotherhood, Cooperation, and Coordination, negotiated by Syria and its post-Ta'if allies in Lebanon, which solidified economic and security ties between the two countries, see *Beirut Review* 1, no. 2 (Fall 1991): 115–19.

89. Zisser, *Asad's Legacy*, pp. 139–43. For example, as Hizballah became an increasingly important factor in Shi'a politics through its performance in the 1992 parliamentary elections, Asad's ties to the group were an important lever for exerting influence over Shi'a affairs. But, at the same time, Asad made sure that Hizballah did not become so important that it could disregard Syrian interests. In particular, Asad used his other means of influence in Lebanon to ensure that Hizballah did not eclipse its chief Shi'a rival, Nabih Berri's Amal Party, in the 1996 parliamentary elections, when popular support for Hizballah had risen significantly as a result of the group's military performance against the Israeli military during Israel's Operation Grapes of Wrath earlier that year. For discussion, see Graham Usher, "Hizballah, Syria, and the Lebanese Elections," *Journal of Palestine Studies* 26, no. 2 (Winter 1997); and Magnus Ranstorp, "The Strategy and Tactics of Hizballah's 'Lebanonization Process,'" *Mediterranean Politics* 3, no. 1 (Summer 1998).

90. For further analysis from two outspoken critics of the Asad regime and Syria's dominant role in Lebanese affairs, see Gary Gambill and Elie Abou Aoun, "How Syria

Orchestrates Lebanon's Elections," *Middle East Intelligence Bulletin* 2, no. 7 (August 2000). Commenting on the candidates in the 2000 parliamentary election, the British journalist Robert Fisk wrote: "Despite the 589 pro- and anti-government candidates standing for the 128 seats in the national assembly, every one of them is pro-Syrian"; see Fisk, "Money Ranks Higher than Democracy in Lebanese Polls," *The Independent* (London), August 27, 2000. On similar Syrian gerrymandering in the first postwar elections, see Farid el-Khazen, "Lebanon's First Postwar Parliamentary Elections, 1993," *Middle East Policy* 3, no. 1 (1994), pp. 120–36.

91. For competing interpretations of the significance of the protests (which erupted on April 13, 2000, the twenty-fifth anniversary of the Lebanese civil war) and ensuing crackdowns, see As'ad AbuKhalil, "Lebanon One Year after the Israeli Withdrawal," *MERIP*, May 29, 2001; and Gary Gambill, "Lebanon's Intifada," *Middle East Intelligence Bulletin* 2, no. 4 (April 2000).

92. United Nations Secretary General Kofi Annan confirmed on June 16, 2000, that Israel had fully complied with UN Security Council Resolution 425.

93. After the 1973 Yom Kippur/October War, Asad reiterated his commitment to a negotiated solution to the conflict with Israel, stressing that he chose war only because he could not bring the Israelis into serious discussions without it: "When they occupied our land, we were faced with two alternatives—either to find some political and diplomatic way to get them to withdraw, or fight to get our land back. Six years of talking led to nothing, so we opted for war. It was the only choice after exhausting all other avenues prior to October 6. . . . As you know, all we want is a just peace. It's not too much to ask. And when the prerequisites for this peace have been realized, there will be no need for special measures such as demilitarized zones." See de Borchgrave, "Hafiz Assad: A Just Peace Can Survive"; and Drysdale and Hinnebusch, *Syria and the Middle East Peace Process*.

94. Drysdale and Hinnebusch, *Syria and the Middle East Peace Process*, pp. 59–62, and Ma'oz, *Asad, the Sphinx of Damascus*, pp. 177–83.

95. Drysdale and Hinnebusch, *Syria and the Middle East Peace Process*, pp. 117–19; Ma'oz, *Asad, the Sphinx of Damascus*, pp. 109–22; Seale, *Asad of Syria*, pp. 312–14.

96. Drysdale and Hinnebusch, *Syria and the Middle East Peace Process*, pp. 135–42; Ma'oz, *Asad, the Sphinx of Damascus*, pp. 177–88. See also Michael Eisenstadt, *Arming for Peace? Syria's Elusive Quest for "Strategic Parity,"* Policy Papers 31 (Washington: Washington Institute for Near East Policy, 1992).

97. Eisenstadt, *Arming for Peace?* pp. 34–37.

98. On the shift toward nonconventional weapons, see Ellen Laipson, "Syria: Can the Myth Be Maintained without Nukes?" in *The Nuclear Tipping Point: Why States Reconsider Their Nuclear Choices,* edited by Kurt M. Campbell, Robert J. Einhorn, and Mitchell B. Reiss (Brookings Institution Press, 2004), p. 86. As noted in chapter 1, Syria began to develop a chemical weapons program in the 1970s. These efforts intensified through the 1980s, accompanied in time by procurement of ballistic missile systems for weaponized chemical warfare agents. On Asad's use of terrorist proxies, see Seale, *Asad of Syria*, pp. 461–91; Ma'oz, *Asad, the Sphinx of Damascus*, pp. 170–77.

99. This proposition would be hotly debated within the Israeli national security establishment and between the Israeli and U.S. intelligence communities during the 1996 Israeli-Syrian "war scare," when the withdrawal of a Syrian special forces division from Lebanon to its traditional garrison area in Syria near the Golan Heights raised concerns

in Israeli military intelligence and in the Mossad that Damascus was preparing to launch a limited land-grab operation on the Golan to force the new government of Binyamin Netanyahu to resume peace talks with Syria on Hafiz al-Asad's terms. U.S. intelligence officers disagreed with this assessment, arguing throughout the episode that Syria had no intention or plans to initiate military conflict with Israel. The Israeli chief of staff at the time, General Amnon Lipkin-Shahak, and the defense minister, Yitzhak Mordechai, also disagreed publicly with the Israeli intelligence assessment, and U.S. officials were able to walk the two sides back from possible confrontation. A Mossad case officer was subsequently convicted of fraud and sentenced to prison for taking money meant to pay a supposedly well-placed Syrian source and fabricating reports about Syrian military planning and intentions, supposedly from that source, that helped generate the erroneous Israeli assessment of the redeployment of the Syrian special forces division. For an account, see Leslie Susser, "The Drums Beat," *Jerusalem Post*, January 23,1997; Jay Bushinsky and Douglas Davis, "'False Info' Scandal Unfolds. Mossad Agent Yehuda Gil to Stand Trial," *Jerusalem Post*, December 7, 1997; and Kenneth Pollack, "Syria's 'War Option': Assessing the Lessons from West Bank/Gaza Riots," Peacewatch 107 (Washington: Washington Institute for Near East Policy, October 8, 1996).

100. Zisser, *Asad's Legacy*, pp. 104–13.

101. On the Syrian perception of the guidelines of a final peace treaty, see Raymond Hinnebusch, "Does Syria Want Peace? Syrian Policy in the Syrian-Israeli Peace Negotiations," *Journal of Palestine Studies* 26, no. 1 (Autumn 1996), pp. 42–57.

102. Zisser, *Asad's Legacy*, pp. 117–21.

103. Ibid., p. 124.

104. Secretary of State Warren Christopher and the Clinton administration's special Middle East coordinator, Dennis Ross, initially conveyed Rabin's offer to Asad in August 1993. For details on Rabin's offer, see Warren Christopher, *Chances of a Lifetime: A Memoir* (New York: Scribner, 2001), pp. 220–24; Itamar Rabinovich, *The Brink of Peace: The Israeli-Syrian Negotiations* (Princeton University Press, 1999); pp. 3–13; and Dennis Ross, *The Missing Peace: The Inside Story of the Fight for Middle East Peace* (New York: Farrar, Straus and Giroux, 2004). During Rabin's tenure in office, as well as during the brief tenure of Shimon Peres as prime minister following Rabin's assassination in 1995 (Peres reaffirmed Rabin's deposit upon becoming prime minister), Asad's fluctuating perception of his Israeli counterpart's commitment to the deposit was the critical variable determining the rate of progress in negotiations. Three separate rounds of Israeli-Syrian negotiations took place under U.S. auspices at Wye: the first on December 27–29, 1995, and January 3–5, 1996; the second round, January 24–26 and January 29–31, 1996. The third round was launched February 28–March 1, 1996, but was suspended when the Israeli delegation withdrew following terrorist bombings in Jerusalem and Tel Aviv and a refusal by the Syrian delegation to express condolences for the victims of those bombings.

105. More detailed analysis of these negotiations can be found in Rabinovich, *The Brink of Peace*; Helena Cobban, *The Israeli-Syrian Peace Talks: 1991–96 and Beyond* (Washington: United States Institute of Peace, 2000); and the relevant portions of Ross, *The Missing Peace*.

106. Prime Minister Netanyahu's evasions over the withdrawal issue reinforced Asad's distrust of Netanyahu, which had taken root with the prime minister's initial advocacy of a "Lebanon first" approach to negotiating peace with Syria in the summer of 1996 and the Israeli-Syrian "war scare" in the late summer and fall of that year. Following the war scare,

Netanyahu used a variety of back channels to explore reviving Israeli-Syrian peace talks. Initially he tried to do this under a policy of tying the depth of withdrawal to the depth of security arrangements, sending three key advisers—Dore Gold, Danny Yatom, and Uzi Arad—in succession to Washington in 1997 with messages for Syrian ambassador Walid al-Mu'allim, who had headed Syria's delegation to the Wye Plantation talks. Mu'allim was adamant that Syria would not begin talks until Netanyahu endorsed the previous contingent commitment to full withdrawal. In January 1998 Netanyahu launched an unofficial initiative to revive the talks using U.S. private citizens as intermediaries, but his unwillingness to clarify his position on the withdrawal issue prompted Syrian officials in early 1999 to refuse to continue back channel contacts.

107. For an account of Israeli-Syrian exchanges from Barak's election in May 1999 until the Shepherdstown discussions, see Ross, *The Missing Peace*, pp. 509–65.

108. According to Ross (*The Missing Peace,* pp. 567–68), Robert Malley, the president's special assistant for Arab-Israeli affairs, described Clinton as having "gone overboard" on the withdrawal issue in a telephone conversation with Asad. Similarly, another member of the peace team who was privy to the conversation has told the author that President Clinton "went too far" in assuring Asad about Barak's position on full withdrawal.

109. On the preparations for and failure of the Geneva summit, see Madeleine Albright, *Madam Secretary: A Memoir* (New York: Miramax, 2003), pp. 473–82; Ross, *The Missing Peace*, pp. 550–90; and Martin Indyk, *Unintended Consequences* (New York: Knopf, forthcoming 2005).

110. Rabinovich, *The Brink of Peace*, p. 214.

111. In an interview on the MacNeil/Lehrer NewsHour on October 1, 1993, Asad said: "To my mind, this is not their [the Palestinians'] best option, nor the best route to the establishment of peace. Yet, we decided not to obstruct the agreement. We said that this is up to the Palestinian people and their organizations. However, no one should expect us to wax enthusiastic over a secret agreement concluded behind our backs." See "Asad on the Israel-PLO Accord," *Middle East Quarterly* 1, no. 1 (March 1994). Asad's critiques of the Oslo process are analyzed in Christopher Hemmer, "I Told You So: Syria, Oslo and the al-Aqsa Intifada," *Middle East Policy* 10, no. 3 (September 22, 2003).

112. For a thoughtful presentation of what an Israeli-Syrian agreement meeting both sides' critical needs could look like, see International Crisis Group, *Middle East Endgame III: Israel, Syria, and Lebanon—How Comprehensive Peace Settlements Would Look*, Middle East Report 4 (www.crisisgroup.org, July 16, 2002).

113. Ma'oz, *Asad, the Sphinx of Damascus*, pp. 109–22; Drysdale and Hinnebusch, *Syria and the Middle East Peace Process*, pp. 59–97.

114. Zisser, *Asad's Legacy*, pp. 79–82, 104–6.

115. Alasdair Drysdale, "Syria's Relations with the Moderate Arab Bloc," paper presented at a U.S. Department of State conference, *Syria's Foreign Policy: Looking Beyond the Gulf Crisis*, Washington (June 20, 1991).

116. Egypt's membership in the Arab League had been suspended in 1979 following the conclusion of the Camp David Accords.

117. The financial pledges, originally earmarked for five years, were made by Gulf states to "frontline states" in the Arab-Israeli conflict at the Baghdad Summit of 1978. See Ma'oz, *Asad, The Sphinx of Damascus*, p. 589.

118. Drysdale, "Syria's Relations with the Moderate Arab Bloc."

119. The most significant sign of renewed cooperation between Syria and the Gulf countries in the aftermath of the 1991 Gulf War was the signing of the Damascus Declaration on March 6, 1991, by the countries of the Gulf Cooperation Council (Bahrain, Kuwait, Oman, Qatar, Saudi Arabia, and the United Arab Emirates), Syria, and Egypt. The declaration announced the intention of the "6+2" signatories to bolster political, economic, and military cooperation. Although the GCC countries soon downplayed the security aspect of the declaration, preferring bilateral agreements with the United States to reliance on Syrian and Egyptian troops first introduced in the region as part of the Gulf War coalition, the new alignment produced a loosely coordinated framework for political and economic cooperation. Syria's central role in the reconstituted postwar regional balance was symbolized by the choice of its capital for issuance of the declaration. The "6+2" framework remained relevant in the 1990s as the Gulf countries used Egypt and Syria as a counterweight for disputes with Iran. For further analysis of the significance of the Damascus Declaration, see F. Gregory Gause III, *Oil Monarchies: Domestic and Security Challenges in the Arab Gulf States* (New York: Council on Foreign Relations Press, 1994), pp. 132–37.

120. In the near term, a protracted military conflict between Iran and Iraq worked to deflect Baghdad's attention away from Damascus, leaving Asad greater freedom to concentrate on dealing with Israel and his Levantine Arab neighbors. For discussion, see Hussein J. Agha and Ahmad S. Khalidi, *Syria and Iran: Rivalry and Cooperation* (London: Pinter Publishers for the Royal Institute of International Affairs, 1994), pp. 10–13.

121. Anoushiravan Ehteshami and Raymond A. Hinnebusch, *Syria and Iran: Middle Powers in a Penetrated Regional System* (London: Routledge, 1997), pp. 101–05.

122. Agha and Khalidi, *Syria and Iran*, pp. 14–25.

123. As was noted earlier, Hizballah's two principal state sponsors have had a rough division of labor. Essentially, Iran has provided the larger part of Hizballah's funds and exercises usually determinative influence over the group's terrorist operations outside the region. Damascus, for its part, has been Hizballah's main point of reference regarding the group's activities inside Lebanon; this includes exercising what is almost always decisive influence regarding the timing, geographic scope, and physical scale of Hizballah's anti-Israeli operations. The two countries' roles with respect to Hizballah have overlapped in ways that impelled their (sometimes uneasy) cooperation. Most important, Tehran had to rely on Syrian cooperation to use Damascus as the principal transit point for shipping weapons and other supplies to Hizballah fighters in Lebanon. When Iran and Syria were of one mind on the appropriate level for Hizballah's anti-Israeli operations, this was an unproblematic part of their bilateral relationship. When Iranian and Syrian perspectives have diverged, as they did intermittently during Israeli-Syrian peace talks in the 1990s, the question of regulating Hizballah's operations could become a point of friction. In particular, when Syria would act to rein in Hizballah's Lebanese operations to encourage progress in the negotiations, Iran would have no meaningful leverage to forestall a reduction in the group's activity. For additional discussion, see Agha and Khalidi, *Syria and Iran*, pp. 77–82.

124. For discussion, see Eberhard Kienle, *Ba'th v. Ba'th: The Conflict between Syria and Iraq, 1968–1989* (London: I.B. Tauris, 1991).

125. The shift became apparent in the first half of 1997 and developed steadily over the remainder of the elder Asad's tenure. In May of that year, Syria allowed an exchange of commercial delegations between the two countries and in June reopened its border

with Iraq for trade, ending a seventeen-year closure. See Robert Danin, "An Iraqi-Syrian Entente? Prospects and Implications," Policywatch 253 (Washington: Washington Institute for Near East Policy, June 11, 1997). Syrian-Iraqi trade grew noticeably during the last three years of Hafiz's presidency, and it was reported that Syria was being used as a transit point for importing goods prohibited by the UN sanctions regime into Iraq. For discussion, see Patrick Clawson, "Can Iraq Reconstitute the Arab Eastern Front against Israel?" Policywatch 509 (Wasington: Washington Institute for Near East Policy, January 8, 2001). In July 1998 Syria and Iraq signed a memorandum of understanding to reopen an oil pipeline between Kirkuk and Banyas. The pipeline had been closed in 1982 and required extensive repairs to become fully operational, but its prospective reopening was a significant threat to the viability of the UN sanctions regime and the oil-for-food program. By late 1999, oil industry sources were claiming in trade publications and media reports that the pipeline was nearly ready to resume operations. See, for example, "Iraq-to-Syria Pipeline Almost Repaired," *Alexander's Gas & Oil Connections* 4, no. 17 (September 8, 1999). Iraqi foreign minister Mohammed Sa'id al-Sahhaf made a public declaration of the pipeline's operational readiness in February 2000.

126. See, for example, Dilip Hiro, "Iraq Making Unlikely Friends with Iran and Syria," Inter Press Service, April 7, 1998; Bill Gertz, "Syria, Iraq Want to Unite against U.S., Report Says," *Washington Times*, January 8, 1998; and Waiel Faleh, "Iraq Moves to Restore Syrian Ties," Associated Press, December 28, 1999.

127. On this point, see also Zisser, *Asad's Legacy*, pp. 82–85.

128. For detailed discussions of Soviet-Syrian relations, see two works by Robert Freedman: *Soviet Policy toward the Middle East since 1970* (New York: Praeger, 1982); and *Moscow and the Middle East: Soviet Policy since the Invasion of Afghanistan* (Cambridge University Press, 1991); see also Galia Golan, *Soviet Policies in the Middle East: From World War II to Gorbachev* (Cambridge University Press, 1990), and Efraim Karsh, *The Soviet Union and Syria: The Asad Years* (London: Routledge for the Royal Institute of International Affairs, 1988).

129. Asad was probably only half-joking when he told Kissinger, during one of their meetings, "The problem should be pictured as Arab against Israel, not as the United States versus the USSR. I was told by other Arabs that you would not allow American arms to be defeated by Soviet arms. So, I would propose that we develop a situation where U.S. arms are against U.S. arms." Kissinger, *Years of Upheaval* (Boston: Little, Brown and Company, 1982), p. 850.

130. For Asad's take on these discussions, see Seale, *Asad of Syria*, pp. 226–49; for Kissinger's, see *Years of Upheaval*. An overview of the postwar diplomacy leading to the 1974 disengagement agreement can also be found in Steven Spiegel, *The Other Arab-Israeli Conflict: Making America's Middle East Policy, From Truman to Reagan* (University of Chicago Press, 1985), pp. 267–83.

131. See Yair Evron, "Washington, Damascus, and the Lebanese Crisis," in *Syria under Assad: Domestic Constraints and Regional Risks*, edited by Moshe Ma'oz and Avner Yaniv (London: Croom Helm, 1986), pp. 209–23.

132. Ma'oz, *Asad, The Sphinx of Damascus*, pp. 136–37.

133. Seale, *Asad of Syria*, pp. 296–97.

134. Spiegel, *The Other Arab-Israeli Conflict*, pp. 337–39.

135. Seale, *Asad of Syria*, p. 336.

136. For discussion, see Itamar Rabinovich, "Syrian Foreign Policy: Goals, Capabilities, Constraints, and Options," *Survival* 24, no. 4 (July/August 1982): 179.

137. Evron, "Washington, Damascus, and the Lebanese Crisis," pp. 209–17.

138. Rabinovich, "Syrian Foreign Policy," p. 181.

139. Drysdale and Hinnebusch, *Syria and the Middle East Peace Process*, p. 191. Habib's disputes with the administration over Lebanon policy and his complicated negotiations with Asad, Ariel Sharon, and various Lebanese parties are recounted in John Boykin, *Cursed Is the Peacemaker: The American Diplomat versus the Israeli General, Beirut 1982* (Belmont, Calif.: Applegate Press, 2002).

140. Drysdale and Hinnebusch, *Syria and the Middle East Peace Process*, pp. 195–96.

141. Zisser, *Asad's Legacy*, pp. 37–51; Neil Quilliam, *Syria and the New World Order* (Reading, U.K.: Ithaca Press, 1999), pp. 128–32.

142. As his secretary of state noted, "President Bush was anxious to engage the Syrians. He had always believed that George Shultz had made a serious mistake by cutting off contacts with Syria after the disastrous 1983 bombing of the U.S. Marine barracks in Beirut. In 1986, Vice President Bush had wanted to visit Damascus on his trip to the Middle East, but had been reluctantly dissuaded by aides fearful of the potential political fallout. . . . He had grudgingly accepted that he shouldn't visit Syria, but he always believed that the United States had dropped the ball and should have engaged Asad, despite serious disagreements over Syria's support of international terrorism and heavy involvement in narcotics trafficking." See James A. Baker III with Thomas M. Defrank, *The Politics of Diplomacy: Revolution, War and Peace 1989–1992* (New York: G. P. Putnam's Sons, 1995), p. 296.

143. An early indication of the new level of "understanding" that had been reached between Damascus and Washington came in October 1990, when Asad ordered Syrian troops to put down the rebellion of the self-styled Maronite prime minister General Michel Aoun, who led a rump Lebanese Army force that continued to resist Syrian hegemony after the signing of the Ta'if Accord. Washington eventually signaled (by withholding formal protest) its tacit endorsement of a final Syrian assault on the holdouts. See Harris, *Faces of Lebanon*, pp. 276–77.

144. Baker, *The Politics of Diplomacy*, pp. 297–98.

145. In addition to extensive involvement in mediating the Syrian track by Secretary Christopher and Special Middle East Coordinator Ross, U.S. engagement with Syria during President Clinton's first term included a Clinton-Asad summit in January 1994. Christopher played an important role in brokering the understandings that ended Israel's Operation Accountability in June 1993 and Operation Grapes of Wrath in April 1996 and in deescalating the Israeli-Syrian war scare in September 1996; see Christopher, *Chances of a Lifetime*, p. 220. In the second term, Ross was heavily involved in the mediated back channel communications between Prime Minister Netanyahu and Asad described earlier. After Prime Minister Barak came to office in 1999, Ross, Secretary of State Madeleine Albright, National Security Adviser Samuel Berger, and President Clinton himself became involved in the reinvigorated Syrian track. These efforts culminated in the Clinton-Asad summit in Geneva in April 2000, which marked the collapse of the track.

146. On this point, see Flynt Leverett, Testimony to the Senate Foreign Relations Committee, October 31, 2003.

Chapter Three

1. Hafiz al-Asad's firstborn child, a daughter named Bushra, died in infancy after falling sick when Hafiz was posted as an air force officer in Egypt during the short-lived United Arab Republic. His second child, a daughter born in October 1960, also during Hafiz's posting in Egypt, was given the same name as her departed sister. See Patrick Seale, *Asad of Syria: The Struggle for the Middle East* (Berkeley, Calif.: University of California Press, 1989), pp. 68–69.

2. Mahir was born in 1968. Biographic information on Majid is not publicly available.

3. The Fraternity School was founded by Franciscan friars during the French occupation but was taken over by the Syrian government and made a "semi-public" school for boys (meaning it could charge tuition, even though it was a public school) in the 1960s. All the Asad sons attended the school; Bushra attended the Laic School, another formerly religious school founded by the French.

4. On Bashar's schooling and personality, see Susan Sachs, "Man in the News: The Shy Young Doctor at Syria's Helm," *New York Times*, June 14, 2000.

5. Zisser cites a 1993 report in the Paris-based Arabic weekly *al-Muharrir* as the earliest mention of Hafiz selecting Basil as his would-be successor; see Eyal Zisser, "The Succession Struggle in Damascus," *Middle East Quarterly* 2, no. 3 (September 1995). For other signals that Basil had become the designated successor, such as the distribution of his photo along with that of Hafiz at public events, see Eyal Zisser, *Asad's Legacy: Syria in Transition* (New York University Press, 2001), pp. 158–59.

6. The elder Asad went so far as to contact St. Joseph's University in Beirut to inquire about studying medicine there, but his family was too poor to send him to Lebanon to fill out the enrollment forms. Seale, *Asad of Syria*, p. 38.

7. Most children of the Syrian elite still do not study abroad or, if they do, go abroad for no more than a year. In a personal communication with the author, a Syrian civil society activist noted, somewhat wryly, that this allows them to develop a taste for Western consumption but does not allow them to develop any sense of democratic or market-oriented values. Cobban has observed that "many non-Westerners who study in the West become even more anti-Western as a result of that experience"; see Helena Cobban, "Syria's New Assad No Sure Thing," *Christian Science Monitor*, June 28, 2000.

8. Press reports vary in their accounting of the length of Bashar's period of residence in London; Bashar told the author in January 2004 that he started his training at the Western Eye Hospital in 1992 and stayed until his brother Basil's death in January 1994.

9. Even Bashar's limited time in the West is significantly more than that of his father or of most members of the old guard who, with the exception of Foreign Minister Faruq al-Shar', have had little direct experience of the West and rarely travel there. Bashar, who applied for and received a visa to come to the United States before his accession to the presidency, has expressed to U.S. visitors an interest in visiting various parts of the United States and, since the September 11, 2001, terrorist attacks, has spoken of his regret that it has not been possible for him to do so.

10. In an interview with the author on January 17, 2004, Bashar said that during his time in London he concentrated, in a manner not unusual for young doctors going through their postgraduate training, on his work at the Western Eye Hospital. He lived near the hospital, and claimed not to have experienced much of London during his time there.

11. Syrians, including some officials, have claimed in private conversations that Basil was on his way to the airport to fly to Germany to visit his brother Majid at a psychiatric treatment facility there.

12. On succession preparations generally, see Zisser, *Asad's Legacy*, pp. 160–71.

13. Benjamin Orbach and David Schenker, "The Rise of Bashar Al-Asad," Policywatch 371 (Washington: Washington Institute for Near East Policy, March 5, 1999).

14. "Bashar al-Asad's Biography," *ArabicNews.com*, June 28, 2000. A story circulated around Damascus for several months after Bashar's graduation from the Higher Military Academy that another officer had ended the course with a slightly higher overall score than Bashar for the command and staff course, putting him at the top of the class. According to the story, this officer withdrew his name from consideration for formal acknowledgment as the top student, allowing Bashar to claim the honor.

15. Orbach and Schenker, "The Rise of Bashar Al-Asad"; "Bashar al-Asad's Biography."

16. Orbach and Schenker, "The Rise of Bashar Al-Asad."

17. Zisser, "The Succession Struggle in Damascus"; Michael Collins Dunn, ed., "The Asad Factor," *The Estimate* (May 10 and 24, 1996); Michael Eisenstadt, "Who Rules Syria? Bashar Al-Asad and the Alawi Barons," Policywatch 472 (Washington: Washington Institute for Near East Policy, June 21, 2000).

18. Eisenstadt, "Who Rules Syria?"; Eyal Zisser, "The Syrian Army: Between the Domestic and External Fronts," *MERIA Journal* 5, no. 1 (March 2001); Zisser, *Asad's Legacy*, p. 162.

19. Following his unsuccessful challenge to Hafiz al-Asad's leadership in the aftermath of his older brother's 1983 heart attack, Rifa't al-Asad was effectively exiled from Syria in 1984. After spending several years in Paris, he was allowed by his older brother to return to Syria for their mother's funeral. Rifa't then remained in Syria until 1998. He currently maintains his principal residence in Spain but was rumored to have returned to Syria in September 2004. See *Akhbar al-Sharq*, September 26, 2004. For additional background on Rifa't and his role in the Asad family and modern Syrian politics, see "Dossier: Rifaat Assad," *Middle East Intelligence Bulletin* 2, no. 5 (1 June 2000).

20. Shihabi, who had described himself in meetings with U.S. and other foreign officials as the second-most powerful man in Syria, was, until Bashar's rise, widely viewed inside and outside Syria as a possible successor to Asad. For discussion of Shihabi's replacement, see "Asad Cleans House," *The Estimate* (July 17, 1998) and Zisser, *Asad's Legacy*, p. 166.

21. Zisser, *Asad's Legacy*, pp. 162–3, 166–7. See also Eyal Zisser, "Clues to the Syrian Puzzle," *Washington Quarterly* 23, no. 2 (Spring 2000).

22. "Asad Cleans House."

23. Eisenstadt, "Who Rules Syria?"

24. Shawkat's rise offers interesting insights into Asad family dynamics. Shawkat was a promising army officer who had been twice married and divorced at the time he met Bushra al-Asad at some point in the early 1990s. Bushra's family was strongly opposed to the relationship, in part because Shawkat was ten years Bushra's senior and in part because of his divorces. Mahir tried actively to break up the couple, and Hafiz al-Asad refused to give his blessing to the couple's wedding plans. In 1995 the couple eloped. Initially, relations with the presidential household were seriously strained, and in 1996 Bushra and her husband apparently inquired at the British Embassy in Damascus about obtaining visas to pursue doctoral studies at Cambridge University. In short order, though, Bushra had

conceived twins, who were born in 1997. Presented with his first grandchildren, Hafiz al-Asad apparently relented in his opposition to the marriage. Shawkat forged a positive relationship with Bashar and has since ascended rapidly in the Syrian power structure. For additional information on Shawkat's background and career, see "Dossier: Maj. Gen. Assef Shawkat," *Middle East Intelligence Bulletin* 2, no. 6 (July 1, 2000).

25. Eisenstadt, "Who Rules Syria?"

26. On Bashar's anticorruption activities, see Zisser, *Asad's Legacy*, p. 167, and Gary Gambill, "Bashar's Two Major Challenges," *Middle East Intelligence Bulletin* 2, no. 6 (July 1, 2000).

27. Personal communications by Syrian observers and foreign journalists with the author.

28. Personal communications with the author by members of the Syrian Computer Society's board.

29. See, for example, the interview that Bashar gave to Patrick Seale in *al-Hayat* (London), March 7, 2000.

30. Alan George, *Syria, Neither Bread Nor Freedom* (London: Zed Books, 2003), p. 129.

31. For an assessment of the March 2000 changes in the Syrian cabinet, see Gary Gambill, "Bashar Reshuffles Syrian Government," *Middle East Intelligence Bulletin* 2, no. 3 (March 2000).

32. For discussion, see two articles by Gary Gambill: "Syria's Night of the Long Knives," *Middle East Intelligence Bulletin* 2, no. 5 (June 1, 2000); and "Syria's Former PM Takes His Secrets with Him to the Grave," *Mideast Mirror*, May 22, 2000.

33. On this point, see "Bashar's Challenges: The Establishment and Its Discontents," *The Estimate* (June 16, 2000).

34. See, for example, Eisenstadt, "Who Rules Syria?"

35. On this point, see "Bashar's Challenges, " and Gary Gambill, "The Assad Family and the Succession in Syria," *Middle East Intelligence Bulletin* 2, no. 6 (July 1, 2000).

36. Eyal Zisser, "Can Bashar Al-Asad Hold On in Syria?" Policywatch 470 (Washington: Washington Institute for Near East Policy, June 12, 2000).

37. Zisser, "The Syrian Army: Between the Domestic and External Fronts."

38. On Tlas's role in ensuring a smooth transition, see Yossi Baidatz, "Bashar's First Year: From Ophthalmology to a National Vision," Policy Focus 41 (Washington: Washington Institute for Near East Policy, July 2001).

39. Two days before Bashar's inauguration, Defense Minister Tlas said publicly: "With the death of the late President we in the leadership were faced with two choices, either to hand the responsibility over to Mr. 'Abd al-Halim Khaddam, since he is Vice President of the Republic, or that I will be appointed. . . . We considered things rationally and found that all the members of the old guard are close to 70-years old, and if we appoint one of them you will face a change of President of the Republic every two years, and this is not in the interest of stability. Therefore, we decided unanimously to appoint the young Dr. Bashar." Interview with *al-Ahram*, July 15, 2000. In considering the key role that Tlas played in ensuring a smooth transition from Hafiz to Bashar, it is interesting to recall the role that Tlas played, forty years before, in seeing Hafiz's wife and infant daughter safely back to Syria during Hafiz's incarceration in Egypt.

40. Rachel Bronson, "Syria: Hanging Together or Hanging Separately," *Washington Quarterly* (Fall 2000).

41. An English translation of Bashar's inaugural address can be found on the Arab Gateway website (www.al-bab.com/arab/countries/syria/bashar00a.htm). This speech is hereafter cited simply as "Inaugural Address."

42. See the interview with Bashar al-Asad in *al-Sharq al-Awsat* on February 8, 2001, located in English translation at (www.al-bab.com/arab/countries/syria/bashar0102b. htm#POLITICAL). This interview is hereafter cited as "February 2001 interview."

43. Baidatz, "Bashar's First Year," p. 2.

44. Interview with the author, January 17, 2004. Perthes observed another sign that political reforms, anticipated by many at the outset of Bashar's presidency, soon took a back seat to economic and social reform: "Increasingly, Syria's media replaced the term 'reform and renewal' (*al-islah wa-l-tajdid*), which had been used to denote the new era, with 'development and modernization' (*al-tatwir wa-l-tahdith*)." See Volker Perthes, *Syria under Bashar al-Asad: Modernisation and the Limits of Change*, Adelphi Paper 366 (Oxford University Press for the International Institute for Strategic Studies, 2004).

45. Interview with the author, January 17, 2004.

46. This point is also made in Perthes, *Syria under Bashar al-Asad*, pp. 9–11.

47. Sukkar's firm is the Syrian Consulting Bureau for Development and Investment, serving domestic and international companies with business activities in Syria; its website (www.scbdi.com) presents some of Sukkar's recent writings on economic reform in Syria.

48. For an authoritative presentation of Sukkar's views, see his interview with *al-Sharq al-Awsat*, November 18, 2002.

49. See Sukkar's interview with Amir Taheri, "An Alternative Syrian Voice: Meet Nabil Sukkar," *National Review Online*, December 2, 2002 (www.nationalreview.com).

50. *All4Syria*'s website is located at (www.all4syria.org).

51. An example is Ratib al-Shallah, the president of the Damascus Chamber of Commerce.

52. Ghassan Qalla', the reformist vice president of the Damascus Chamber of Commerce, also falls in this category.

53. The SEBC website is located at (www.sebcsyria.org).

54. Seifan's firm was started as Economic and Business Consultants, based in Damascus, and was later renamed the Arab Development Center.

55. On this point, see Stephen Glain, "Middle East Beset by Fiscal Chaos and Lack of Capital," *Alexander's Oil & Gas Connections*, August 24, 2003.

56. Sami al-Khiami was sworn in as ambassador to the United Kingdom on October 18, 2004. See *Tishrin* (Damascus), October 18, 2004.

57. Personal communication by Dr. al-Akhras with the author.

58. For more information on Asma's background, see Anne Applebaum, "When You Wish upon Bashar," *Slate*, January 29, 2001; Gary Gambill, "Dossier: Asma Assad, First Lady of Syria," *Middle East Intelligence Bulletin* 3, no. 6 (June 2001); and Peter Beaumont, "From Schoolgirl Emma to Asma, the Syrian Icon," *Observer* (London), December 15, 2002.

59. On Rifa'i's career, see "Ghassan El-Rifai Appointed Minister in New Syrian Government," World Bank press release, January 28, 2002.

60. Personal communications by former colleagues of Kana'an at Damascus University.

61. Perthes (*Syria under Bashar al-Asad*) points out that involvement in the Syrian Computer Society is another important common denominator for some members of Bashar's personal network.

62. By any serious measure, only about half a dozen of the new ministers could be considered true champions of reform. Moreover, as noted in chapter 2, the reformists' impact within the cabinet was limited by their encirclement by a much larger number of entrenched defenders of the status quo. Bashar still obviously felt himself bound by many of the traditional parameters for selecting cabinet ministers, which limits his room for advancing outspoken reformists. Seventeen of the ministers in the September 2003 cabinet were members of the Ba'th Party, and seven were members of other National Progressive Front parties, leaving only six ministers not affiliated with established parties. See "The Baath Party Keeps the Upperhand in the New Government," *Syria Report*, October 2003.

63. On the range of possible interpretations of the reformist character of the October 2004 cabinet, see Nicholas Blanford, "Questions Remain about Syrian Cabinet Reshuffle," *The Daily Star*, October 6, 2004, and three postings by Joshua Landis on (http://syriacomment.com): "What Does the New Syrian Cabinet Portend?" October 5, 2004; "More on New Syrian Ministers," October 8, 2004; and "Asad's Alawi Dilemma," October 8, 2004.

64. For discussion, see Gary Gambill, "The Military-Intelligence Shakeup in Syria," *Middle East Intelligence Bulletin* 4, no. 2 (February 2002).

65. On Kana'an's background, see Daniel Nassif, "Maj. Gen. Ghazi Kanaan," *Middle East Intelligence Bulletin* 2, no. 1 (January 2000).

66. Syrian Arab TV (Damascus), January 22, 2002.

67. Gambill, "The Military-Intelligence Shakeup in Syria."

68. To minimize the potential for a backlash, the president made all three deputy defense ministers—a position in which they would no longer command troops.

69. *Al-Safir* (Beirut), May 4, 2004; Agence France-Presse, May 13, 2004.

70. Tlas also noted that he would remain president of the Ba'th party committee for the armed services until party elections scheduled for 2005 but explicitly denied that he would assume any role as a "deputy" to Bashar; see *Elaph* (United Kingdom), April 16, 2004.

71. On the resurgence of Kurdish activism, see Gary Gambill, "The Kurdish Reawakening in Syria," *Middle East Intelligence Bulletin* 6, no. 4 (April 2004), Havel Yusuf, "The Emergence of the Kurdish Question in Syria," *The Tharwa Project*, April 5, 2004, and Ammar Abdulhamid, "Out of the Dark: Syria's Kurdish Question Reborn," *The Daily Star* (Beirut), April 9, 2004.

72. For the regime's official account of the attack, see "Small 'Fundamentalist Group' Carried Out Damascus Attack: Official," Agence France-Presse, May 15, 2004. Syrian officials concluded that a "homegrown" terrorist organization—led by a Syrian who had smuggled weapons into Iraq and possibly fought on the side of insurgents there—was responsible. Numerous alternative theories on who was behind the attack have been floated in the Arabic and Western press. One theory attributed the attacks to a larger network of Islamists with ties to al-Qaeda and the al-Zarqawi group, through the 'Usbat al-Ansar group based in Lebanon's 'Ayn al-Helweh Palestinian refugee camp. The exile opposition Reform Party of Syria claimed the attacks were staged by the regime. And a Syrian intellectual told the author that the word on the street in Damascus was that the incident was a dispute between two security agencies over a smuggling ring and was an indication of Bashar's loss of control. See *All4Syria*, June 24, 2004, and *Jerusalem Post*, April 27, 2004; for an account of the suspicious circumstances surrounding the attack, see "The Bombing in Damascus: Ten Reasons to Doubt Syria's Claim," *The Middle East Intelligence Bulletin* 6, no. 5 (May 2004).

73. Salary increases were implemented in August 2000; Associated Press, August 26, 2000. The first credit cards were issued at the end of 2000; Agence France-Presse, December 25, 2000. Relevant decrees to allow private auto imports were issued in July 2000; Agence France-Presse, July 8, 2000.

74. Regulations permitting the operation of private Lebanese banks in free trade zones along the Lebanese-Syrian border were promulgated in August 2000. The first set of regulations permitting private Syrian banks were issued in December 2000, with additional guidelines published in March 2001. Agence France-Presse, August 8, 2000; SANA, December 2, 2000; United Press International, March 19, 2001; Associated Press, March 29, 2001.

75. As Nabil Sukkar has pointed out, banking reform was also necessary to mobilize domestic and foreign savings, help attract capital inflow, and improve allocation of resources in the national economy. See Sukkar, "Commentary on Banking Reform and Bank Restructuring," Presentation to the Arab National Committees of the International Chamber of Commerce, Damascus (September 17, 2002).

76. *Middle East Economic Digest*, February 2, 2001.

77. Personal communications by Syrian businessmen and officials with the author.

78. See, for example, Nabil Sukkar, "Opportunities in Syria's Economic Reforms," *Arab Banker* (Summer 2001), and Samir Seifan, "The Controversial Economic Reform in Syria," Arab Development Center (2000), available at (www.adc-syria.com).

79. Gareth Smyth, "Does Bashar Mean Business?" Reuters, February 16, 2002.

80. For an overview of the private financial sector in Syria, see *Banking in Syria 2003*, prepared by *Syria Report* and published by the Middle East Information and Communication Agency in Paris.

81. See, for example, Seifan, "The Controversial Economic Reform in Syria."

82. Interview with the author, January 17, 2004.

83. According to Western diplomats in Damascus, Rifa'i himself has questioned the wisdom of establishing free trade zones, saying that he would rather work to reform the whole system. For more details on the plan, see "Government to Set-Up Special Economic Zones," *Syria Report*, May 2004.

84. Personal communications with the author.

85. Personal communication by Syrian officials with the author.

86. Personal communications by European diplomats with the author.

87. Interview with the author, January 17, 2004. See also "Syria: Public Priorities," Oxford Business Group *Online Briefing*, 55 (www.oxfordbusinessgroup.com, June 21, 2004).

88. Personal communications by French officials with the author.

89. Stanley Reed, "The Rough Road to Reform," *Business Week* (September 4, 2000); Perthes, *Syria under Bashar al-Asad*, p. 37.

90. As a result of Khaddam's long handling of the Lebanon portfolio, his family also has extensive reconstruction and telecommunications interests in Lebanon, including what Middle East telecommunications experts say is a significant stake in the Cellis Corporation.

91. See the website of Firas Tlas (www.firastlass.com) and MAS Group (www.masgroup.net).

92. Personal communications by Syrian and Syrian expatriate businessmen with the author.

93. For example, Rami Makhluf reportedly tried to usurp the role of agent for Mercedes in Syria by having a law passed forcing the company to use him as the exclusive agent for importing spare parts. Mercedes had wanted to retain the services of Omar Sanqar and Sons, the longtime owner of the concession. *Elaph* (United Kingdom), June 24, 2004.

94. Corruption in Syria's telecommunications sector may be connected to Bashar through an additional channel. During Bashar's grooming for the presidency, as he became involved in management of the Lebanese portfolio for his father, the younger Asad appears to have developed relationships with the Lebanese brothers Taha and Azmi Miqati (brothers of Najib Miqati, the Lebanese minister of public works and transport under the government of Prime Minister Hariri; left out of the new cabinet formed by Omar Karami in November 2004). According to Lebanese journalists and officials, as well as U.S. diplomats, Taha and Azmi—both telecommunications executives—became Bashar's "go to guys" for high-technology personal items that are difficult to obtain in Syria; in return, the two brothers have reportedly been allowed to participate in the Makhlufs' telecommunications business in Syria.

95. For further discussion, see Gary Gambill, "The Political Obstacles to Economic Reform in Syria," *Middle East Intelligence Bulletin* 3, no. 7 (July 2001).

96. The Barcelona process, which began with the Barcelona Declaration of 1995, initiated negotiations between twelve Mediterranean countries and the European Union intended to lead to the establishment of a Euro-Mediterranean free trade area by 2010.

97. Personal communication by Syrian officials with the author.

98. Agence France-Presse, December 10, 2003; personal communications by European officials with the author.

99. See Daniel Williams, "Syria-EU Trade Deal Stalls over Chemical Weapons Issue," *Washington Post*, April 8, 2004.

100. Personal communications by European diplomats and EU officials with the author.

101. Quoted in Douglas Davis, "EU Proceeds with Syrian Trade Agreement," *Jerusalem Post*, May 14, 2004.

102. A special clause in the agreement will allow it to go into effect immediately after its official signing, before its ratification by the individual parliaments of the EU states and Syria. Agence France-Presse, October 19, 2004; *Syria Report*, November 2004.

103. "Filling Syria Line, Iraq Stokes Sanctions Fire," *Oil Daily*, November 22, 2000.

104. Estimates ranged from 180,000 to 230,000 barrels a day.

105. For discussion, see Gary Gambill, "Syria's Foreign Relations: Iraq," *Middle East Intelligence Bulletin* 3, no. 3 (March 2001).

106. Economist Intelligence Unit, *Syria: Country Profile 2003* (www.eiu.com), p. 44.

107. For discussion, see Department of Energy: Energy Information Administration, "Country Analysis Brief: Syria" (www.eia.doe.gov/emeu/cabs/syria.html).

108. In addition to calling for the removal of posters bearing his likeness, Bashar instructed the media to forswear using the phrase "immortal leader" to describe either him or his late father. See "Syria: Bashar Calls on Media to Use 'Calm, Balanced, Logical' Information," *Tishrin* (Damascus), July 17, 2000.

109. For discussion, see George, *Syria*, 129–34.

110. *Al-Thawra*, October 1, 2000. For a summary of the main points in Dalilah's article in English, see Roueida Mabardi, "A Breath of Fresh Air Blows through Syria's Press," Agence France-Presse, October 2, 2000.

111. The Committees for the Defense of Democratic Freedoms and Human Rights in Syria (CDF) had been created in 1989 but was suppressed by the regime in 1991, when its chairman, Aktham Nu'aysa, and other officers were arrested. Nu'aysa was released from prison in 1998; other CDF officials were released during the late 1990s. In September 2000, two months after Bashar's inauguration, the CDF met for the first time since 1991 and elected a new board of trustees under Nu'aysa's leadership; see George, *Syria*, p. 41. In December 2000, the CDF issued its own public call for the suspension of martial law, amnesty for all political detainees, the guaranteed safe return of those in political exile, and fair and open trials for those accused of crimes against state security—echoing many of the themes of the Statement of 99, discussed later. At the same time, Nu'aysa said that only one member of his original group remained in prison; that individual, the journalist Nizar Nayyuf, who had edited the CDF's monthly newsletter during 1989–91, was released in May 2001. On Nayyuf's ordeal, see George, *Syria*, pp. 121–24; the CDF website is currently hosted at (www.cdfsyr.de).

112. The Syrian Human Rights Committee (SHRC, also known as the Syrian Human Rights Association) describes itself, on its website, as "an independent and neutral human rights organization concerned fundamentally with defending general liberties and human rights of the Syrian people through several practices." For additional background, see the SHRC website (www.shrc.org.uk) and George, *Syria*, p. 41.

113. "Syrian President Orders Release of 600 Political Prisoners," Associated Press, November 16, 2000; "Syrian Rights Group Says Amnesty 'First Important' Step by Assad," Agence France-Presse, November 17, 2000.

114. George, *Syria*, p. 40.

115. Ibid.; "Notorious Prison to Become a Modern Hospital," Associated Press, November 21, 2000.

116. It does not appear that this order was carried out, as political prisoners were still reported held at Tadmur prison three years later in 2003. Eyal Zisser, "A False Spring in Damascus," *Orient* 44, no. 1 (2003), p. 43.

117. George, *Syria*, pp. 36, 55–56.

118. *Al-Sharq al-Awsat*, August 6, 2000. *Al-Ahram* cited a report that Bashar al-Asad met with his interior minister in January 2001 to discuss the lifting of martial law, but "the February 2001 election of Israeli Prime Minister Ariel Sharon brought the idea to a grinding halt. Al-Assad feared that an all-out war with Israel could be on the horizon and it was argued that domestic freedoms needed to be restricted to avoid the outbreak of political chaos." See Sami Moubayed, "Pushing the Limits," *al-Ahram Weekly* (Cairo), January 2002, pp. 24–30.

119. See George, *Syria*, pp. 30–46, for a summary account of the Damascus Spring.

120. See appendix B for the translated text of the Statement of 99 and its signatories. The text of the statement first appeared in the Lebanese press and was reprinted for a regional and international audience in *al-Hayat* on September 27, 2000.

121. George, *Syria*, pp. 39–42.

122. Ibid., pp. 33, 51–52. At the civil society movement's height, an estimated 300 political "salons" were operating in Syria. This number had dwindled to 14 by July 2002. See "Syrian Rights Activists Convicted of Trying to Change the Constitution, Sent to Jail for 5–10 Years," Associated Press, July 31, 2002.

123. See "Open Sesame," *Middle East Economic Digest*, December 22, 2000.

124. This group centered around Michel Kilo and his political forum. See George, *Syria*, pp. 42–46.

125. Riyad Sayf was one of the more remarkable figures to emerge in Syrian political life during the last decade of Hafiz al-Asad's presidency. One of the few examples of an essentially self-made entrepreneurial businessman, Sayf founded and developed one of Syria's largest clothing manufacturing enterprises. He won election to the National Assembly as an independent; despite regime opposition, he was reelected in 1998. In addition to founding the Friends of Civil Society in Syria, Sayf circulated a memorandum in early 2001 calling for a government investigation into mobile telephone contracts won by Bashar's billionaire cousin, Rami Makhluf. For a profile, see Raed al-Kharrat, "Riyad Sayf: Syrian Member of Parliament," *Middle East Intelligence Bulletin* 3, no. 3 (March 2001). Explaining his opposition to Sayf's more radical reformist agenda, Michel Kilo said that Sayf "thought that he was Lech Walesa and that Syria was Poland and that the Syrian regime was about to fall." See George, *Syria*, p. 42.

126. Mabardi, "A Breath of Fresh Air Blows through Syria's Press"; see also "Intelligence Briefs: Syria," *Middle East Intelligence Bulletin* 2, no. 10 (November 2000).

127. George, *Syria*, pp. 45–46.

128. Beirut's *al-Safir* published an article quoting sections of the leaked draft of the Statement of 1,000 on January 11, 2001, days before its official release to the press. For discussion, see George, *Syria*, pp. 42–45. The full text of the statement is reprinted in appendix B.

129. See, for example, then–information minister 'Adnan 'Omran's accusations that the civil society movements were in the pay of foreign embassies, and that "neocolonialism no longer relies on armies." 'Abd al-Halim al-Khaddam was apparently at the head of the regime counterattack, overseeing the changed tone of dialogue with the new civil society activists. See George, *Syria*, pp. 47–63, and Zisser, "A False Spring in Damascus," pp. 52–61.

130. See, for example, Bashar's interview with *al-Sharq al-Awsat* in February 2001. In a June 2001 interview, Bashar said "The word spring does not concern us. We said spring is a temporary season. Some might like spring. Others might like winter. If we want to go deeper into analysis, we say fruits come out in summer. However, there are no fruits without spring, when the trees blossom. Nor is there spring without the rains of winter, and so on and so forth. . . . Modernization does not conform to the word spring or any other season. We are not looking for the four seasons. We are looking for a real process of modernization." Interview broadcast on Syrian Arab Republic Radio (Damascus), June 27, 2001.

131. On the regime counterattack, see George, *Syria,* pp. 47–63; Nicholas Blanford, "As Reform Falters, Syrian Elites Tighten Grip," *Christian Science Monitor*, September 30, 2003; Bassam Haddad, "Business As Usual in Syria?" *Middle East Report*, September 7, 2001; and International Crisis Group, "Syria under Bashar (II): Domestic Policy Challenges," ICG Middle East Report 24 (Brussels: February 11, 2004), pp. 7–14.

132. On Mahmud Salameh's dismissal and its implications, see George, *Syria*, pp. 132–34, and "'Change' Still Eludes Syria," *Mideast Mirror*, May 30, 2001.

133. Although *al-Dommari* resumed publication after a three-week suspension, it continued to face regime-enforced hardships and was finally forced to close in August 2003. During the U.S.-led war against Iraq, *al-Dommari* owner and editor 'Ali Firzat was

accused of insulting the Iraqi people and army; the Syrian regime seized upon this as a pretext for forcing the magazine's final closure. See Kim Ghattas, "Syrian Satirist Finds Himself in Front Line Damascus," *Financial Times* (London), August 3, 2003; and Roula Khalaf, "Withdrawing the Licence for the Country's First Private Publication Has Dulled Hopes for a Freer Syrian Press," *Financial Times* (London), August 8, 2003. For a discussion of the short life of the publication, see George, *Syria*, pp. 130-32.

134. On Sayf and Homsi's arrest and trial, see George, *Syria*, pp. 49–50, 56–61; and Sami Moubayed, "The Damascus Spring Ends," *Gulf News*, November 22, 2001.

135. On 'Aref Dalilah's arrest and imprisonment, see George, *Syria*, pp. 58–61, 146–47; and "Syrian Rights Activists Convicted of Trying to Change the Constitution."

136. Turk was eventually released on humanitarian grounds in November 2002. Despite a July 2004 amnesty for political detainees on the occasion of the fourth anniversary of Bashar's accession, in which 257 prisoners were released, the other detainees mentioned here remained in prison at the end of 2004. See "Syria: Political Prisoners Released," *Arabicnews.com*, July 21, 2004.

137. The website of the Syrian Human Rights Committee states, "Until SHRC is permitted to open a head office in Damascus and branches in the Syrian provinces, SHRC will be temporarily based in London."

138. Alan Makovsky, "Syria under Bashar Al-Asad: The Domestic Scene and the 'Chinese Model' of Reform," Policywatch 512 (Washington: Washington Institute for Near East Policy, January 17, 2001); and Baidatz, "Bashar's First Year," p. 22. For an insightful critique on the inapplicability of the China model to Syria, see the article by well-known Syrian reformist intellectual Burhan Ghalyun, "*al-taharrur min wahm al-tariq al-sini* [Liberation from the Illusion of the Chinese Path]," July 8, 2004 (aljazeera.net). See also Ibrahim Hamidi, "*al-islah al-suri bayn 'al-tajribatayn' al-malayzia wa al-sinia . . . wa al-'alaqa bayn al-b'udayn al-siyasi wa al-iqtisadi* [Syrian Reform between the Malaysian and Chinese Experiences . . . and the Relationship between the Political and Economic Dimensions]," *al-Hayat*, May 8, 2004.

139. See, for example, Baidatz, *Bashar's First Year*, p. 23.

140. On this point, see Ammar Abdulhamid, "Cradle of Contradictions," *The Tharwa Project*, April 2004.

141. On FIRDOS, see Samar Farah, "Syrians 'Click' via a Rolling Internet Café," *Christian Science Monitor*, November 25, 2003, and the profile at the International Fund for Agricultural Development: (www.ifad.org/ngo/ecp/2002/pn/syria.htm). The organization's acronym means *paradise* in Arabic.

142. The SYEA website is located at (www.syea.org). The word *mawred* means *resource* in Arabic; the organization's website is www.mawred-syria.org.

143. Personal communications by Syrian civil society activists with the author.

144. In the interest of full disclosure, the author acknowledges that he is a member of the *Tharwa* Project's advisory board, along with the Egyptian sociologist and civil society advocate Sa'd Eddin Ibrahim and the French scholar Gilles Kepel.

145. Personal communications by SEBC officers and Syrian civil society activists with the author.

146. "The First Virtual University in the Middle East Opens in Syria," *Syria Report* (September 9, 2002). The Syrian Virtual University is accessible at (www.svuonline.org/sy/eng). In the September 2003 cabinet reshuffle, Murtada was named the minister of higher education.

147. "Four Private Universities Are Licensed," *Syria Report*, October 2003.

148. See also the posting at ⟨http://syriacomment.com⟩ by David Lesch, "Bashar Is Recasting Syria's Operational Philosophy," September 15, 2004.

149. See two postings at ⟨http://syriacomment.com⟩ by Josh Landis: "Issa Touma: 'Artists Still Have Hopes,'" September 19, 2004; and "Nabil Fayyad Arrested," October 3, 2004. Fayyad, a fierce critic of the Islamizing trend in Syrian society, ran a website called al-Naqd (the critic), which posted reformist articles and criticism by himself and other Syrians (www.annaqed.com). He was also a spokesman for the Liberal Gathering party in Syria, which was dissolved soon after his arrest. Fayyad was detained without charge for at least a month before he was released on November 3, 2004; Associated Press, November 5, 2004. The Syrian authorities never issued an explanation for his arrest, but the "Nabil Fayyad Arrested" posting listed above speculates on the regime's motives. Touma has not been arrested, but regime officials have ordered him to desist from his politically and religiously charged artistic expositions.

150. Some of the security and police officials, reports the same source, will be charged with embezzlement and exploitation of their positions for monetary gain. See *Akhbar al-Sharq*, November 28, 2004.

151. When slated to become the next director of Syrian Military Intelligence, Shawkat was deprived of his own bailiwick as the head of the subdivision within the SMI known as the "*fara' amin al-quwwat*," from which he was able to wield independent influence. The subdivision was dissolved with Shawkat's elevation to his new position, its duties incorporated into the SMI. Although a personal ally and relative of Bashar, Shawkat was rumored to have had a bad relationship with Khalil. See *Akhbar al-Sharq*, November 20, 2004.

152. On Dakhlallah's appointment, see Landis, "Asad's Alawi Dilemma" and "What Does the New Syrian Cabinet Portend?"

153. *Syria Report*, "The Syrian Media Takes New Steps," December 2004. The same report mentions other instances of loosening strictures on public criticism. Despite the obvious progress on respect for freedom of speech, Syrian journalists continue to suffer under an atmosphere of intimidation. Journalists are especially subject to harassment if they single out instances of corruption by high-level officials, or if they write on Kurdish affairs. See the report by the press freedom watchdog Reporters sans frontières on December 8, 2004.

154. For the original editorial, see *Tishrin*, November 23, 2004. Dakhlallah was directly criticized in the editorial but still permitted its publication. See also *Syria Report*, December 2004. It should be noted here that Ghazi Kana'an is also an advocate of greater press freedom, having once remarked that Syrian newspapers were "unreadable." See *Akhbar al-Sharq*, November 24, 2004.

155. The decree (no. 408) issued by the Ba'th leadership read: "The task of the 'Leading Party' is to plan, supervise, guide, review and necessitate reports. The Party electors and institutions must refrain from intervening in the daily working of the governmental institutions and allow the comrades appointed to those institutions to discharge their duties. . . . Every appointment to managerial and executive positions in the governmental offices will be made on the basis of the suitability of the candidate to his job regardless of his party affiliation." For further discussion, see Eyal Zisser, "Bashar al-Asad and His Regime: Between Continuity and Change," *Orient* 45, no. 2 (2004), p. 251. The decree was not passed without resistance; party stalwarts fiercely argued against their marginalization from the political life of the country.

156. After the National Progressive Front charter was amended, nine parties were listed under the umbrella organization: the Ba'th Party (headed by Bashar al-Asad), the SCP-Bakdash Wing (Wisal Farhat Bakdash), the SCP-Faysal wing (Yusef Faysal), the ASU (Safwan Qudsi), the MSU (Fayiz Isma'il), the ASM (Ahmed al-Ahmed), the Democratic Socialist Unionist Party (a faction which broke from the MSU in 1974—Fadlallah Nasir al-Din), the Democratic Arab Union Party (Ghassan Ahmed 'Uthman), and the National Covenant *('Ahd)* Party. On the new NPF charter, see "The Amended Charter of the 'Front': Increase in the Number of Members and the Control of the Ba'th," *Akhbar al-Sharq*, October 18, 2004. See also the discussion of political parties in the Bashar al-Asad era in Zisser, "Bashar al-Asad and his Regime," pp. 251–56.

Chapter Four

1. Eyal Zisser, "Syria's Asad—The Approach of a Fifth Term of Office," Policywatch 366 (Washington: Washington Institute for Near East Policy, February 6, 1999).

2. Benjamin Orbach and David Schenker, "The Rise of Bashar Al-Asad," Policywatch 371 (Washington: Washington Institute for Near East Policy, March 5, 1999).

3. Gary Gambill and Ziad Abdelnour, "Dossier: Rafiq Hariri, Prime Minister of Lebanon," *Middle East Intelligence Bulletin* 3, no. 7 (July 2001).

4. Orbach and Schenker, "The Rise of Bashar Al-Asad."

5. Zisser wrote in 1999 that Bashar "[had] gotten involved in the incipient peace process with Israel," but the author is unaware of any other source attributing to Bashar a role in peace process diplomacy before his accession. Eyal Zisser, "Heir Apparent," *New Republic*, October 11, 1999.

6. The English translation of Bashar's inaugural address, issued by the Syrian Arab News Agency, can be found on the Arab Gateway site at (www.al-bab.com/arab/countries/syria/bashar00a.htm). This speech is cited hereafter as "Inaugural Address."

7. The withdrawal took place during May 22–24, 2000.

8. "Report of the Secretary-General on the Implementation of Security Council Resolutions 425 (1978) and 426 (1978)" (New York: United Nations, June 16, 2000).

9. Frederic C. Hof, *Beyond the Boundary: Lebanon, Israel, and the Challenge of Change* (Washington: Middle East Insight, 2000); International Crisis Group, *Old Games, New Rules: Conflict on the Israel-Lebanon Border*, ICG Middle East Report 7 (Brussels: November 18, 2002), p. 7 (www.crisisgroup.org).

10. Sharon was elected to his first term as prime minister on February 6, 2001, and took office on March 7.

11. U.S. and other foreign visitors to Damascus who have dealt with the cadre of young staffers in Sha'ban's department at the Foreign Ministry were uniformly impressed with their quality.

12. Although, under Ta'if's terms, the Lebanese presidency is effectively reserved for a Maronite, the two post-Ta'if presidents so far, Elias Hrawi and Emile Lahud, have been viewed by old-line Maronites as too subservient to Syrian interests and demands. (Maronite partisans, although disunited, typically see Lebanese Christian leaders forcibly shut out of the political order by Syria through exile or imprisonment as more legitimate representatives of their community. The most revanchist partisans have focused on former Lebanese Armed Forces commander and self-declared prime minister Michel 'Aoun, now in exile in France.)

13. In September 2000, the Council of Maronite Bishops, under the leadership of the Maronite patriarch, Mar Nasrallah Butros Cardinal Sfayr, issued a statement calling for full implementation of the Ta'if Accord, including redeployment of Syrian troops to the Biqa'a and deployment of the Lebanese Armed Forces to the south, as well as an eventual withdrawal of all Syrian forces from the country. See Gary Gambill, "Dossier: Nasrallah Boutros Sfeir, 76th Patriarch of the Maronite Church," *Middle East Intelligence Bulletin* 5, no. 5 (May 2003). Over the next several months, Maronite intellectuals, politicians, and political parties coalesced around Sfayr's questioning of continued Syrian dominance in Lebanon, forming the so-called "Gathering" of Qornet Shehwan (the name of the Maronite monastery where the group first met); see Gambill, "Dossier: Nasrallah Boutros Sfeir." On the Gathering's agenda, see the group's pamphlet *Liqa' Qornat Shehwan fi Sanatihi al-'Ula, Mawaqif wa Bayanaat*, April 2001–April 2002 (The Gathering of Qornet Shehwan in Its First Year, Positions and Statements).

14. Gary Gambill, "The Weakening of Syria's Political Patronage in Lebanon," and Maha Melhem, "Thousands Demonstrate against Syrian Presence on Independence Day," both in *Middle East Intelligence Bulletin* 2, no. 11 (December 2000); Marlin Dick, "Thirteen-Year Itch: The Demise of Lebanon's Taif Agreement?" *Middle East Report Online* (www.merip.org, August 13, 2002); and ICG, *Old Games, New Rules*, pp. 27–28.

15. Hariri is a Lebanese Sunni from Sidon who became a billionaire as a construction contractor in Saudi Arabia. He played a key role in Saudi efforts to broker the Ta'if Accord in the late 1980s, returning home at the end of the Lebanese civil war to enter politics. He was appointed prime minister in 1992 and reappointed in 1995. For further information on Hariri's background and career, see "Lebanon: The Return (?) of Rafiq al Hariri," *The Estimate* 8, no. 18 (September 8, 2000); and Gary Gambill and Ziad Abdelnour, "Dossier: Rafiq Hariri, Prime Minister of Lebanon," *Middle East Intelligence Bulletin* 3, no. 7 (July 2001). Hariri's platform as prime minister emphasized Lebanon's physical reconstruction and creation of a business-friendly environment so that the country would emerge as a regional financial and services center. See Volker Perthes, "Myths and Money: Four Years of Hariri and Lebanon's Preparation for a New Middle East," *Middle East Report* 27, no. 2 (Spring 1997); John Roberts, "Hariri: Renewal and Relative Recovery," and Tom Najem, "Horizon 2000: Economic Viability and Political Realities, " both in *Mediterranean Politics* 3, no. 1 (Spring 1998); and Franck Debie and Danuta Pieter, *La paix et la crise: le Liban reconstruit?* (Peace and Crisis: Lebanon Reconstructed?) (Paris: Presses Universitaires de France, 2003), pp. 115–24. Hariri drove several landmark reconstruction projects during his initial stint as prime minister, including the Beirut International Airport, the coastal highway, and the rebuilding of Beirut's city center; see Debie and Pieter, *La paix et la crise*, chapters 5 and 6. (These projects were not without controversy in Lebanon; charges that Hariri, his friends, and political cronies were enriching themselves in the process circulated in Lebanese political circles throughout his tenure.)

16. Personal communications by French officials with the author. Hariri has a long-standing relationship with French president Jacques Chirac and is said by some in France to have been a major financial backer of Chirac's presidential campaigns.

17. For further discussion, see As'ad Abu Khalil, "Lebanon One Year after the Israeli Withdrawal," *Middle East Report Online* (May 29, 2001); Gary Gambill, "Is Syria Losing Control of Lebanon?" *Middle East Quarterly* 8, no. 2 (Spring 2001); and Gary Gambill, "Can Syria Put the Lebanese Regime Back Together?" *Middle East Intelligence Bulletin* 3, no. 6 (June 2001).

18. This point is made by Patrick Seale in an analysis of Bashar's performance in his first half-year as president, published in al-*Hayat* on January 26, 2001. Seale presented an English version of this article, entitled "President Bashar al-Asad's First Six Months: Reform in a Dangerous Environment," as a lecture at the Royal Institute of International Affairs in London on January 25, 2001; it is available at (www.mafhoum.com/press/chttam.html).

19. Bashar has lowered the number of Syrian troops in Lebanon from roughly 25,000 at the time of his inauguration to roughly 15,000 at the end of 2004. See Dalal Saoud, "Analysis: Syria's New Re-Deployment Move," United Press International, July 16, 2003; Ziad Abdelnour and Gary Gambill, "Syria's Fourth Redeployment from Lebanon," *Middle East Intelligence Bulletin* 5, no. 7 (July 2003); and Scott Wilson, "Syria Begins Dismantling Some Outposts in Lebanon," *Washington Post*, September 22, 2004.

20. See "President al-Asad Discusses Regional Issues, Challenges Facing Syria," *al-Sharq al-Awsat*, February 8, 2001.

21. On this point, see also Eyal Zisser, "Leaving Lebanon?" *Tel Aviv Notes* 20 (Tel Aviv University, Jaffee Center for Strategic Studies, July 5, 2001).

22. Gary Gambill and Daniel Nassif, "Lebanon's Parliamentary Elections: Manufacturing Dissent," *Middle East Intelligence Bulletin* 2, no. 8 (September 2000).

23. On this point, see Yossi Baidatz, "Bashar's First Year: From Opthalmology to a National Vision," Policy Focus 41 (Washington: Washington Institute for Near East Policy, July 2001), pp. 38–41.

24. Zisser ("Leaving Lebanon?") also makes the point that "Bashar's action does not signify that the Syrians are losing their control of Lebanon or their ability to suppress those that challenge it. . . . In sum, the Syrian redeployment out of Lebanon does not foreshadow the end of Syrian presence and control in Lebanon, or even the beginning of the end."

25. U.S. Department of State, "Lebanon: Country Report on Human Rights Practices," 2001 and 2002.

26. Hariri and Hizballah have long been antagonists on the Lebanese political scene. For background on tensions between the two during Hariri's initial stint as prime minister, see Graham Usher, "Hizballah, Syria, and the Lebanese Elections," *Journal of Palestine Studies* 26 (Winter 1997): 59–67.

27. The phrase comes from Gal Luft, "Hizballahland," *Commentary* (July-August 2003), and Eyal Zisser, "The Return of Hizballah," *Middle East Quarterly* 9, no. 4 (Fall 2002). In the August-September 2000 parliamentary elections, the Hizballah leadership struck a deal with Damascus that all of its candidates would be guaranteed election if it did not run a larger slate of candidates; as a consequence, the group did not gain seats. In return, Damascus effectively gave the group a dominant position in the south. Michael Young, "Hizballah Outside and In," *Middle East Report Online* (October 26, 2000). As a side note, Bashar's willingness to boost Hizballah's standing in the south of the country briefly elevated the risk of renewed military conflict along the Israeli-Lebanese border in the summer and fall of 2002. This episode is particularly interesting because Hizballah's paramilitary activities were not an immediate provocation. Rather, Hizballah's rising stature following the withdrawal of the Israel Defense Forces prompted a backlash from its chief Shi'a rival, Amal, and its leader, National Assembly speaker Nabih Berri. Berri's efforts to cope with this situation set another potentially escalatory spiral in motion. Concerned about a relative loss of popular standing, Berri sought some

way to demonstrate to southern Shi'a that he could "deliver" for them in ways that Hizballah could not. Berri found his comparative advantage in his ability to channel classic, pork-barrel infrastructure projects to his constituents. In particular, he focused on increasing the water supply to residents of the recently liberated security zone in the south by pumping water from the Wazzani River, a tributary of Lake Kinneret and the Jordan River, from which Israel also draws water. Israel, concerned about a troublesome precedent for future cooperation on water sharing and the possible diminution of its deterrent posture along its border with Lebanon in the aftermath of the IDF's withdrawal, responded in September 2002 with a threat of military action if the Lebanese began pumping significantly elevated amounts of water from the Wazzani. In the end, neither the Israeli government nor any of the major players in Lebanon (nor Syria, for that matter) wanted to risk escalation to a regional conflict over a relatively mundane dispute about water sharing. With U.S. facilitation in the fall of October 2002, the parties were able to walk back from possible conflict. (The author, at the time acting senior director for Middle East affairs at the National Security Council, was on the U.S. team that, as part of a regional tour, traveled to Lebanon and Israel in October 2002 to forestall further escalation of the dispute.) For further discussion of the episode, see Eyal Zisser, "Israel and Lebanon: The Battle for the Wazzani," *Tel Aviv Notes* 50 (Tel Aviv University, Jaffee Center for Strategic Studies, October 14, 2002).

28. Zisser, "The Return of Hizballah."

29. One particularly personal piece of evidence supporting this assessment was Bashar's invitation to Nasrallah to speak at the ceremonies in June 2001 in Qurdaha, Syria, commemorating the first anniversary of Hafiz al-Asad's death.

30. The "Paris II" conference was called, under the sponsorship of French president Chirac, to seek bilateral assistance that would allow Lebanon to restructure its debt at lower rates of interest. The "Paris I" conference of February 2001 had secured a loose conference of donors to Lebanon to aid in its reconstruction efforts. Delilah Heakal, "What Happened at the 'Paris II' Donors Conference?" (arabfinance.com), undated.

31. "The Controversy over Aoun's Return," *Middle East Intelligence Bulletin* 3, no. 1 (January 2001).

32. For an analysis of the cabinet changes, see Dalal Saoud, "Lebanon's New 30-Member Cabinet Formed," United Press International, April 17, 2003.

33. Personal communications with the author by Lebanese and Syrian journalists.

34. This pressure culminated in the passage of United Nations Security Council Resolution 1559 in September 2004.

35. Scott Wilson, "Lebanese Premier Quits in Sign of Tension on Syria," *Washington Post*, October 21, 2004.

36. Following the collapse of the Syrian track at the Clinton-Asad summit in March 2000, Barak had shifted emphasis in his strategy for the peace process to seeking a final-status deal with the Palestinians; this task would consume his diplomatic energies for the remainder of his term in office.

37. Debie and Pieter, *La paix et la crise*; International Crisis Group, *Hizbollah: Rebel without a Cause?* Middle East Briefing (July 30, 2003): 7–9.

38. Hizballah has seized upon the pretext of Israel's occupation of the Sheba'a Farms to justify its continued military posture on the border zone. However, the UN considers the Sheba'a Syrian territory, as it was occupied in the 1967 war when Israel took the Golan and has been monitored by the UN contingent dispatched there ever since. Syria

and Lebanon have refused to settle the issue officially by registering their claims on the map with the UN, preferring to exploit the open-ended dispute. Even if ownership of the Sheba'a were to be settled, Hizballah has at times mentioned two other border claims that the Israeli withdrawal of 2000 did not resolve to its satisfaction. Hizballah charges Israel with slight encroachments into Lebanese territory in four locations (to leave the Israeli side with the more defensible position), and has also raised the claim of the "Seven Villages." This claim stems from seven primarily Shi'a-populated villages whose inhabitants fled from Mandatory Palestine to Lebanon during the 1948 war and registered as Palestinian refugees. Hizballah claims the villages are Lebanese (the refugees' descendants were belatedly granted citizenship in 1994), but some have criticized Hizballah for making a specious argument for sectarian purposes. Hizballah has pointedly not raised the issue of Christian villages located near the seven Shi'a ones in the Galilee, whose inhabitants also fled to Lebanon in 1948 (the Lebanese state has not backed either claim). A resolution of the Sheba'a dispute might only drive Hizballah to tout another territorial claim to justify continued militancy. See Hof, *Beyond the Boundary*, and Avi Jorisch, "Hizballah's Vision of the Lebanon-Israel Border," Policywatch 368 (Washington: Washington Institute for Near East Policy, March 4, 2002).

39. Ely Karmon, *Fight on All Fronts: Hizballah, the War on Terror, and the War in Iraq*, Policy Focus 46 (Washington: Washington Institute for Near East Policy, December 2003), p. 15.

40. Nasrallah used the phrase in his victory speech, delivered on May 26, only two days after the Israelis departed. ICG, *Old Games, New Rules*, pp. 8, 13.

41. Zisser, "The Return of Hizballah"; Gary Gambill and Ziad Abdelnour, "Hezbollah: Between Tehran and Damascus," *Middle East Intelligence Bulletin* 4, no. 2 (February 2002); and testimony by Patrick Clawson, deputy director of the Washington Institute for Near East Policy, before the Senate Foreign Relations Committee on October 30, 2003: (foreign.senate.gov/testimony/2003/ClawsonTestimony031030.pdf). For a critical assessment of early Israeli portrayals of Bashar reflecting this view, see Patrick Seale, "Syria-Israel-Palestine-Lebanon: Four Partners in a Dangerous Dance," *al-Hayat*, December 24, 2000; an English translation of this piece is available at (www.mafhoum. com/press/sealeh10.htm).

42. Personal communications by U.S. and Jordanian officials with the author.

43. For example, at the ninth summit of the Organization of the Islamic Conference in Doha in November 2000, Bashar explained that "some call for jihad. But this does not imply that those people want war. All of us assess the circumstances and know the capabilities. They do not ask for more than the possible which our states can provide, particularly as a conviction has been generated amongst a lot of those peoples that many states, especially Israel, do not wish us good and they endeavor to keep us within our current conditions of poverty and backwardness so that we keep on paying the price and they receive the payment materially and morally." This speech is hereafter cited as "OIC Doha address."

44. This Hizballah campaign began in early October 2000, when the group launched its first attack on Israeli positions in the Sheba'a Farms area, using as justification the Lebanese-Syrian claim that the Israeli withdrawal from southern Lebanon had been incomplete. Hizballah would continue these attacks, on an intensifying scale, for the next nine months. At the same time, Hizballah sought to up the ante by carrying out two kidnapping operations that October. The first entailed the apparent abduction of three

Israeli soldiers from an IDF position in the Sheba'a Farms area that had been overrun by Hizballah fighters; in reality, the three soldiers were all mortally wounded in the attack. The second involved the enticement of an Israeli businessman and IDF reserve officer to Lebanon, where he was taken hostage by Hizballah. ICG, *Old Games, New Rules*, pp. 8–9; Daniel Sobelman, *New Rules of the Game: Israel and Hizballah after the Withdrawal from Lebanon*, Memorandum 69 (Tel Aviv University, Jaffee Center for Strategic Studies, January 2004), p. 62. Hizballah cited the ongoing intifada in the occupied territories as justification for the kidnappings; the group was also collecting bargaining chips to use in negotiation with Israel for the release of Lebanese prisoners from Israeli custody. Young, "Hizballah Outside and In."

45. In April 2001, a month after he took office, Sharon responded to a Hizballah missile attack on an Israeli tank in the Sheba'a Farms area by ordering the Israeli Air Force to bomb a Syrian radar post in Lebanon. Officials in the prime minister's office made clear that, with this reaction, Sharon was out to establish escalation dominance over Hizballah and its Syrian patron; see "Israeli Warplanes Hit Syrian Radar Station in Lebanon, Killing Three Soldiers," *Ha'aretz* (Tel Aviv), April 16, 2001. Syria and the Hizballah leadership were temporarily chastened by Sharon's tougher line but still interested in finding a way to continue armed operations against Israel while forestalling larger-scale Israeli retaliation. For a similar assessment, see Eyal Zisser, "Bashar's First Test," *Tel Aviv Notes* 16 (Tel Aviv University, Jaffee Center for Strategic Studies, April 19, 2001). Following the April 2001 Israeli air strike on the Syrian radar post, Damascus responded with public bluster declaring international calls for restraint "no longer effective" and asserting Syria's right to retaliate against Israel "in the way we see fit." For a description and analysis of Syria's initial response to the April 2001 Israeli air strike, see Yotam Feldner, "Escalation Games: Syria's Deterrent Policy, Part I—Brinksmanship," Inquiry and Analysis Series 56 (Washington: Middle East Media Research Institute, May 24, 2001). Within a couple of weeks, though, the Syrian leadership was making clear that it had no interest in further escalation. On a visit to Spain in early May, for example, Bashar told the Madrid daily *El Pais* that "a military retaliation to the attack on the Syrian radar would mean fulfilling Ariel Sharon's wish to push the region into war," adding that "Syria has never supported war and there are different ways to respond to an Israeli attack." See Jesús Ceberio and Ángeles Espinosa, "Siria no quiere la escalada militar y no creo que Israel se lance a esa aventura," *El Pais*, May 2, 2001.

46. In an article published April 30, 2001, in the London-based Arabic weekly *al-Wasat*, Damascus correspondent Ibrahim Hamidi offered considerable insight into the calculations going on at the highest levels of the Syrian government. Working from anonymous sources—but almost certainly with leaks from the office of Foreign Minister Shar', if not from Shar' himself—Hamidi reported, "The Syrian leadership understands that Israel is militarily stronger than Syria." Nevertheless, according to Hamidi, Damascus wanted to continue supporting Hizballah operations against Israeli positions in the Sheba'a Farms area "without being dragged into an unnecessary confrontation and without giving up Syria's right to respond to the Israeli bombing." In keeping with the established rules of the game, Israel could respond to such operations by striking Hizballah-related or other Lebanese targets.

47. ICG, *Old Games, New Rules*, pp. 8–9. As Hizballah and its Syrian patrons sorted out their relative priorities during this stand-down, the possibility of continuing some level of paramilitary activity against Israel while limiting escalatory risks seemed to

trump the perpetuation of Hizballah's terrorist operations outside the region. U.S. and Lebanese officials have told the author that during the fall of 2001 Hizballah sought through various intermediaries to explore the possibility of an understanding with the United States, whereby the group would restrict its activities to relatively small-scale attacks in the Sheba'a Farms at roughly six- to eight-week intervals, but would desist entirely from terrorist activities and preparations outside the region. In this regard, it was reported in the press that British ambassador to Lebanon Brian Kinchen met with Hizballah officials on December 12, 2001, in Beirut. See Gareth Smyth, "UK Ambassador Opens Contact with Hizbollah Militants," *Financial Times*, December 13, 2001. Although these overtures came to naught, they are an interesting reflection of the complicated calculations that the Hizballah, Syrian, and (almost certainly) Iranian leaderships had to make during this period.

48. On this period, see Eyal Zisser, "Hizbullah Attacks: Motives and Implications," *Tel Aviv Notes* 30 (Tel Aviv University, Jaffee Center for Strategic Studies, January 28, 2002).

49. The Israeli military has continued to overfly Lebanese airspace and patrol Lebanese coastal waters since the withdrawal of the IDF from southern Lebanon; see the semi-annual "Report of the Secretary-General on the United Nations Interim Force in Lebanon," and ICG, *Hizbollah*, p. 8. In June 2001, Hizballah began intermittently firing antiaircraft rounds at Israeli military planes violating Lebanese airspace. In early 2002 the group's paramilitary cadres began firing antiaircraft rounds into Israeli airspace, often well after Israeli planes had passed; see ICG, *Old Games, New Rules*, p. 9. Hizballah's antiaircraft guns were incapable of hitting the Israeli planes, but rounds sometimes were purposely aimed across the Blue Line, where they sometimes landed on kibbutzim in northern Israel and caused occasional casualties and property damage; see Sobelman, *New Rules of the Game*, pp. 70–78.

50. U.S. concern about the growing risk of regional conflict was clearly reflected in President Bush's February 2002 announcement that he was sending his Middle East envoy at the time, retired Marine Corps general Anthony Zinni, back to the region, and in his April 4, 2002, Rose Garden address on the Middle East, in which he announced the dispatch of Secretary of State Colin Powell to the region.

51. On Powell's April 2002 Middle East trip, see Bob Woodward, *Bush at War* (New York: Simon and Schuster, 2002), pp. 323–26. According to Woodward, National Security Advisor Condoleezza Rice undercut Powell's efforts to restart a political process between Israel and the Palestinians; as the National Security Council representative on the trip, the author can confirm the essential accuracy of Woodward's account.

52. Hizballah launched approximately ten separate groups of attacks over a period of two years (August 2002–August 2004), usually in response to an escalation of violence in the Palestinian-Israeli arena or a perceived violation of Lebanon's sovereignty. These totals do not include Hizballah antiaircraft fire in response to Israel's flyovers of Lebanese territory, both of which occur with regularity. On the strategy behind Hizballah's attacks, see Nicholas Blanford, "Hizballah and Syria's 'Lebanese Card,'" *Middle East Report Online* (September 14, 2004).

53. For discussion, see ICG, *Hizbollah*, pp. 6–8. In this regard, it is interesting to note that Lebanese prime minister Hariri and Hariri-controlled media publicly complained in the spring of 2001 about Hizballah's continued military operations on the border with Israel after the Israeli air strike against the Syrian radar post in April. Hariri and his

camp complained again during the escalation of March–April 2002, calling into question one of Syria's main points of leverage with Israel.

54. Hizballah continues to seek new ways to change the military equation along the border region in its favor, such as when it managed to fly an Iranian-built observation drone over northern Israel in November 2004 without IDF forces detecting it in time to bring it down. Although the drone was unarmed and of scant value as a surveillance tool, Israeli observers warned that the drone could in the future be outfitted with explosives or even chemical weapons. Hizballah proclaimed that the spy drones would be used again so long as Israeli aircraft continue to overfly Lebanon. Clearly, Hizballah will continue to search for a deterrent to Israeli surveillance flights that will not appear threatening enough to prompt an intolerable level of IDF military retaliation. *Al-Jazeera.Net,* November 8 (aljazeera.net); 2004; *al-Nahar,* November 9, 2004.

55. In this regard, Dennis Ross has said that Bashar "still thinks that Israel will stay within certain boundaries. He needs to hear from us that, if he provokes a war, don't expect us to come to your rescue." Jeffrey Goldberg, "In the Party of God," *New Yorker* 78, no. 31 (October 14, 2002).

56. Some analysts have described this as the "Palestinianization" of Hizballah; see, for example, ICG, *Hizbollah,* p. 9.

57. "Hasan Nasrala, líder de Hizbulá: 'Arafat no es el representante legítimo del pueblo palestino,'" *El Mundo* (Madrid), December 18, 2001.

58. See Karmon, *Fight on All Fronts,* p. 25.

59. The ship was intercepted in the Red Sea by the Israeli Navy. For details, see Robert Satloff, "Karine-A: The Strategic Implications of Iranian-Palestinian Collusion," PolicyWatch 593 (Washington: Washington Institute for Near East Policy, January 15, 2002).

60. This operation was broken up by Jordanian security services. The story of Hizballah and Iran's collaboration in arms smuggling and attacks on Israel through Jordan was first reported in Amir Taheri, "Jordan Uncovers Iranian Plans to Launch Attacks on Israel from Its Land," *al-Sharq al-Awsat,* February 5, 2002.

61. For discussion, see Goldberg, "In the Party of God," and Karmon, *Fight on All Fronts,* pp. 16–17.

62. Ibid. See also Matthew Levitt, "Hizballah's West Bank Foothold," PeaceWatch 429 (Washington: Washington Institute for Near East Policy, August 20, 2003).

63. Arieh O'Sullivan, "Hizbullah Recruiting Israeli Arabs," *Jerusalem Post,* February 19, 2002; Gary Gambill, "Hezbollah's Israeli Operatives," *Middle East Intelligence Bulletin* 4, no. 9 (September 2002); Goldberg, "In the Party of God."

64. The camp had apparently been used by several different terrorist groups, including Islamic Jihad, which claimed responsibility for the Haifa attack. Douglas Jehl, "Construction Was Spotted at Syrian Camp Hit by Israel," *New York Times,* October 10, 2003.

65. Personal communications by Egyptian and Israeli officials with the author.

66. Agence France-Presse, December 9, 2004; *Akhbar al-Sharq,* December 8, 2004.

67. For details, see Gary Gambill, "Hezbollah's Strategic Rocket Arsenal," *Middle East Intelligence Bulletin* 4, no. 11 (November-December 2002). Sharon began complaining publicly about the scope of Iran's resupply of Hizballah and the nature of the weapons being provided in March 2001.

68. Ibid.

69. For example, Goldberg ("Inside the Party of God)" gives a figure of more than 8,000; Karmon (*Fight on All Fronts*) estimates 9,000; Gambill ("Hezbollah's Strategic Rocket Arsenal") gives a figure of 10,000.

70. Inaugural address.

71. See "Egyptian, Syrian Presidents Call for Arab Summit," Egyptian Satellite Channel (Cairo), BBC Summary of World Broadcasts, October 2, 2000; henceforth "Mubarak-Asad joint press conference."

72. On this point, see Christopher Hemmer, "I Told You So: Syria, Oslo and the al-Aqsa Intifada," *Middle East Policy* 10, no. 3 (September 22, 2003).

73. *Al-Sharq al-Awsat*, February 8, 2001.

74. Ibid.

75. The official Syrian translation of Bashar's address to the summit was taken from the Syrian Ministry of Information website at (www.moi-syria.com/bassad.html); hereafter "Arab League Amman Summit address." The site has since been removed. The author has made revisions in the Syrian translation to improve the quality of the English.

76. On this point, see the testimony of Paul O'Neill, former secretary of the treasury, recounted in Ron Suskind, *The Price of Loyalty: George W. Bush, the White House, and the Education of Paul O'Neill* (New York: Simon and Schuster, 2004), pp. 70–72. During his first year in office, President Bush's sole action of significance with regard to Arab-Israeli peacemaking was entirely rhetorical—his endorsement, in a speech to the United Nations General Assembly in November 2001, of the creation of a state of Palestine as part of a two-state solution to the Israeli-Palestinian conflict.

77. The Quartet—consisting of the United States, Russia, the European Union, and the Secretary-General of the United Nations—was launched in Madrid in April 2002 to coordinate international efforts to mediate the Arab-Israeli conflict. The efforts of the group, however, have been focused almost exclusively on the Palestinian track. As a participant in the creation of the Quartet and the drafting of its initial and several subsequent statements, the author can testify that the Bush White House was always reluctant to include references to Syria in Quartet documents; generally the Quartet could only agree to passing references to Syria in its public statements. The president's June 24 speech—the administration's benchmark statement on Arab-Israeli peace—focused almost entirely on the Israeli-Palestinian conflict. The only reference to Syria noted: "We must also resolve questions concerning ... a final peace between Israel and Lebanon, and Israel and a Syria that supports peace and fights terror"; the text can be found at (www. whitehouse.gov/news/releases/2002/06/20020624-3.html). The roadmap, intended as a step-by-step plan for operationalizing the president's June speech, is formally entitled "A Performance-Based Roadmap to a Permanent Two-State Solution to the Israeli-Palestinian Conflict"; the text can be found at (www.state.gov/r/pa/prs/ps/2003/20062.htm). Not only is Syria left out of the title, but it is not mentioned in the body of the text until Phase II, where the plan envisions an international conference convened by the Quartet to "support Palestinian economic recovery and launch a process, leading to the establishment of an Palestinian state with provisional borders." The document notes that such a conference should be "inclusive, based on the goal of a comprehensive Middle East peace (including between Israel and Syria, and Israel and Lebanon)." In Phase III, which focuses primarily on negotiation of a "comprehensive permanent status agreement" between Israel and the new state of Palestine, the document calls only for inter-

national efforts "to support progress toward a comprehensive settlement between Israel and Lebanon, and Israel and Syria, to be achieved as soon as possible."

78. Mubarak-Asad joint press conference.

79. Arab League Amman Summit address.

80. OIC Doha address.

81. Arab League Amman Summit address.

82. SANA posted an official English translation of the speech on its website on May 5, 2001, but has since removed it. See Eyal Zisser, "The Damascus Blood Libel," *Tel Aviv Notes* 18 (Tel Aviv University, Jaffee Center for Strategic Studies, May 10, 2001).

83. S/RES/1397 (2002) was adopted on March 12, 2002.

84. Personal communications by U.S. and European officials with the author.

85. Syria responded to the Gaza First initiative and Bush's assurances to Sharon by declaring: "In spite of the Israeli violations of international legitimacy, U.S. President Bush has urged the world to thank the terrorist Sharon because he will withdraw from Gaza, as if the withdrawal represents a concession from Israel which had delayed this incomplete withdrawal more than 25 years in light of UNSC Resolution No. 242." Damascus Radio, April 22, 2004.

86. Syria began hinting at its willingness to restart negotiations with Israel at the end of April. On Syrian statements to this effect made to the foreign ministers of Turkey and Japan, see "Syria Interested in 'Just and Comprehensive' Peace in Mideast, Foreign Minister Says," Associated Press, April 29, 2003. On May 7, 2003, a Syrian Foreign Ministry spokesman renewed Syria's "lasting readiness to return to negotiations based on the Madrid conference, related Security Council resolutions, and the land-for-peace principle," while simultaneously denying that it had undertaken secret talks with Israel in the previous months; see "Syria Denies Secret Talks with Israel," United Press International, May 7, 2003. Three days later the Syrian government daily *Tishrin* posted an article declaring its willingness to renew negotiations. For Syria's announcement and Israel's response, see "Israel Ready to Negotiate with Syria If It Comes with 'Clean Hands': Shalom," Agence France-Presse, May 10, 2003. See also Herb Keinon, "Lantos Lists Steps for Syria," *Jerusalem Post*, April 29, 2003.

87. "Israel Skeptical of Syrian Talks Offer," Agence France-Presse, April 29, 2003; "Israeli PM Views Unconditional Talks with Syria, Relations with Abu-Mazin," Israeli TV Channel 1, May 8, 2003.

88. Lally Weymouth, "Syrian President Bashar al-Asad Talks about Iraq, Israel, and Weapons of Mass Destruction," *Newsweek*, May 19, 2003.

89. Neil McFarquhar, "Syria Pressing for Israel Talks," *New York Times*, December 1, 2003.

90. Herb Keinon, "Sharon Wary of Syrian Overtures," *Jerusalem Post*, December 29, 2003.

91. On the debate in Israel over how to respond to the Syrian overtures, see Herb Keinon, "PM, Shalom Differ on Syrian Overtures," *Jerusalem Post*, December 31, 2003; Peter Enav, "Reports: Ministers Press Israel on Talks," Associated Press, January 8, 2004; and Hazel Ward, "Israel Says Syria Must End Support for 'Terrorism' for Revival of Talks," Agence France-Presse, January 11, 2004.

92. Claude Salhani, "Analysis: Golan Settlements Hinder Peace," United Press International, December 31, 2003.

93. Katsav first made his initial offer on Israeli public radio and renewed the invitation in an interview on *al-Jazeera* television two days later. See Rawya Rageh, "Israeli President Urges Syria to Visit," Associated Press, January 14, 2004.

94. Syrian prime minister Muhammad Naji al-'Utri called Katsav's offer an "advertising invitation," and said there was "no hope of achieving a just and comprehensive peace with this Zionist administration." See Rageh, "Israeli President Urges Syria to Visit," and Edith M. Lederer, "Syria Envoy Rejects Israeli Bid for Talks," Associated Press, January 13, 2004. See also, for example, the editorial by Hisham Bashir in the state-run daily *Tishrin* on January 17, 2004, entitled, "The Challenge of Peace," in which the author writes: "If Israel is truly serious in its proposals, it must explicitly announce its absolute commitment to the relevant resolutions of international law and its readiness to resume negotiations from the point where they left off."

95. As, for example, in an interview with the author on January 17, 2004.

96. Personal communications by Turkish officials with the author.

97. On Larsen's comments, see Nina Gilbert, "Larsen: Call Assad's 'Bluff,'" *Jerusalem Post*, December 1, 2004. Mubarak's comments after his meeting with Bashar are cited by MENA (Cairo), November 30, 2004 (www.mena.org.eg) Although both Larsen and Mubarak said Bashar told them he was willing to negotiate with no preconditions, Bashar told Lebanese prime minister Emile Lahud that the Syrian stance was a resumption of negotiations from where they left off. This position was reiterated by Information Minister Mehdi Dakhlallah in a television interview; see SANA, November 30, 2004, and al-Jazeera television, November 30, 2004. Shortly after Larsen's comments, Israeli president Moshe Katsav revealed that he had conducted secret talks with Asad in May 2004, offering to meet with the Syrian president in Israel, Syria, or a third country. Asad reportedly responded, "I will be happy to meet with you—if you come as a representative of the Israeli government." When Katsav answered that he could only come as a "representative of the state of Israel, but not of the government," Asad turned him down. See *Ma'ariv* (Tel Aviv), December 9, 2004. Katsav also asked Asad to prove he was serious with his new call for peace negotiations by making a gesture of good faith such as returning the remains of Israeli spy Eli Cohen, executed by the Syrian regime in 1965; Associated Press, December 9, 2004.

98. Personal communications by Israeli officials with the author; the author is also grateful to Martin Indyk for his insights on this point.

99. Against this argument, Turkish officials claim that the most important factor contributing to the breakdown in their efforts to restart Israeli-Syrian discussion was the Israeli assassination of Hamas leader Shaykh Ahmed Yassin in March 2004.

100. The crown prince's initiative was first articulated in an interview with Thomas Friedman: "An Intriguing Signal from the Saudi Crown Prince," *New York Times*, February 17, 2002. More Saudi clarifications on the parameters of the initiative were revealed in Henry Siegman, "Will Israel Take a Chance?" *New York Times*, February 21, 2002. See also commentary on the inter-Arab debate over the initiative prior to the March 2002 Arab Summit in Serge Schmemann, "Quickly, a Saudi Peace Idea Gains Momentum in Mideast," *New York Times*, March 3, 2002, and Thomas Friedman, "Say That Again?" *New York Times*, March 13, 2002.

101. The text of the Arab League Peace Initiative 2002 can be viewed in English translation at the Arab Gateway (*al-Bab*) website: (www.al-bab.com/arab/docs/league/peace02.htm).

102. Personal communications by U.S. and Jordanian officials with the author.

103. See Lamia Radi, "Mubarak, Asad Want Syria Involved in New Peace Process with Israel," Agence France-Presse, July 7, 2003, and "Asad and Mubarak Call for the 'Roadmap' to Include Syria and Lebanon," *al-Nahar* (Beirut), July 8, 2003.

104. The notion of a separate roadmap for the Syrian track failed to gain traction within the Quartet, largely because of resistance from the Bush administration. The idea effectively died when Moratinos left the special envoy's post at the end of June 2003 and was replaced by the Belgian diplomat Marc Otte on July 4. Moratinos went on to become foreign minister in the Zapatero government in Spain, elected in March 2004 following an al-Qaeda attack on Madrid's commuter train network.

105. On tensions in the Iran-Syria relationship in the aftermath of Operation Iraqi Freedom, see Haytham Mouzahem and Anders Strindberg, "Syria and Iran: Strained Relations in a Changed Environment," *Jane's Intelligence Review* (October 2003).

106. Significant from the Syria-Iraq point of view was the first provision stated in the final communiqué of the Sharm al-Shaykh conference: "Reaffirming Iraq's sovereignty, political independence and territorial integrity, as well as its national unity, in accordance with the principles of non-interference in internal affairs and the relations of good neighborliness between states as stated in the UN Charter." The Tehran conference of Iraq's neighboring states reaffirmed the outcome of the Sharm al-Shaykh conference and further emphasized their commitment to preventing the breakup of Iraq in the first point of their communiqué: "[The interior ministers at the conference] stressed the provisions of UN Security Council Resolution 1546 and the statements of the previous sessions of Iraq's neighboring countries including the recent sessions in Cairo and Sharm al-Shaykh and stressed also on the sovereignty, political independence, territorial integrity and national unity of Iraq as well as on the right of the people of Iraq to a secure and stable life." See "Text of the Sharm al-Shaykh Conference on Iraq," *al-Akhbar* (Cairo), November 24, 2004; "Full Text of the Final Communiqué of the Tehran Conference on Iraq," *IRNA* (Tehran), December 1, 2004.

107. Personal communications by Iranian officials and scholars with the author.

108. See Ze'ev Schiff, "Syria Buys Arms for Iraq in Eastern Europe," *Ha'aretz*, July 15, 2002; Gary Gambill, "Syria Rearms Iraq," *Middle East Intelligence Bulletin* 4, no. 9 (September 2002); and Daniel Williams and Nicholas Wood, "E. Europe Armaments Find Way to Iraq; Some Suppliers Are about to Be Offered NATO Membership," *Washington Post*, November 20, 2002.

109. Personal communications by U.S. officials with the author.

110. Alan Sipress, "U.S. Favors Easing Iraq Sanctions; On Mideast Tour, Powell Outlines Plan to Focus Efforts against Military," *Washington Post*, February 27, 2001; Jane Perlez, "Powell Goes on the Road and Scores Some Points," *New York Times*, March 2, 2001; Alan Sipress and Colum Lynch, "U.S. Avoids Confronting Syrians on Iraqi Oil," *Washington Post*, February 14, 2002. En route to his May 2003 visit to Damascus, Powell remarked to reporters: "I am sure there will be occasion to remind my Syrian colleagues that two years ago I got an assurance about oil going into the pipeline that turned out not to be the case. I will always have that in my background software and on my hard drive." See Glenn Kessler, "Powell to Detail Concerns to Syria; At Meeting Intended to Ease Tensions, Secretary to Seek 'Specific Action,'" *Washington Post*, May 3, 2003.

111. As late as October 2002, Assistant Secretary of State William Burns met with Bashar and delivered a letter from President Bush reiterating U.S. concerns about Syria's

posture toward Iraq and demanding changes in Syrian behavior; Burns repeated this message in a follow-up visit to Baghdad in January 2003.

112. See, for example, Bashar's interview with Reuters editor Geert Linnebank in October 2002: "Our concern is with the unknown. Even the United Sates does not know how a war in Iraq is going to end. You cannot change the regime without killing millions of Iraqis." See "President Assad Received Media Editors," *SyriaLive.net*, October 19, 2002.

113. S/RES/1441 (2002) was adopted on November 8, 2002. Among other things, the resolution declared Iraq in material breach of relevant Security Council resolutions, invoked Chapter VII of the United Nations Charter, and warned Iraq that it would face "serious consequences as a result of continued violations of its obligations."

114. For example, see Eyal Zisser, "Syria and the War in Iraq," *Middle East Review of International Affairs* 7, no. 2 (June 2003), and International Crisis Group, "Syria under Bashar (I): Foreign Policy Challenges," ICG Middle East Report 23 (Brussels: February 11, 2004), pp. 3–4, 17.

115. In perhaps the most notorious episode of such activity, British Special Air Service troops operating in Iraq's western desert intercepted four busloads of "suspected suicide bombers and would-be fighters"; although the combatants hailed from various Arab countries, "all carried Syrian passports." See "Syria Gives Passports to Suicide Bombers," *Times* (London), April 2, 2003. U.S. forces operating in western Iraq during the last week of the war intercepted a "bus with 59 men of military age carrying $650,000 in cash and a letter offering rewards for killing American soldiers"; the bus was "headed for Syria." See Hans Griemel, "Foreign Fighters Remain Threat in Iraq," Associated Press, April 15, 2003. For a first-hand account by a young Palestinian from Lebanon who joined other foreign "jihadis" in Damascus to be bused into the war zone in Iraq, see Jonathan Steele, "War in the Gulf: On a Convoy to Doom, Arabs Who Wanted to Help Their Iraqi Brothers," *Guardian* (London), April 3, 2003.

116. Personal communications by U.S. officials with the author.

117. On Rumsfeld's remarks that Syria was committing "hostile acts" for which it would be held accountable, see David E. Sanger and Eric Schmitt, "Rumsfeld Cautions Iran and Syria on Aid to Iraq," *New York Times*, March 29, 2003. Various administration threats and cautions to Syria during the Iraq war are cited in Romesh Ratnesar, "Next Stop Syria?" *Time* 161, no. 17 (April 28, 2003). See also Eyal Zisser, "Syria and the United States: Bad Habits Die Hard," *Middle East Quarterly* (Summer 2003).

118. On April 17, 2003, Powell stated in an interview on the television program *News-Hour with Jim Lehrer*, "As I have said previously, and the President has certainly indicated in his own remarks, there is no war plan on anyone's desk right now to go marching on Syria."

119. On April 21, 2003, President Bush played down concerns that Syria was an impending target, remarking, "I'm confident the Syrian government has heard us, and I believe it when they say they want to cooperate with us." See Richard W. Stevenson, "Bush Now Says He Believes Syria Wants to Cooperate," *New York Times*, April 21, 2003.

120. The quotes are taken from Bashar's interview with Reuters editor Geert Linnebank; see *SyriaLive.net*, October 19, 2002.

121. Syria hosted a two-day meeting of the foreign ministers of Iran, Turkey, Saudi Arabia, Kuwait, and Jordan in November 2003. See Sam Ghattas, "Regional States Call for Iraq Border Cooperation, Urge America to Restore Order," Associated Press, November 2, 2003.

122. See Vernon Loeb, "Commanders Doubt Syria Is Entry Point," *Washington Post*, October 29, 2003.

123. ICG, "Syria under Bashar (I)," p. 6.

124. See, for example, the testimony of Assistant Secretary of State for Near Eastern Affairs William Burns to the Senate Foreign Relations Committee, October 30, 2003.

125. U.S. and Syrian officials have told the author that Syrian ambassador Mustafa was informed that a request for U.S.-Syrian military-to-military coordination in controlling the Syrian-Iraqi border would be made to Deputy Foreign Minister Mu'allim. By the time the U.S. chargé d'affaires in Damascus had his meeting with Mu'allim a few days later, the Office of the Secretary of Defense had fought a successful bureaucratic rear guard action against the idea, and the proposal was never formally made.

126. Robin Wright and Glenn Kessler, "Some on Hill Seek to Punish Syria for Broken Promises on Iraq," *Washington Post*, April 20, 2004.

127. Personal communications by U.S. officials with the author.

128. Carla Ann Robbins and Greg Jaffe, "U.S. Sees Efforts by Syria to Control Border with Iraq," *Wall Street Journal*, December 10, 2004.

129. Ibid., and Thomas E. Ricks, "Rebels Aided by Allies in Syria, U.S. Says," *Washington Post*, December 8, 2004.

130. Burns testimony, October 30, 2003.

131. Wright and Kessler, "Some on Hill Seek to Punish Syria for Broken Promises on Iraq." During Iraqi prime minister Iyad Allawi's visit to Damascus in July 2004, the two governments appeared to settle on the amount of former Iraqi regime funds in Syrian banks (estimated at $800 million), but Syrian officials hinted that they would not release the monies until "occupation forces" departed Iraq. *al-Safir*, July 27, 2004; *al-Ba'th*, July 27, 2004; Oxford Business Group (www.oxfordbusinessgroup.com), July 27, 2004.

132. Clifford Krauss, "U.S. Welcomes Thaw in Relations with 'Pragmatic' Syria," *New York Times*, January 2, 2002. Earlier hints that Syria was willing to help the CIA were reported in James Risen and Tim Weiner, "C.I.A. Is Said to Have Sought Help from Syria," *New York Times*, October 30, 2001.

133. Seymour Hersh, "The Syrian Bet," *New Yorker* 79, no. 20 (July 28, 2003).

134. Testimony of David Satterfield, deputy assistant secretary of state for Near Eastern affairs, to the House Committee on International Relations on September 18, 2002; Burns testimony, October 30, 2003.

135. Hersh, "The Syrian Bet." As the National Security Council's senior director for Middle East affairs, the author accompanied Assistant Secretary Burns at this meeting.

136. Personal communications by French officials with the author. Chirac has also been a strong backer of Lebanese prime minister Hariri in his efforts to chart a somewhat more independent policy course.

137. Interviews with the author, January 2004; see also ICG, "Syria under Bashar (I)," p. 6. Characteristic of the administration's strategy of simply recycling long-standing grievances with Syria were Secretary Powell's comments to the press while en route to Damascus for his May 2, 2003, visit: "The President has written to President Assad previously. They know what we are interested in, they know the things that we frankly disapprove of, and so I will repeat them all as every interlocutor who has gone to Syria has laid them out. They are not unknown, and we will go over each and every one of them. . . . We will go over all of the things that have been in dispute with them over the

years, from terrorism to weapons of mass destruction to some of their actions in the last six or seven weeks in the run-up to the conflict in Iraq and then during the conflict in Iraq, their support for particular organizations, organizations that have a presence in Lebanon and that have a presence in Syria." "On-the-Record Briefing en Route to Damascus, Syria," Secretary of State press release, May 2, 2003.

138. Louis Meixler, "Syrian, Turkish Leaders Meet amid Concern over Kurds in Iraq," Associated Press, January 7, 2004. Syria also used Turkey as an intermediary through which to send messages to Israel. "Khaddam: Syria Sent Messages to Israel via Turkey to Revive Peace Talks," *Associated Press*, February 18, 2004.

Chapter Five

1. President Bush announced the implementation of the Syria Accountability and Lebanese Sovereignty Restoration Act sanctions on May 11, 2004. In addition to the mandatory ban on the export of dual-use items to Syria, the president also chose to implement a ban on all American exports except food and medicine, a prohibition on flights between Syria and the United States, and the freezing of certain Syrian assets in the United States. Significantly, Bush chose not to employ some of the harsher options from the "basket" of sanctions proposed by the law, such as a strict ban on the travel of Syrian diplomatic personnel in the United States, the prohibition of investment by U.S. companies in Syria, or the downgrading U.S.-Syrian diplomatic contacts. See the president's announcement to Congress at (www.whitehouse.gov/news/releases/2004/05/20040511-8.html) and Christopher Marquis, "Bush Imposes Sanctions on Syria, Citing Terrorism," *New York Times*, May 12, 2004.

2. Robin Wright and Glenn Kessler, "Some on Hill Seek to Punish Syria for Broken Promises on Iraq," *Washington Post*, April 30, 2004.

3. See the case studies in Richard Haass and Meghan O'Sullivan, eds., *Honey and Vinegar: Incentives, Sanctions, and Foreign Policy* (Brookings, 2000) and the updated analysis in Meghan O'Sullivan, *Shrewd Sanctions* (Brookings, 2003). Unilateral sanctions in the modern globalized world usually only prompt the targeted state to diversify its trade partners. O'Sullivan's assessment (p. 306) of the overall utility of this type of sanction is that "although the goals touted have often called for the target to abandon certain actions, the rigid comprehensive sanctions regimes usually employed and the instruments that accompany them (or, in more cases than not, the lack of instruments used alongside sanctions) have been more suited toward containment." Uncoupled from positive inducements, the effect of unilateral sanctions, however strict they may be, is quickly dissipated. O'Sullivan (p. 295) also makes the point that sanctions regimes are rarely structured for specific strategic outcomes; instead, "when new goals are adopted toward a regime or country, additional sanctions are simply added to the existing body of restrictions. If all the relevant contacts are already severed, lawmakers have shown no reluctance to 'double' or 'triple' sanctions against a country, that is, to impose redundant measures on it."

4. Hadley spoke at the Washington Institute for Near East Policy's Weinberg Founders Conference at Landsdowne, Virginia, on October 15, 2004. See the text of his keynote address at (www.washingtoninstitute.org/media/speakers/hadley101504.htm).

5. See President Bush's remarks at his December 19, 2003, press conference announcing Libya's pledge to dismantle its WMD programs: (www.whitehouse.gov/news/releases/2003/12/20031219-9.html).

6. Institute for Advanced Strategic and Political Studies, *A Clean Break: A New Strategy for Securing the Realm, Report of the Study Group on a New Israeli Strategy toward 2000* (Jerusalem: 1996).

7. Jim Lobe, "New Cheney Adviser Has Sights on Syria," *Asia Times*, October 22, 2003.

8. Ibid.

9. On this point, see also Michael O'Hanlon, "Why Americans Feel Safer with Bush," *Financial Times*, November 8, 2004.

10. After the U.S. invasion of Iraq, Pentagon proposals called for cutting back on U.S. troops stationed in Europe and South Korea to cope with the increasing military burdens in the Middle East. Thom Shanker, "US Debates Global Troop Buildup; Pentagon Weighs Best Use of Increasingly Strained Forces," *New York Times*, July 23, 2003; Thom Shanker, "After the War: Military Plan; Army Is Devising Ways to Reorganize Its Forces," *New York Times*, August 6, 2003; Robert Burns, "Strapped for Troops, the Pentagon Wants to Redeploy U.S. Troops in South Korea to Iraq," Associated Press, May 17, 2004; Michael R. Gordon, "A Pentagon Plan Would Cut Back G.I.'s in Germany," *New York Times*, June 4, 2004. The Army has also resorted to mandatory recalls of retired veterans under the Individual Ready Reserve program to fill the gaps in manpower needs in Iraq and Afghanistan; see Josh White, "Army to Recall Soldiers for Iraq, Afghan Wars," *Washington Post*, June 30, 2004.

11. Secretary of Defense Donald Rumsfeld, in a memo issued to Pentagon advisers and published in *USA Today* on October 22, 2003, called into question the administration's military-first approach to the war on terror, citing "mixed results" from the current policy.

12. On this point, see the United Nations Security Council Counter-Terrorism Committee report, November 2003 (www.un.org/docs/sc/committees/1373).

13. In the immediate aftermath of the September 11 attacks, all members of the UN Security Council "departed from tradition and stood to unanimously adopt resolution 1368" on bringing the perpetrators to justice and combating all forms of terrorism (Press Release SC/7143, Security Council 4370th Meeting, September 12, 2001). The General Assembly adopted a similar resolution without a vote (Press Release GA/9903, Fifty-sixth General Assembly, September 12, 2001). The Security Council unanimously adopted another strong resolution a month later calling on all states to cooperate in the fight against terrorism and authorizing the UN Counter-Terrorism Committee to coordinate the international effort (S/RES/1377, November 12, 2001). NATO demonstrated its solidarity with the United States when it invoked Article 5 of the Washington Treaty on September 12, 2001, triggering for the first time in NATO history a collective response against a threat to one member: (www.nato.int/terrorism/five.htm). The "Six Plus Two" committee—Afghanistan's neighboring states plus Russia and the United States—issued a joint communiqué calling on Afghanistan to cooperate against al-Qaeda and agreeing upon the need for "a broad-based, multiethnic, politically balanced, freely chosen Afghan administration representative of their aspirations and at peace with its neighbors"; see Betsy Pisik, "'Six Plus Two' Speeds to Create New Government; Troops nearby Kabul Press Need," *Washington Times*, November 13, 2001.

14. According to U.S. Central Command, more than seventy nations joined Operation Enduring Freedom in Afghanistan, with twenty-one coalition partners providing over half of the troops deployed. The White House listed nearly fifty coalition countries participating in Operation Iraqi Freedom, but only thirty-one nations were willing to publicly state their support before the war began. Of the 300,000-plus coalition troops, only two countries besides the United States committed sizable detachments—Britain (45,000) and Australia (2,000)—while a handful of other nations contributed token forces. Jonathan Weisman, "War Will Be Mostly an American Effort," *Washington Post*, March 19, 2003; Pamela Hess, "DOD: 13 Nations Join Coalition of Willing," United Press International, March 20, 2003; and William J. Kole, "Iraq Coalition Weaker than 1991 Alliance," Associated Press Online, March 19, 2003.

15. For analysis of the difficulties of successful regime change, see Minxin Pei and Sara Kasper, *Lessons from the Past: The American Record on Nation-Building*, Policy Brief 24 (Washington: Carnegie Endowment for International Peace, May 2003); and James Dobbins, *America's Role in Nation-Building: From Germany to Iraq* (Santa Monica, Calif.: RAND Corporation, 2003).

16. The Reform Party of Syria (RPS) describes itself as "a US-based opposition party that has emerged as a result of September 11" that "is governed by secular, peace-committed American-Syrians, Euro-Syrians, and native Syrians who are determined to see that a 'New Syria' is reborn that embraces real democratic and economic reforms." See the RPS website at (www.reformsyria.org/).

17. For example, this is the approach recommended in Steven Simon and Jonathan Stevenson, "The Road to Damascus," *Foreign Affairs* 83, no. 3 (May/June 2004).

18. See, for example, the testimony of Ambassador Richard Murphy to the Senate Foreign Relations Committee, October 30, 2003.

19. On this point, see Martin Indyk, "Achieving Arab-Israeli Peace," in *The Road Ahead: Middle East Policy in the Bush Administration's Second Term*, edited by Flynt Leverett (Brookings, 2005).

20. Randolph Martin, "Sudan's Perfect War," *Foreign Affairs* 81, no. 2 (March/April 2002); Michael M. Phillips, "Bush Diplomats Gain in Sudan; White House Targets Terrorism without Using Military," *Wall Street Journal*, October 22, 2003; Marc Lacey, "From Rogue State to Pariah State," *New York Times*, May 16, 2004.

21. Flynt Leverett, "Why Libya Gave Up the Bomb," *New York Times*, January 23, 2004; Martin Indyk, "The Iraq War Did Not Force Gaddafi's Hand," *Financial Times*, March 9, 2004.

22. See also Stephen Fidler, Mark Huband, and Roula Khalaf, "Return to the Fold: How Gadaffi Was Persuaded to Give Up His Nuclear Goals," *Financial Times*, January 27, 2004.

23. Sonni Efron and Douglas Frantz, "Kadafi Fulfills Vow to Cede Nuclear Materials," *Los Angeles Times*, January 28, 2004. An unnamed U.S. diplomat voiced this attitude in reference to Syria in a May 2003 interview with the International Crisis Group: "[We] will not pay for them to undo what they ought not to have done in the first place. They don't deserve a prize for it. We want strategic, irreversible steps." International Crisis Group, "Syria under Bashar (I): Foreign Policy Challenges," *ICG Middle East Report* 23 (February 11, 2004): 3.

24. Nayla Assaf, "Israel Report Lauds Syrian Presence in Lebanon: Argues Withdrawal Strengthens Hizbullah," *Daily Star*, December 2, 2004.

25. See President Bush's post–September 11 radio addresses on September 15 and 29, 2001; his State of the Union speeches on January 29, 2002, and January 28, 2003; and his speech at the National Endowment for Democracy on November 6, 2003. The speeches are available under their respective dates at ⟨www.whitehouse.gov/news/⟩.

26. The Middle East Partnership Initiative (MEPI) was announced by Secretary of State Colin Powell in a speech on December 12, 2002. President Bush reaffirmed his commitment to the MEPI and proposed the Middle East Trade Initiative (METI) in a speech at the University of South Carolina on May 9, 2003.

27. See MEPI project goals and funding at ⟨http://mepi.state.gov/⟩. The administration spent $98 million on MEPI programs in fiscal 2002 and 2003 and allocated $150 million for fiscal 2004. The 2004 allocation is equivalent to only fifty-eight cents for each man, woman, and child in the Arab world. For these calculations and more details on MEPI, see two articles by Tamara Cofman Wittes: "Arab Democracy, American Ambivalence," *Weekly Standard*, February 23, 2004; and "The Promise of Arab Liberalism," *Policy Review* 125 (June/July 2004). See the list of MEPI-eligible countries at ⟨http://mepi.state.gov/c10128.htm⟩. The lack of programs for those Middle Eastern countries with the most problematic relationships with the United States is not outwardly mentioned anywhere in the protocols of the initiative; rather, it is subtly indicated by an interactive feature on the MEPI website. Running the cursor of your mouse over countries on the map of the Middle East who have favorable relationships with the United States will reveal pop-up links for programs sponsored by MEPI, but pointing the cursor at Syria, Libya, or Iran brings up nothing—these are considered noninteractive regions by MEPI standards.

28. See more details on the METI at ⟨www.ustr.gov/new/fta/middleeast.htm⟩. U.S. trade representative Robert Zoellick waxed eloquent on the now-dormant "free trade 'Spirit of the Levant'" in his speech at the World Economic Forum in Jordan on June 23, 2003, extolling the glories of Syria and its Arab neighbors in their long-ago golden age. He ignored modern-day Syria in his remarks.

29. In this context, the United States should note that a "just and agreed" resolution to the refugee issue, as described in the 2002 Beirut summit declaration, should and would not mean an outcome that threatened Israel's Jewish character.

Index